Speculative Fictions
Contemporary Canadian Novelists and the Writing of History

Herb Wyile provides a comparative analysis of the historical concerns and textual strategies of twenty novels published since the appearance of Rudy Wiebe's groundbreaking *The Temptations of Big Bear* in 1973. Drawing on the work of theorists and critics such as Hayden White, Mikhail Bakhtin, Fredric Jameson, Linda Hutcheon, and Michel De Certeau, *Speculative Fictions* examines the nature of these novels' engagement with Canadian history, historiography, and the writing of historical fiction.

In the 1970s and early 1980s writers such as Wiebe, Joy Kogawa, and Timothy Findley set the stage for a predominantly postcolonial and postmodern interrogation of traditional conceptions of Canadian history, the writing of history and fiction, and the idea of nation. Through his comparative approach, Wyile emphasizes the ways in which this spirit has been sustained in more recent historical novels by Jane Urquhart, Guy Vanderhaeghe, Thomas Wharton, Margaret Atwood, and others. He concludes that the writing of history in English-Canadian fiction over the last thirty years makes a substantial contribution to a revisioning of history and to a postcolonial renegotiation of Canada and Canadian society as we enter into a new century.

HERB WYILE is assistant professor in the Department of English, Acadia University.

Speculative Fictions

Contemporary Canadian Novelists and the Writing of History

HERB WYILE

McGill-Queen's University Press
Montreal & Kingston · London · Ithaca

© McGill-Queen's University Press 2002
ISBN 0-7735-2315-4

Legal deposit second quarter 2002
Bibliothèque nationale du Québec

Printed in Canada on acid-free paper

This book has been published with the help of a grant
from the Humanities and Social Sciences Federation of
Canada, using funds provided by the Social Sciences
and Humanities Research Council of Canada.

McGill-Queen's University Press acknowledges the
financial support of the Government of Canada
through the Book Publishing Industry Development
Program (BPIDP) for its activities. It also acknowledges
the support of the Canada Council for the Arts for its
publishing program.

**National Library of Canada Cataloguing
in Publication Data**

Wyile, Herb, 1961–
    Speculative fictions : contemporary Canadian novelists
and the writing of history
Includes bibliographical references and index.
    ISBN 0-7735-2315-4
    1. Historical fiction, Canadian (English) – History and
criticism. 2. Canadian fiction (English) – 20th century –
History and criticism. 3. Novelists, Canadian (English)
– 20th century. I. Title.
PS8191.H5W94 2002   c813'.08109054   C2001-902811-3
PR9192.6.H5W94 2002

Typeset in Palatino 10/12
by Caractéra inc., Quebec City

Contents

Illustrations

Acknowledgments

This book emerged as a result of a senior-level course I taught at the University of Alberta in the spring of 1998, so my thanks go to the students in that class for joining me, for reassuring me that the subject was of interest, and for prompting me with their many insights to think through the topic in more detail. I would like to express my gratitude to Bill Parenteau, Ann Howey, and Tom Wharton for aiding this project in various ways. Thanks also to staff at the City of Toronto Archives, the National Archives, the *Montreal Gazette*, the Public Archives of Manitoba, the Public Archives of Nova Scotia, the City of St John's Archives, and the Centre for Newfoundland Studies for their help in tracking down illustrations for the book. I gratefully acknowledge the City of Toronto Archives, the *Montreal Gazette*, and the Public Archives of Nova Scotia for granting permission to reproduce photos from their respective collections. My thanks to Barry Cameron, Frank Davey, Jeanette Lynes, and Paul Hjartarson for their ongoing support of my work. And, last but not least, my gratitude to, and for, my family.

The discussions of *The Englishman's Boy* and *Away* appeared in slightly different form as "Dances With Wolfers: Choreographing History in *The Englishman's Boy*," in *Essays on Canadian Writing* 67 (1999): 23–52, and "'The Opposite of History is Forgetfulness': Myth, History and the New Dominion in Jane Urquhart's *Away*," in *Studies in Canadian Literature* 24.1 (1999): 20–45. My thanks to the editors for their kind permission to reprint that material here.

Preface

Speaking of the lack of historical fiction during the flourishing of Canadian literature in the 1960s, Margaret Atwood recently observed that the writers of that generation "were instead taken up by the momentous discovery that we ourselves existed, in what was then the here and now, and we were busily exploring the implications of that."[1] Since that time, however, writing about history has been a tremendously important part of Canadian literature's proliferation and growing popularity. If the writers of the 60s were obsessed with the here and now, contemporary Canadian historical novelists have been engaged in coming to terms with both the present and the past. The question posed by Northrop Frye and echoed by Atwood in *Survival*, "where is here?" has been extended to "what is now and where did it come from?" Robert Kroetsch once observed that "we haven't got an identity until somebody tells our story. The fiction makes us real."[2] Contemporary Canadian historical novels can be seen as an important extension of that narrating into existence, but one that also inscribes a recognition of the problems with such an identity-making process and with notions of the real. They reflect a confidence not in fiction's ability to provide the stuff of the past, but in the past's ability to provide the stuff of fiction.

The title of this book, *Speculative Fictions: Contemporary Canadian Novelists and the Writing of History*, was suggested by the recurring characterization of the historical novel as a mirror image or inversion of science fiction.[3] Such an image goes against the common assumption that because history is, well, in the past, it is somehow much more of a known quantity than the future. Indeed, instead of exhibiting a retrospective certainty, contemporary historical novels are undeniably increasingly speculative. They have departed in various ways from the traditional historical novel's aim of realistically depicting historical figures, episodes, or eras and to a great degree reflect the widespread scepticism in historical and literary studies today about historical knowledge and its literary representation. Speculative fiction is not an objective, detached, authentic glimpse into the future, but rather usually a very purposeful, subjective, and rhetorical extrapolation from present circumstances, and the same might be said of historical fiction. Except, of course, that it faces in the opposite direction.

The subtitle of the book, however, is intended to modify this emphasis on the represented world of such fiction; though the phrase "the writing of history" can be taken as synonymous with writing about the past, it is intended here to suggest contemporary Canadian novelists' preoccupation with historiography itself. Historical novels like Michael Ondaatje's *In the Skin of a Lion*, Timothy Findley's *The Wars*, and Daphne Marlatt's *Ana Historic* are as much about the writing of history as they are about the past, and indeed much of the work of these and other novelists collapses the distinction between the two. This book thus examines the general departure of contemporary Canadian historical novels from the customary aims of the traditional historical novel; the historiographical, ontological, and epistemological implications of that departure; and the many key considerations pertinent to English-Canadian literature that these writers address in the process: nationalism, postcolonialism, postmodernism, gender and sexuality, ethnicity and race, aestheticism and politics, time and place.

These considerations, of course, have been the focus of critical attention for close to three decades. Studies such as Linda Hutcheon's *The Canadian Postmodern*, Frank Davey's *Post-National Arguments*, Marie Vautier's *New World Myth*, Martin Kuester's *Framing Truths*, Marlene Goldman's *Paths of Desire*, and books and articles by many others in various ways explored the centrality of history in Canadian fiction in the latter part of the twentieth century. This book is obviously indebted to the work that has been done on Canadian historical fiction and seeks to extend these considerations to more recent Canadian historical novels. The largely postcolonial, revisionist illumination of Canadian history and historiography initiated by novelists like Findley, Rudy Wiebe, and Joy Kogawa in the 1970s and early 80s has very much been sustained by more recently acclaimed novelists like Wayne Johnston, Jane Urquhart, Guy Vanderhaeghe, and Thomas

Wharton. English-Canadian historical fiction published in the last decade and a half, however, seems less radical and more ambivalent in its challenging of the underpinnings of empiricist historiography and the form of the traditional historical novel. This difference, *Speculative Fictions* argues, reflects the difficulties of negotiating a more postcolonial presentation of Canadian history within the context of a postmodern culture characterized on the one hand by scepticism of official history and on the other by strong pressures to render history in a commodified and dehistoricized form.

To develop this argument, *Speculative Fictions* is structured not around individual texts and writers but around particular features of contemporary Canadian historical novels. While the book provides some commentary on much-analyzed texts such as *The Wars*, Kogawa's *Obasan*, and Wiebe's *The Temptations of Big Bear*, for the most part that commentary serves to contextualize and provide a point of comparison for recently published novels like Urquhart's *Away*, Vanderhaeghe's *The Englishman's Boy*, and Johnston's *The Colony of Unrequited Dreams* (along with Heather Robertson's neglected *The King Years* trilogy, which appeared during the 1980s). Thus *Speculative Fictions* provides a sense of the broad scope of contemporary Canadian historical novels while concentrating on the concerns and the directions of fiction of the last decade.

The introduction situates developments in English-Canadian historical fiction in the context of debates about historiography and representation. Both historiography and literary studies have been sites of profound philosophical, ideological, and methodological debate in recent decades, and a discussion of contemporary historical fiction needs to take into account how the two halves of the term have been thoroughly contested, reconceptualized, and, perhaps most significantly, increasingly dovetailed. Drawing on the work of various theorists, including Michel Foucault, Julia Kristeva, Michel de Certau, and particularly Hayden White, the introduction considers the implications for historiography of structuralist and poststructuralist conceptions of language, discourse, subjectivity, and narrative, looking in particular at the role of representation, narrative form, and intertextuality in historical discourse. Drawing especially on the work of Naomi Jacobs and Linda Hutcheon, the introduction examines the ways in which these conceptual shifts are evident in the aesthetic, philosophical, political, and cultural reconfiguration of the contemporary historical novel in Canada, providing the theoretical framework for the more detailed textual analysis in the rest of the book.

The second chapter of *Speculative Fictions*, "Historical Sites," looks at the "sites" of these novels not so much in terms of significant historical figures and events, but as part of a prevalent and largely revisionist interest in questioning the imperatives of colonialism, drawing attention to the historically marginalized or misrepresented and undermining unified and glorified notions of nationhood. The first section highlights the general resistance of contemporary historical novels to monologic and Eurocentric versions of Canadian history, employing postcolonial theory to provide a framework for charting this resistance. I look at how novels like Wiebe's *A Discovery of Strangers*, George Bowering's *Burning Water*, *The Englishman's Boy*, and Wharton's *Icefields* undermine the neat colonial trajectory of exploration, settlement, and nation-building and suggest how the birth of a nation is, from a less Eurocentric perspective, the death of others. The next part of the chapter considers how, like Marlatt, Kogawa, and Ondaatje, novelists such as Urquhart, Robertson, Atwood, Sky Lee, and Margaret Sweatman have exposed, and pushed beyond, the barriers of class, gender, race, and ethnicity that "official" history both constructs and naturalizes. The final part of the chapter focuses on the nation itself as a significant historical "site," examining how novels such as Robertson's *Willie* and Johnston's *The Colony of Unrequited Dreams*, like Susan Swan's *The Biggest Modern Woman of the World*, subvert the historical novel's customary function of serving as a kind of national allegory.

For most of these novelists, the writing of history is as important as – indeed is usually inseperable from – the historical sites themselves. Thus the third chapter of the book, "The Content of the Form," looks at various ways in which these novels test the limits of history and thematize or foreground different elements of the writing of history. Drawing especially on theories of postmodern fiction postulated by Hutcheon, Brian McHale, and Patricia Waugh, the chapter first examines the preoccupation with historical research and writing, focusing on *The Wars*, *Ana Historic*, Robertson's *Igor: A Novel of Intrigue*, and *The Colony of Unrequited Dreams*. The chapter then probes the relationship between history, orality, and literacy; here the discussion draws on the work of Walter Ong and looks at Jack Hodgins's *The Invention of the World*, *The Englishman's Boy*, Wiebe's *The Scorched-Wood People*, and John Steffler's *The Afterlife of George Cartwright* in the context of metafictional strategies and oral historiography. Finally, taking cues from Mircea Eliade's work on myth and Vautier's postcolonial treatment of myth in *New World Myth*, I examine various novels that explore the complex and problematic interpenetration of history and myth, such as *The Wars*, *In the Skin of a Lion*, *The Invention of the World*, and *Away*.

In the final chapter, "Speculating in Fiction: Commodity Culture and the Crisis of Historicity," historical discourse and historical fiction are viewed primarily as a reflection of the present rather than the past. This chapter studies the relation between the increasing interest in history on the part of contemporary English-Canadian historical novelists and our own historical moment: how that interest has been shaped by postmodern culture but also how those historical novels themselves serve to comment on contemporary society. Evoking the work of theorists both critical and supportive of post-modernism, this chapter explores the ambivalent relation between contemporary historical fiction and the commodity culture of which it is a part. Looking at works such as *Away*, *In the Skin of a Lion*, *Icefields*, *The Biggest Modern Woman of the World*, and *The Englishman's Boy*, the chapter considers the implications of historical fiction's tenuous balance between politics and aesthetics in the context of consumerism, and examines the strategies these novels employ to critique postmodern culture and contemporary capitalism.

Speculative Fictions does not aspire to be a comprehensive taxonomy of English-Canadian historical novels of the late twentieth century. Its main aim is to suggest some significant developments, shared interests, and recurrent strategies in the writing of history by these novelists. One of the obvious consequences of these parameters is that the discussion of the various novels is fragmented, limited, and uneven. Many of the novels covered could easily be discussed in most sections of the book, but because a great deal of criticism already exists on works such as *The Wars*, *Obasan*, *The Temptations of Big Bear*, and *In the Skin of a Lion*, I have tried to concentrate on more recent and less prominent texts.

Another result of the scope of the book is that, while I have made some effort to explore the histories with which these novels deal, that research, especially by historical standards, is fairly sketchy.[4] A thorough investigation of the histories that serve as the bases for these texts is, I feel, a necessary enterprise, not just for a better appreciation of the texts themselves but for a deeper appreciation of the relationship between history and literature, particularly since surprisingly little of the critical attention these texts have received has been directed to the history behind them. Unfortunately, at least as far as this book is concerned, there is neither world enough nor time. The illustrations are intended to serve as a similar link to the historical contexts of the novels. They provide, as in many history books, visual supplements to the history at hand and connect the critical analysis of these novels to their historical intertexts and the material history they engage. They are not be taken as immediate, unmediated glimpses of the past, but as visual traces of the histories with which these novelists are in constant dialogue.

The discussion, furthermore, is obviously limited to English-Canadian historical novels; those looking for a comparative exami-nation of the treatment of history in English-Canadian and Québécois novels have to look no further than Vautier's *New World Myth*. The discussion also is restricted to English-Canadian novels that deal with Canadian history, however much such a boundary is to be undermined in the discussion that follows. Novels like Ondaatje's *Coming Through Slaughter* and *The English Patient*, Findley's *Famous Last Words*, Anne Michaels's *Fugitive Pieces*, and others could easily figure in the argument of *Speculative Fictions*; they serve as an impor-tant reminder that these novelists are also citizens of a larger world, their concerns far from limited to the borders of Canada.

Last but not least, conspicuous in this discussion of postcolonial-ism and historical fiction is the absence of historical novels by native writers. One could well draw the conclusion that the historical novel is a fundamentally European and Eurocentric form and that the dis-cussion has simply neglected native alternatives to the historical novel. Yet writers all over the postcolonial world – perhaps most notably in Latin America – have adapted the historical novel form in myriad creative ways for clearly postcolonial purposes, and native writers in Canada have for some time been creatively reworking not just traditional oral forms but also various literary forms of the dom-inant culture.[5] So the relative absence of historical fiction in their work, I would argue, is not just a perceived one. One reason for the lack of such historical fiction may be that so much psychic energy has been spent on breaking the dominant culture's association of native people with the past that stressing contemporary existence has been first and foremost a decolonizing literary strategy.[6] More gen-erally, the persistence of colonial assumptions hampers both the pro-duction and reception of historical writing by natives.

Nonetheless, given the increasing variety, innovation, and postco-lonial complexity of work by native writers, I would venture that it is just a matter of time (no pun intended) before we see native writers producing their own historical fiction. Given the dominant culture's continued ignorance concerning the significance of the historical con-text of land claims, the effect of residential schools on cultural prac-tices and family structures, and the question of self-government, the past is bound to become more prominent as a territory to which native writers turn. Thomas King's *Green Grass, Running Water* is substantially concerned with subverting Eurocentric conceptions of the history of colonialism, but ultimately the novel is too compendiously carnivalesque to be considered a historical novel, even within the expanded conception of the term in this study. Lee Maracle's *Ravensong*, like Tomson Highway's *Kiss of the Fur Queen*, Richard Wagamese's *Keeper 'n Me*, and Jeannette Armstrong's *Slash*, concentrates on a more proximate past, though it contains hints of a longer historical perspective. Soon, I suspect, we will be seeing such a perspective developed in more detail.

Speculative Fictions

"Only the Devil ain't tired of history"
        – George Elliott Clarke, *Whylah Falls*

"The past is a flowering minefield"
        – Alasdair Gray, *1982 Janine*

1 History, Theory, and the Contemporary Canadian Historical Novel

In the fall of 2000, *The Globe & Mail* ran a week-long series of opinion pieces under the suspense-ending title "The Death of History." Though some contributors took issue with the conclusion that Canadian history was critically ill, the series reflected the anxious tone (and titular question-begging) of conservative historian J.L. Granatstein's polemical book *Who Killed Canadian History?*. The narrative of the nation, according to Granatstein and to Rudyard Griffiths, one of the contributors, is under threat from an atomizing, ideological, revisionist social history that passes over the "political drama of Confederation, the heroism and terror of Vimy ... for homilies on the conscription crisis and the internment of minorities in the Second World War."[1] Despite the conclusion of three contributors that Canadian history is alive and well and in no need of reclaiming, the editorial reflecting back on the series reinforced the attack on social history. It intoned that "the main stream of history is being neglected" and supported the conservative call for resurrecting the narrative of nation: "Every nation, like every life, has a story. It is time we remembered ours."[2]

What the series reflected, in part, was the growing interest of corporate Canada in the fate of Canadian history, an interest grounded in anxiety over the declining influence of the political and military history that has traditionally underpinned the narrative of the nation's past and that is more compatible with corporate conceptions of order, leadership, and national identity.[3] The questions that such anxiety begs, as the series's dissenting voices underscored, are "the death of history *for whom*?" or "the death of *what kind of* history?"

"There is," retorted contributor Patrick Watson, "a hunger for narrative about our past" evident in the audience for history on stage, on television, on computers, and in heritage fairs.[4]

This hunger has also been evident in the appearance, almost yearly over the last three decades, of a wealth of historical fiction that has helped push Canadian literature to international prominence. Within the last decade alone, historical novels set partly or entirely in Canada, such as Guy Vanderhaeghe's *The Englishman's Boy*, Jane Urquhart's *Away* and *The Underpainter*, Anne Michaels's *Fugitive Pieces*, and Thomas Wharton's *Icefields*, have received international acclaim, and established writers like Michael Ondaatje, Rudy Wiebe, and Timothy Findley have continued to enjoy success in the genre. As Wiebe has observed of the consistent concern with history in his own fiction, there is really no need to invent stories when Canada's past is filled with a wealth of material for writers to develop in their fiction, something Canadian novelists seem increasingly inclined to do.[5] Writing in 1981, W.J. Keith could rightly say that "serious historical fiction does not yet form a prominent part of Canadian literature," but now, some twenty years later, it would be hard to deny that it most certainly does.[6]

Whereas most contemporary English-Canadian novelists would agree that history is far from dead, what history is and how it might be approached in fiction is clearly a trickier subject than it was for previous historical novelists such as Thomas Raddall, Philip Child, and Thomas Costain. Reading novels such as Findley's *The Wars*, Ondaatje's *In the Skin of a Lion*, Susan Swan's *The Biggest Modern Woman of the World*, Daphne Marlatt's *Ana Historic*, and Wiebe's *The Temptations of Big Bear*, one is bound to be struck by the degree to which these novels disturb the customary illusion of holding up a mirror to history. Their presentation of history is fragmented, self-conscious, and discursively and generically heterogeneous, reflecting a wariness about the terms of – even the possibility of – historical representation. This disruption is part of a much broader reconfiguration of history and literature, and the necessary starting point for an examination of some of the significant features of contemporary historical fiction in English Canada is the general scepticism about historical discourse and the subversion of the traditional view of history as a picture of the past, which is perhaps one of the most significant "metanarratives" under scrutiny at the end of the twentieth century.[7] Contemporary historical fiction is part of a larger fray, and it is helpful to situate the propensities of that fiction within the ideological, philosophical and disciplinary turmoil that historiography has experienced over the last forty years.

Writers of fiction, like their counterparts in the discipline of history, have increasingly occupied themselves with finding and telling the stories of those left out of traditional history. At the same time, however, many of those writers have become more aware of the interrelation between finding and telling that is such a preoccupation of current theorizing about historical discourse. As a result, the historical novel, in Canada as elsewhere, has undergone substantial reformulation in various ways that parallel developments in historiography, particularly politically and epistemologically. In the process of unearthing the untold or obscure stories of the past, or revisiting established stories, contemporary novelists are also contributing to an investigation of the process of historical representation – what history is and what it means to try to depict the past. More specifically, they are contributing to an investigation of the role of representations of the past in the construction of social, political, cultural, and, not least of all, national discourse.

This self-awareness has precipitated a substantial reshaping of historical fiction. Customarily, it has been assumed that historical fiction differs from other literature in that at least some recognizably "historical" events are to be portrayed and that there will be a mingling of recognizably historical characters with fictional ones. As Avrom Fleishman contends, "the plot must include a number of 'historical' events, particularly those in the public sphere (war, politics, economic change, etc.), mingled with and affecting the personal fortunes of the characters."[8] In Gyorgy Lukács's terms, the historical novel engages with a politically pivotal historical era, one characterized by "the radical sharpening of social trends in an historical crisis."[9]

Over the course of the last century, however, many questions have been raised about what counts as history, and historians have taken a pronounced turn towards a more heterogeneous social history. Perhaps the principal cause of the current upheaval in historiography is simply that history has been so exclusively defined, prompting many people to question the objectivity of a history that left them out. Resistance to history as a kind of unified story about the past has been reflected in a variety of ways in the discipline, particularly in the emergence of social history and the focus on gender, class, race and ethnicity, and culture. Many historians have sought to replace the idea of "history as a sequence of events orchestrated by a small and powerful elite" – a public, political history largely defined in Eurocentric, upper-class, and male terms – with a view of history "as an arena in which classes, cultural groups, and individual men and women struggled to control the values that shaped their collective lives."[10] The result has been a more demographically varied social history reflecting the interests of groups previously marginalized in or excluded from the story of traditional history, such as workers, women, and minorities.

This shift has been mirrored in literary circles: in Canada as elsewhere, the last few decades have seen a proliferation of revisionist historical fiction and historical fiction about previously neglected or marginalized histories, underlining that what is historically significant has been narrowly defined and ideologically overdetermined, and that there's much more to Canadian history than meets the European male eye. This revisionist approach is more than evident in contemporary Canadian historical novels. In *The Temptations of Big Bear*, Rudy Wiebe presents the Plains Cree chief Big Bear not as a sullen rebel defying Her Majesty's authority at the time of the second Riel "rebellion," but as a tragic figure caught between the extremes of hopeless, violent resistance and acquiescence to extinction as he seeks to allay the impact on his dying people of the encroachment of white civilization. In *Burning Water*, George Bowering portrays George Vancouver as an insecure, disappointed functionary whose overbearing behaviour prompts his ship's surgeon to murder him. Finally, in *Igor*, Heather Robertson provides a critical and demythologizing account of the enigmatic defector Igor Gouzenko, heralded for exposing the operation of Soviet spies in Canada (and credited with starting the Cold War in the process). Recasting the accepted history, Robertson presents his defection as part of an orchestrated post-war consolidation of power by the United States. Writers like Guy Vanderhaeghe, Michael Ondaatje, and Susan Swan bring to the fore relatively obscure historical figures and episodes such as the Cypress Hills Massacre, the building of the Bloor St Viaduct in Toronto, and the Nova Scotia giantess Anna Swan's carnival(esque) career. In questioning and/or questing beyond received history in Canada, these writers raise important concerns about the cultural, racial, gender, class, and colonial biases of that history, illustrating that while Canada does indeed have a rich history, it may not necessarily be the kind of history or version of history that has typically been provided.

Part of this revisionist turn away from an established, public history is that the contemporary historical novel, rather than serving to reinforce nationalist myths, as in the work of Scott and Tolstoy, in such nineteenth-century Canadian works as Gilbert Parker's *The Seats of the Mighty*, and in twentieth-century novels like Raddall's *His Majesty's Yankees* and Costain's *High Towers*, has been more inclined to deconstruct those myths, revealing their excluding effects. Instead of contributing to the ideological consolidation of the nation as an "imagined community" (to use Benedict Anderson's phrase),[11] much contemporary Canadian historical fiction can be seen in terms of

Homi Bhabha's essay "DissemiNation." In reponse to Anderson's formulation, Bhabha argues that "[c]ounter-narratives of the nation that continually evoke and erase its totalizing boundaries – both actual and conceptual – disturb those ideological manœuvres through which 'imagined communities' are given essentialist identities."[12] Thus in Wiebe's work the process of the peaceful settlement of Western Canada is refigured as a coercive and violent appropriation, and in Swan's *The Biggest Modern Woman of the World* stereotypes of Canadians as self-effacing consensus-builders are parodied in terms of feminist critiques of patriarchy and postcolonial critiques of imperialism. Contemporary Canadian novelists are much less inclined to construct patriotic narratives of the building of a nation and of a unitary Canadian character than to dramatize the exploitation, appropriation, and exclusion that such narratives of nation have often served to efface.

This revisionist bent and diversification of the "objects" of historical discourse and historical fiction, however, are part of a much more substantial reshaping of attitudes towards history. Historians have increasingly concerned themselves not just with the recovery of the neglected history of women, of working people, and of marginalized ethnic groups, but also with reshaping the very terms in which history is written. Perhaps more important than the recognition that history has been narrowly defined has been the increasing recognition of history as a kind of constructed consensus about the past rather than a narrative about a "given" historical reality.[13] This has led to a revamping of history that involves not just expanding the boundaries of what counts as "historical," but also reinterpreting and deconstructing the historiographical and ideological assumptions of received history. As Joan Scott argues about women and history, "the discipline of history, through its practices, produces (rather than gathers or reflects) knowledge about the past generally and, inevitably, about sexual differences as well. In that way, history operates as a particular kind of cultural institution endorsing and announcing constructions of gender."[14] For many historians, these new histories are not just about illuminating what traditional history has overshadowed, but also involve turning the spotlight on history itself, questioning and reworking the very ideological, philosophical, and methodological principles of historical writing.

How history is theorized, defined, and practised, therefore, has been dramatically reconfigured. Profound doubts have been raised about various aspects of the authority of history: as a discipline with a particular methodology, as a scientific discourse aspiring to objectivity, and as a narrative of the past. Many have come to view historical discourse as a metanarrative naturalizing unequal relations of power through its selection, interpretation, and exclusion of material – in short, through its deeming of what is "historical." The illusion that historical discourse draws back the curtain that separates us from the past has been shattered; what we have instead, it is often suggested, is something akin to a puppet show orchestrated by the historian. Such a reconfiguration of history and denaturalizing of the activity of historians has amounted, in Michel de Certau's view, to "a fundamental revolution, to be sure, since it replaced the historical *given* by historiographical *process*. It transformed the search for meaning unveiled by observed reality into analysis of the options or organizations of meaning implied by interpretive operations."[15]

These insights have significantly reshaped not only the discipline of history but also the whole genre of historical fiction, breaking down the traditional distinctions between history and literature. This dissolution of the epistemological, ontological, and ideological borders between history and literature is manifested in contemporary Canadian historical fiction in a range of ways. In particular, the continuities between the two, and how these shifts in historiographical theory are reflected in historical fiction, can be seen in three key areas: historical representation, narrative, and intertextuality.

"AS IT REALLY WAS": HISTORY, REPRESENTATION, AND OBJECTIVITY

One of the principal functions of the historical novel in its classical or traditional formulation, according to Allesandro Manzoni, is "to give a faithful representation of history."[16] The historical novel in this sense shares the ideal of representing the past, to use Leopold von Ranke's famous formulation, *wie es eigentlich gewesen*, "as it really was." According to this view of history, a historian is able to construct an accurate representation of the past on its own terms in the same fashion as a realistic novel provides a replica – a kind of verbal mirror image – of the world. The underlying assumption, as Hayden White observes, is that, "insofar as it is an accurate imitation, it is to be considered a truthful account thereof."[17]

The generic imperatives of the historical novel, seen as a perfectly suitable vehicle for conveying a sense of the lived experience of past eras, have been molded by similar empiricist expectations and mimetic conventions. Though critics recognize that, in general, historical fiction does not sustain the same concern with veracity as historical writing, at least some make the argument that historical fiction can indeed provide a "truer" representation of the past. Herbert Butterfield argues that "history cannot come so near to human hearts and human passions as a good novel can; its very fidelity to facts makes it not perhaps less true to life, but farther away from the heart of things."[18] Likewise, Fleishman believes in the capability of the historical novel to provide a more complete – in his terms, more "intellectually acceptable" or universal, rather than factual – truth: "The historical novel is pre-eminently suited to telling how individual lives were shaped at specific moments of history, and how this shaping reveals the character of those historical periods."[19]

The ease of such "telling," however, has been undermined by sustained questioning of models of representation. "Recent reflection on history, like recent reflection on literature," as Lionel Gossman observes, "has tended increasingly to question the mimetic ideal itself."[20] In the latter half of the twentieth century, theorists such as Michel Foucault, Roland Barthes, Jacques Derrida, Julia Kristeva, and others engaged in a thorough deconstruction of the model of language as a medium for referring to an external world, and historical discourse has not escaped scrutiny (to say the least). "History," writes Foucault in *The Archaeology of Knowledge*, "must be detached from the image that satisfied it for so long, and through which it found its anthropological justification: that of an age-old collective consciousness that made use of material documents to refresh its memory."[21]

Structuralist and poststructuralist theorists have steadily undermined the model of language as an unproblematic signifying system with a neat correspondence between the language used to signify and the thing being signified, a correspondence on which defenses of the possibility of a historically objective or "true" discourse tend to rely. As Foucault, Barthes, and others have pointed out, historical discourse presumes the existence of an observable past by which the accuracy of a historical representation can be judged and is ultimately based on, to use Derrida's term, a "metaphysics of presence." Barthes describes the reliance of historical discourse on what he calls "the reality effect" and argues that although historical discourse pretends to be representative, it is instead merely assertive: "historical discourse does not follow reality, it only signifies it; it asserts at every moment: this happened, but the meaning conveyed is only that someone is making that assertion."[22]

Derridean linguistics, with their rejection of reference as the basis of language and their emphasis on difference and linguistic relations, on the free play of the signifier, and on the infinite deferral of meaning, have played a key role in problematizing the entire activity of reference and the possibility of a language in which the past real can be "captured." "Reading," Derrida observes, "cannot legitimately transgress the text toward something other than it, toward a referent (a reality that is metaphysical, historical, psychobiographical, etc.) or toward a signified outside the text whose content could take place, could have taken place outside of language, that is to say, in the sense that we give here to that word, outside of writing in general."[23] As Derridean linguistics suggest, this redrawing of epistemological and ontological boundaries involves a pronounced shift away from the Cartesian relation between the subject and the objective world, and away from the subject's use of language to capture or reflect that world, to a concern with how that world is constructed through the discourses of which it is an effect.

This, in turn, has reconfigured what is perhaps the key epistemological question in historiography: the problem of the absence of the past, the problem of describing something that is not, or is no longer, there. This problem customarily has been addressed as a hermeneutic one, the assumption being that through proper methodological procedures and critical awareness, the past can be made present in such a fashion that we can "see it." This ideal, however, has long been seen as compromised by the tendency of historians to project their contemporary concerns on representations of the past. As Benedetto Croce formulates it, "the practical requirements which underlie every historical judgment give to all history the character of 'contemporary history' because, however remote in time events there recounted may seem to be, the history in reality refers to present needs and present situations wherein those events vibrate."[24] As many critics have argued, the historian's subjectivity and ideological orientation have a necessary (and thus, to varying degrees, distorting) effect on his or her representation of the past. "The belief in a hard core of historical facts existing objectively and independently of the interpretation of the historian," observes E.H. Carr, "is a preposterous fallacy, but one which it is very hard to eradicate."[25] This recognition of the subjectivity and selectivity of the historian has long been seen as undermining the possibility of representing the past "as it really was."

To be sure, the mimetic ideal of historical writing holding up a mirror to the past has for most historians always been an unachievable ideal because of the fragmentary nature of historical evidence – the fact that historical study "is not the study of the past but the study of present traces of the past."[26] Historical evidence is the residue of the past, "the surviving deposit of an historical event"[27] – the statistics, testimonies, documents, and reports through which, along with other historians' commentaries, historians reconstruct a more complete picture of that past. Defenders of the traditional empirical "practice of history" such as G.R. Elton recognize that subjectivity is an unavoidable aspect of historical writing but argue that bias can be reduced through methodological rigor and critical questioning of historical evidence and the historians' own assumptions. Taking such precautions, historians can come close to presenting a "true" picture of the past.[28]

Such an ideal, however, presumes an ontological break between the present and the past – an ontological break, furthermore, that is very much grounded in assumptions about language and historical representation. In presuming a false detachment from their image of the past, White argues, professional or proper historians overlook the impossibility of bracketing one's ideological assumptions, rhetorical intentions, and presuppositions about history.[29] Rather than "uncovering" the past or finding observable patterns in all its multiplicity, historians, according to White, overdetermine their findings by making assumptions that prefigure the field of evidence. "Historical accounts purport to be verbal models, or icons, of specific segments of the historical process. But such models are needed because the documentary record does not figure forth an unambiguous image of the structure of events attested in them. In order to figure 'what *really* happened' in the past, therefore, the historian must first *pre*figure as a possible object of knowledge the whole set of events reported in the documents."[30]

This prefigurative act, of which the historian is not conscious, White argues, is a poetic one and has constitutive effects on the historian's conceptual framework, field of investigation, and the structure of his or her representation of the past. There is, "in short, an elective affinity between the act of prefiguration of the historical field and the explanatory strategies used by the historian in a given work."[31] De Certau puts it even more bluntly: "historiography stages the condition of possibility of production, and it is itself the subject on which it endlessly writes."[32] In consequence, historians like White, de Certau, and Dominick LaCapra have consistently advocated a more self-conscious historiography.

This reconception of history as a discursive construct has considerable political ramifications, as Foucault's work in particular highlights. Foucault describes his task in *Archaeology* as one "that consists of not – of no longer – treating discourses as groups of signs (signifying elements referring to contents or representations) but as practices that systematically form the objects of which they speak. Of course, discourses are composed of signs; but what they do is more than use these signs to designate things."[33] That is, discourse does not merely provide a reflection of some determinate, transcendental ground that lies outside of it, but neither is it reducible to a limitless and arbitrary textual play. Instead, Foucault contends, it is structured by discursive regularities, a set of "relations that characterizes discursive practice itself" or "a group of *rules* that are immanent in a practice, and define it in its specificity" – an insight that has significant implications for a reconsideration of historical discourse.[34]

Moreover, as the term "regulation" suggests, Foucault's work insistently emphasizes the necessarily ideological and political character of discursive formations. In all societies, he argues, "the production of discourse is at once controlled, selected, organised and redistributed by a certain number of procedures whose role is to ward off its powers and dangers, to gain mastery over its chance events, to evade its ponderous, formidable materiality."[35] Discourse, Foucault argues, "appears as an asset – finite, limited, desirable, useful – that has its own rules of appearance, but also its own conditions of appropriation and operation"; it "poses the question of power" and "is, by nature, the object of a struggle, a political struggle."[36]

Such a view of discourse resituates history as the product, rather than the object, of discourse and suggests the importance of articulating the underlying ideological assumptions that set the limits of historical discourse and the intricate relations between power and knowledge those limits inscribe. In this light, historical discourse appears as an act of power, the assertion of a particular reading of the past that involves particular power relations, the exclusion of certain historical material and certain points of view, and the projection of a particular ideology, which traditionally, unsurprisingly, has been that of the victor. Indeed, one of the crucial repercussions of the undermining of history as a grand narrative of the past has been the exposing of the triumphalist and exclusionary character of such an ideal – the use of history to justify and celebrate the status quo and consolidate the establishment's grip on power.

This emphasis on the linguistic dimensions of historical discourse and the consciousness of its speculative and textual character has had important consequences for the historical novel, first of all because it has served to destabilize the distinction between history and literature. The prevailing view through most of the twentieth century was that history and literature are separate orders, or at least have separate intentions, different relations towards time and reality, and different attitudes towards rhetorical, stylistic, formal, and figurative features. Usually the distinction is based on the assumption that history is representationally accurate; thus it is often evoked to consolidate the validity or truth of historical discourse. Robin Collingwood, for instance, argues in *The Idea of History* that the novelist "has a single task only: to construct a coherent picture, one that makes sense. The historian has a double task: he has both to do this, and to construct a picture of things as they really were and of events as they really happened." For the historian to accomplish this, argues Collingwood, "his picture must be localized in space and time ... must be consistent with itself" (whereas "purely imaginary worlds cannot clash and need not agree"), and must be related to the available historical evidence.[37]

However, this model of historical discourse as a unitary language referentially related to historical evidence and capable of presenting a "picture" of the historical past has been systematically undermined in contemporary fiction as well as in contemporary theory. The decline of the mimetic ideal in particular has had a profound influence on writers' attitudes towards history. Consequently, historical fiction has been revitalized on very different grounds from traditional historical fiction and often with very different political and rhetorical aims. Historical fiction of the last thirty or forty years has likewise raised epistemological questions concerning *what* and *how* we know about the past. These concerns in turn, and necessarily, have entailed ontological questions, particularly about the autonomy of the subject and the relationship between subjectivity and the discursive frameworks that shape subjectivity, as well as political issues, particularly about the intentions and ideological assumptions that structure representations of the past.

The historiographical and literary assumptions about the constraints under which the historical novelist must operate, as Naomi Jacobs argues, tended to limit the appeal of the genre during the ascendancy of realist and modernist poetics. However, "with the weakening of the hegemony of realism in the twentieth century, brought about in part by challenges to the concept of objective representation, writers have increasingly come to believe that whatever problems have been felt in the past evaporate along with the epistemological presuppositions of realism."[38] The notion that historical discourse is essentially speculative rather than mimetic has certainly given novelists the elbow room to develop their own speculative fictions, probing the gaps or "dark areas" of received history, "those aspects about which the 'official' record has nothing to report," as in the work of E.L. Doctorow and D.M. Thomas.[39] In many cases, however, writers such as Thomas Pynchon and Robert Coover have gone further, openly turning that received history on its head, undermining the ideology on which it is based and/or self-consciously raising questions about the writing of history itself and about the relationship between history and literature.

As a consequence, historical fiction has become more self-conscious and self-reflexive, less concerned with creating and sustaining the illusion of a perceivable past. It reflects the prevalent influence of an increasingly postmodern art, an "art that is self-consciously art (or artifice), literature that is openly aware of the fact that it is written and read as part of a particular culture."[40] In light of the questioning of the possibility of historical objectivity and the undercutting of any ontological privileging of the historical over the fictional, Helen Hughes argues, "the presentation of history" in historical fiction is arguably "as much a part of the 'myth of the past' as the invented story." Indeed, an important aspect of contemporary historical fiction is the use of "the invented story," as Hughes puts it, "to effect an interrogation of 'the presentation of history.'"[41] As part of their engagement with historiography and with the writing of particular kinds of history, writers of historical fiction such as John Fowles and Salman Rushdie have opted for devices that openly question or complicate the distinction between the writing of fiction and the writing of history or that lay bare the process of construction that historical discourse and realistic fiction generally strive to efface.

Self-reflexive, parodic, and metafictional devices that call attention to the text as text, as imaginative construct, are similarly prevalent in Canadian fiction. Timothy Findley presents the story of Robert Ross in *The Wars* not as a mimetic account of Robert's family history and his experiences at the front during World War I, but as a narrative of a researcher's reconstruction of that story through the examination of photographs, through interviews, and so on – what Manina Jones calls a "documentary-collage."[42] In *The Invention of the World*, Jack Hodgins parodies the figure of the oral historian in his portrayal of Strabo Becker's struggle to piece together the history of the Revelations Colony of Truth and its mythic founder Donal Keneally. Anna Swan's tale in Susan Swan's *The Biggest Modern Woman of the World* parodies the *Bildungsroman* and, in its patchwork form and carnivalesque style, subverts historiography's and literary realism's conventions of unity and plausibility. These concerns with form are also evident in more recent novels such as Margaret Sweatman's *Fox*, Sky Lee's *Disappearing Moon Café*, and Rudy Wiebe's *A Discovery of Strangers*.

Another sign of the questioning of the epistemological underpinning of historical representation is a resistance to established notions of historical progression and the "pastness" of the past. The use of the past for the purposes of the present is for many historians a fundamental shortcoming (commonly attributed to historicism) because it undermines the objective presentation of the past. The projection of the present onto representations of the past therefore has been an important consideration in theorizing about the historical novel. In *The Historical Novel*, Lukács addresses the problem of historicism by citing Hegel's belief "that 'necessary anachronism' can emerge organically from historical material, if the past portrayed is clearly recognized and experienced by contemporary writers as the necessary prehistory of the present."[43] Lukács argues that "Scott's 'necessary anachronism' consists, therefore, simply in allowing his characters to express feelings and thoughts about real, historical relationships in a much clearer way than the actual men and women of the time could have done. But the content of these feelings and thoughts, their relation to the real object is always socially and historically correct."[44] In other words, a little historicist heightening in fact strengthens the clarity and accuracy of a historical portrait.

Contemporary formulations of history, however, as de Certau observes, have breached the gap that traditional historiography assumes between the present and the past: "It is thrown topsy-turvy, it is displaced, it moves forward. This movement is precisely due to the fact that this gap was posited, *and* that now it cannot be maintained."[45] Likewise, in contemporary historical fiction, such as Fowles's continually proleptic *The French Lieutenant's Woman*, the present intrudes more openly and disruptively on the representation of the past than Lukács has in mind. In some cases, writers are becoming more blatantly anachronistic, their use of anachronism, Jacobs argues, serving to highlight our assumptions about historical progression; the "judgment that something is anachronistic," for instance, "assumes that certain objects or ways of thinking belong to a particular time and to no other."[46]

A number of Canadian novelists raise these issues by representing or mingling historical figures in fairly carnivalesque ways, disregarding respect for historical periodization and ontological separation of the present and the past. Susan Swan's Anna Swan, for example, possesses a modern feminist consciousness. George Bowering's *Burning Water* is openly anachronistic in its portrayal of George Vancouver and in its blending of the writer George with the historical George. At one point the former observes that "then was then and now was now. [And now *is* now, but we're forgetting that for the moment.]" – both stating and parodying the operating principle of the historical novelist, the bracketing of contemporary perspective in order to better approximate a historical milieu.[47] And Daphne Marlatt demonstrates that "received history" is thoroughly patriarchal and that the past (at least for Mrs Richards of *Ana Historic*) must be imagined in more liberatory ways, requiring the active – or, rather, retroactive – intervention of her contemporary protagonist Annie. Such a purposeful use of anachronism, as Jacobs argues, serves to breach the historicist divide "between the original, 'correct' context and the new, 'incorrect' one," leading readers to see the two as similar rather than distinct.[48]

If these novels are intended as period pieces, there is some (obviously intentional) confusion about the period. In more recent fiction, such as *The Englishman's Boy*, Thomas Wharton's *Icefields*, and Jane Urquhart's *Away*, anachronism is present in more subtle ways but important nonetheless.

Another significant dimension of the contemporary historical novel that likewise subverts empiricist constraints and questions their ideological underpinnings is the undermining of the boundary between the real and the fictional. One of the challenging aspects in theorizing about the historical novel is that from the start it has been seen as a hybrid genre, combining the real and the historical with the fictional and the literary in often problematic ways. It necessarily raises ontological anxieties because it is neither purely history nor purely fiction. A key convention of the historical novel, it can be said, is a sign of such ontological anxiety: as Lukács observes, the main character of historical fiction is usually not the world-historical figure of Hegelian history but marginal in relation to the world-historical figure.[49] In Sir Walter Scott's writing, Lukács argues, such a character illustrates historical forces and represents Scott's conservative middle course between political extremes in a context of historical crisis.[50]

There is, however, another, more pragmatic reason for such marginality. By focusing on a minor historical player or a fictional character and minimizing the appearances of the world-historical figure, Marina Allemano observes, writers avoid the "problems that would arise from having to deal with the many known factual aspects of the historical figures" and the constraints of molding "the fictional aspects of the story ... to fit around the factual aspects."[51] The underlying "realist aesthetic" of the historical novel, as Jacobs points out, "assumes that a recognizable historical figure in fiction must not 'do things' its model did not do in real life; it follows that historical figures can be used only in very limited ways."[52]

In contemporary historical fiction, the blurring of the real and the fictional is far more substantial than in traditional historical novels. The latter, as Brian McHale observes, "typically involve some violation of ontological boundaries" but "strive to suppress these violations, to hide the ontological 'seams' between fictional projections and real-world facts. They do so by tactfully avoiding contradictions between their versions of historical figures and the familiar facts of these figures' careers, and by making the background norms governing their projected worlds conform to accepted real-world norms."[53] If there is no access to the historical outside of the framework through which the historian constructs the past, rather than there being "real" historical elements to be mingled with "constructed" fictional ones, writers have different ground rules for the construction of a fictional world and can be (indeed, obviously are) less concerned with "building" around received history. Findley's *Famous Last Words*, for instance, is narrated by Hugh Selwyn Mauberley, a character out of Ezra Pound's *Cantos* who seems, Martin Kuester feels, more real than the historical figures who populate the novel.[54] The Métis bard Pierre Falcon narrates Rudy Wiebe's *The Scorched-Wood People* from beyond the grave. Daphne Marlatt defends her invention of a past beyond existing historical records for Mrs Richards, the "historical" protagonist of *Ana Historic*, by saying, "As a novelist I'm allowed to do anything."[55] Such invention likewise plays an important part in John Steffler's *The Afterlife of George Cartwright* and Heather Robertson's *The King Years* trilogy.

In the wake of the questioning of mimetic models of representation, the hybridity of the historical novel, so troubling for those insistent on distinctions between the fictional and the real, has provided the departure point for a sustained challenging of the epistemological and ontological assumptions behind that insistence. The result is not just a more historiographically liberated form, in which the materials of history are highly malleable, but a much more diverse, heterogeneous, and self-conscious form.

HISTORY AND NARRATIVE

If the interpretation of historical evidence and the act of historical representation have been problematized as necessarily bound up with the subjectivity and interpretive systems of historians, the media through which such evidence is presented have likewise come under scrutiny. This further troubles the distinction between history and literature and projects the writing of historical fiction in a very different light. Because of its traditional reliance on narrative, history has long been at close quarters with literature, the two at times seen as separate discourses, at times as related. In twentieth-century historiography, the dominant trend was a shift of history away from literature. Under the influence of empiricism and positivism, history has increasingly aspired to achieve the status of a science. One of the central considerations in this aspiration has been the problematic character of the form of historical representation and the problem of subjectivity in such patterning of the past – exemplified in the empiricist distrust of historicism. While many historians have emphasized the specificity and uniqueness of history (that it is not repeatable and predictable) and the importance of the narrative aspects of history (that it is not just an assemblage of facts but a story about the past),[56] other historians have de-emphasized narrative, have emphasized evidence, fact, and statistics, and have striven to submit historical processes and events to the same kinds of general laws that govern the natural sciences. Much twentieth-century historiography thus displayed an empiricist suspicion of those imaginative formal and stylistic features that are taken as distinguishing literary writing from historical writing.

The underlying premise is that the poetic and/or narrative elements writers employ in their treatment of history transform that material beyond a particularized mimetic depiction, rendering it idealized or "fictional" rather than real. This rhetorical and stylistic distinction between history and literature goes back at least to Aristotle, who argues in *The Poetics* that the historian and the poet "differ in this, that while the former speaks of incidents that have come to be, the latter speaks of incidents that might come to be." Poetry therefore "is both more philosophic and more worthy than history, for making speaks more of universals while history speaks more of particulars."[57] Fleishman argues that the historical novel "is unashamedly a hybrid; it contemplates the universal but does not depart from the rich factuality of history in order to reach that elevation." The effect of literary representation, according to Fleishman, is thus to transform the particular into the archetypal. Historical or fictional characters become figures "in a universal pattern: not the repetitive patterns of the philosophies of history, but those of literature," which have "the same universalizing function when applied to historical situations. In the historical novel, the generic properties of plot, character, setting, thought, and diction ... operate on the materials of history to lend esthetic form to historical men's experience."[58]

Though such a distinction has been used to establish the boundaries between history and literature, contemporary historiography has served to muddy them, as well as to problematize the Aristotelian distinction between the specificity of history and the universality of literature. White puts into perspective the assumptions, and lack of ultimate objectivity, of both scientific and narrative history through his drawing attention to what he calls "the content of the form"[59] – the effects of the discursive conventions through which historians render their findings. All historical writing relies on discursive conventions that impose a certain shape, rhythm, and meaning on historical material – conventions that, particularly in the work of narrative historians, have great affinities with literature. Those events seen to be historical, White argues, "are made into a story by the suppression or subordination of certain of them and the highlighting of others, by characterization, motific repetition, variation of tone and point of view, alternative descriptive strategies, and the like – in short, all of the techniques that we would normally expect to find in the emplotment of a novel or a play."[60] Though White's focus is on narrative history, in which the selectivity of historical discourse is most pronounced, that selectivity is nonetheless evident to some degree in the most "scientific" and least "narrative" of histories.

White's emphasis on the shared figurative qualities of history and literature effects a *rapprochement* between the two which is especially important in the context of historical fiction. White underlines the essentially poetic nature of historians' narrative strategies, and contends that historical discourse, rather than representational, is essentially figurative and allegorical: "As a symbolic structure, the historical narrative does not *reproduce* the events it describes; it tells us in what direction to think about the events and charges our thought about the events with different emotional valences ... Properly understood, histories ought never to be read as unambiguous signs of the events they report, but rather as symbolic structures, extended metaphors, that 'liken' the events reported in them to some form with which we have already become familiar in our literary culture."[61] Historical representation is allegorical because it relies on interpretation, and interpretation, as Fredric Jameson argues, is essentially allegorical: "the question 'What does it mean?' constitutes something like an allegorical operation in which a text is systematically *rewritten* in terms of some fundamental master code or 'ultimately determining instance.'"[62]

Of course, debates about the relationship between history and literature and about the imaginative element of historical discourse have a long history themselves. What distinguishes White's reconceptualizing of history in this regard is how it undermines the empiricist ideal of the eradication of the subjective or imaginative elements in historical discourse and underlines that historical discourse, in the attempt to present the past in the form of narrative, necessarily makes use of discursive conventions that are continuous with, rather than distinct from, the discursive conventions of imaginative literature. Furthermore, the idea that these discursive conventions render the act of historical representation a figurative and symbolic, rather than mimetic, one serves to distinguish White's position from that of traditional defenders of narrative history.

White's shifting of the description of historical writing's operations from mimetic to allegorical obviously undermines the traditional distinction between history and literature and also has considerable implications for the historical novel. While it still might be said that writers of historical fiction do not generally operate within the same constraints or with the same aims as historians and that they are much more conscious of the aesthetic, linguistic, and figurative elements of their work, White's model of history suggests that those elements can no longer be used as the basis on which literature can be denied the representational function that is accorded to history. Indeed, Fleishman's view that "generic properties ... operate on the materials of history to lend esthetic form to historical men's experiences" sounds a lot like White's characterization of nineteenth-century historiography in *Metahistory*.[63] However, Fleishman effects a form-content distinction, presuming a separation between the historical material and the genres used to present it. In contrast, White underlines the necessary relationship between them, specifically the act of prefiguring the historical field that accompanies the choice of narrative mode, a choice that for White is fundamentally ideological and poetic. Ultimately, both historical discourse and historical fiction are marked by the dual function White describes – that is, both by aesthetic and allegorical imperatives and by a gesture towards the perceived past.

Another important implication of White's work is that to render the past as narrative involves not just putting it in story form, but giving it epistemological and ideological contours as well. Drawing on Hegel's rooting of history in the rule of law, White argues that "narrativity, certainly in factual storytelling and probably in fictional storytelling as well, is intimately related to, if not a function of, the impulse to moralize reality, that is, to identify it with the social system that is the source of any morality we can imagine."[64] A polished historical narrative that presents the illusion of a ready-made, coherent past, he suggests, is essentially a socially instrumental and ideological fiction.[65] In this sense, a historical narrative is not an objective representation of the past because it is already moralized, ideologically inscribed, due to the necessarily figurative character of its narrative form, and because the assumption that it represents the past is itself ideological.[66]

White's emphasis on the structuring effects of discourse, however, does not amount to a complete banishing of reference. Drawing on the work of Northrop Frye, White argues that "historical narrative points in two directions simultaneously: *toward* the events described in the narrative and *toward* the story type or mythos which the historian has chosen to serve as the icon of the structure of the events." The historical narrative structures our reading of the past by mediating "between the events reported in it on the one side and pregeneric plot structures conventionally used in our culture to endow unfamiliar events and situations with meanings, on the other."[67] Thus contemporary historiographical theory, especially that of White, has dispelled the naive construction of narrative in historical discourse as "simply a medium for the message" or "a code that served as a vehicle for transmitting messages about reality."[68] A deconstructive historiography, Alun Munslow argues, modifies the notion of history as a mode of knowing "by declaring that the past exists as history only because a narrative or story structure has been imposed by the historian on the evidence."[69]

Furthermore, if history has much of the fictive and figurative qualities of imaginative literature, literature, it can be argued, shares some of the epistemological value of history. An important implication of White's notorious and often misrepresented description of history as a "fiction-making operation" is that underlining history's affinities with literature reworks but does not completely undermine history's epistemological value:

How a given historical situation is to be configured depends on the historian's subtlety in matching up a specific plot structure with the set of historical events that he wishes to endow with a meaning of a particular kind. This is essentially a literary, that is to say fiction-making operation. And to call it that in no way detracts from the status of historical narratives as providing a kind of knowledge. For not only are the pregeneric plot structures by which sets of events can be constituted as stories of a particular kind limited in number, as Frye and other archetypal critics suggest, but the encodation of events in terms of such plot structures is one of the ways that a culture has of making sense of both personal and public pasts.[70]

Both history and literature, then, make meaning of the past, and any attempt to see the one as "science" and the other as "entertainment" is reductive, to say the least – especially when it comes to a genre like historical fiction. Narrative, in short, makes history possible, but in doing so it also shapes the appearance of history. Thus an awareness of the nature and extent of that shaping is crucial to our understanding of history.[71]

Furthermore, the implication that both the use of historical material and "the encodation of events" must be assessed is no less relevant for historical fiction. Summarizing the implications of contemporary theory's underlining of the discursive and mediated nature of our perception of the past, Hutcheon observes that "while all knowledge of the past may be provisional, historicized, and discursive, this does not mean we do not MAKE MEANING of that past."[72] While contemporary theorists have stressed the implications of the duality of that phrase for historiography, it is also crucial for understanding the writing and reception of historical fiction. In light of Hutcheon's formula, which mingles aesthetic considerations with epistemological ones, it is tempting to observe that the historical novel privileges the "making" and that historiography privileges the "meaning." Yet, while emphasizing the "making" – that is, the shared textual and figurative dimension of literature and historical discourse – it is important not to lose sight of the "meaning" that is mixed with it. In other words, just as it is problematic for the "making" in historical discourse to be overlooked or effaced in characterizing it as an objective, mimetic representation of the past, it is equally problematic to see the historical novel as simply an aestheticizing transformation of historical material into a purely textual entity with no referential relation to the material past.

Thus, even though the model of historical discourse as transparently mimetic has been undermined, history to some degree still presents the illusion of the past or at least in some way gestures to it. Furthermore, because that gesture is nonetheless taken very seriously and very materially, representing the past is not just a matter of a metaphorical play of texts with no referential inclination. And the same is true of historical fiction. An important focus of debate, then, is the relationship between, on the one hand, the particularity of historical events and contexts and, on the other hand, the aestheticizing and symbolic dimensions of literature and history as (in White's terms) necessarily tropological and allegorical discourses. Thus it is not irrelevant to consider the relationship between epistemological choices and narrative form, and to assess the compatibility of a text's aesthetic and rhetorical aspirations with its handling of "the materials of history." If history is necessarily allegorical, in other words, then aesthetic choices are inextricably bound up with epistemological choices.

Like historical writing, historical fiction has always worked against notions of what are considered appropriate uses of historical material (the issue of libel being the extreme legal edge of this concern). A key consideration in this regard is the importance of observing the letter or the spirit of the law of history, as it were – that is, the accuracy of the "materials of history" or the appropriateness of the tropological form in which they are presented. Lukács argues that the great achievement of writers of realistic fiction, including the historical novel, is due in part to "the freedom with which they handle their material: ... they are sufficiently familiar with popular life to be able to devise situations in which the deepest truths emerge more clearly and luminously than in everyday life itself." Consequently, what Lukács calls the "'cult of facts' is a miserable surrogate for this intimacy with the people's historical life."[73] This emphasis on spirit over historical precision is succinctly emphasized by Wiebe, who observes that, "unless they are very carefully handled, facts are invariable tyrants of story. They are inhibiting as fences and railroad."[74]

This balance, however, is more strenuously put to the test in an atmosphere of epistemological liberation and formal innovation. Scepticism about history may have destabilized epistemological considerations, but it certainly has not banished them. The benefits of this freedom notwithstanding, a historical novel's version of a particular figure or episode may be controversial or questionable because, as result of the way in which "the materials of history" have been selected, interpreted, or supplemented, it deviates from or runs counter to prevailing accounts.[75] Thus Salman Rushdie has come under fire for historical inaccuracies and the negative portrayal of Indian nationalism in *Midnight's Children*, and the cloud of legal action has hovered over the career of Robert Coover's *The Public Burning* because of its portrait of Richard Nixon and other public figures.[76] Similar departures are evident in Canadian fiction. Susan Swan's *The Biggest Modern Woman of the World* gives the celebrated Nova Scotia giants Anna Swan and Angus McAskill the opportunity to meet and fall in love, an opportunity the historical giants appear not to have had. In *Willie*, Robertson depicts Mackenzie King as having a secret mistress whom at one point he tries to rape, and in *Igor: A Novel of Intrigue* she entertains the possibility that Gouzenko might himself have been a Soviet plant. These and other historical novels present a considerable affront to those whose attitude towards history is "a place for everything and everything in its place."

The way in which "meaning" is "made" of the past is also an important and often controversial consideration. In historical fiction, as in historical discourse, the allegorizing of historical material will differ in its political and rhetorical effects depending on what kinds of strategies are employed, and often exception is taken to the balance between the allegorical or aesthetic pattern and the historical detail that is given shape through that pattern. Magic realist texts that deal with Third-World histories are a good example, as they have been accused of presenting exoticized and dehistoricized accounts of struggles against imperialism.[77] In Canada, Wiebe's efforts to counter the Eurocentric historical record's injustices against native leaders like Louis Riel and Big Bear in his novels *The Temptations of Big Bear* and *The Scorched-Wood People* have led to concerns about appropriation because of the Christian teleology that is the overriding pattern in his presentation of their stories. Likewise, Ondaatje's *In the Skin of a Lion* has been criticized for its representation of working-class, revolutionary activism in Depression-era

Toronto in a potentially aestheticizing and depoliticizing fashion. Thus, despite all the scepticism about, and reconfiguration of, historical and literary representation, epistemological questions continue to be relevant because the historical novel is, like history, one of the ways in which we make meaning of the past.

While the emphasis White and others place on the importance of narrativity would seem to dissolve the borders between literature and history, it is crucial to recognize the role of certain "discursive regularities" in both. Writers, it seems fair to generalize, are more inclined to be self-consciously aesthetic and less rigorously empirical than historians in their prefiguring, narrativizing, and allegorizing of historical material. But this is only relatively valid, and there are certainly writers and historians whose work defies such a distinction. Ultimately, postmodern historiography's emphasis on narrative, and on history as allegory, undermines the epistemological and ontological boundaries between history and literature, and underlines the importance of assessing "the content of the form" of both. As novels like *Fox*, *Away*, *Icefields*, and *Willie* show, the interplay between historical material and literary form continues to be a crucial consideration in Canadian historical fiction.

HISTORY AND INTERTEXTUALITY

The narrative form of the contemporary historical novel, as texts like *The Temptations of Big Bear*, *The Biggest Modern Woman*, and *Ana Historic* reflect, is much more heterogeneous and intertextual. This shift in narrative form points to another dimension of the traditional distinction between history and literature that has been reconfigured in contemporary theory: their relations to their sources. The two kinds of discourse have generally been seen as synthesizing their narratives out of different kinds of material: writers draw on their personal experiences, social circumstances, the mythologies of past and present cultures, and so on, while historians rely on documents, eyewitness testimony, statistics, historical accounts, and the like. Historical fiction, however, representing a mixture of the two, obviously complicates this distinction, because most historical novelists have typically made use of sources similar to those used by historians. Furthermore, in the case of many historical novelists, the sources have been used to the same effect – to create a sense of historical verisimilitude and veracity – but without the same attention to footnotes. Raddall's *His Majesty's Yankees*, for instance, draws heavily on archival research and on the work of various historians of the

Maritimes and the American Revolution in its fictional recreation of revolutionary-era Nova Scotia.[78] Indeed, Raddall viewed the book as being "history with a very thin coating of fiction. Much of it is pure fact, even to the minor conversations of minor characters."[79]

Contemporary theory and contemporary historical fiction, however, have much more profoundly complicated the relationship between historical writing and historical sources. If, in White's terms, the historical narrative "mediates" between "events in the historical record" and culturally relative narrative forms, the historical record, as White, LaCapra, and others have noted, is itself textual, not only posing epistemological problems about the possibility of historical knowledge, but also posing ontological problems about historical discourse and subjectivity. Rather than being the transparent, unproblematic, residual presence of the past, historical evidence is already textualized, shaped by the signifying systems of its time, and already framed as evidence, as "historical" or "significant," through the interpretive systems of historians. As Jameson puts it, "history is not a text, for it is fundamentally non-narrative and nonrepresentational; what can be added, however, is the proviso that history is inaccessible to us except in textual form, or in other words, that it can be approached only by way of prior (re)textualization."[80]

These considerations are further complicated by theories of intertextuality stressing the radical heterogeneity rather than unity of discourse. Attention increasingly has been drawn to the illusory unity of historical discourse, to how historians customarily strive to provide a coherent, homogeneous picture of the past on the basis of fragmentary and heterogeneous evidence. Though good historians traditionally have tended to be meticulous about documenting sources and evidence and about proving their familiarity with the historical writing on the subject at hand, they have also been good surgeons, suturing together the scraps that contribute to what is usually assumed, and asserted, to be a unified picture. Now critics are increasingly inclined to point out that history, instead of being a smooth fabric, is more like a quilt, the pieces for which, furthermore, historians have cut and dyed rather than found ready-to-hand.

This notion of intertextuality has been theorized most prominently by Julia Kristeva, and her model of a text as "a heterogeneous mosaic of texts" has definite implications for historiography.[81] In a particularly relevant formulation of intertextuality, Kristeva presents novelistic discourse as an ongoing relationship between narration (or what we might call representation) and citation: "The author-actor's utterance unfolds, divides, and faces in two directions: first, towards a referential utterance, *narration* – the speech assumed by he who inscribes himself as actor-author; and second, toward textual premises, *citation* – speech attributed to an other and whose authority he who inscribes himself as actor-author acknowledges."[82] These contrasting modes – reminiscent of the duality noted in White's model of historical narrative – are integrated within a novelistic totality: "The novel is thus structured as dual space: it is both phonetic utterance and scriptural level, overwhelmingly dominated by discursive (phonetic) order."[83]

Historical discourse likewise, and perhaps more conspicuously, involves a quilting of textual scraps, an amalgam of different voices and discourses contained within the historian's account of the past – with the seams generally concealed. De Certau describes historical writing as a "stratification of discourse" that, instead of taking an openly intertextual "form of a 'dialogue' or a 'collage,'" subsumes that discursive plurality to buttress its own (singular) authority. Quoted language "introduces into the text an effect of reality; and through its crumbling, it discreetly refers to a locus of authority. From this angle, the split structure of discourse functions like a machinery that extracts from the citation a verisimilitude of narrative and a validation of knowledge. It produces a sense of reliability."[84] Thus, somewhat ironically, historians convince readers of the veracity of historical accounts by imposing on them an illusory unity and suppressing the actual heterogeneity of the texts on which they are based. The quilt, in other words, is easier to sell as a blanket – and, indeed, the attempt to present it as such provides a further instance of the mediating, rhetorical, and allegorical character of historical discourse. LaCapra observes that, since literature and history parted ways in the nineteenth century, the novel, unlike historical writing, has steadily become more self-reflexive, experimental, and carnivalesque, and he calls for the reinjection into history of a long-suppressed carnivalesque element.[85]

That both historical discourse and literary discourse comprise a fabric of citations, a weave of other texts, illustrates once again the continuities between the two. Just as Kristeva's work undermines the idea of a correspondence between a unified, pure language and a represented world, it also does the same for the relation between historical discourse and the past it presumes to represent. It suggests the degree to which historical discourse is an "ordering" of other texts rather than a discovery of an "order" in the past. In this "ordering," furthermore, the repertoire of conventions associated with what Kristeva calls "narration," as opposed to citation, is also an intertextual formation, the cumulative reverberations of prior texts. This description of history as a kind of intertextual discursive synthesis highlights its affinities with fiction, which Jacobs describes as "scrap art compiled from old conversations, rumors, memories, and visions, which are cut into patterns and stitched together or simply relabeled like old bottles, retaining their original shapes but wearing new names and containing different potions."[86]

This intertextual "ordering," moreover, is not so much an orderly mosaic as it is the site of discursive contestation. Rather, historical discourse can be viewed, in the spirit of Mikhail Bakhtin's treatment of the novel, as fundamentally dialogic. For Bakhtin, the model of speech as expressive signification is profoundly complicated by the fact that any utterance is intertextual, rather than a unitary "thing that articulates the intention of the person uttering it, ... a direct, single-voiced vehicle for expression."[87] A significant proportion of an individual's social utterances, of whatever complexity, will be "implicitly or explicitly admitted as someone else's."[88] This heterogeneity is, furthermore, not comfortably harmonious: "Within the arena of almost every utterance an intense interaction and struggle between one's own and another's word is being waged, a process in which they oppose or dialogically interanimate each other."[89]

If speech is so profoundly and dialogically heterogeneous, then history in turn must be recognized as a discourse that strives to contain other texts – particularly those traces of the past that constitute the historical record, but also the work of other historians – in the process of asserting a particular representation of the past. As LaCapra observes, history is both externally and internally dialogic: "a 'conversation' with the past involves the historian in argument and even polemic – both with others and within the self – over approaches to understanding that are bound up with institutional and political issues."[90] That suppressing the intertextuality of historical discourse has been the custom in the past and that at present it is, instead, increasingly being foregrounded certainly suggests the operation of certain discursive regularities in historical practice (and suggests, furthermore, that such regularities are subject to historical change). But whether a historian's preferred form is the monologue or the dialogue, what theories of intertextuality suggest is that the activity of historians consists less of providing some Olympian, retrospective play-by-play of the past than of drawing on a repertoire of historiographical conventions to synthesize and choreograph a wide array of texts, discourses, and voices. Rather than training their eyes on the past as through a telescope, this model suggests, historians look to the past through a kaleidoscope of fragments of their own choosing.

The application of theories of narrative and intertextuality to the conception of subjectivity has further undermined the model of history as a Cartesian encounter between the subjectivity of the historian and the traces of the past that constitute the historical record. Attention is increasingly being drawn to the role of narrative in the construction of the self, to the idea that it "is in and through various forms of narrative emplotment that our lives – and thereby ... our very selves – attain meaning."[91] Rather than being the organic, unified entity of Enlightenment progress, Donald Polkinghorne argues, the individual establishes a coherent sense of self "by understanding it as an expression of a single unfolding and developing story." The self, as a result, "is not a static thing nor a substance, but a configuring of personal events into a historical unity which includes not only what one has been but also anticipations of what one will be."[92]

This emphasis on the intertextuality of the subject reinforces once again the continuity, rather than difference, between history and literature. Anthony Kerby, for instance, emphasizes not only the subject's position within semiotic systems, comprising "speech, texts, art works, and meaningful action generally," but also "the active intertextuality that such participation involves." For Kerby, personal development relies on "a reflective grasp of, and habitual participation in, this network of social communication and praxis. The human subject must thus be situated within the structures that sustain it rather than posited as transcendent to them; it must be implicated in the production of such structures but need not be taken as foundational."[93] The convergence between historical and literary discourse entailed by this intertextual orientation is nicely summarized by Jacobs, who cites a "growing sense that all character is a fiction, constructed by imagination as well as observation."[94]

One implication of this convergence is that the intertextuality of the literary imagination is thus ultimately not of a different order from that of the historian, but simply a composite of a different variety of textual scraps, and perhaps a different methodology and set of rhetorical strategies – in particular a less sustained gestural intention. As Jacobs argues, "the process of reconstructing a historical subject differs very little from the process of constructing a wholly fictional character."[95] The intertextuality of the historical novel, however, comes closer to that of historical discourse. That is, the two tend to be made up of more of the same kinds of scraps; you might find the quilts in different departments, but the material is much the same.

This blurring of the generic and even ontological boundaries between historical discourse and historical fiction has been accelerated by contemporary writers of historical fiction. One distinguishing feature of contemporary historical fiction is that its intertexts are more likely to be deployed to question the possibility of an authentic history than to emulate it, in the manner of Raddall, in a work of fiction. As Kuester points out, while historical novels quite obviously "differ from other novelistic genres in their use of parodic strategies because the textual material they incorporate is often of non-fictional origin," the "integration of 'real' elements into the fictional universe then leads to new metafictional, or rather metahistorical, questions about the quality of 'realism' in these novels."[96] Traditional historical novels have often displayed the evidence of exhaustive research and at least the appearance of historical fidelity (an ideal that typically distinguishes them from the obvious costume drama of much historical romance). However, contemporary writers, while often likewise exhaustively engaged in research, are less inclined to apply that research to the creation of the appearance of history "as it really was." Instead, the intertextuality of their work is often connected to its social, political, cultural, and epistemological concerns.

Foregrounding rather than submerging the intertextuality of representations of the past is a key strategy evident in much contemporary Canadian fiction. Wiebe, for instance, integrates the discourses of eye-witnesses, historians, and government officials into the narrative of *The Temptations of Big Bear* in a fashion that both highlights perspective and ideology and subjects these discourses to scrutiny. The narrative thus recognizes the varied, conflicting, and interpenetrating world-views of the characters and underlines that, if anything is invented, it is the idea of a homogeneous, cohesive view of the past – not least of the history of the Prairies. Marlatt inserts scraps of both newspaper clippings and other texts into the narrative of *Ana Historic* to burlesque their masculine assumptions and language. Finally, Susan Swan's narrative of Anna Swan's picaresque adventures as a carnival attraction in *The Biggest Modern Woman of the World* is itself a parodic carnival of different texts, deconstructing the role of documents in the reconstruction of a historical figure. If, as Bakhtin argues, the novel is a fundamentally heteroglossic genre, "*an artistically organized system for bringing different languages in contact with one another,* a system having as its goal the illumination of one language by means of another,"[97] the contemporary historical novel presents a site in which such engagements are a significant part of the text and very often foregrounded in the narrative. More recent fiction – such as Wiebe's *A Discovery of Strangers*, Sweatman's *Fox*, and Steffler's *The Afterlife of George Cartwright* – continues the tradition.

This self-consciously dialogic relationship exists not just between ostensibly fictional intertexts and ostensibly non-fictional intertexts, but also between different kinds of literary intertexts and different kinds of discourses. The historical novel, as an extension of the realistic novel, has always been dialogic (witness the mix of realism, romance, folklore, and the supernatural in Scott), but the contemporary historical novel is much more openly and systematically carnivalized, flooding over the boundaries of literary realism and mingling with other genres such as fantasy, myth, magic realism, documentary, and so on. In Urquhart's *Away,* Celtic mythology and historical fiction interpenetrate in problematic but productive ways. Vanderhaeghe subverts the Hollywood Western in *The Englishman's Boy.* Robertson's *Igor* draws heavily on non-fictional accounts of Gouzenko's celebrated defection but in a narrative structure that parodies popular genres such as the detective story and the thriller. In other words, the complex relationship between ostensibly literary conventions and texts and ostensibly historical conventions and texts is complicated by the interaction between different literary genres. Ever a hybrid form, the historical novel is only becoming more so, as novelists explore the myriad possibilities of intertextuality. The most valuable forms of engagement with history, their work reflects, emerge not from insisting on an objective and unified discourse but by permitting – indeed stressing – the interplay between different perspectives, different voices, different genres, and different texts.

In the wake of contemporary theory's deconstruction of the foundations on which ideologies of scientific objectivity, artistic realism, and historical authenticity are based, historical discourse and historical fiction are tenuously poised between a discredited objectivism and an aestheticized textual play in a language cut off from any ontological ground (as Derrida's notorious phrase "il n'y a de hors-texte" suggests).[98] The emphasis on intertextuality, like the undermining of the ontology of mimesis and the reconfiguration of historical narrative as allegory, seems to lead down the murky ethical path of textual relativism, in which there is no "real" or "extra-textual" ground beyond the text and historical discourse's relation to the past is arbitrarily metaphorical or allegorical. This is, unsurprisingly, an unpopular conclusion among most historians, and even some who appreciate the implications of the "linguistic turn" in historiography resist the idea of historical discourse as completely arbitrary and relative – as a playful, nostalgic *plaisir du texte.*[99]

Georg Iggers, for one, observes that, although contemporary theory has cultivated a greater scepticism about historical sources, historians' methodology and reliance on those sources in large part remain the same: "We have become more aware of the extent to

which they do not directly convey reality but are themselves narrative constructs that reconstruct these realities, not willy-nilly, but
guided by scholarly findings and by a scholarly discourse."[100] The
guiding principle or aim, Iggers argues, drawing on Peter Novick's
work, is not objectivity but a rational determination of what is plausible. The assumption remains that historical discourse "relates to a
historical reality, no matter how complex and indirect the process is
by which the historian approximates this reality," because most historians are not ready to embrace the principle "that the texts with
which they work have no reference to reality. To be sure every historical account is a construct, but a construct arising from a dialog
between the historian and the past, one that does not occur in a
vacuum but within a community of inquiring minds who share cri-
teria of plausibility."[101] The model of "practical realism" developed
by Appleby, Hunt, and Jacob in *Telling the Truth About History* is
likewise seen as a way around relativism because of their insistence
"that some words and conventions, however socially constructed,
reach out to the world and give a reasonably true description of its
contents"; in short, realism "permits historians to aim language at
things outside themselves."[102]

Although obviously sceptical about historical discourse and the
possibility of representing the past, Iggers, Appleby, Hunt, and Jacob
provide compelling defences against constructions of historical discourse as completely arbitrary and essentially mythical or metaphoric in its relation to the past. However, the model of a scholarly
community committed to plausibility (reminiscent of Stanley Fish's
insistence on the role of "interpretive communities" in prefiguring
one's critical engagement with literary texts[103]) and the concept of
practical realism reflect a residual assumption of an ontological split
between the historian and the historical past, not sufficiently credit-
ing how the two are inextricably entwined. In this respect, the two
models illustrate the importance of resisting a radically relativist historiography not through upholding the mimetic validity of historical
discourse, but through recognizing the "discursive regularities" that
govern historical writing.

If poststructuralist theorizing of language, representation, and subjectivity has created a certain ontological insecurity, Foucault's
description of the operation of discursive regularities and White's
view of historical discourse as figurative and allegorical limit the
arbitrariness that is seen as the inevitable and disturbing outcome of
critiques of reference. Discourse, in short, may not refer to a transcendent, objective reality, but it is nonetheless highly regulated rather

than boundless. Recognizing the importance of methodological and linguistic practices, as de Certau argues, does not mean that historiography simply "turns in on itself to take pleasure in examining its procedures." Instead, it underlines that "meaning cannot be apprehended in the form of a specific knowledge that would either be drawn from the real or might be added to it, ... because every 'historical fact' results from a praxis," that is, "from procedures which have allowed a mode of comprehension to be articulated as a discourse of 'facts.'"[104] Thus have the traditional epistemological and ontological boundaries between historical evidence and the historian been profoundly blurred: we cannot see through lenses without understanding how they make vision possible.

Much has been written about the structuralist and poststructuralist collapse of the world into text and about the apparent abolition of any ontological ground behind language; an examination of this collapse's implications for historiography can fill, indeed has filled, entire books.[105] Nonetheless, the assumption underlying the argument to follow in this book is that, if historical and representational discourse assumes, constantly gestures to, a phenomenal world, then keeping the gestural nature of that discourse in view is as important as foregrounding its conventional, discursive, and textual nature. This position leaves necessary room for resisting a radically relative and anti-materialist historiography, especially given the implications of, for instance, viewing the Holocaust or colonialism as a fiction, a historical construct in the purely textual sense. Recognizing what Munslow calls the "impositionalism" of historical discourse does not mean "that we construct the past without any sense of what is morally right just because we do not know what is true. This is a bleak argument that does not do justice to the dissenting and questioning nature of much historiography."[106] Postmodern historiography has been recurrently dismissed as cultivating an irresponsible "anything goes" mentality, but it should be clear from the preceding discussion that this is not necessarily the case.

Taking a glimpse at the profound shifts in historiography and the debates they have occasioned not only facilitates an understanding of the philosophical and ideological underpinnings of shifts in the genre of historical fiction, but also helps to put into perspective what is at stake when the conventions of that genre are deployed in different ways. Underlining the limited relativism of postmodern historiography, for instance, is important because most contemporary historical novels in Canada likewise inscribe a recognition that discourses on history "reach out to the world" – though contemporary novelists are implicitly wary of concluding from this that their texts "give a reasonably true description of its contents." Instead, to varying degrees they highlight the codes and discursive conventions that govern historical writing and reflect the sense that the politics and technologies of representation of traditional history and historical fiction need to be questioned. Their doing so amounts to a reconfiguration, rather than repudiation, of material history – again, to varying degrees. Some texts are more historiographically sceptical, anti-mimetic, or revisionist than others, and hence it is necessary to explore in more detail the nature and implications of that variety.

2 Historical Sites

Historical novels are, in their own fashion, "markers" of what are deemed to be significant historical "sites." They have customarily served as textual monuments to pivotal figures or events in a very public, official national history. In contrast, many contemporary historical novels, reflecting the influence of postmodernism and postcolonialism, for the most part focus on what has been left out of that history or on what that history has served to override. The centrifugal energies of postmodernism, Robert Young argues in *White Mythologies*, are very much tied to throwing off the legacy of colonialism. Thus postmodernism marks "not just the central effects of a new stage of 'late' capitalism, but the sense of loss of European history and culture as History and Culture, the loss of their unquestioned place at the centre of the world."[1]

This reversal of the pre-eminence of European history is, of course, a response to that history's own erasures. Writing of the genesis of *The Temptations of Big Bear*, Rudy Wiebe expresses his indignation at discovering that the trail of Big Bear's life crossed and recrossed the ground on which he himself was raised, provoking his anger at how such history so close to home could be effaced: "in forcing me to discover the past of my place on my own as an adult, my public school inadvertently roused an anger in me which has ever since given an impetus to my writing which I trust it will never lose."[2] This sense of recovering a past elided by an exclusionary "public" version of Canadian history informs the work of the vast majority of the historical novels written in Canada since the publication of *Big*

Bear. Over the last thirty years, Canadian novelists have been rede-fining, on a number of terrains, both the terms of the nation and history as a medium for recording its past, bringing greater demo-graphic variety to representations of Canadian history, with a distinctly revisionist and largely postcolonial slant. They have concerned them-selves with those who have been either left out of history, as it were, or misrepresented within a narrowly defined sense of what is his-torically important. They have increasingly opted out of the idea that the story of a nation is necessarily a unified narrative and a narrative about unity. In the process they have raised important ques-tions about the assumptions underlying choices of what counts as history.

Seeing this literary reconfiguring of Canadian history as postcolo-nial, however, is complicated by Canada's status as one of a number of settler-invader cultures or "breakaway settler colonies," which are distinct from other postcolonial societies by virtue of "their formal independence from the founding metropolitan country, along with continued control over the appropriated colony (thus displacing con-trol from the metropolis to the colony itself)."[3] If postcolonialism involves a writing back to the empire, this gesture is obviously com-plicated when those doing the writing are of the same cultural back-ground and heritage as those being addressed.[4] As a result, in the whirlwind of debates raging over the definition and application of the term "postcolonialism," settler-invader cultures like Canada, Australia, and New Zealand have occupied an uneasy place.

In the context of Canada, the obvious problem of a settler culture's complicity with colonialism has prompted differing responses. Linda Hutcheon suggests that the term "post-colonial" is more appropri-ately applicable to the writing of indigenous peoples.[5] In contrast, Diana Brydon responds that using the term to establish an exclusive domain of the postcolonial in some ways replicates colonial thinking. She contends instead that "postcolonial frames of interpretation are most enabling when they facilitate distinctions between different orders of colonial experience, rather than, on the one hand, conflating Third World and invader-settler societies as equally victimized or, on the other, banishing settler colonies from the sphere of 'properly' postcolonial subject matter."[6] Furthermore, the idea that settler-invader cultures fail to qualify as postcolonial on the basis of their European heritage elides the fact that all postcolonial societies have been marked by colonialism and that the idea of a return to an unco-lonial, prelapsarian state is a dangerously essentialist ideal that has led to troubling forms of nationalism and tribalism. "To overlook the particularity of the settler site, to collapse it into some larger or unspecified narrative of empire or metropolis, or even to exclude it from the field of the postcolonial altogether," as Alan Lawson argues, "is to engage in a strategic disavowal of the actual process of colonization, a self-serving forgetting of the entangled agency of one's history as a subject with that of the displaced Native/colonized subject."[7]

To say this, however, is not to reduce everything to a state of postcolonial equivalence; as Elleke Boehmer notes, "post-imperial realities are far more contradictory, agitated, and diverse than any one critical approach could hope to describe."[8] Distinctions are still in order, and an investigation of contemporary Canadian historical fiction provides a good illustration of how concerns with race, ethnicity, gender, and constructions of nation have been shaped in response to the legacy of colonialism. The aim of this chapter, therefore, is to explore some of the fronts along which these novelists respond to such historical imbalances, not just supplementing Canadian history but questioning, revising, and redefining it in largely (but not unequivocally) postcolonial terms. Emphasizing that these historical "sites" are interconnected rather than discrete, this chapter examines the treatment of colonization and the history of native-white relations in Canada, clearly a preoccupation of historical novelists old and new; the redefining of Canadian history through the lens of a social history that emphasizes concerns of gender, sexuality, ethnicity, race, and class; and, finally, the reconfiguring of nation and national identity.

FIRST NATIONS TO COLONY TO NATION: DECOLONIZING OR RECOLONIZING CANADIAN HISTORY?

Colonial discourse "has always operated by making the local (colonised) place secondary to the metropolitan centre, its history calibrated according to an external norm." Consequently, part of the reconstitutive work of a counter-hegemonic, postcolonial response is "to begin to understand local geographies and histories to allow them to count in a way previously denied."[9] As Wiebe's description of the suppression of indigenous local history underscores, colonialism is a kind of palimpsest, a writing over the aboriginal past. It is no surprise, then, that responding to this erasure has been a central objective of recent Canadian historical novels, many of which seek to reopen what is too often seen as a closed book: the history of colonialism and of relations between native people and the dominant culture.

The delicate navigation that delineating the postcolonial status of settler-invader cultures requires is particularly evident in what can be seen as postcolonial attempts to rework colonial history in fiction. The historical novel has certainly played a part in this colonial erasure, contributing to a confirmation of the project of colonialism that has as its complement the marginalization or caricature of native characters; Thomas Costain's *High Towers*, Philip Child's *The Village of Souls*, and Raddall's *His Majesty's Yankees* all work to this effect. Contemporary historical novelists, however, are much more inclined to be critical of the colonial project and to allow the histories colonialism attempts to erase "to count in a way previously denied."

This shift in attitude can be seen particularly in the treatment of colonial figures involved in the "discovery" and exploration of Canada and in the treatment of the process of settlement. Rather than fleshing out stages in a narrative of national emergence, contemporary portrayals of discovery and settlement tend to emphasize the role those portrayals play in a process of appropriation and imposition. However, the historical novel is still predominantly the preserve of writers of European heritage, whose participation in the decolonizing of Canadian history raises issues of cultural politics and appropriation. Thus the recurring question with such attempts is whether they truly contribute to a decolonization of Canadian history or simply perpetuate colonial domination.

Chronicling the courageous penetration of European trailblazers into a new world, narratives of discovery and exploration are obviously an important part of the colonial project and of the foundational myths of a Eurocentric view of Canadian history. Within this view, the appropriation underlying this project has been elided either through depictions of Canada as a blank slate waiting to be filled by Europe or through depictions of the original inhabitants as obstacles to be overcome in the inevitable fulfilment of imperial or national destiny. Such accounts generally reflect in North American terms what Abdul R. JanMohamed sees as "the central feature of the colonialist cognitive framework and colonialist literary representation: the manichean allegory – a field of diverse yet interchangeable oppositions between white and black, good and evil, superiority and inferiority, civilization and savagery, intelligence and emotion, rationality and sensuality, self and Other, subject and object."[10] Recent historical novels, however, have resisted such a manichean depiction of native people and have been more inclined to dramatize rather than submerge that appropriation. Rudy Wiebe's *A Discovery of Strangers* and Thomas Wharton's *Icefields*, like George Bowering's earlier *Burning Water*, in many ways reverse and even parody the terms and the perspective of colonial representations of exploration and discovery. The question remains, however, whether these novels are ultimately different from their predecessors in kind or just in degree.

The title of Wiebe's *A Discovery of Strangers* (1994), about the 1819–22 Franklin expedition, gives a good indication of its revisionist thrust. The programed response is to read the "discovery" as the customary, active pursuit of the explorer. Here, however, the use of "strangers" suggests that it is the explorers themselves who are discovered, in this case by the Tetsot'ine or Dene, whom the members of the expedition expect to help them chart a route up the Coppermine to the Arctic Ocean and back. The title's inversion of the trajectory of colonial exploration mirrors the general inversion of the narrative as a whole, which focuses largely on the reaction of the Tetsot'ine to the coming of the whites.

Wiebe's aim in telling the story of this particular expedition (as opposed to the more notorious and final 1845 expedition, whose members disappeared in pursuit of the Northwest passage, providing a tantalizing mystery for generations of historians) is consistent with the postcolonial reappraisal of the history of colonization in much of his fiction. In writing about the failure of the earlier expedition, Wiebe unearths one of many suppressed narratives of colonization, exposing an episode that blurs the manichean opposition of the civilized and the savage through which colonial appropriation is so often justified. As Heather Robertson notes, by 1848 rumours of cannibalism had surfaced about the 1845 expedition, but the story was suppressed for over a century, presumably in an effort to make an unsavoury incident go away; the truth was "so grisly it has been considered literally unspeakable."[11] Having become intrigued during his research with the character of Robert Hood, Wiebe began to pursue the issue of cannibalism in the context of the earlier expedition, taking this particular episode as the focus for an exploration of colonial assumptions in *A Discovery of Strangers*.

Wiebe draws on a vast array of sources to construct the story of the expedition's disastrous journey north from Fort Enterprise in the summer of 1821. He juxtaposes actual and reworked or imagined journal entries, letters, and narrative segments from the perspective of members of the expedition (principally Robert Hood and John Richardson) with third-person-omniscient or limited-omniscient narration from the perspective of members of the Tetsot'ine hunter Keskarrah's family. Wiebe's intent in constructing an aboriginal perspective is to highlight the incomprehensibility and implacable, irrational resolution of the expedition and its inevitable defeat by the land itself.

A recurring strategy in postcolonial writing is the deliberate disruption of "European notions of 'history' and the ordering of time."[12] Wiebe achieves this in *Discovery* by juxtaposing "the journal extracts, [which,] through their dated succession, provoked a reassuring linear narrative," with a Tetsot'ine cosmology "based on a circular notion of time" that disrupts the linear teleology of colonial discovery.[13] There is little suspense about the ultimate outcome of the expedition, as Wiebe signals its failure at the beginning of the novel, noting that "when those who were still alive appeared again out of the north fifteen months later, they were quite incapable of seeing anything at all" (*Discovery of Strangers* 13). By focusing on Keskarrah and his family, however, Wiebe presents the pursuit of the expedition's mandate not just as Eurocentrically stubborn, but as almost masochistic because of the doom that awaits it from the very beginning. Keskarrah and more so his wife, Birdseye, are aware that the expedition is destined to fail. Throughout the long winter before the northern trek, Birdseye unravels "the inevitability of the future" (119), that is, the story of the disastrous outcome of the expedition prior to its departure for the north. She foretells the explorers' defeat by the ice, their elliptic return overland and near defeat at the double rapids on the Coppermine River, the succumbing of most of the voyageurs, and the death of Hood.

Birdseye's own telling, however, is not so chronological. The looping, enigmatic course of her story disrupts the relentless progress and pace of colonial exploration: "the ceaseless travel of the Whitemuds begins to tire her and she forces them to move more slowly." She "teaches them to savour details, whether they wish to or not. Sometimes for an entire day she describes one single rock they must pass in the crooked river of their journey" (147). Thus the narrative is governed by a circular and elastic, rather than linear and chronometric, sense of time, in which the determination of the whites is merely the impetus that leads to the completion of a foreordained circle. The "trek of These English coming," reflects Keskarrah, "has always been here waiting for them. It was already waiting before they decided (as they still seem to think *they decide* everything, as if they could determine or change what will happen), before they marked down and decided what should happen" (153).

This non-linear sense of time provides a framework that intensifies the novel's critique of colonialism in a number of ways, highlighting the naive, condescending self-confidence of the colonizer in an alien land. Through the reactions of Keskarrah, his daughter Greenstockings, and others, Wiebe emphasizes the arrogance of whites in abrogating everything – people, technology, the land – to the furthering of their designs. At various points in the narrative, *Wiebe* stresses the supreme presumption of the English in expecting the Tetsot'ine to play support staff to the expedition, an imposition that upsets their balance of life and exposes them to unnecessary privation, especially when the survivors of the expedition make their way back to Fort Enterprise and have to appeal to the generosity of the Tetsot'ine to be saved.[14]

Wiebe emphasizes the expectation of the English that their new environs should adapt to suit them rather than vice versa, for instance by highlighting the stark inappropriateness of the technology of exploration. The weapons they provide for the Tetsot'ine hunters are thoroughly disruptive – loud, clumsy, and unreliable – and threaten to upset the established ecological balance and the spiritual bond the People have with the animal world. "What kind of hunting is that," Keskarrah asks at one point, "when a hunter no longer touches an animal until it is dead and its life is spreading out in the snow?" (115). Throughout the novel Keskarrah cautions the Tetsot'ine against inevitable destruction if they adapt to the needs and the ways of the Whites, become reliant on their technology, expose themselves to disease, and develop an exploitative attitude toward the land.

Mapping and recording serve as a key metaphor for colonial control, a gesture whose arrogance is starkly highlighted in contrast to the humility of the Tetsot'ine in the face of the magnitude of the world. As Graham Huggan has persuasively argued, cartography symbolizes the colonial desire for a systematic organization of space grounded in a mimetic, logocentric relation between the map and the mapped. In response, many postcolonial texts deploy cartographic tropes to expose and deconstruct the imposition of colonial perception: "The 'contradictory coherence' implied by the map's systematic inscription on a supposedly 'uninscribed' earth reveals it, moreover, as a palimpsest covering over alternative spacial configurations which, once brought to light, indicate both the plurality of possible perspectives on, and the inadequacy of any single model of, the world."[15]

In *A Discovery of Strangers* Wiebe repeatedly foregrounds the impertinence of such an imposition. Keskarrah is described as "powerful and old enough to draw the picture of the world in the sand and name a few places what they are" (20). In contrast, the English – newcomers who are completely reliant on the Tetsot'ine to guide them through the land – nonetheless set about naming its features, "every lake and river with whatever sound slips from their mouths" (22), imprinting the land with a chronicle of their colonial drama.[16] Their desire to be the omniscient narrators of any book they open leads them to an uncritical faith in measurement and recording – in their maps, drawings, and journals: "Sometime, somewhere, they have decided to believe this simplicity of *mark*, and they will live their lives straight to the end believing that" (147). Yet Wiebe emphasizes the slippage that necessarily intervenes, both through physical privation and mishaps (lost notebooks and such) and through the actions of the colonial censor (the officers' accounts of the expedition, he suggests, have suppressed incidents unflattering to the English). As Michael Krans observes of the original expedition, "they were intent on writing for an elsewhere."[17] Thus their cartographic and scientific activities are intended to fix the land, freeze it within their colonial designs, oblivious to the fact that the environment, as Keskarrah reflects, is constantly in flux: "everything changes when they come, and yet they mark it down as if it will always be the same and they can use it" (75).

In their preoccupation with mastering the land, the English are portrayed as having a singular and catastrophic lack of respect for its strength. Franklin tries to impress the Tetsot'ine by predicting an eclipse, a characteristic colonial sleight-of-hand, but the eclipse is clouded over. Franklin's attempt to show mastery over the environment is further deflated by Keskarrah's scepticism about Franklin's refusal to delay an expedition to the Coppermine River despite the coming of winter. Thus the English are portrayed as being in a state of perilous denial; in their determination to reach the Arctic Ocean, the land is something they "do not ever want to be there" (146). When warned by Keskarrah of the prophesied failure of the expedition and of the double rapids that will obstruct their return, Franklin smugly and arrogantly instructs the intrepreter to reassure Keskarrah, "their land being so very large as we already know, that with his warning we will thankfully be able to avoid, wherever they may be, those fatal double rapids" (207). Ian MacLaren argues that the Franklin expedition displayed an "understandable dependence on the sublime and the picturesque – aesthetics devised to treat European nature," which reflected "a dangerous, if unconscious blindness to nature which could only end in accidents or ... full blown catastrophes."[18] Wiebe's Keskarrah puts it yet more succinctly: "Whitemuds hear only what they want to hear" (131). Indeed, in the novel the expedition's fate illustrates the fatal consequences of such arrogance in an unforgiving environment that requires accommodation, humility, and equanimity if one is to survive.

Franklin's insouciance is all the more objectionable because the "discovery of strangers" has apocalyptic ramifications for the Tetsot'ine. The expedition is portrayed as disrupting a sense of equilibrium that, while far from utopian, is nonetheless in keeping with the environment. This disruption is evident, for instance, in the hunter Bigfoot's adoption of European notions of individualistic and hierarchical politics and in the undermining of communal consensus. Also threatened is the Tetsot'ine sense of the sacred; at one point Keskarrah entertains his people with a parodic version of the story of Adam and Eve, but then muses more seriously, in an anachronistic gesture to the role of the church in the project of European colonialism, that "a story can tangle you up so badly you start to think different. I think these strange Whitemud stories could be strong enough to tie us down" (127). Even the relations between the sexes are reshaped by the coming of the English. Wiebe makes use of evidence that Robert Hood was enamoured of and had a child by Greenstockings and that he competed for her affections with fellow officer George Back. As the English make their mark on the Tetsot'ine, Keskarrah begins to absorb their presence into his larger sense of time and to consider that their coming may amount to a catastrophe from which it will be difficult for the People to recover. The influence of the Whites, he reflects, leaves the People poised between "power or anni-hilation" (305). At the end of the novel, it is affirmed that it will be the latter: "sickness and the men's unrelenting aggression will destroy Greenstockings' People" (316).

Wiebe thus depicts colonial penetration as catastrophically mega-lomaniacal and deluded, as profoundly disruptive of the harmonious relation between the People and their environment in pursuit of an incomprehensible goal. The colonial arrogance that characterizes Franklin and his officers (with Hood something of an exception) sets up a hegemonic binary that the debacle of the expedition, and espe-cially the resorting of the survivors to cannibalism, works to demol-ish. Wiebe clearly conveys the sense that a suppressed story is being unearthed; indeed, Richardson considers burning his notes because admitting cannibalism would violate the sense of propriety expected by Franklin: "Things have taken place that would not be understood properly, they may be there in memories, like ineradicable teeth" (247–8).

An important innovation in dramatizing this violation is Wiebe's use of the perspective of seaman John Hepburn to provide a correc-tive to colonial glorification. Though Hepburn has a definite admi-ration for the character and determination of his officers, he provides the perspective of "a blunt seaman" (95) on the hardships and lack of glory of colonial service. Most importantly, he serves to "correct" John Richardson's account of the survivors' resorting to cannibalism, the blame for which Richardson foists on Michel Terohaute, the Mohawk voyageur responsible for the death of Hood. Richardson suspects Michel of killing other starving voyageurs and feeding them to the English officers, and in his account, reported (at least in part) verbatim in Wiebe's novel, he takes credit for overcoming and killing Michel in self-defense. After Hepburn offers to do the deed himself,

Richardson observes: "I determined, however, as I was thoroughly convinced of the necessity of such a dreadful act, to take the whole responsibility on myself; and immediately on Michel's coming up, I put an end to his life by shooting him through the head with a pistol."[19] In *Discovery*, Hepburn contests Richardson's neat and self-aggrandizing account: "A clean, legal, proper – execution? Hah! Life on the polar Barrens ain't no Admiralty report" (289). He describes how, instead, he approached and then tackled Michel himself before Richardson came up to deliver the fatal shot.

Hepburn also contests the dismissal of cannibalism as an impossible recourse for the civilized English. Richardson in his account pauses to justify his killing of Michel by characterizing him as a savage overwhelmed by hunger: "His principles, however, unsupported by a belief in the divine truths of Christianity, were unable to withstand the pressure of severe distress."[20] Richardson's rhetoric illustrates the manichean operation of colonialist literature; as JanMohamed argues, if it "can demonstrate that the barbarism of the native is irrevocable, or at least very deeply ingrained, then the European's attempt to civilize him can continue indefinitely, the exploitation of his resources can proceed without hindrance, and the European can persist in enjoying a position of moral superiority."[21] In contrast, Wiebe's Hepburn frankly confesses that after Michel's death he "ate a lot of him" (291) and suggests that Richardson, though he refused to, had earlier been willing to eat what Michel had brought even though he suspected the meat to be human. Hepburn furthermore goes on to question how those who survived had managed to do so, implying that it had been necessary for them to dine, like many an English sailor, on "long pig." Thus, through Hepburn, Wiebe upsets the savagery/civilization binary that, he implicitly suggests, accounts of the expedition strived to uphold: "stand an English tar to a few pints and he'll tell you that, long pig it is. An' any officer'll tell you the same, if he don't lie" (293). Hepburn thus provides a very vocal example of Wiebe's general intent in *Discovery*, which is not to let the official accounts of the expedition go unchallenged.

Wiebe's strategy of presenting the story of the failed expedition predominantly through the construction of a Tetsot'ine perspective and a dialogic undermining of the colonial record provides a good illustration of the precariousness of decolonizing history in a settler-invader culture. Tony Tremblay, writing about *A Discovery of Strangers* (as well as historical novels of exploration by Joan Clark and John Steffler), argues that such revisionist histories, although intended to critique colonial ideology, are unreflexive about their own practices, particularly about their making use of an aboriginal perspective.[22]

Tremblay contends that the novels ultimately deconstruct themselves by practicing themselves what they criticize in the Eurocentric discourse of the explorers they portray. Their appropriation of an aboriginal vernacular or perspective, furthermore, is grounded in a colonial guilt and ultimately results in a complicitous reinscribing of colonial assumptions: "even though the versions change, the story ... remains essentially the same: explorers, whether historical or modern, trespass, and in their trespass leave trace, the white figure of which fades easily into a white ground."[23] Thus Tremblay extends to these contemporary writers JanMohamed's critique of colonialist discourse: that instead "of being an exploration of the racial Other, such literature merely affirms its own ethnocentric assumptions; instead of actually depicting the outer limits of 'civilization,' it simply codifies and preserves the structures of its own mentality."[24]

It does seem fair to say that Wiebe's novel offers itself as a historically legitimate representation of the expedition and that it provides no evident narrative self-reflexiveness or questioning of the authority of the narrative voice – no sense that the novel is no less ideological and constructed than it shows the whites' journals to be. It lacks the self-reflexiveness that has been an important strategy of postcolonial and postmodern writers for inscribing a resistance to the troublesome pretensions of omniscience and omnipotence characteristic of colonial discourse and much Western canonical literature. Less convincing, however, is Tremblay's characterization of Wiebe's novel, along with the others, as incredibly naive: "The more important lesson about knowledge and power appears to be that history – the impulse to narrative – solves history."[25] Moreover, Tremblay's contention that "[h]istorical revisionist fiction can never be about anything more than itself"[26] suggests a binary of inside/outside to both language and culture that Wiebe is obviously keen to upset in *Discovery*. Wiebe compels readers to read the impact of colonialism through the perspective of aboriginal people, however narratively and ideologically unreflective about that strategy the novel may appear. As the preoccupations of his fiction suggest, Wiebe is all too keenly aware of the structuring effects of culture and language, but neither is he ready to concede that they construct impermeable spheres around a people.[27]

While the narrative practice of *Discovery* may seem to replicate colonial appropriation, it is at the same time the impressive result of a sustained attempt to know the Other, which has been such an important part of the decolonizing impulse of Wiebe's fiction. JanMohamed argues that colonialist literature "is essentially specular: instead of seeing the native as a bridge toward syncretic possibility, it uses him as a mirror that reflects the colonialist's self-image."[28] What Wiebe's work demonstrates is that this is not an either/or proposition and that, for a "settler" in a settler-invader culture, the movement towards a more syncretic discourse will continue to be partly marked by the kind of specularity JanMohamed describes, but this is a very different thing from engaging in naive revisionist historiography that replicates colonialist discourse. The narrative is driven by a desire to redress the distortions of history in the colonial record but also strives to develop a culturally alternative perspective on that history.

George Bowering's earlier *Burning Water* (1980) is worth revisiting in the context of such questions about revisionist history and narrative form. A parodic and metafictional rendering of George Vancouver's explorations off the Pacific coast in the late 1700s, *Burning Water* certainly provides a good example of the postmodern, self-reflexive, "contingent" kind of fiction Tremblay has in mind as the standard of which *A Discovery of Strangers* falls short. As Wiebe does with Franklin, *Burning Water* subversively offers a less-than-flattering portrait of Vancouver and of the project of colonial exploration, but the novel also self-consciously parallels Vancouver's voyages with the author's peregrinations away from his Vancouver home while struggling to write Vancouver's story and is much more parodic and anti-mimetic in its presentation of history.

Though *Burning Water* to a degree reflects a certain admiration for Vancouver's tenacity and accomplishments, Bowering nonetheless has a great deal of fun at Vancouver's expense, particularly through his cheeky presentation of Vancouver's frustrated ambitions. Whereas explorers are typically heroized as trailblazers, Vancouver's mission is distinctly unheroic, as Bowering's flippant summary emphasizes: "He was supposed to chart the coast, be friendly but firm with the Spanish, and if he had any time left over, keep an eye open for gold and the Northwest Passage" (*Burning Water* 26). Following in the wake of his idol James Cook, Vancouver is sceptical of Cook's claim about a North-West passage, but all the same is dismayed by the fact that there is little left to discover; he enviously thinks of "Champlain and de Maisonneuve, who got to climb hills with big crosses and plant Christ in the soil of a new world" (27). He chafes at his mundane task, annoyed that it is motivated primarily by trade, and wishes that "he could be firing grapeshot at a French rig instead of dropping sounding lines into a pacific brine" (22). An important part of postcolonial representations echoed here is the baring of the crass exploitation and self-interest lying behind the putatively noble and civilizing enterprise of exploration and colonization.

Even more than *Discovery*, *Burning Water* dramatizes charting as a central feature of the colonizer's presence. Frustrated in his desire for accomplishment as an explorer, Vancouver transfers his desire to be the *ne plus ultra* to his cartographic task. Through Vancouver's desire for cartographic completeness and plenitude, Bowering parodies the Enlightenment obsession with scientific accuracy: "The most exercisable beauty of all was the ability to trace that coast true, representing it as no more even and no more odd than it was" (59). Though *Burning Water* is very much concerned with the creative and imaginative dimension of exploration – both as a literary and as a geographical pursuit – ultimately the mission of Vancouver and his ship, the *Discovery*, is constructed as rationalist drudgery, as opposed to imaginative exploration: "Whatever the edge of the world was made of, this craft at the nose of the eighteenth century was turning it day by day into facts. Fathoms, leagues, rainfall, names, all facts. The *Discovery* was a fact factory" (186). Vancouver's obsessions ultimately position him not as an artist but as a cog in the larger colonial machine concerned with fixing, naming, and appropriating the "uncharted."

The obverse of Vancouver's determined, colonial rationalism, however, is a kind of megalomania, a desire to make his mark on history: "He wanted to be a famous story very much, the kind of story that is known before you read it. He wanted his name and its exploits to be a part of the world any Englishman would walk through" (62–3). Vancouver leaves his stamp cartographically "all over the globe" so that, at the very least, by virtue of his cartographic accomplishments, if those exposed to his work "did not love him they would not be able to avoid him" (63). Vancouver's megalomania and ambition, products of a very English anal retentiveness and lack of imagination, are in turn tied to a very colonial imposition of power and naming: "He never wrote down on his charts any names that were there before he got there. He didn't imagine that one should" (63). Vancouver's expedient state of denial provides a good illustration of Lawson's insight into how colonial experience disturbs and even deconstructs "the coherence of European epistemology" and how, for "epistemological reasons, ... but also for professional ones, the colonial explorer had to empty the land of prior signification – what is already known cannot be discovered, what already has a name cannot be named."[29]

Bowering develops this very postcolonial presentation of Vancouver as a colonial flunky and hero manqué particularly by focusing on Vancouver's shipboard relationships. For instance, Bowering transforms the historical Vancouver's warm relationship with the Spanish officer Bodega y Quadra into a homosexual one, which is repeatedly the subject of lewd comments on the part of other crew members and helps to deflate the masculinist, heterosexual stereotype of the explorer. More significant to *Burning Water*, however, is Bowering's use of Archibald Menzies, the botanist who doubles as ship's doctor, as a foil for Vancouver. Menzies is depicted as the archetypal "eighteenth century man," "satisfied to accumulate knowledge" (50) and thus at odds with the ambitious and stern Vancouver, to whom he refuses to defer.

Menzies also serves to highlight Vancouver's colonial rigidity, particularly his resistance to genuine cross-cultural contact. When Vancouver expresses a colonially instrumentalist appreciation of language – "Learning a naked foreigner's tongue is the first step in creating some form of government" – Menzies replies, "I cannot help thinking that languages have purposes beyond allowing one man to tell the other his demands upon his behaviour" (42). Later, Menzies argues that Vancouver is too suspicious of natives "because you learn their language in order to practise your control over them, while you never get close enough to them to listen to that language for a while and find out what they want" (150). Vancouver's behaviour, in contrast with Menzies's Enlightenment curiosity, certainly illustrates JanMohamed's insight that "the colonizer's invariable assumption about his moral superiority means that he will rarely question the validity of either his own or his society's formation and that he will not be inclined to expend any energy in understanding the worthless alterity of the colonized."[30]

Throughout the novel, the tension between the two men is connected to the Romantic distinction between fancy and imagination, which in Bowering's terms, Edward Lobb argues, "is essentially between idle dreaming and real perception."[31] Vancouver at one point Anglocentrically lectures two Spanish officers that the "imagination depends on facts, it feeds on them in order to produce beauty or invention, or discovery" and that the "true enemy of the imagination is laziness, habit, leisure. The enemy of the imagination is the idleness that provides fancy" (155). However, Vancouver himself is constructed, particularly through his relationship with Menzies, as lacking imagination; he is, Lobb contends, "a figure of failed or false imagination."[32] Indeed, the final confrontation between Menzies and Vancouver is set in motion when Menzies refuses to turn his journals and sketches over to Vancouver, rejecting his authority as captain. In refusing, Menzies observes that he does "not accede to fancy" (252), here construed as arbitrary, authoritarian whim. An argument ensues when Menzies discovers that all his botanical discoveries – contained in a cold frame that has taken up much of Vancouver's space on deck and the better part of his patience – have been left unprotected and ostensibly destroyed during a squall. Bowering gives dramatic closure to the debate between the two men by having the enraged Menzies murder Vancouver, who tumbles "over the rail and into the unsolicitous sea" (258), instead of considerately allowing him to die six years later, as do most historians.[33] Bowering's somewhat sympathetic view of Vancouver, it might be said, avoids the reverse manicheanism of many postcolonial revisionist accounts, as he sees him as a potentially creative figure with a stultifying rationalist fixation and a thwarted desire to be the stereotypical colonial hero, a trajectory that, at least in the novel, brings about his demise.

Bowering's presentation of European contact with native people emphasizes, like Wiebe's *Discovery*, the importance of cultural perspective to the perception of colonialism, but it does so in a much more playful manner. Like Wiebe, Bowering subverts the Eurocentric mythos of discovery from the very beginning by having the whites seen arriving from the viewpoint of natives who are obviously long-established in the so-called New World. Rather than striving for verisimilitude as does Wiebe, however, Bowering renders his Indians as subversive caricatures, anachronistically lancing various myths of colonization and deflating Eurocentric representations of aboriginals' awed first impressions. As one Indian says to another: "You must never believe you have seen a god when you have seen a man on a large boat" (17). As well as deflating the grandeur of discovery, Bowering also obviously intends to link the colonial assumptions that govern Vancouver's rigid, "civilized" treatment of the natives he encounters with contemporary stereotypes of native people, and to lampoon both. The narrator observes, for instance: "A lot of people think that Indians are just naturally patient, but that's not true. Before the white 'settlers' arrived there were lots of impatient Indians. It's only in the last two hundred years that Indians have been looking patient whenever there were any white men around" (92). Thus Bowering underlines the Eurocentric perspectival conventions and ideological assumptions that not only governed narratives of exploration and discovery, but also have persisted to present times.

Such a strategy, however, is somewhat ambivalent and potentially problematic. In many contemporary novels, Marie Vautier argues, "a self-conscious postcolonial urge to demythologize the superiority of the European or white colonizer and to explore self/other tensions … coexists with a postmodern play with the figure of the Amerindian."[34] Though these texts generally approach colonization with a postcolonial agenda, "they sometimes *use* the figure of the Amerindian or Métis to further the postcolonial arguments of the nonnative cultural majorities."[35] Bowering thus could, like Wiebe, be accused of appropriating, however playfully, the image of the Amerindian as a semiotic counter in his portrait of colonialism. More seriously, he could be accused of perpetuating a long tradition of Eurocentric caricature of indigenous peoples.

However, as Vautier subsequently observes, the "overriding pressure of the self/other paradigm in politically correct academic circles appears to be working *against* the postcolonial practices" of mainstream non-native writers trying "to open up a textual space in which to explore various manifestations of differing cultural representations," a caution that is particularly applicable to Bowering's novel.[36] Bowering's caricatures are grounded in a fairly clear project of subverting Eurocentric assumptions about discovery, history, and colonial relations. The fun in *Burning Water*, in short, comes at the expense of the colonists and not of the colonized. Moreover – and herein lies a significant distinction from *Discovery* – it also comes at the expense of any sense of historical authenticity. We know that the caricatures are caricatures, and that knowledge turns our attention to the colonial mindset that the caricatures – and *Burning Water* as a whole – subversively expose. More important, the postcolonial inversions in *Burning Water* avoid the presumption of objectivity and the demonizing of the explorer that render Wiebe's novel susceptible to criticism.

The imperious explorer has proved to be a continuing attraction in historical fiction, appearing as the central character of John Steffler's *The Afterlife of George Cartwright* (to be examined in the next chapter) and playing an important role in Thomas Wharton's 1995 novel *Icefields*. *Icefields* is set predominantly in the first few decades of the twentieth century and does not treat a prominent explorer like Franklin or Vancouver. Yet the novel presents a similarly critical view of European exploration and discovery, addressing Canada's reinscription within a Eurocentric perspective by focusing on the transformation of the Rocky Mountains into a mecca for tourists. This transformation begins with a Royal Geographical Society expedition in the region of the Columbia icefields, during which the novel's main character, Edward Byrne, falls into a crevasse, where he catches a glimpse of an angel frozen in ice. *Icefields* centres on Byrne's patient, enigmatic vigil as he waits for the angel to emerge from the melting glacier, but the novel also loops back to an earlier expedition, that of the Earl of Sexsmith, who manifests a colonial imperiousness reminiscent of Wiebe's Franklin and Bowering's Vancouver. The story of his search is juxtaposed with Byrne's narrative, particularly as that story is related to Byrne by the daughter of Athabasca, the young Snake woman whom Sexsmith uses as a guide. The figure of the explorer thus serves as the fulcrum of the postcolonial reverberations in *Icefields*: the novel charts the Europeans' appropriation of the mountains from their aboriginal precursors; details Sexsmith's sojourn in the mountains, parodically reworking that of the historical Earl of Southesk; and through the character of Viraj, Sexsmith's East Indian servant, voices a resistance to colonial servitude.

Wharton borrows the rough outlines for the character of Sexsmith from James Carnegie, Earl of Southesk, one of a number of British "sports" who made hunting trips to the Rocky Mountains in the nineteenth century as guests of the Hudson's Bay Company. From 1859 to 1860, Southesk, a Scottish nobleman, travelled from Lachine to Fort Edmonton, and from there through the Athabasca valley before returning east via Edmonton. What Wharton principally preserves from Southesk, otherwise, are his eccentricities: like Sexsmith, Southesk did indeed travel with an India-rubber bath and was fond of reading Shakespeare and other uplifting classics at the end of a day's travel: "I believe intellectual reading, in moderation, to be a rest for the body after hard labour: it seems to act as a counter-irritant, drawing off fatigue from the muscles in the brain."[37] Unlike Sexsmith, however, Southesk during his time in the Rockies seemed to be interested in little other than shooting every beast in sight.

Sexsmith, in contrast, has come in search of a climate more amenable to his flagging health, and though he does, like Southesk, dream of bagging a grizzly bear, he is also led on by a vision of the Grail. After seeing moonlight gleaming on a distant mountain top, Sexsmith has a dream about the grail, in which he encounters an "old man in rusted armour" (Icefields 40).

Who are you? he asked the old man.
    There were seven of us. I am the last one. We took an oath to follow the king into the west, and to keep the Grail hidden.
The old man stumbled at last and sank into the long grass. A gust of wind lifted the cloth and swept it away. The old man was holding a silver cup. At that moment the sun caught the lip of the cup and filled it with fire. The blazing light spilled over onto his armour, burnished it into white gold. (41)[38]

Following a map on the palm of Athabasca, Sexsmith and his Stoney guides come upon Arcturus glacier, and Sexsmith feels himself closer to the goal, particularly due to Athabasca's reticence about the glacier because it is "a spirit place. Not for the living" (43). Heedless of such distinctions, and interpreting the significance of the glacier in the Eurocentric, Christian terms of Arthurian romance, Sexsmith ventures out on to the icefield and discovers it to be … just that. After he turns back, in his journal he "writes nothing about the plain of ice" and records but one word: "*Disappointment*" (181). Sexsmith returns from his excursion to the glacier deflated, in ill health and foul humour, reflecting to Viraj, "*I wish I could be transported back to England without leaving this tent. That would be pleasant indeed*" (47).

Sexsmith is very much the arrogant European interloper in the manner of Franklin, and his turn for the worse is implicitly tied to his violation of a sacred site. As Sara, Athabasca's daughter, later reflects to Byrne: "In my father's country ... , the mountains are gods, or at least the palaces of gods. And, I think, for my mother's people as well. Spirit places. It was enough for us that we could see them from the valley" (51). This passage, furthermore, serves to highlight Sexsmith's expedition as the precursor to the later development and commodification of the icefields.

The presence of Sexsmith's East Indian servant, Viraj, fortifies the impression of Sexsmith as the archetypal colonial bully, and their relationship replays that of Ariel and Prospero in what is seen to be a key allegory of colonialism, Shakespeare's *The Tempest*. The half-white, half-caste Viraj (Southesk's principal sidekick, in contrast, was a Métis named Antoine Blandoine) is taken into Sexsmith's service in Rajasthan and accompanies his master to the Rockies after Sexsmith, like Conrad's Marlow, "stabbed a finger at that blank, wordless space in the atlas" (29). Wharton underlines Viraj's colonial subservience through references to *The Tempest*, which Sexsmith is reading, with Viraj playing Ariel to Sexsmith's Prospero (hence Sexsmith's possession of books is doubly appropriate). Sexsmith is "musing on Caliban's beautiful speech in the third act of *The Tempest*" (27) at the moment he starts to flounder on a slope of scree, and as Viraj bounds across the rock to rescue him, Sexsmith reflects, "*Like feather'd Mercury... Vaulting with such ease*" (28). Wharton is presumably alluding to Caliban's lyrical description of his enchanted isle, but Caliban's other principal speech in the third act, in which he urges Stephano to murder Prospero, has appropriate overtones for Viraj's chafing under his servitude to Sexsmith: "Burn but his books. / He has brave utensils, – for so he calls them, – / Which, when he has a house, he'll deck withal."[39]

Like Ariel, Viraj obtains his release, but it comes after a confrontation in which Sexsmith physically asserts his authority (unlike Prospero, for whom threats of punishment are sufficient in dealing with Ariel). When Sexsmith's health takes a turn for the worse after his disappointment on Arcturus glacier, Viraj suggests that the young Snake woman might be able to help him; thus Viraj, unlike Ariel, who collaborates with Prospero in sustaining his domination over Caliban, seeks to bridge the gap between the European and the indigene. Sexsmith upbraids him when he persists with this advice, striking him with his copy of *The Tempest*: "*You forget your place.*" Viraj's response, "*You are quite right*" (47), is defiant rather than submissive, signalling his break with Sexsmith. Viraj stays behind, subsequently taking Athabasca as his wife (though she leaves with her people shortly after Sara is born). Thus Wharton reconfigures *The Tempest*, aligning Viraj with Caliban as a figure of postcolonial resistance, to envision a more syncretic and less appropriated "brave new world."[40]

Unlike Wiebe's Franklin and Bowering's Vancouver, Sexsmith plays a relatively limited role in *Icefields*. His tantrum upon failing to gain the grail serves to provide an anterior narrative against which to juxtapose Byrne's search for the angel. Nonetheless, Sexsmith illustrates the handiness of the trope of the explorer/discoverer as an agent of appropriation and as a representative of colonial ideology. Like Franklin and Vancouver, Sexsmith exhibits an imperious determination and callous disregard for the Other, and his activities are portrayed as reconfiguring and effacing indigenous geography, culture, and spirituality in accordance with European modes of thought.

Subverting the heroic image of the explorer/discoverer, however, threatens to become, indeed has become, a postcolonial cliché, an archetype susceptible to a simplistic revisionism that does little to disturb the binary oppositions that plague postcolonial negotiations of identity, culture, and politics. In this respect, the parodic and self-reflexive qualities of Bowering's *Burning Water* provide a more nuanced view of colonialism than do the other two novels. But the popularity of the colonial bully as a target of revisionist history is nonetheless a testament to the entrenched power of imperialist narratives of discovery and to how the power of these narratives still needs to be subjected to scrutiny and destabilized. Furthermore, even though one has to be wary of looking at decolonization itself as a linear, teleological, evolving history, it might be argued that such revisionism, cliché as it has become, is paving the way for a more productively postcolonial reckoning with the much more complicated nature of origins and political and cultural foundations in a settler-invader society such as Canada – one which explores the murky, conflicted territory that lies between the poles of such binaries as aggressor/victim, savage/civilized, colonizer/colonized.

If contemporary historical novels complicate the idea of "discovery," they do much the same for "settlement." As the hyphenated term "settler-invader culture" suggests, settlement is an uncomfortably euphemistic term for the consolidation of the territorial claims that accompany colonial exploration and discovery. It suggests reaching a stage of comfort rather than displacing a population and provides a good illustration of the epistemological adjustment on the part of the colonizer that settlement, like exploration, requires: "For the settler, too, the land had to be empty. Empty land can be settled, but occupied land can only be invaded."[41] A common, consolatory myth about the process of settlement in Canada, particularly of settlement in the West, is that it was less violent, less imposed, less imperial than in the United States, as properly befitting Canada's self-image as a nation of conciliators. Contemporary historical novels, however, provide a much less sanguine view of that process. Rudy Wiebe's *The Temptations of Big Bear* and *The Scorched-Wood People* depict the settlement of the Prairies in the late nineteenth century as a violent imposition of European military and cultural domination, and Guy Vanderhaeghe's more recent portrait of that era in *The Englishman's Boy* presents a similar perspective.

The Englishman's Boy* has much in common with *The Temptations of Big Bear* because it provides a postcolonial treatment of a fairly key, if relatively obscure, incident in the history of the Canadian West – the 1873 killing of the inhabitants of an Assiniboine camp in the Cypress Hills on the Alberta-Saskatchewan border by a party of wolfers up from Montana in search of stolen horses. Rather than emphasizing what the Cypress Hills Massacre precipitated – the westward march of the newly formed North West Mounted Police – Vanderhaeghe focuses on the anarchic, exploitative, and racist frontier mentality that led to it. As Wiebe's novels suggest, however, the narrative and historiographical strategies necessary for a postcolonial revisionist history of settlement can prove to be problematic, and the pitfalls of Wiebe's work are to some degree encountered in Vanderhaeghe's novel as well. A brief foray into Wiebe's history of the West thus provides a useful preamble to an examination of *The Englishman's Boy*.

One of the primary challenges of a revisionist approach to the history of settlement, as with exploration and discovery, is the necessity of countering narratives that are entrenched, legitimized, and heroized. Vanderhaeghe's strategy in *The Englishman's Boy* is to write against the heroic colonial trajectory of the Western. In *The Scorched-Wood People* (1977), Wiebe writes against a centrist history of the West. His account of the rise and fall of the Métis Nation from the beginning of the first uprising to the end of the second and the execution of Louis Riel is far more sympathetic to the Métis and critical of the federal government, and in general counters an eastern bias in the representation of those events. Penny van Toorn succinctly frames Wiebe's revisionist intent through an appropriate legal image: "Like *The Temptations of Big Bear*, *The Scorched-Wood People* reopens a court case closed officially many years ago. Wiebe enlists readers to perform jury duty, and instructs them to judge Riel's and the Government's actions and words in the light of Mennonite morality, not Canadian law."[42]

Wiebe's revisionist "instructions" emphasize how differently these political and military developments are seen in the West, as the title of an article Wiebe wrote for *The Globe & Mail* at the time suggests: "In the West, Sir John A. is a Bastard and Riel a Saint. Ever Ask Why?"[43] After reading *The Scorched-Wood People*, the answer is pretty clear. The novel dramatically presents the Riel "rebellions" not as a treasonous challenge to the legitimate authority of the federal government but as the legitimate response of a desperate people near-genocidally abandoned by a Machiavellian government that purports to represent them. The military response to both uprisings thus comes across as a draconian, bloodthirsty, and double-crossing violence on the part of a racist government driven by political expediency and corrupt financial interest. In short, some nation building.[44]

Wiebe's revisionist history in the novel does not simply reverse the terms of the centrist version of the rebellions, especially in his portrait of Riel. While Wiebe's account undeniably favours the Métis cause, it does not present Riel uncritically as martyred saviour. Rather than coming across as a political maverick messianically leading his people down the garden path, Riel is construed as a visionary leader trying to stem the devastating consequences of the federal government's negligence. Yet Wiebe portrays Riel's vision as wavering, vulnerable to self-doubt and to a prophetic, other-worldly distraction that proves to be politically and militarily disastrous for the Métis. Though Wiebe underlines the strength and significance of Riel's commitment to his people, he certainly does not present him as an unblemished, unproblematic saviour.

His main strategy nonetheless is to illustrate how Riel, for all his shortcomings, is principled and committed to justice for his people, compared to the eastern politicians who preside over their fate. However compromised, Riel's commitment stands in stark contrast to the lack of integrity of Macdonald and his cronies. In *The Scorched-Wood People* the government, not Riel, is on trial. Wiebe highlights the brutal hypocrisy of Macdonald's Tories in crushing the democratic aspirations of a people with legitimate grievances, whose armed uprising the federal government, through its neglect, was responsible for causing in the first place. The sense that the novel is righting the historical balance is highlighted in Métis narrator Pierre Falcon's rhetorical reflection on the outcome of Riel's trial: "Poor fool; it was immoral to hang him; clearly he was mad. The necessity of hanging him was simply, clearly Sir John A.'s Conservative politics. You believe that? Many Canadians, even many Métis believe and will believe it; but I cannot. I agree with white-haired Dr. Augustus Jukes, senior surgeon of the North-West Mounted Police, that we are too likely to call men whose understanding of life goes counter to our usual opinion, insane. Sanity becomes then a mere matter of majority opinion, not a test of the wisdom of what is spoken" (*The Scorched-Wood People* 330).

Despite his errors in judgment, which are at least to a degree attributable to his desire to avoid violence, Riel looks like a paragon next to Macdonald. Even Riel's execution of the inflammatory Orange settler Thomas Scott retains a sense of integrity when compared to Macdonald's treachery in seeming to support negotiation and the right of the Métis to self-determination while in private being dismissive and racist towards the Métis and quite happy to bend to the racist fervor of Orange Ontario for a military quashing of these half-breed upstarts in the wake of Scott's execution. To put it simply, the real traitor in *The Scorched-Wood People* is Macdonald, not Riel.

The Scorched-Wood People is not an unequivocal achievement, however, as Wiebe's revisionist view of the uprisings, reflected in his postmodern historiographical narrative strategies, is compromised by his belief in an ultimate truth and his Mennonite ideology. Van Toorn, for instance, argues that Wiebe's portrait of Riel is intentionally ambivalent. Wiebe's attraction to and portrait of Riel is motivated by the resemblance between their religious visions and their commitments to social justice: "Wiebe's patronage of Riel may be explained by the fact that Riel's ideological position corresponds closely in several respects with Wiebe's Mennonite Brethren beliefs and values: rejection of alcohol, advocacy of peace and of goodwill towards enemies, resistance to an over-institutionalized church and the importance of individual communication with God."[45] Riel's appeals to political justice accord with Wiebe's Mennonite pacifism, but his support of violence and political coercion does not. More problematically, Wiebe's use of Falcon as the novel's spectral narrator, to be examined in the next chapter, raises another spectre – that of appropriation. The overriding tension of *The Scorched-Wood People*, then, is that an attempt to revise the history of the settlement of the West – to dramatize just how completely the concerns of the Métis were bulldozed – is rendered in aesthetic and moral terms that are not altogether compatible with those concerns.

Similar doubts raised about *The Temptations of Big Bear* (1973) are yet more useful in providing context for an investigation of *The Englishman's Boy*. Focusing on Big Bear, the last of the plains chiefs to sign a treaty, *Big Bear* provides a panoramic view of the cultural and political cataclysm that European expansion onto the Prairies represented for native people. Wiebe conveys the story of Big Bear from a variety of perspectives, those of white officials and soldiers, white settlers, and various Cree characters, but principally that of Big Bear. He portrays Big Bear essentially as a tragic, noble figure, caught between two cultural systems, increasingly recognizing the inevitable hegemony of white authority over the decreasingly nomadic plains tribes, and trying to do the best thing for his people without unnecessarily provoking either side.[46]

As in *The Scorched-Wood People*, Wiebe's narrative strategies are a fundamental part of a revisionist view of the settlement of the West. The book is a prime example of historiographical metafiction, in that the heterogeneity of history, the reliance on sources in representing the past, and the presence of conflicting viewpoints are all fairly openly foregrounded in the novel.[47] In this manner, Wiebe breaks the illusion of historical presence and foregrounds the difficulty of trying to reconstruct historical experience in all its diversity. If, following Bakhtin, the novel is the genre *par excellence* for bringing various voices into dialogic relation, in *Big Bear* Wiebe illustrates the potential of that heteroglossia to represent the complexity of a pivotal historical situation and to harness the novel's dialogic energies for postcolonial purposes. Instead of providing a linear, consistent, cohesive historical perspective, Wiebe forces the reader to navigate and assess a wide array of discourses that represent very different and often conflicting ideologies – evident particularly in the ironic undertones given the discourse of white officials such as Alexander Morris, Edgar Dewdney, and Francis Dickens through the way their texts are reworked and intertextually situated in the larger narrative. The novel thus underlines that history is not a single, unified story but a clash of different perspectives, in which what passes as history is usually the official version, that of the victors.

The somewhat jarring experience of reading the novel – a result of not being afforded a stable position from which to view and interpret developments in the situation – eloquently makes Wiebe's point: that it is an illusion to think that we are afforded such a position. The relative heterogeneity and dialogism of the narrative underlines the central feature of the story: representing the often violent encounter of two very different cultures from a single, unified perspective would replicate the kind of appropriation and coercion characteristic of the European takeover of the Prairies. The difference in perspectives not only underlines how there is no single, authoritative story, but also effectively counters the predominant, eastern vision of the "peaceful" settlement of the west. In most respects Wiebe demonstrates through this discursive and political struggle that history is itself historically and culturally relative, not a timeless, immutable account conveyed from an Archimedean position outside of culture and historicity. Certainly *Big Bear* conveys the lesson, to rework a cliché, that it's never over even when it's over.[48] History is subject to revision, supplementation, its final meaning always deferred and therefore always contestable.[49]

Although Wiebe's dialogic and heteroglot representation of the history of Big Bear seems a compelling response to the cultural clash of settlement, his commitment to dialogism is somewhat undermined by his commitment to a unitary truth. First of all, while Wiebe's narrative strategies certainly work to relativize and historicize our experience of the past, he has suggested in an interview that such an approach ultimately lends itself to a kind of truth: "I have a sense of trying to get at the truth of things – I think the truth of things can be gotten at still – by setting the diamond of the document in the artificial set of the fictive situation. The diamond shines so much more clearly, it shows its true nature."[50] Furthermore, the power of Wiebe's portrait of Big Bear suggests that Wiebe, though underscoring the relativity and heterogeneity of our perception of such a historical struggle, recuperates the intertextuality and heteroglossia of the narrative into a fairly coherent and monologic view of history.

Brian McHale cautions that it "is important to distinguish between the formal and stylistic heteroglossia of a text and its ideological polyphony, for heteroglossic texts are not inevitably polyphonic," and *The Temptations of Big Bear* provides a good example.[51] Frank Davey, for one, argues that despite the novel's dialogic interplay between different narrative voices and discourses, its ultimate effect is monologic and historically authoritative; the third-person narration serves to choreograph the various voices in a fashion that clearly privileges Big Bear's perspective.[52] Wiebe himself acknowledges that, although he wanted to juxtapose the various perspectives, "forcing the reader to do the interpreting, of bringing these many elements together," the book as a whole "affirms what Big Bear is doing."[53] The result of this discursive hierarchy, as both Davey and van Toorn argue, is that Wiebe's novel, though formally heteroglossic and dialogic, is ultimately ideologically monologic, inscribing a unitary, Christian vision.

Big Bear's struggle to lead his people wisely against an overwhelming and intractable imperializing force is contained, as the title of the novel suggests, within an allegorical framework informed by Wiebe's Mennonite principles. This framework, in which Big Bear is equated with Christ and with the Biblical prophets, suggests, as van Toorn argues, that there is ultimately a truth that is not historically and culturally relative, a truth that is outside historicity. Indeed, Wiebe responds in an interview that, while the novel is historically honest but not impartial, "I do think that, say, the Biblical prophets and Big Bear had a great deal in common, the sense of a heritage that has been sold out, that through ignorance or neglect has simply been left."[54] Given the problematic and substantially imperializing role played by the church in the history not just of the Prairies but of Canada in general, it is not surprising that giving the story of one of the great Cree chiefs a Christian resonance should be controversial. Looking at how the narrative consistently moves "towards recovering or redeeming a suppressed Christian voice and meaning," van Toorn concludes that, although Wiebe "records history from the point of view of societies subjugated to various forms of imperialism, he adopts the strategies of an imperialistic power when it comes to using language. As an evangelical Christian, Wiebe attempts to establish, both within and outside the text of the novel, an 'empire' of God's word."[55] Certainly, *The Temptations of Big Bear* can readily be seen as a Eurocentric appropriation of the story of a Cree leader; as with *Discovery*, what starts out as a counter-imperialist revisioning of history, in short, threatens to become an imperializing novelistic history.

Wiebe's view of his own marginality, however, puts these concerns in an interesting light. Wiebe has argued of *Big Bear* that, because of his own religious sensibility, his belonging to a dispossessed group marginalized by imperial culture, and his opposition to that culture, he feels that he is, in a way, "well-suited to try to tell the story."[56] Wiebe's defence thus serves to modify the tendency to wards homogenizing majority culture as monolithically white and Anglocentric and to efface the complex and hierarchical politics that have in turn been an important part of Canadian history and its postcolonial negotiations of cultural identity.

Rather than underscoring the essential futility of even such an esteemed revisionist history as *Big Bear*, however, the ambivalent achievement of the novel serves as a reminder of how revising historical tradition is more likely to be achieved in increments rather than wholesale. Terry Goldie argues of Wiebe's fiction that "the standard commodities remain the same, no matter how subtly they are presented," despite Wiebe's "careful scholarly research and extraordinary sensitivity to native cultures."[57] Because Eurocentric representations of indigenous people seem to have "created a semiotic field of such power that no textual representations ... can escape it," Goldie suggests that the best possible response "is to establish an awareness of our semiotic snare and reverse it so that it becomes a device of genealogy."[58] I would argue, however, that the commodities are the same but different and that such a response is already in effect in Wiebe's texts. This semiotic field, though ideologically pervasive and powerful, is not immutable but historical, and, while Wiebe's underlining of historicity stands in uneasy relation to his privileging of a Christian truth, his texts represent a significant step in making us aware of such a semiotic snare.[59]

Wiebe's historiographical and narrative choices in *Big Bear* and their uneasy relation to the semiotic field Goldie describes provide a useful background to an investigation of Vanderhaeghe's strategies in *The Englishman's Boy* (1996). In chronicling the Englishman's boy's reluctant participation in the wolfers' cause and the massacre itself, the novel, like *Big Bear*, resists identification with the colonialist triumph of the whites and instead underlines the racist imperialism of most of the wolfers. Furthermore, in a narrative move reminiscent of Wiebe's fiction, the story of the massacre – and of its later reworking in film – is "contained" within the story of Fine Man and Broken Horn's successful absconding with the wolfers' horses, subverting the conventional outcome of the Western by ending with their triumphant return to their camp. These choices, however, raise the question of whether the novel – as Tremblay and Goldie observe of Wiebe's work – is mired within the semiotic field of Eurocentric representations of natives and is ultimately a consolatory and compensatory fiction expressive of white guilt.

An immediate potential sticking point of a postcolonial analysis of *The Englishman's Boy* is that, while the novel gains a lot of its impetus by subverting the conventions and ideology of the Western, it also consistently focuses on white protagonists. The nineteenth-century history of Shorty McAdoo, the Englishman's boy, who joins the party of wolfers who ultimately perpetrate the massacre in the Cypress Hills, is juxtaposed with the history of early twentieth-century Hollywood during the advent of talking pictures, a time when megalomaniacal directors and producers such as Cecil B. De Mille, Samuel Goldwyn, Carl Laemmle, and Louis B. Mayer ruled the roost. In the Hollywood sequences, narrated by Harry Vincent, a Canadian eking out an existence in Hollywood as a title writer, Shorty is an old man who has reached the end of a career as a Hollywood cowboy. Harry has been dispatched to interview him in order to provide Hollywood mogul Damon Ira Chance with the material for the epic Western he wants to make.

As in *Big Bear*, Vanderhaeghe's narrative strategies are a key part of the novel's postcolonial treatment of the history of the West. Shorty ultimately divulges his story, and Vanderhaeghe skilfully interweaves segments of it – from the Englishman's boy's arrival in Montana up to the massacre – with Harry's first-person narrative of his being conscripted by the reclusive and enigmatic Chance to track down Shorty and his story. Through the contrast between Chance's imperialist vision of the Western and the "realism" of the narrative of the Cypress Hills Massacre, Vanderhaeghe clearly intends to subvert the colonial assumptions of the traditional Western and of the history of the West. However, it could be further argued that, despite the novel's attempt to provide a less Eurocentric and even postcolonial Western, and despite its critique of white imperialism, Vanderhaeghe makes whites (Vincent and McAdoo) the heroes of the novel and relegates natives to the margins. Jane Tompkins's observation that "Indians are repressed in Westerns – there but not there – in the same way that women are" is applicable to *The Englishman's Boy* and thus raises, as with Wiebe's work, the issue of appropriation.[60]

The principal effect of the contrapuntal structure of *The Englishman's Boy* is to emphasize that imperialism is a thing of the past – and of the present. Rather than inserting Shorty's history into the chronology of Harry's search for Shorty, Vanderhaeghe breaks up and synchronizes the progression of each narrative. The climax of the nineteenth-century sequences (the description of the massacre itself) is interwoven with the climax of the twentieth-century sequences, in which Shorty's sidekick, Wylie, after the premiere of Chance's film *Besieged*, kills Chance's right-hand man, Denis Fitzsimmons, and then guns down Chance. In this way, Shorty's reaction to the wolfers' violence towards the Assiniboine is choreographed with his and Wylie's response to the violence Chance does to his story. This technique of alternating between the two historical periods obviously serves to delay disclosure of the outcome of Shorty's story and to sustain suspense. More importantly, however, it serves to synchronize a critique of the wolfers' attack on the Assiniboine camp with a critique of what amounts to Chance's repetition of the outrage.

Vanderhaeghe's depiction of the wolfers' venture clearly departs from the celebratory atmosphere of most Westerns, especially his portrait of the leaders of the party. The confrontation with the Assiniboine is fuelled by the racist hatred and contempt of the wolfers' leader, Tom Hardwick, and of the notorious chief of the Spitzee Cavalry, John Evans, and by the reciprocal animosity of the Assiniboine. However, a though this part of the narrative exploits the conventions of the Western as it tracks the progress of the wolfers from Montana to the Cypress Hills, it subverts the racial polarization and triumphalist rhetoric typical of the genre. The narrative draws on such Western conventions as the young loner proving himself in a barroom confrontation, the "posse" in pursuit of Indian horse thieves that the Englishman's boy joins, and the imposition of authority by the hard-bitten Hardwick.[61] However, Vanderhaeghe subverts the progress towards the conventional terminus of such narratives. Rather than constructing the Assiniboine as the bloodthirsty aggressors and the wolfers as heroic representatives of white superiority and righteousness, he depicts the confrontation in the Cypress Hills as the product of the wolfers' racism, their unpopular reputation among the Assiniboine, and their belligerent provocation of armed conflict.

While Shorty and Harry are complicit in these acts of racist violence, literal and filmic, they are pushed towards complicity in response to financial exigencies and coercion by more powerful figures, and both strive to make amends by defecting from these imperialist enterprises. Shorty throws his lot in with the wolfers in Fort Benton after his patron, the Englishman of the title, dies and after he makes himself *persona non grata* by defending himself against a belligerent assault at the hands of the owner of the hotel in which he has left the Englishman's body. As their pursuit of the Indians progresses, Shorty grows to distrust rather than emulate Hardwick and Evans and ultimately breaks with the wolfers after a gunfight with the Assiniboine, refusing to let them scalp those he has killed and putting an end to their gang-raping of an Assiniboine girl. Indeed, he confides to Harry that the wolfers "knew what was coming" as a result of Hardwick's belligerence and that the "only mistake is one us of never shot him in his blankets when he slept" (*Englishman's Boy* 205). Later, in Hollywood, he overcomes his desire to "let the dead bury the dead" and agrees to sell his story to Harry only in order to earn enough money to go north to Canada with the dependent and unpredictable Wylie. Likewise, Harry is compelled to aid Chance in his search for Shorty in order to keep his invalided mother in a respectable rest home but becomes increasingly distrustful of Chance's racist revisioning of history, ultimately resigning from the project.

The contrapuntal structure of the narrative of *The Englishman's Boy* in various ways works effectively to dramatize an imperialist writing and rewriting of history, especially because of the way Chance seeks to rework Shorty's story to underscore white superiority rather than white brutality. At the same time, however, as with *Big Bear*, the structure of *The Englishman's Boy* raises questions about its own reworking of history. One of the main problems with *The Englishman's Boy* in this regard is the question of the ontological status of the three main levels of narration. Vanderhaeghe's use of Fine Man and Broken Horn's successful coup to frame the narrative, especially because of Chance's appropriation of Shorty's story, raises the important question about whether Vanderhaeghe intends his version to be taken as historically "authentic." Vanderhaeghe is obviously focusing on a historical "gap" in *The Englishman's Boy* since Shorty's story is a narrative of a somewhat marginal but nonetheless catalytic episode in Canadian history. Vanderhaeghe's presentation of the Cypress Hills Massacre effects the kind of detailed historicizing typical of the historical novel, providing insight into the immediate and larger background to the massacre, including the starvation caused by the decimation of the buffalo, the general notoriety of the wolfers, and the politics of the whisky trade and its effects on the native population. Nonetheless, he ultimately presents this complex and pivotal historical stage in the settlement of the West with an undeniable rhetorical slant.

Questions about the ontological status of the various levels of narration in the novel are further complicated by historiographical questions, considerations about the relationship of the novel's version of the massacre to the versions of various historians. Shorty's version is generally unambiguous: the wolfers are fundamentally responsible for the massacre, their leaders racist, belligerent, and brutal. In contrast, most historical accounts are less unequivocal, particularly about responsibility for the incident and the extent of the killings; historians tend to agree that these aspects of the incident are murky. Estimates of the death toll generally range between twenty and thirty – consistent with Shorty's observation, when Harry offers him fifteen hundred dollars for his story, that "the going rate on a dead Indian" is "fifty dollars a head" (204).[62]

The question of responsibility, however, is subject to more substantial variation, with some historians demonizing the wolfers and some arguing that the wolfers were not as bad, or as culpable, as they were made out to be. For the most part, Vanderhaeghe's generally damning portrait of the wolfers seems to accord with the testimony of trader Abe Farwell – the key witness at the subsequent extradition hearing in Montana and the trial of some of the wolfers in Winnipeg – whose questionable reliability has been a central focus of debate in reconstructions of the incident (he was an employee of a rival trading firm). In constructing Shorty's version of the massacre, Vanderhaeghe generally sticks to those details about which there is general historical consensus but also makes use of details about which there is uncertainty or contradictory evidence in the historical record.[63] For instance, he has George Hammond fire the first shot in the conflict, has Ed Grace shot in the throat with an arrow (instead of being killed with a bullet), and has the wolfers decapitating Little Soldier and parading his head on a stake (which may not have happened or may have happened to another Assiniboine leader). Thus, while Vanderhaeghe chooses to focus on a relatively obscure historical episode about which there is a certain amount of disagreement among historians, making use of the creative elbow room such a strategy affords, his choices clearly lead to an indictment of the wolfers.

Where, then, do Vanderhaeghe's narrative and historiographical choices situate *The Englishman's Boy* in relation to historiographical metafictions such as *Big Bear*, Findley's *The Wars*, or Swan's *The Biggest Modern Woman of the World*? The dialogic interaction between different discourses and the narrative self-reflexivity characteristic of historiographic metafiction is conspicuously absent from the nineteenth-century sequences in *The Englishman's Boy*, which seem fairly unselfconscious and monoglossic, especially when placed beside the heterogeneous narrative of *Big Bear*. Vanderhaeghe does set Shorty's account against another, that of Chance's epic *Besieged*; even though we are never privy to the actual contents of the film, it is safe to assume that readers familiar with the Western will get the picture. But Chance's rendering of the incident is constructed by Harry as polemically and imperialistically revisionist, reducing the effect of the dialogue between the two versions. Thus there is not the same plurality of perspective nor the encouragement to consider, compare, and critique different perspectives as there is in Wiebe's novel. Considering the variation in historical perspectives on the Cypress Hills Massacre, the rendering of that history in *The Englishman's Boy* seems fairly monophonic and cohesive when compared with overtly heteroglossic and historiographical fictions such as *The Wars* and *Big Bear*, with their multiple perspectives, testimonies, and "documents."

The Englishman's Boy, then, is not as visibly heteroglossic or stylistically heterogeneous as *Big Bear* and does not, like *The Wars* or Daphne Marlatt's *Ana Historic*, openly undermine or inscribe a scepticism about the accuracy of the historical events it presents. However, the formally monoglossic nineteenth-century sequences are nonetheless somewhat polyphonic in their effect, creating a certain dialogue between different ideological perspectives. Bakhtin observes that even the language of a novel that is assumed to be "unitary and direct," lacking "any distancing, refraction or qualifications," nonetheless "is polemical and apologetic, that is, is interrelated dialogically with heteroglossia."[64] The segments focusing on the Englishman's boy parody the discourse of the Western and challenge the racist othering characteristic of Hardwick's speech, and put in contrapuntal relation the figurative, colloquial, earthy discourse of the cowboy, the mythic discourse of the Old Testament, and the imagistic lyricism of literary modernism.

While this modulation of registers effects a dialogic engagement with codes of race, masculinity, and representation – thus contributing to the novel's contesting of colonial discourse – Vanderhaeghe's text, ultimately, does not exhibit the democracy intrinsic to Bakhtin's notion of the polyphonic novel, in which "every voice, including the author's, enjoys equal validity."[65] The more subtle discursive heterogeneity of these sequences is contained, as in Wiebe's novel, within a fairly monologic discursive hierarchy and a unified purpose, one that favours the Englishman's boy's perspective. The reader participation typically favoured in historiographical metafiction is thus cultivated to a lesser degree. Nonetheless, the depiction of the settlement of the West (as with Wiebe) is a predominantly postcolonial, counterimperialist one. If, from a Bakhtinian perspective, one is tempted to say that the cup is half empty, it is, in other respects, half full. Furthermore, Vanderhaeghe's treatment of continental colonization in the past is juxtaposed with and complicated by his treatment of global colonization in the present (a subject addressed in the final chapter), making it possible to view the historiographical concerns that qualify the novel's postcolonial aims in a wider and ultimately much more favourable framework.

Historical novels that depict the history of native-white relations in Canada recurrently reflect a desire to reverse the terms of colonialism – to render that which was assumed to be heroic, despicable; that which was peaceful, violent; that which was necessary, expedient. Yet these novels also suggest that reconfiguring that history is much more messy, nuanced, and perilous than such a neat reversal would indicate. These novels certainly reflect Hutcheon's contention that an uncontaminated postcolonial identity is an impossible, essentialist ideal: "just as the *word* post-colonialism holds within it its own 'contamination' by colonialism, so too does the culture itself and its various artistic manifestations, in Canada as elsewhere."[66] While, in comparison with earlier historical novels that tended to consolidate a colonial perspective, recent historical fiction is predominantly concerned with decolonizing Canadian history, it also consistently runs the risk of perpetuating colonial assumptions and appropriation. At the same time, the shift in intent is not to be disparaged, and it is important not to fall victim to what Donna Bennett sees as an occupational hazard of postcolonial criticism: that it cultivates "contestation as the only valid methodology and practice."[67] The conclusion that we can never think or write our way out of colonialism seems too despairing and profoundly ahistorical, and efforts to rewrite Canadian history in considerably less colonial terms deserve appreciation. At the same time, it is also important for members of the dominant culture to resist self-congratulation as much as self-castigation, both of which foster a politically disastrous passivity.

Because there is no going back, that is, no way of undoing a colonial past that has transpired, negotiating what form that postcolonial culture will take seems a much more pressing issue than who has the qualifications to enter into those negotiations. At the same time, the idea that there is no going back has certainly been perversely interpreted as meaning that the past does not matter and that things like aboriginal land claims, the abuses of the residential school system, and debates about the extinguishing of native sovereignty are ancient (i.e., irrelevant) history. However compromised these historical novels may be, they dispute such a conclusion and open up that past for debate. The settler, as Lawson points out, served as "the go-between for the European First World with the strategically named Third" and thus "acted as a mediator rather than as a simple transmitter of imperialism's uncomfortable mirroring of itself. Colonial space, then, is occupied by vectors of difference. The in between of the settlers is not unbounded space but a place of negotiation."[68] These historical novels demonstrate, I would argue, that such a liminal position is subject to evolution and change. In short, they are marked by significant differences from the colonial discourse of the explorers and settlers they depict and are not simply a contemporary replication of it.

"BRUSHING HISTORY AGAINST THE GRAIN": SOCIAL HISTORY AND THE BUILDING OF NATION

"Never again will a single story be told as though it were the only one." John Berger's observation, which serves as one of the epigraphs for Michael Ondaatje's *In the Skin of a Lion,* captures the mood of many contemporary novelists writing about history. Like those writers unearthing the material and narrative strife behind Canada's movement "from colony to nation" by focusing on the exploration and settlement of the country by Europeans, other contemporary novelists have emphasized the multiple, often conflicting, and historically marginalized narratives behind the "building" of a nation. Recent historical fiction dramatizes how decolonizing Canadian history requires much more than a revisionist look at native-white relations. It underlines how, largely as a legacy of colonialism, the building of Canada and the whole edifice of Canadian history have been narrowly defined along lines of gender, race, ethnicity, region, class, and sexual orientation. These concerns, dramatized in prominent novels such as Marlatt's *Ana Historic,* Joy Kogawa's *Obasan,* and *In the Skin of a Lion,* have continued to be visible in more recent historical fiction, reflecting the degree to which the scope and definition of Canadian history need to be not just broadened but interrogated and reworked.

Certainly the most vigorously contested "site" in this (re)construction project has been that of gender. Traditionally, Canadian historians have opted, as Veronica Strong-Boag notes, "to focus on a tiny group of elite white men: to know John A. Macdonald, Henri Bourassa, Joseph Flavelle, James S. Woodsworth, Lionel Groulx, William Lyon Mackenzie King, Pierre E. Trudeau, we are told, implicitly if not explicitly, is to know Canada."[69] Over the last three decades, however, social historians, particularly feminist historians, have suggested that there is much more to knowing Canada and that looking at the history of the other half of the population is a good place to start. A number of novelists have deployed the historical novel for much the same purposes.

This recognition of the contestatory potential of the genre marks a conspicuous departure from the politics of the traditional historical romance so popular with women readers. The historical romance, as Helen Hughes argues, privileges the "sphere of public activity," particularly masculine activity, and subordinates the role of women.[70] Thus it tends to affirm that in a patriarchal society subordination is not just the fate of women but the ideal, and, as in George Eliot's famous phrase, "The happiest women, like the happiest nations, have no history."[71] Though this is applicable to a degree to the traditional historical novel, the latter arguably has greater subversive potential, and many recent historical novels suggest that to have no history is not a happy fate and challenge the terms in which women, unhappily, have a history. If one of the recurrent features of social history is a consciousness of the pervasiveness and importance of power relations, Marlatt's *Ana Historic*, along with Findley's *The Wars* and Swan's *The Biggest Modern Woman of the World*, highlights the dynamics of power behind the construction of gender and sexuality. Historical novels such as Margaret Atwood's *Alias Grace*, Heather Robertson's *The King Years* trilogy, Sky Lee's *Disappearing Moon Café*, and others have continued the trend.

Perhaps the most ambitious and compelling English-Canadian historiographical novel, *Ana Historic* (1988) emphasizes that "happiness" in the terms of Eliot's maxim amounts to marginality or erasure. The work of feminist historians and "the emergence of a large literature on women's history has done more than 'add women and stir'; it has challenged many of the conclusions reached by historians who examined only the rhetoric and behaviour of male elites" and has recognized and subverted the masculinist biases of historiography itself.[72]

Marlatt's protagonist Annie undertakes this dual program as she becomes obsessed with how Ana Richards, a schoolteacher in the early days of Vancouver, has been written into, but more so out of, history. The play on words in the book's title signals these concerns: on the one hand, "an ahistoric" suggests something that has been left out of history (both Ana Richards and women on the whole, as Annie's narrative indicates), while "Ana historic" reinscribes Ana's historicity and significance. As numerous critics have underlined, Annie's preoccupation with Ana's fate (and by extension her own) helps to foreground a principal insight of feminist historiography: that the "story is no longer about the things that have happened to women and men and how they have reacted to them; instead it is about how the subjective and collective meanings of women and men as categories of identity have been constructed."[73]

Historiography and historical sources, *Ana Historic* emphasizes, are thoroughly gendered and, in that respect, far from the neutrality to which most history aspires. As Strong-Boag observes, "historical sources have been defined by a focus on the public realm, where women's influence has been more indirect. No wonder women frequently seem not to exist as historical actors."[74] In *Ana Historic*, the fate of women in this kind of history, represented by Annie's historian husband, Richard, and by Annie's historical sources, is to be "sized-up in a glance, objectified. that's what history offers, that's its allure, its pretence. 'history says of her … '" (*Ana Historic* 56). The flip-side of this summary dismissal of women, Annie realizes, is a preoccupation with phallocentric endeavour, as reflected in the accounts of colonial Vancouver Annie peruses. Women merit but brief mention in the course of a narrative of masculine activity, and "only the briefest mention is made of Mrs. Richards who takes over the job of schoolteacher" (48). Furthermore, *Ana Historic* emphasizes (like so much of Marlatt's work) that language is loaded – and historical discourse is far from exceptional.[75]

The challenge for Annie is to counter the erasure or containment of women that both language and masculine history inscribe, a gesture that involves exposing the constructed "drama" of male history and undermining the binary oppositions of traditional historiography: "once history's onstage, histrionic as usual (all those wars, all those historic judgements), the a-historic hasn't a speaking part. what's imagination next to the weight of the (f)actual?" (139). Historiography's privileging of public accomplishment and documentation skews history in favour of men and banishes women to the wings. Annie expresses her solution (and by extension Marlatt's): "but when you're so framed, caught in the act, the (f) stop of act, fact – what recourse? step inside the picture and open it up" (56). Mrs Richards's past is not being represented, cannot be represented, "as it really was"; thus Annie writes her back into history through an act of imaginative intervention, imagining "the 'historic' Ana's story differently, since to repeat the probable story would mean never changing it."[76]

Annie's historiographical choices, moreover, are very much bound up with shifting directions in her emotional and sexual life. As Marlene Goldman argues, "Annie's impulse to generate an alternative version of history is clearly tied to the process of individuation and the struggle to invent a life that can account for women's buried or repressed experience."[77] Her researching and writing of Ana's story signals her opting out of an obviously symbolic relationship with Richard, for whom she has been serving as a research assistant (later to be "replaced" by an enthusiastic, and female, graduate student). Richard's work, which is "built on a groundwork of fact" and in which "one missing piece can change the shape of the whole picture" (134), represents the unitary, empiricist, and masculine model of history – "the real story the city fathers tell of the only important events in the world" (28) – against which Annie's work, and her conception of self, is increasingly defined. Marlatt thus emphasizes the necessary connection between writing women back into history and writing women into a less subordinate and constrained place in the present. Though the ambitiousness of *Ana Historic*'s narrative style sets it dramatically apart, Marlatt's "historic" achievement compresses key themes of feminist historiography that have been echoed by other contemporary Canadian writers.

If women's history contests the construction of history as male-centred, another important site of contestation has been that of ethnicity, race, and culture. As with gender, the redressing of the Eurocentric biases of Canadian history is not simply a matter of supplementing the history of European accomplishment, of listing others in supporting roles in the credits of Canadian history. Rather, it involves the recognition of patterns of racial and cultural marginalization, exploitation, and contestation, as well as of accommodation and collaboration, in the construction of that history. Just as with gender, such a corrective is more than "add pluralism and stir." No novel makes this clearer than Joy Kogawa's *Obasan* (1981), one of the most critically acclaimed, and dissected, works of Canadian literature. If the image of Canada as a multicultural haven is sustained by the suppression of historical episodes that contradict that myth of "tolerance," "*Obasan* effectively counters the country's preferred image of itself and attests that the national metaphor of the mosaic is sometimes honoured more in the breach than in the observance."[78]

Obasan has a singular place in English-Canadian literature as the book that brought home to many Canadian readers (or at least to the vast unenlightened majority) the fundamentally Anglocentric character of Canadian history and the understanding that the past is a culturally and racially "contested terrain" in which "events must be analyzed from a variety of perspectives."[79]

Obasan does this, as numerous critics have noted, by actively interrogating the public record, unearthing a marginalized historical story, and pressing for recognition of a historically suppressed injustice. Kogawa compels her readers to piece together a buried history, to turn the pages of (rather than on) a shameful chapter in Canada's past. *Obasan* chronicles the oppressive treatment of Canadians of Japanese descent in reaction to the bombing of Pearl Harbor: their being stripped of their possessions and herded like animals into the barracks at Hastings Park; the breaking up of the Japanese-Canadian community through deportation and dispersal; and the upholding of discriminatory legislation well beyond the crisis of the war to prevent the re-establishment of that community. "In seeking to make audible what has been forcibly silenced and conveniently forgotten," Coral Ann Howells observes, "Kogawa's novel is a historical engagement on behalf of an oppressed minority."[80] Indeed, as Arnold Davidson notes, the novel played a key role in building the momentum for the Mulroney government's official apology and pledging of restitution in 1988.[81]

Obasan succeeds in dissecting the infrastructure of racism through its deep concern with the effects of such sanctioned exclusion and persecution on individuals, families, and the community as a whole. By following what Marilyn Russell Rose describes as Naomi's family's "descent into ever-deepening circles of hell"[82] – from Hastings Park to Slocan and Granton and ultimately to Nagasaki – the novel reveals the damage inflicted not just by official policy but also by the internalized effects of racism. The crippling emotional, psychic, and physical toll these experiences take on Naomi's parents, her brother, Stephen, her uncle Isamu, and her aunts Emily and Obasan, are a microcosm of the effects on the larger community. The legacy of this devastation, however, is reflected most prominently by Naomi's struggles with uncovering past injustices and with the suppressed knowledge about the fate of her mother. As Naomi moves through the narrative towards a thorough unearthing of the past and towards the revelation of her mother's fate, the novel underlines that disclosure is necessary for psychic and emotional health.

It is also necessary for a more culturally and racially harmonious society. "The theory proposed by the book," Gary Willis maintains, "is not just for Japanese Canadians, but for all Canadians, as Canada's future health as a democracy depends, at least in part, on its recognition of (and reparation for) its past failings."[83] That conclusion, however, is one that emerges dialectically through *Obasan*'s metafictive foregrounding of debates about the need to confront the past, particularly as Naomi navigates between her Aunt Emily's resolute activism and Obasan's stoic silence. Instead of unremitting polemic, the novel aims to "pull with control rather than push with force."[84] Naomi's private search makes possible the unearthing of the larger suppressed story, putting into context the racist discourse of public opinion and official pronouncements, and it provides an opportunity to deconstruct the assumptions underlying that discourse and to highlight the sweeping violation of human rights it represents.

While *Obasan* is far from radically postmodern in its deployment of these strategies, the result is a compelling historiographical metafiction, in which "much of the novel's power lies not in its historical indictment nor in the story of Naomi's private quest but in the lyric intensity of its vision."[85] *Obasan* works *not* by "writ[ing] the vision and mak[ing] it plain" but through a complex, intertextual engagement with official and unofficial racism that connects the personal and the communal, the familial and the political, the lyrical and the historical.[86] Its achievement is nonetheless unequivocal: *Obasan* makes all too clear the implications of telling a single story "as if it were the only one," and numerous novels published since have likewise underlined the influence of race, ethnicity, and culture on perspectives on history.

Increasingly foregrounded in social history and the contemporary historical novel, finally, are considerations of class and the suppressed narratives of class conflict. If history has often been presented as a pageant, hidden behind the scenes is the violence involved in building the floats and clearing the parade route. "Whoever has emerged victorious," writes Walter Benjamin, "participates to this day in the triumphal procession in which the present rulers step over those who are lying prostrate."[87] Benjamin's image of history has important implications both for class relations and for historiography. The accomplishments of civilization, he observes, "owe their existence not only to the efforts of the great minds and talents who have created them, but also to the anonymous toil of their contemporaries. There is no document of civilization which is not at the same time a document of barbarism. And just as such a document is not free of barbarism, barbarism taints also the manner in which it was transmitted from one owner to another. A historical materialist therefore dissociates himself from it as far as possible. He regards it as his task to brush history against the grain."[88]

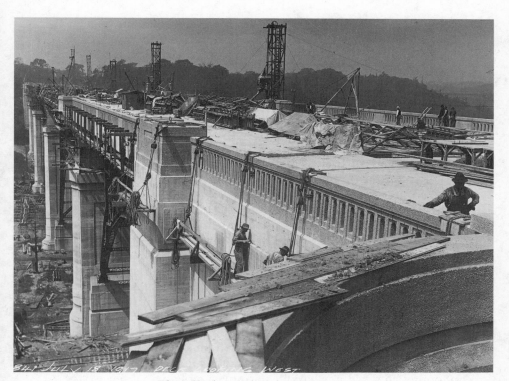

Bloor Viaduct – deck looking west.
One of the few photographs of the construction of the bridge
in which the workers are in the picture.

Michael Ondaatje's novel *In the Skin of a Lion* (1987) brushes history against the grain by striving to put a human face on the anonymous toil behind the emergence of modern Toronto between the two world wars. In *In the Skin of a Lion*, as Winfried Siemerling puts it, "the historical possibility (and probability) of another history of Toronto comes to life, and with it a multi-faceted mural of the city that its dominant historiography has left in the dark."[89] Ondaatje renders this history in such a way that his portrait of working-class immigrants – one redressing of the imbalance of official history – overlaps with dominant tropes and narrative strategies that likewise undermine the problematic methodologies and emphases of traditional historiography. While researching the building of the Bloor Street Viaduct (one of the principal construction projects on which the novel focuses), Ondaatje's protagonist Patrick Lewis evokes the American photographer Lewis Hine, whose photographs of workers and immigrants "betray official history and put together another family." *In the Skin of a Lion* provides a fictional analogue to such an aim. While the novel does portray historical figures like Commissioner of Public Works Rowland Harris and the millionaire Ambrose Small, its main intent is clearly to concentrate on those workers and/or immigrants who have been written out of a history circumscribed by class, ethnicity, and civic achievement, ironically while making that history possible through their labour.

Ondaatje redresses this imbalance by focusing much of his novel on the suppressed stories of modernity: the arduous and dangerous labour behind such civic monuments as Harris's viaduct and the waterworks, the communal solidarity and agitation of the immigrant workers to whom Patrick becomes bonded, and the revolutionary activity to which the authorities respond with draconian force. Thus Ondaatje presents the construction of modern Toronto not as a moment of civic, even national, achievement but as a configuring of urban space within a larger narrative of the rich, in which the participation of the workers is not a sign of shared enthusiasm but the end result of exploitation. These suppressed narratives of capitalist modernity are reinstated in *In the Skin of a Lion* particularly through Patrick's gradual realization that his life "was no longer a single story but part of a mural, which was a falling together of accomplices," and through Ondaatje's dramatizing of the human costs of capitalism.[90]

In the Skin of a Lion is, of course, much more than a lyrical litany of oppression, and much of the narrative emphasizes a sense of class solidarity and resistance to the "single story" of capitalism, underlining the class and ethnic conflicts that historical narratives of modern progress tend to suppress. Ondaatje portrays the immigrant workers as being doubly marginalized within an Anglocentric, capitalist society, reflecting the interpenetration of labour exploitation and the pressure to assimilate to an Anglocentric norm. However, though Ondaatje emphasizes the borders of class, ethnicity, and language that define the world of modern Toronto, his narrative strategies consistently serve to blur and displace these borders. Ondaatje's achievement in *In the Skin of a Lion*, as Susan Spearey has argued, is that, in probing the darkness beyond the lighted world of a history circumscribed by class, ethnicity, and, indeed, by gender as well, he does not simply reinscribe the teleological, realist narratives that in the past have helped to shore up such history.[91] While Ondaatje's narrative style, by virtue of its very fluidity, fragmentation, and resistance to social realism, raises interesting questions of aesthetics and politics, *In the Skin of a Lion* has proved to be a prominent and influential text because it concentrates on historical agents different from those of conventional historical fiction, writing in those workers and immigrants who have heretofore been written out.

Ana Historic, In the Skin of a Lion, and particularly *Obasan* have received a great deal of critical attention, but the historical concerns and revisionist politics of the three novels are evident in a wide range of contemporary Canadian novels that share their objective of expanding the range of perspectives on the building of Canada. Heather Robertson's *The King Years* trilogy and more recent historical novels by Margaret Atwood, Jane Urquhart, Sky Lee, and Margaret Sweatman illustrate Canadian novelists' continuing concern not just with broadening the demographics of Canadian history but with exploring the structuring effects of, and interplay between, gender, sexuality, class, ethnicity, and race in the formation of that history.

Part of what irks many historians about social history is its emphasis on what Catherine Gallagher, writing about New Historicist criticism, describes as "the micro-politics of daily life": "the traditionally important economic and political agents and events have been displaced or supplemented by people and phenomena that once seemed wholly insignificant, indeed outside of history: women, criminals, the insane, sexual practices and discourses, fairs, festivals, plays of all kinds."[92] Gallagher's list provides most of the menu of interests in Atwood's 1996 novel *Alias Grace*, the story of Grace Marks, a "celebrated murderess" in mid-nineteenth-century Toronto. In contrast with *Ana Historic*'s emphasis on the marginalizing of women in history, *Alias Grace* displays the contrary fate of women within a patriarchally circumscribed history: a plenitude of unwelcome attention and notoriety resulting from a distorted image of femininity and its boundaries. Atwood's foray into the genre of historical fiction thus makes an important contribution to the highlighting of both gender politics and assumptions about class in constructions of the past.

In July 1843, Thomas Kinnear and Nancy Montgomery were found murdered in Kinnear's home in Richmond Hill, and Kinnear's servants James McDermott and Grace Marks were convicted of Kinnear's murder; McDermott was hung, and Grace Marks's sentence was reduced to life imprisonment. In *Alias Grace*, Atwood constructs a quasi-fictional situation in which to explore her protagonist's background and to revisit the context in which the murders took place. Atwood, however, is less interested in reconstituting and offering a plausible fictional version of events – and in the process rendering judgment on her protagonist's guilt – than in exploring the strictures and restrictions of nineteenth-century patriarchy. As a result, the enduring enigma of the murders and of those alleged to have committed them is ultimately sustained.[93]

Because of the uncertainty about her participation in the crime and the consequent swirl of speculation, Grace Marks, as *Alias Grace* makes clear, was a *cause celebre*, an object of fascination, titillation, and moral condemnation (or defence) for proto-criminologists, humanitarians, religious zealots, and other, less specialized members of the curious public. Atwood structures the bulk of the novel around a series of interviews between Grace and Simon Jordan, a Yankee doctor who has been hired by a humanitarian committee promoting Grace's release and who is interested in testing his theories of criminal psychology on Grace. As the initially suspicious Grace warms to Jordan, she relates to him the story of her life leading up to the murders, a narrative that reveals not the pathological inclinations of a nineteenth-century murderess but the pathology of class and gender power relations in a rigidly stratified nineteenth-century society. From her drunken, abusive immigrant Irish father through to the sexual exploitation of domestic servants by the gentlemen of Toronto, Grace spins a tale of patriarchal abuse and upper-class privilege that conveys on the murders a sense of appropriate justice and on the ending a sense of ultimate vindication.

Such an overview makes the novel sound like the feminist dissection of, and turning of the tables on, patriarchy that are familiar staples of Atwood's fiction. But in *Alias Grace* her evocation of that constricting, hierarchical, and (especially for servant women) perilous world is more detailed, atmospheric, and ideologically nuanced, a moderation that may be a result of Atwood trying her hand at the historical novel and of her immersion in (and satirical subversion of) a more genteel nineteenth-century discourse. Those familiar objectives are more subtly interwoven with other thematic considerations and narrative textures, as Atwood draws on a wide range of intertexts to address an array of nineteenth-century social, cultural, intellectual, and spiritual preoccupations. At the heart of *Alias Grace*, however, is a sophisticated, subversive reworking of melodrama, of which Grace is the self-narrated heroine who runs a gamut of perils on her way into, and ultimately out of, Kingston Penitentiary.

From a very young age, Grace learns that life for an Irish servant girl is subject to an unforgiving and perilous pecking order. Grace describes to Simon how her shiftless, unfaithful, alcoholic, and abusive father prompts the emigration of her family from Ireland to Canada and later compels her to leave the rest of her family behind when she finds a live-in position as a housekeeper in class-bound Anglocentric Toronto. Working in the home of the upper-class, Anglican Mrs Alderman Parkinson, Grace also learns that subordination in terms of class is very much bound up with subordination in terms of gender. Her roommate, Mary Whitney, undertakes to educate Grace in the politics of service, class, and sexual relations, and to help her succeed within the narrow limits of achievement and mobility that their station in life affords.

As the authors of *Canadian Women: A History* note, during the nine-teenth century "the most serious problem of the domestic servant, if she was far from the protection of friends or family, was her vulner-ability to sexual exploitation."[94] Such is the case with Mary, who is seduced by a gentleman (Grace's narrative clearly casts suspicion on her employer's son) and abandoned when she becomes pregnant; to avoid disgrace and dismissal, she resorts to an abortion and dies of complications. Thus Grace loses a friend but gains important insight into the sexual brutalities of "service," and it is this dark episode that sets the stage for the rest of the novel. In portraying Mary's demise, Atwood takes a story encountered during her research into the med-ical records of the time and makes it a central imperative in Grace's life story, in more ways than one.[95] The death of Mary makes Grace acutely aware of the social inequities that beset her all around and projects a spectre over her subsequent career as a "murderess."

Tempted by a new position working for Kinnear, Grace is subtly forewarned about, but takes some time to truly absorb, that Kinnear's housekeeper, Nancy Montgomery, is his mistress. That liminal posi-tion – not quite servant, not quite wife – compels Nancy to be "very changeable, two-faced you might call her, and it wasn't easy to tell what she wanted from one hour to the next" (*Alias Grace* 224). In her behaviour toward Grace, Nancy is suspicious and domineering when Kinnear is at home, amicable and conciliatory in his absence. Com-plicating their uneasy relationship is the simmering violence of McDermott, who is bitterly resentful of Nancy's ascendancy in the household (because she is both a servant and a woman) and further embittered by Grace's rebuffing of his crude sexual advances. In short, it is an incendiary situation.

The crisis of this tangle of class, gender, and sexual politics is pre-cipitated by Nancy's consciousness of her expendability. Grace's effi-ciency as a servant and her potential as a replacement mistress (making her doubly admirable in Kinnear's eyes) increase the strain on the relationship between the two women. The possibility of Grace succeeding to Nancy's place is intensified by the realization that Nancy is pregnant – a repetition of Mary's dilemma that brings things to a head. Nancy's impatience with the unreliable McDermott and her resentment of Grace compel her to give them both their notice; as Grace observes to Simon, "she was in the family way, and it often happens like that with a man; they'll change from a woman in that condition to one who is not, and it's the same with cows and horses; and if that happened, she'd be out on the road, her and her bastard" (309).

In Atwood's version, the murders are presented as the result of the competitive politics and bitter resentment occasioned by a hierarchy of both class and gender. McDermott, already inclined to violent revenge for being mistreated, and having boasted that he will kill both Nancy and Kinnear, is galvanized into action (though his resolve is less than steely, according to Grace) and Grace is sucked into the vortex of complicity. He first bludgeons Nancy and throws her into the cellar, descending later to finish her off by strangling her, and then shoots Kinnear. In the conflicting versions that swarmed around the trial itself and that led to her conviction, Grace was presented as encouraging McDermott and participating in the strangling of Nancy. In Grace's narrative in *Alias Grace*, however, she is at most an unwilling accomplice, coerced to go along with McDermott's plan to murder Nancy and Kinnear to avoid being killed herself. Thus she has no choice but to escape with him and is arrested when they reach the United States.

Atwood's version is, of course, predominantly her fictional Grace's version, and the complexity of her narrative raises important considerations about gender, class, and history. Numerous subtle metafictional moments prompt readers (if not always the principal listener, Simon) to question the veracity of Grace's account and to consider the discursive and ideological vagaries that plague any effort at historical reconstruction. In Grace's case, these vagaries in particular comprise problems of memory, the relative and ideological nature of definitions of sanity, and the subjectivity of and motivation behind attempts to recover the past. In this last respect, a key feature of *Alias Grace* is the relation between Grace's narrative and her survival. Grace is something of a Scheherazade figure because a positive report from Simon may well bolster the efforts of a committee of well-meaning (if naive) humanitarians to have Grace released from prison. Thus, as with Scheherazade tantalizing King Shahriar with her interminable tales and infinitely stalling her execution, Grace's life is on the line, her fortunes reliant on her ability to tell her story.

This narratorial self-interest complicates the reception of Grace's story's inadequacies and lapses, and makes the novel an interesting study in narratorial reliability. The long confession that comprises most of *Alias Grace* is riddled with ambiguities, contradictions, and unlikely developments that put the reader in the position of judging Grace, not just on the limited evidence considered at the murder trial, but on the evidence of the broader terrain of her struggle to survive in a stratified world. As a result, Simon's goal in interviewing Grace becomes progressively complicated (and, for that matter, compromised) as he becomes, despite his residual scepticism, increasingly sympathetic. The ambiguity is sustained at the climax of Grace's account when Simon does not get what he is really looking for –

confirmation or rejection of Grace's participation in the strangling of Nancy. Grace maintains that there is a gap in her memory of events and that her confessing to having seen McDermott drag Nancy to the trapdoor and throw her into the cellar was advised by her lawyer merely to save herself from hanging: "He said it was not a lie, as that is what must have happened, whether I could remember it or not" (317). She is likewise unable to disconfirm McDermott's accusation that she took part in strangling Nancy.[96] Furthermore, most of Grace's account of her subsequent fate. is narrated in Simon's absence, as he travels to Toronto to interview her defense lawyer and later flees Kingston before seeing Grace's case through to the end. Thus Grace manages to elude his grasp, to tantalize him, on the one hand, with the coherence and integrity of her narrative, and, on the other, with its gaping holes and ambiguities.

In that respect, Grace's narrative is, like Scheherazade's, a kind of performance, which makes the novel also an interesting study in the construction of gender. In her groundbreaking analysis of gender, Judith Butler argues that gender is performative rather than a natural attribute: "Gender is, thus, a construction that regularly conceals its genesis; the tacit collective agreement to perform, produce, and sustain discrete and polar genders as cultural fictions is obscured by the credibility of those productions – and the punishments that attend not agreeing to believe in them; the construction 'compels' our belief in its necessity and naturalness."[97] Such a model of gender helps to put into perspective how Grace's behaviour is "assessed" not according to objective, scientific, behavioural taxonomies but according to patriarchal expectations of feminine performance.

Moreover, in light of Butler's model of gender, one can see Grace's narrative as the product of a consciously directed performance of femininity. Responding to scepticism about the effects of dispensing with the idea of gender as the core of identity, Butler argues that recognizing gender as constructed provides new possibilities for agency, rather than undermining the foundation it requires: "Construction is not opposed to agency; it is the necessary scene of agency, the very terms in which agency is articulated and becomes culturally intelligible." Because there is no ground outside constructed identities on which to establish a feminist politics, the task instead is "to locate strategies of subversive repetition enabled by those constructions, to affirm the local possibilities of intervention through participating in precisely those practices of repetition that constitute identity and, therefore, present the immanent possibility of contesting them."[98]

Grace's narration, then, and the interplay of desire with which it is charged, can be viewed as a discursive performance in which she manipulates social, sexual, and generic codes, within the limited agency her position affords, to achieve her goal of release from incarceration and, more implicitly, to deliver a critique of class and gender relations. Elizabeth Rose nicely ties this performance to Grace's métier as a seamstress: "Grace, then, is an evocative object onto which those around her project their expectations and assumptions about women and the poor. Grace pieces these expectations into the quilt of her identity, along with scraps of Mary Whitney and Nancy Montgomery. In the end, her ability to survive is based upon her qualities as a seamstress – her ability, that is, to stitch all these bits together into a recognizable pattern, an identity that is 'fashionable' according to the lights of her time. The title of the book hints at the tenuousness of this identity."[99]

Grace's narration, however, is not the only performance that demands assessment in the novel, since what is perhaps the climactic moment of Atwood's narrative – the moment in which, in some sense, a "theory" or explanation of Grace's role in the murders is put forth – comes when Grace submits to being induced into a neuro-hypnotic sleep by an ostensible expert in the procedure, Dr Jerome DuPont. In this state Grace speaks in a voice that is ultimately identified by Simon to be that of Mary Whitney, who "only borrowed her [Grace's] clothing for a time" (402) and encouraged McDermott to commit the murders, which avoided a repetition of the circumstances of Mary's demise and constituted a kind of retribution: "She had to die. The wages of sin is death. And this time the gentleman died as well, for once. Share and share alike!" (401). DuPont, however, is another alias for Grace's itinerant peddler friend and latter-day Sam Slick, Jeremiah Pontelli, with whom she contemplated running away prior to the murders. As a past master of confidence tricks, Jeremiah fools the assembled company (most of whom are credulous members of The Committee to Pardon Grace Marks) into taking him for an expert and is able to alert Grace to cooperate in the procedure. Thus the immediate temptation is to read the result as a clever conspiracy to help exonerate Grace from blame, if not in the readers' eyes, at least in those of her upper-class supporters.

Atwood, however, does not make things so simple, but instead leaves readers in the position of having to "assess" Grace's behaviour. While the opportunity for Grace's collusion with Jeremiah arrives unexpectedly, the possibility of such a "double consciousness" has been prepared for earlier in Grace's narrative, in segments she has obviously already related to Simon. Just after Mary's death, Grace hears Mary's voice saying "Let me in" and rushes to open the window to release her soul. Her fear that she might have been too late seems to be confirmed when she falls into a ten-hour faint, during which, it is suggested, she is possessed by Mary. The possibility of possession raises its head elsewhere at various points in her account – in her behaviour when she is sent to the Lunatic Asylum in Toronto and during her description of the murder – and it is a recurring motif in her dreams. As the voice says, it borrowed Grace's "earthly shell. Her fleshly garment. She forgot to open the window, and so I couldn't get out!" (403). It appeals to the assembled gathering not to tell Grace because such manifestations, which were not taken seriously at the Asylum, would no doubt have Grace promptly sent back.

While it might be argued that the voice's revelation is Grace merely taking the opportunity profferred by Jeremiah to reap the harvest from narrative seeds she has been sowing all along, the voice is also uncannily clairvoyant, reading Simon's hidden motives, including his lust for Grace, and perceiving his actions in the dark (as he clutches the hand of his hostess's eligible daughter). The ultimate effect is one of uncertainty. Atwood makes use of a psychological theory seriously entertained at the time in order to provide a potential explanation for the enigmatic contradictions of the historical Grace Marks, but she also cultivates the suspicion that that explanation might well have been an illusion created by a consummate performer.[100]

This tension reflects Atwood's concern with the relation between sanity and gender in the novel, her dissection of the patriarchal assumptions underlying nineteenth-century psychological assessments of women. As Grace considers the legacy of her notorious reputation, she highlights the dubious condemnations and equally dubious defences of her role in the murder: "that I am an inhuman female demon, that I am an innocent victim of a blackguard forced against my will and in danger of my own life, that I was too ignorant to know how to act and that to hang me would be judicial murder." She then underlines the mutual incompatibility of (and therefore implicitly discredits) the heterogeneous barrage of reactions to her: "I wonder, how can I be all of these different things at once?" (23). Through Grace, Atwood exposes the manichean binaries that spring from patriarchal assumptions about women, sanity, and capability. The only avenues for exoneration for Grace seem to be ignorance or insanity, neither particularly complimentary nor empowering alternatives. Her lawyer, for instance, contends that ignorance is her best defence, as a sign of intelligence would necessarily render her suspect – a neat patriarchal catch-22. And Susanna Moodie's account of Grace in the asylum in Toronto in *Life in the Clearings* (which provided Atwood's initial encounter with the story and is cited and commented upon at various points in the novel) sensationally and melodramatically depicts her as a raving lunatic, in her loss of sanity doing penance for her misdeeds.[101]

The structure of *Alias Grace*, however, allows for the consideration (and subversive dissection) of these alternatives and for the restoration to Grace – through her skillful, compelling, and ultimately ambiguous narrative – of a sense of agency and power. Through the questions of reliability and intention that the novel raises, Grace's honesty and sanity are certainly put to the test, but readers must consider the very real possibility that Grace, as the one who is in control of what she tells, is very sanely, very carefully steering the ship of her story to the destination of her choosing, rather than having it commandeered by others – which has been the story of her life. Grace is very much defined by the principle that women achieve historicity only through unhappy fates, but her fate also provides the opportunity to break out of the melodramatic position of victim to which her class and gender have consigned her.[102] Putting the question of Grace's guilt aside, the murders precipitate a destabilization of the social hierarchy, which Grace is able to harness to achieve a greater degree of mobility and prominence (however ambivalent) than she otherwise would have had.

Despite the novel's unsurprising preoccupation with the character and history of Grace Marks, *Alias Grace* to a substantial degree shifts the focus from the fictional reconstruction of the past to a narrative frame in which the assessment of that reconstruction is foregrounded.[103] Simon is forced to enter Grace's story and to make decisions about what happened, ostensibly analytically assessing it within the framework of his theories of criminal behaviour. But this scientific relationship of observer-observed is soon destabilized, and the borders between the events of Grace's narrative and Simon's status as a professional and a gentleman dissolve. In the process, Simon's complicity with those who have plagued Grace in the past – demanding employers, sexually motivated gentlemen, the prurient public – becomes increasingly more of an issue than Grace's participation in the murders.

Though comparatively sympathetic (in a novel in which the bar for masculine behaviour is held pretty low), Simon, like the other doctors Grace encounters, is initially interested in her as an object of scientific scrutiny. In order to fund his dream of establishing a private (and more humane) asylum, he needs "to be able to offer something novel, some new discovery or cure, in a field that is already crowded and also very contentious" (56). Thus he seeks to gain Grace's confidence and penetrate the enigma of her role in the murders; securing her release is a potential subsidiary outcome and by no means the principal goal. Initially suspecting that Simon is trying to use her (as have, in one way or another, most men she has encountered), Grace gradually realizes that he has developed other, less professional interests.

The scientific detachment on which Simon at first prides himself erodes as he falls for Grace (and, indeed, as it seems she falls for him). Their interviews expose Simon to some, if not all, of the most intimate of Grace's experiences (she refuses, for instance, to satisfy his curiosity about the possibility of sexual relations with McDermott), and Simon becomes increasingly plagued by desire for her. Thus he follows the example of so many of the men who haunt Grace's past and present. In this respect, an important part of the novel is Atwood's exploration of how Grace is, to begin with, "marked" for sexual exploitation because of her class and gender, but becomes much more so because of her notoriety and the assumptions men (both professional and lay) make about her guilt.

If Simon thus becomes the misogynistic Shahriar to Grace's Scheherazade, the attraction is not consummated, and eventually the beneficiary of Simon's repressed lust is his landlady, Rachel Humphries, who melodramatically finds herself threatened with ruin after being abandoned by her dipsomaniacal husband. Initially disgusted by Rachel's quietly pleading manner, Simon wakes from a dream about Grace to find himself in bed with Rachel, after which he guiltily and coldly exploits her vulnerability for his own sexual pleasure. When Rachel's husband announces his imminent return, however, Simon is jogged out of his complacency. In his callous reaction to the dilemma in which he suddenly finds himself, he abolishes the distance he has condescendingly assumed from the sordid business of Grace's history. The desperate Rachel suggests to Simon that her husband might be conveniently done away with, echoing the role Grace is said to have played with McDermott in the murders. Simon briefly entertains the thought but recognizes the absurd, melodramatic conventionality of it all – "like some third-rate shocker, Ainsworth or Bulwer-Lytton at their most bloodthirsty and banal" (410) – and realizes that he would thereafter be chained to Rachel, his grateful rescued damsel but also the only material witness to murder. He even contemplates doing away with her once they have fled to the States, displaying the kind of menace that Grace in her narrative attributes to McDermott.

Simon, however, decides that discretion is the better (read: selfishly expedient) part of valour. He quickly skips town, leaving Rachel some financial compensation and a callous Dear Jane letter, indicating the unlikelihood of his ever returning to Kingston. Such behaviour replicates that of the sexually exploitative gentlemen who figure so prominently as the villains of Grace's narrative. Thus, ironically, by virtue of his becoming implicated in the violences of a rigidly stratified society, Simon fails to finish his study of Grace – having concluded that he cannot give credence to the "double consciousness" theory without ruining his scientific reputation – and essentially abandons her to her fate as well.

By the end of the novel, the tables have been turned even more so. Serving in the Civil War, Simon is deprived of part of his memory (as was presumably the case with Grace), while Grace is the unlikely beneficiary of a happy, or at least not unhappy, ending: released from prison after being pardoned, she manages to retrieve some of the disrupted narrative of her life by marrying Jamie Walsh, the young neighbour who had testified against her at her trial. As Stephanie Lovelady rightly points out, this "is an improvement, but not a triumph."[104] This outcome, ironically, is reported by Grace in the letters she mentally composes to Simon – though she is unaware of his whereabouts – in which she displays a concern for him that he proved too self-absorbed and self-indulgent to reciprocate. Thus Atwood takes advantage of a historical "dark area" – Grace Marks moved to the United States soon after her release, and there seems to be no record of her subsequent fate – to construct an ending that to a degree turns the tables on patriarchy.

Alias Grace very much demonstrates the truth of the adage Simon's mother cites in a letter to Rachel, pouring cold water on her romantic hopes and essentially blaming her for the ill-advised liaison: "What is believed in society, is not always the equivalent of what is true; but as regards a woman's reputation, it amounts to the same thing" (421). Women must do nothing to provide fodder for speculation, whereas men, the novel makes clear, have no such responsibilities. Within such a rigid paradigm, Grace's notoriety is the price she pays for allowing herself to be drawn into a compromising situation. Her life thus proves to be the converse of Eliot's maxim: she is unhappily historical. The comparative uneventfulness of Canadian history may suggest that a lack of event can be salutary, but the nineteenth-century patriarchal context of *Alias Grace* underlines that it can also be stifling and violent. Atwood shows that, within the limits of such a rigid hierarchy, a career of crime was one of only a few avenues for women to achieve social distinction. More significantly, however, she also redresses the masculinist inscription of the historical Grace Marks by having the Grace of *Alias Grace* manipulate that distinction to her advantage.

That Grace is Irish is also a significant factor in her uphill struggle in a nineteenth-century Upper Canada dominated by English Prot-estants, though as a Protestant herself she has an easier time of assim-ilating. In this respect, *Alias Grace* contributes to the broader concern with race, ethnicity, and culture in Canadian history. Like many his-torians, Canadian novelists have sought to emphasize that Canadian history is fundamentally multicultural and to challenge the racial and cultural biases of Canadian history. In doing so, however, they have had to navigate what Smaro Kamboureli describes as the ambivalent reception of multiculturalism: "while multiculturalism is expected to facilitate the process of decolonizing the inherited representations of Canadian history, the literary tradition, and other forms of culture, it is also seen as essentializing race and ethnicity, namely assigning to racial and ethnic differences, as well as their various expressions, attributes that are taken to be 'natural,' and therefore stable."[105]

In highlighting the cultural plurality of Canadian history, then, it is important at the same time to destabilize cultural and racial boundaries and to underscore their fluidity. Kamboureli sees, in recent "Canadian multicultural history, the beginning of an attempt to understand how distinct identities can converge and dialogue with each other within Canada, how boundaries of difference must be repositioned – not in relation to the signs of 'centre' and 'margins' but in relation to new and productive alignments."[106] Likewise, Winfried Siemerling argues that "approaches that deemphasize static patterns of difference and identity (defined in terms of pure opposi-tion and negation) promise to continue to be productive fields of research."[107] Historical novels such as Jane Urquhart's *Away* and Sky Lee's *Disappearing Moon Café* recognize the importance of that dual negotiation. They go beyond the provision of a supplemental, polemic, and potentially essentializing history of marginalized communities to a decolonization that involves not just recognizing the inequities of a dominant Anglocentric community, but also imagining how those communities might be more positively realigned.

Urquhart's 1993 novel *Away* dramatizes the cohesion and defen-siveness of a minority culture within a hostile dominant society but also the perils of a radical adhesion to one's cultural heritage. *Away* follows five generations of the Irish Catholic O'Malley family from Rathlin Island in Ireland during the great famine of the 1860s to the backwoods of Upper Canada, to post-Confederation Ottawa and the assassination of Thomas D'Arcy McGee, and ultimately to the present. Like *Alias Grace*, *Away* dramatizes the ethnic distinctions and tensions within what is too often seen as Canada's monolithic

European heritage. It counters Anglocentric accounts of Confederation as a moment of nation-building unity by illustrating not only the history of oppression by the English behind the emigration of so many Irish to Canada, but also the background of intense cultural negotiation, oppression, and violence behind that apparent consensus.

Urquhart addresses these issues of colonialism and cultural politics particularly in her portrait of Irish Catholic nationalism as a blend of the mythic, the historical, and the political in Irish culture and folklore, and in her examination of the effect of immigration on cultural and political identity. This sense of nationalism is established during the famine, in which scenes of dire suffering and cultural oppression mingle with episodes of spectral enchantment and lyrical ethnic nationalism. The transportation of that nationalism to Canada, however, is portrayed as problematic and tied to a larger pattern in which immigration is, in a fashion, another form of being "away." This central trope of the novel blends the immigrant's sense of departure and exile with the belief, prevalent in West Irish folklore, in being "away."[108] While working on *Away*, Urquhart commented that she was writing about cultural identity, immigration, and generations of Irish Catholics who are "tribal, hysterically Anglophobic and very sentimental about their lost homeland" but noted that she intended the novel to "show the parallels between all immigrants' experiences."[109] Thus running through *Away* is a portrait of ethnic nationalism as a legacy of cultural cohesion, beauty, and oppression that is both lyrical and political but whose transportation to a new context raises important – and certainly postcolonial – questions about the nature of history and cultural memory.

The portion of the novel set on Rathlin Island gives *Away* a strong nationalist momentum, underscoring the history of oppression by the English: the religious persecution, the deforestation of Ireland, and, during the era of the famine, the banning of hedge schools, the exploitation leading to the famine, and the forced exodus as an expedient solution. Urquhart dramatizes the injustice of the situation through, for instance, the brilliantly executed scenes of evocative, wearied stasis as Brian O'Malley's family starves to death and through Brian's eloquent nationalist lamentations: "The old language will disappear forever, and all the magic and the legends. It's what they want, what they've always wanted, to be rid of us one way or another" (*Away* 74). At the same time, Urquhart steers away from melodrama, not least through her choice of antagonists; the Sedgewick brothers, the O'Malleys' non-absentee landlords, are well-meaning and eccentric rather than blatantly exploitative villains. In some ways, the Sedgewicks underscore the politics of exploitation perhaps more forcefully because of their oddball behaviour – their fiddling while Ireland burns, so to speak. Their esoteric naturalist and folkorist pursuits – Granville Sedgewick composes romanticizing laments "concerning the sorrows of Ireland" (39) – reflect a detached possessiveness and patronizing superiority towards nature and their peasant tenants alike. The Sedgewicks subsequently opt to solve their tenants' misery by quite naively exporting them across the Atlantic – "the ships are clean and well maintained ... and the food on them is of the highest quality, yes?" (121) Osbert ingenuously asks a land agent.

The bitterness of such a history of exploitation is, of course, not left behind; the Promised Land, in many respects, is more of the same. This is signalled, before the O'Malleys' departure, by Colonel Tarbutt's Anglocentric colonial settler's guide to Canada, which demoralizes the inhabitants of Rathlin Island by listing as things that "should be taken along on a journey to the northern portion of the new world" such staples of Irish Catholic peasant life as "engraved prints of Windsor Castle, Buckingham Palace, and the Queen, Epsom salts, field-glasses, folio for pressed wildflowers, golf clubs, two good hounds for hunting" (117), and so on. After the family has settled, Brian is dismayed to find that Orangeism has likewise been exported to Upper Canada and that "many of his Protestant neighbours had taken the pledge to eliminate Catholicism wherever they might find it" (198). In a replay of the prejudice he experienced in Ireland, his career as a schoolteacher comes to an end when, after his teaching of history takes a nationalist turn, hysterical reaction to Fenian raids in 1866 prompts the Board of Trustees of his township to request his retirement. To further underline the migration of oppression across the Atlantic, after the deaths of Mary and Brian, Osbert Sedgewick reappears, his estate having collapsed because the brothers "sent so many away that there was no one left to work the estate and no money left either" (218). When Brian's daughter Eileen reveals that there is gold on their property, Osbert buys out the children with the money from the sale of his estate, once again taking into his possession Brian and Mary, around whose graves he has a hired man "install a decorative wrought-iron fence" (282). Thus the spirit of Irish Catholic nationalist feelings on the part of the O'Malleys and others is to a great degree sustained by the persistence of the factors that cultivated that nationalism back in Ireland.

Mysticism and ethnic nationalism in *Away*, furthermore, are very much bound up with gender. While sentiments of Irish cultural and political nationalism are expressed most explicitly by male characters like Brian, the Captains O'Shaunessey, and Eileen's patriot lover, Aidan Lanighan (who turns out, instead, to be an agent of D'Arcy

McGee), that sense of the past is also more privately and mystically present both in Mary, who "had fragments of the old beliefs" that "had not been completely stolen from her" (75), and in Eileen. Before the family leaves for Canada, Mary's daemon lover, under whose spell she has gone "away," shows her visions of the passion and suffering of her history, which "are not being shed" but rather "accumulated" (127), and of her participation in one of the great waves of emigration: "when you go, this is what you become part of" (128). Later, Mary's conversation with her Ojibway friend Exodus Crow underlines a history of colonial exploitation that sounds very familiar to him: "After she had been in the forest for several winters she told him dark things; about the time of the stolen lands of her island, and of the disease, and of the lost language and the empty villages and how the people who once sang were now silent, how the people who once danced were now still" (184). The exchange between Mary and Exodus gives a particularly postcolonial twist to Leonard Cohen's phrase "let us compare mythologies."[110]

With Eileen and Liam, the next generation of O'Malleys, however, the portrait of nationalism takes a more ambivalent turn, the relationship between the two showing how burdensome the weight of cultural heritage can be in a new land. Liam, Ireland-born, has forgotten the motherland: "All he remembered of Ireland was a flat stone beyond the threshold of a door, the rest of the past had fallen away" (166). Bitter over his mother's abandonment of the family to go in search of her daemon lover and having had responsibility thrust upon him, Liam has no time for the preservation of his Irish heritage. He rejects the mythological account that Exodus gives of her death and confronts Brian over the validity of Exodus's story: "Do you believe in this spirit? ... Do you believe in this fairy tale?" (190). Brian answers only, "I didn't used to" (190), and it is Eileen who completes the thought: "He believes it ... because it is true" (191). Eileen thus illustrates how belief in the supernatural in the novel is very much bound up with the preservation of cultural identity, but so does the pragmatic Liam through his rejection of both.

After Brian's death, Liam reflects, mystified, on the resilience of his father's nationalism: "What was it that lodged the homeland so permanently and so painfully in the heart of his father?" (207). When Liam discovers from *The Canadian Geological Survey* the existence of the Canadian Shield, which lies beneath their property and has been frustrating his efforts to farm, he repudiates Brian, "thinking of men more enterprising than his father" and realizing that none "of them was Irish" (209). Liam ultimately plays the role of the colonized Irishman, identifying with the capitalist ethic of Osbert Sedgewick, whereas Eileen sees Osbert simply as her parents' former landlord. Indeed, when Liam achieves his dream of owning the white house that he sees as a child on the long voyage to the backwoods of Upper Canada, he buys land in a Loyalist village, becoming a landlord and thus one of the oppressors himself. Eileen is quick to point out the irony: "I think that the English took the land from the Indians same as they took it from the Irish. Then they just starve everybody out, or ... they evict them, or both" (279). In a context of political, cultural, and economic domination by the English, the pragmatic Liam thus becomes a "mimic man," an ambivalent position that is "the effect of a flawed colonial mimesis," Homi Bhabha argues, "in which to be Anglicized, is emphatically not to be English."[111] Liam thus shows the perils of one extreme of the experience of the immigrant – an attempt to completely jettison one's inherited mythology and culture.

Though Liam's apparent neo-colonialist behaviour and betrayal of his heritage is checked by his accommodation of his Irish squatter, Thomas Doherty (and his marrying of Doherty's daughter, Molly), it is Eileen who carries on her father's nationalist aspirations (as well as her mother's more mystical burden of her people's history). In her flirtation with Fenianism in the final section of *Away*, Eileen leans towards a mystic nationalism that inverts but is no less problematic than Liam's desire for a cultural and historical *tabula rasa*. Eileen, like Mary, absorbs in a more lyrical and spiritual fashion the legacy of her people's history through listening to Brian's songs and stories: "She who was born into a raw, bright new world would always look back towards lost landscapes and inward towards inherited souvenirs, while he sought the forward momentum of change and growth, the axe in the flesh of the tree, the blade breaking open new soil" (207–8). Liam, who has experienced the privations of the old land, repudiates it. In contrast, the Canadian-born Eileen by age thirteen has absorbed her father's "Irish revolutionary songs" and "cheerfully sang about the hanging of brave young men, wild colonial boys, the curse of Cromwell, cruel landlords, the impossibility of requited love, and the robbery of landscape while she built snow castles" (199).

Her commitment to the revolutionary cause, however, is catalyzed, and compromised, by her relationship with Aidan. After her first encounter with Aidan, Eileen becomes an avid reader of the nationalist and Catholic newspaper *The Irish Canadian*; her mooning over Aidan is mixed with politics, and her perception of Irish nationalism is constructed as a naive romanticism. Evoking the mythological Irish hero Finn MacCool, she envisions Aidan as part of a band of gallant patriots, galloping "over hills with the wind in their hair or [leaping] back and forth on the trunks of enormous, floating trees ... They were

brothers-in-arms, fiercely loyal, and their arena was the new dominion." She believes, furthermore, that although she is a woman,
"Aidan Lanighan's touch had guaranteed her a role in the theatre,
the performances, that made up their lives" (293).

In her patriotic enthusiasm, Eileen demonizes D'Arcy McGee and
becomes fixated upon him. "[T]ranslating from myth to life the songs
her father had taught her" (296) and spurred by McGee's rejection of
Aidan's "petition" (the dance expressive of the spirit of Irish nationalism he vows to perform before McGee in Ottawa), Eileen comes to
view him as a traitor. This naiveté about McGee's politics is compounded by her misreading of Aidan's attitude towards McGee,
which is quite conveniently never voiced but expressed in his dancing,
with which his audience soulfully (but apparently gullibly) communes.
Resenting McGee for his hold on Aidan, Eileen in her devotion to the
cause is dangerously uncritical, her patriotic ideals constructed as
myth moving further from reality: "The idea of the oneness of the
tribe, the imagined collective voice, calmed her. There were no uncertainties" (330). Her desire for "the power, the collusion, the potential
for tragedy" (298) is conveyed as being fairly extremist: "I've come
to help you ruin the traitor McGee" (310), she tells Aidan when she
searches him out in Montreal. However, when it seems that Aidan is
about to carry through with the assassination, "Eileen was appalled
by the anticipated act shaping itself in her mind" (341), suggesting
that there are limits to her revolutionary ardour.

The surprise ending of *Away*, in which the primary protagonists
are revealed respectively as a political ingènue and a spy, somewhat
abruptly reconfigures the portrait of Irish Catholic nationalism in the
novel (even if, in retrospect, there are signs both of Eileen's naiveté
and Aidan's disagreement with Eileen's nationalist clichés). The
novel cumulatively builds a strong consciousness both of a history
of colonial oppression and of the continuity of a heritage whose eradication has been an ongoing part of that exploitation, but the force
of that consciousness becomes complicated in the new and fairly
volatile political environment of Confederation-era Canada. Through
the contrast between Liam and Eileen, Urquhart suggests the need
in such a situation for moderate accommodation: Liam's attempt to
slough off his Irish heritage comes across as a distorted, extreme
assimilation, a form of colonial cringe, whereas Eileen's clinging to a
fetishized mythology, on the other hand, is portrayed as a distorted,
extreme resistance to accommodation that has serious – potentially
disastrous – consequences.

Urquhart's somewhat oblique portrait of D'Arcy McGee is likewise
tied to the interplay between history, myth, cultural identity, and

immigration in the novel. The view of McGee in *Away* is restricted to a highly filtered and generally hostile response on the part of Brian, Eileen, and other Irish Catholics. Associated with the republican Young Ireland movement in the 1840s, McGee was initially an eloquent North American exponent of Irish Catholic political and cultural nationalism; as Brian reflects, McGee "understands the injustice, ... the terrible black heart of it" (166). However, Brian later repudiates McGee after his notorious speech in Wexford during a visit to Ireland in 1865, in which he denounces Fenianism in North America and criticizes republicanism and "the flaws in the Irish Catholic character that left that group open to manipulation by such creatures" (199). That McGee is hardly the turncoat and villain Brian, Eileen, and the O'Shaunesseys make him out to be is suggested only somewhat subtly by Urquhart's presentation of him as an eloquent and persecuted supporter of Confederation: "when he opened his mouth to speak, the world around him stood at silent attention," though in "recent months he had opened his mouth to speak far too often" (283). Absent from the novel is the image of McGee in nationalist iconography as "one of the founding Fathers of the Confederation of Canada" and "a peacemaker in racial conflicts and the prophet of a federal nation,"[112] or even as a "dynamic social visionar[y]."[113]

The ambivalence towards McGee reflects the legacy of colonialism and the difficulties it poses to negotiating the cultural configuration of the new dominion. Urquhart does suggest his populist appeal and conciliatory sentiments through the speech he gives just before his assassination, in which he emphasizes renewal, unity, and the erasing of divisions: "there would be no factions, no revenge for old sorrows, old grievances. Everything ... was to be new, clear; a landscape distanced by an ocean from the zones of terror. A sweeping territory, free of wounds, belonging to all, owned by no one" (337–8). Eileen, however, though impressed with his eloquence, feels all the more a sense of betrayal: "Lost landscapes through which she had never walked were unfolding, hill by hill, in Eileen's thoughts. To her, McGee was the worst kind of enemy, the truly guilty; the one who knows the beauty and betrays it" (339). Here Urquhart captures the paradoxical difficulties posed by the persistence of anti-colonial sentiment to McGee's vision of a more equitable, less hierarchical, and in that sense postcolonial, state. The loyalty to their new home that McGee preached to his fellow Irish Canadians, as Isabel Skelton argues, for many Irish Catholics had connotations of "truckling to alien rulers, that unworthy acceptance of arrogant pretensions, against which every Irishman of spirit had struggled for centuries," and Eileen obviously reads his words in this light.[114] The continuation of English domination makes cultural accommodation less palatable, a kind of colonial surrender.

Urquhart's presentation of the assassination is particularly oblique, throwing the emphasis back on the O'Malleys' responses to the cultural tensions of the new dominion. Historically, Patrick James Whelan was charged and hanged for the assassination, which was attributed to McGee's Fenian opponents (of which he had many). However, according to Isabel Skelton, "it was never felt that the whole truth was known. Much of the evidence which hanged Whelan was purely circumstantial, and he, to the last, maintained he was innocent."[115] Furthermore, T.P. Slattery argues, it seems unlikely that Fenians were ultimately responsible.[116]

Urquhart, like many historical novelists, is cagey in her presentation of the actual event, which in the novel comes as an interruption of the heated discussion between Aidan and Eileen over the whereabouts of the pistol that she has been concealing for him: "Then her words were cancelled by the sound of a single shot and the sight of a white top hat rolling away, cartwheeling down a wooden sidewalk" (342). As Urquhart observes in her acknowledgments, *Away* "does not pretend to solve the mystery" (n.p.); rather, as Janet McNaughton argues, "Urquhart uses this assassination to explore what it meant to be Irish and Catholic in 19th-century Canada, the nature of nationalism, and the wisdom of nursing old political wounds in a new land."[117]

Rather than focusing her narrative energies on unravelling a historical enigma, Urquhart uses that enigma as the focal point of a dissection of the historical tensions that McGee's notoriety and assassination reflected. Part of colonialism's legacy, Urquhart suggests, is a cultural hegemony that reinforces an oppositional ethnic nationalism and presents a substantial, if not insurmountable, obstacle to the formation of a more democratic and postcolonial culture. As a narrative of immigration, *Away* depicts in Brian the cultivation of a resilient anti-colonial nationalism in the face of poverty and prejudice, and dramatizes, through the contrast between Eileen and Liam, what a delicate balancing act the sustaining of the past in a new home can be, raising particularly postcolonial questions about identity, power, and the force of nationalism.

Sky Lee's *Disappearing Moon Café* (1990) does much the same for Vancouver's Chinese-Canadian community. Though it is tempting to see the novel more as a family saga than a historical novel, the same might be said of *Away*, with which Lee's novel has much in common. Playing an important part in what Lien Chao sees as Chinese-Canadian writers' transformation of "the collective historical silence into a contemporary community-based literature,"[118] *Disappearing Moon Café* similarly develops a multi-generational genealogy of an immigrant family within a larger society that constructs that community as culturally, but also racially, other. Like *Away*, Lee's novel explores the uneasy equilibrium between the internal politics of a cultural community and its external relations with the larger society and suggests perhaps more dramatically the dangers of an obsession with purity and separation.

Though social history is often preoccupied with relations between minority cultures and the dominant culture, *Disappearing Moon Café* is notable for its preoccupation with internal relations – in a couple of senses. At the heart of the complicated history and genealogy of the Wong family, which the narrative of *Disappearing Moon Café* recounts, is a desire for patrilineal and racial continuity, as well as the suppressed disruption of that continuity by the patriarch Wong Gwei Chang's marriage to the mixed-race Kelora Chen. This disruption and the attempt to keep it secret fuel the increasingly tense dynamics within the family and lead to repeated generational resistance, all of which is less than reverently chronicled by Gwei Chang's great-granddaughter Kae.

Tracing the fallout of the family secrets through the next three generations gives the novel a broad historical scope and a sustained concern with gender, sexuality, and race. The source of the family's miscegenated and incestuous history – qualities that disrupt their desire for genealogical purity – is established in the prologue, in which Gwei Chang, sent to Canada on a search for his ancestors' bones in 1892, meets and marries Kelora, born of white and native parents but raised by a Chinese man. Once he has completed his task of delivering the bones to Victoria, Gwei Chang, instead of returning to Kelora, chooses the more conventional option of an arranged marriage in the old country. This decision comes back to haunt him, not just through the genealogical complications that ensue, but because on his deathbed he realizes his love for Kelora and the life that he failed to pursue. Their union and the presence of their son, Wong Ting An, is suppressed, forbidden knowledge, and that suppression, combined with an often hysterical obsession with patrilineal continuity, wreaks havoc on subsequent generations.

The complications, which are sufficiently convoluted that Lee considerately provides a genealogical chart, are fueled by patriarchal imperatives and a duplicitous need to conceal the undermining of those imperatives. The result is a series of situational ironies in which the family's erstwhile racial and gender objectives completely unravel. The machinations of Gwei Chang's shrewish wife, Mui Lan, come back to haunt her after she conspires to find a mistress for her son, Choy Fuk, wrongly assuming that his wife, Chan Fong Mei, is responsible for the lack of children in their marriage. The browbeaten Fong Mei bears three children through a liaison with Ting An, the first child coming at the same time as that of Choy Fuk's mistress, Song Ang, who has had a child by another man in order to save face for Choy Fuk.

With the next generation, the genealogical complications and situational ironies are exponentially intensified. Keeping open the wounds of the previous generation's duplicity, Fong Mei's daughter Beatrice falls for Keeman Woo, Song Ang's son, who is ostensibly Choy Fuk's illegitimate son and thus Beatrice's half-brother; the irony, of course, is that biologically neither is descended from Choy Fuk, and therefore what appears to be an incestuous relationship is not. On the other side of the family tree, the incestuous relationship between Morgan and Beatrice's sister Suzanne (both Ting An's offspring) is not recognized as such because Suzanne is supposed to be Choy Fuk's daughter. Love makes the world go round in a fairly dizzying way. Furthermore, history repeats itself with a particularly perverse vengeance, as Fong Mei's suppressed affair with Ting An (which, like Gwei Chang, Fong Mei is too timid to sustain) leads her to become an overbearing, interfering matriarch much like her nemesis Mui Lan.

The ironic outcome of all of this machination to sustain genealogical purity is the unravelling of patrilineal continuity and of the heterosexist assumptions on which it is based. Suzanne, rebelling against her mother and grandmother's oppressive authority, becomes an unwed mother, her baby (the last male Wong) dies at birth, and she ultimately commits suicide. Kae's mother, Beatrice, another domineering figure, tries to keep Morgan and the family secret from Kae and, at least initially, is successful: Kae enters a conventional marriage, becomes a successful businesswoman very much in the authoritative mould of her mother, grandmother, and great-grandmother, and has a son (though he is a Lee, not a Wong). Ultimately, however, the outcome of the family history that she has been narrating, much like Annie in *Ana Historic*, is that she appears to reject both the sexual model and occupational model of her predecessors. She decides to become a writer and moves to Hong Kong, where she has been invited to "LIVE HAPPILY EVER AFTER TOGETHER" with her long-time friend Hermia Chow (*Disappearing Moon Café* 216) – a relationship which, if not lesbian, certainly has homoerotic overtones.

The structure of the narrative mirrors this undermining of constrictive cultural and patriarchal traditions. The sweeping, anachronistic narrative of the family saga, which Chao succinctly describes as "a symbolic bone-hunting journey," is punctuated by continual returns to the frame narrative, during which Kae takes the opportunity to self-consciously comment on the family story.[119] She foregrounds the effects of her own interests on her construction of the past, particularly her resistance to demonizing the women in her family and her recognition of the way in which patriarchal imperatives have constricted their choices: "In each of their woman-hating worlds, each did what she could. If there is a simple truth beneath their survival stories, then it must be that women's lives, being what they are, are linked together" (145–6). The structure likewise helps to keep in focus Kae's own life choices as, in some ways, the culmination of the family history. Finally, the fragmented, proleptic, self-conscious narration breaks up the traditional chronology of the family epic as a narrative of continuity and progress, undercutting the suspense of finding out the fate of the next generation and also subsequently undermining or rewriting the story of previous generations.

The ending of the novel in particular underlines the significance of Kae's resistance to cultural and sexual conformity. Given the isolation that is the fate of so many of her female forebears, it is hard not to see Kae's decision to bail out of a conventional marriage as a rejection of the pressures that the patriarchal family history has exerted in the past. Furthermore, her desire to become a writer (hardly a choice to be approved of in such a success-oriented family) also serves as a commentary on the dangers of a preoccupation with power and social respectability, a lesson clearly demonstrated by the alienation caused by Mui Lan and Fong Mei. An important strategy that Kae employs at the end of her narrative is her placement of Gwei Chang's deathbed reminiscence about Kelora, dated 1939, after her own decision (in 1987) to join Hermia in Hong Kong. At this point, when all of the family's tortuous secrets have been disclosed and Gwei Chang's love for Kelora is no longer a secret, Kae's decision displays a willingness to break free of patrilineal purity that Gwei Chang lacked, a failure that caused so much misery and regret. Kae's relocation to Hong Kong is also a return to Gwei Chang's origins – but with a difference. Her return is not exactly to China and not exactly to the patriarchal traditions of Chinese village culture, symbolizing her breaking free of the family obsession with cultural, racial, and sexual conformity.

Such an insulated, incestuous, private preoccupation with family – which mirrors the novel's depiction of the general insularity of the Chinese community in Vancouver – would seem to preclude *Disappearing Moon Café* from consideration as a historical novel. Like *Ana*

Historic, however, *Disappearing Moon Café* suggests the problems with the genre's traditional preoccupation with "public" history, particularly through the way the novel situates that insularity and self-absorption within the larger context of a hostile, Anglocentric majority. The genealogical agonies of the Wong family are set against the background of the marginalized and suppressed history of Chinese immigrants in the West, and the novel portrays the internal conflicts of the family and the community as the product not simply of hegemonic Chinese cultural codes, but also of the racist double standards of a majority that both demands and fears assimilation, fears and reinforces otherness. Indeed, Kae observes of Beatrice and Keeman's forbidden post-war romance that, as a result of the 1923 Chinese Exclusion Act, the "rapidly diminishing chinese-canadian community had withdrawn into itself, ripe for incest" (147).

Graham Huggan argues that the novel harnesses the ambivalence of romance – its revolutionary and conservative energies – "to celebrate the collective identity of an ethnic (Chinese-Canadian) community, without isolating that community from its wider social context or attempting, through the mystifications of memory, to mould it into a harmonious whole." Huggan sees Lee as striking an important balance between a problematic cultural unity and a reinscribing of victimhood, uncovering "the repressed history of the Chinese-Canadian community, without indulging in the false glories of nostalgia or succumbing to the paralysis of remorse."[120] Where Kae's family history uncovers repressed knowledge, *Disappearing Moon Café* does the same for the Chinese-Canadian community within the broader (and frayed) fabric of Canadian society.

Though Kae presents the decisions and behaviour of her ancestors with a substantial degree of criticism and irony, she nonetheless also recognizes the intense social and cultural pressures that shaped them. To begin with, Gwei Chang's mission to retrieve the bones of railroad workers and transport them back to Victoria underlines the exploitative background of Chinese immigration. Initially repulsed by his task, Gwei Chang comes to recognize the injustice of the railroad company, as he thinks of those whose lives were sacrificed during the building of the railroad while "the real culprits held out blood-spattered chinamen in front of them like a protective talisman" (13). He sees the survivors "toiling, poor – left behind to rot because the CPR had reneged on its contract to pay the chinese railway workers' passage home" (12). Here Lee evokes a recurrent figure in Chinese-Canadian writing, the sojourner, whom Bennett Lee describes as "stuck between two worlds: too poor to stay in China, not rich enough to return, yet cut off from integrating into Canadian society by discriminatory laws and the habits of his own tradition."[121]

Constantly in the background of the family history is discrimination against Chinese immigrants – manifest in race riots in 1907 and in official policies such as disenfranchisement in 1875, a series of head taxes on Chinese immigrants, and the 1923 Immigration Act, which terminated Chinese immigration into Canada (and was not repealed until 1947). This larger context partially explains the dictatorial behaviour of Mui Lan, whose role as guardian of patrimony is a product of her marginal status as well as of Gwei Chang's divided loyalties: "She was simply the mother of Gwei Chang's only son. Stamped on her entry papers: 'A merchant's wife.' A wife in name only, she relied heavily on him for her identity in this land" (28). Fong Mei's position is likewise precarious. After her arrival from China, having been protected by the older women from being dragged off and raped by "ghosts," she is at the mercy of her husband's family for her security in Canada. Ultimately, for all her resistance to Mui Lan, she ends up vigorously protecting the patriarchal order and resisting assimilation. However, with each succeeding generation the exposure to the larger society increases and the internal bonds grow weaker, a tension between external accommodation and internal solidarity that, as in *Away*, is a key theme in the novel.

The focal incident in this respect, and that which provides a significant link to the tradition of the historical novel, is the novel's treatment of the 1924 murder of a white woman, Janet Smith, allegedly by a Chinese houseboy. As Kay Anderson notes, the Janet Smith case, headed by xenophobic provincial attorney-general Alex Manson, erupted in the wake of the 1923 Immigration Act at a time of intensified isolation and marginalization of Chinatown. The legislation served as "confirmation of the relative entitlements of a socially constructed order of insider and outsider, the contours of which were decisively drawn in Vancouver society and space ... 'Chinatown' was for its representers an incubator of vice and disease that threatened to corrode the pure 'stock' of race and nation."[122] Despite the case ending in acquittal, "the provincial legislature and, in particular, the press played wickedly on the notoriety of Chinatown. Manson also lobbied Ottawa for repatriation of Orientals on the familiar grounds that 'Oriental and European blood' could not be 'mixed with advantage.'"[123]

In *Disappearing Moon Café*, the incident threatens, Gwei Chang fears, to ignite the already volatile and hostile relations between the Chinese community and the majority society: "Those whites who hated yellow people never needed an excuse to spit on chinese. So the idea of a young, lone, yellow-skinned male standing over the inert body of a white-skinned female would send them into a bloodthirsty frenzy" (70). The case, which is used to push a punitive law prohibiting Chinese men from working closely with white women, precipitates a crisis, as the community adopts tactics that not only create internal divisions, but also mark a profound change in their relation to the dominant culture. In that respect, the case puts Gwei Chang, as Chinatown's most prominent businessman and elder, in a dilemma as profound as the choice with which he is faced at the beginning of the novel.

Initially, the community leaders' response is an isolationist one, the us-against-them mentality implicitly signalling a sense of guilt and an acceptance of victimization. Gwei Chang, however, recognizes in the automatically defensive response of the old guard the self-defeating resignation of the outcast: "Under the strain of bigotry, they were outlaws. Chinamen didn't make the law of the land, so they would always live outside of it. In fact, it was a crime for them just to be here. The result was submerged, but always there: violence, with the same, sour odour of trapped bodies under duress" (221). Recognizing the necessity of interaction to counter victimization, Gwei Chang defers to a younger generation of community leaders proposing a boycott in response to the Janet Smith bill. The pressure the new guard exerts, using the political and economic levers of the dominant culture, helps to deflect attention away from the Chinese community and precipitates an atmosphere of internal scandal and mutual accusation within the dominant society that defuses the threat to Chinatown. However, the success of the new guard – "statesmen, smooth liars in good english" who "said the correct phrases" (227) – alienates Gwei Chang from the other elders and signals an irrevocable breach in the cultural wall erected by the old guard. It consolidates the exposure of the community to the dominant society, something the older generation had almost pathologically guarded against and which, they believe, had triggered the present crisis. The tradeoff for inter-ethnic accommodation, they suggest, is the decline of cultural unity and racial purity, but Gwei Chang sees some middle ground between solidarity and surrender.

In this sense, Gwei Chang's decision compensates for his initial conservatism in abandoning Kelora, which wreaks so much havoc on his descendants and prefigures Kae's own decision to buck tradition in the interests of her emotional well-being. However, Gwei Chang is unable to be so compromising with his own family when, eight years later, his attempts to convince Ting An not to marry a white woman and to "take a real wife from China" lead finally to open acknowledgement of his paternity. "Like your real wife from China?" Ting An responds, before he repudiates Gwei Chang once and for all. "Not a dirty half-breed, buried somewhere in the bush?" (233). Gwei Chang's bitter failure with Ting An is a result of his hypocritical adhesion to principles he has already compromised, and his descendant Kae achieves her freedom by learning from his example, just as in *Away* Eileen's granddaughter Esther is to learn a crucial lesson in life from Eileen's errant infatuation with Aidan and Fenianism.

Drawing on Homi Bhabha, Stuart Hall argues that in a world increasingly marked by migration and diasporas, translation becomes an important notion for defining identity for those "who have been dispersed forever from their homelands. Such people retain strong links with their places of origin and their traditions, but they are without the illusion of a return to the past. They are obliged to come to terms with the new cultures they inhabit, without simply assimilating to them and losing their identities completely. They bear upon them the traces of the particular cultures, traditions, languages, and histories by which they were shaped."[124] In *Disappearing Moon Café*, Lee provides not only a genealogy of translation but a politics of it as well. Like *Away*, Lee's novel dramatizes the Anglocentrism and cultural constrictions of Canadian society but also suggests that cultural negotiation, compromise, and ultimately translation, rather than cultural separatism or assimilation, are necessary to establish a more secure place in that society. Both novels dramatize the cultural boundaries erected around the foundation of the nation but resist narratives of historical victimization that risk reinforcing those boundaries from a minority position. Furthermore, they suggest that to do so ultimately fosters accommodation – however resistant and gradual – on the part of the dominant culture as well.

As novels about immigrants climbing their way up from the bottom of the social ladder, *Away* and *Disappearing Moon Café* also reflect how, in much social history, brushing history "against the grain" involves a questioning of history as a narrative of the accomplishments of the elite. The stereotype of Canada as culturally harmonious has its counterpart in the image of Canada as free of class strife, and these and other recent historical novels, like the work of a growing number of historians, serve to counter that image of social harmony. They question such triumphalist narratives and ask at what cost to those who work for them the triumphs of the elite come, illuminating the lives of workers, farmers, domestic servants, the unemployed, and others traditionally left in the shadows beside the spotlight on "public" figures and events. In doing so, they complement a shift in the work of some social historians towards taking in the entirety of working-class experience rather than just that of the labour movement.[125]

In the "labour revolt of 1917–20," Gregory Kealey and Douglas Cruikshank note, "there were 1,384 strikes involving almost 360,000 workers."[126] The centrepiece of that revolt was the Winnipeg general strike of 1919, which is the focus of Margaret Sweatman's *Fox* (1991), a panoramic view of Winnipeg during the strike. A collage of news-paper headlines, diary entries, official directives, poems, mono-logues, and limited-omniscient narrative segments, *Fox* provides multiple perspectives, from both sides of the class divide, on one of the most notorious labour-management clashes in Canadian history, in which Winnipeg's business elite, with the cooperation of the fed-eral government, called in mounted police to restore "order" and to coerce labour leaders to end the month-old strike. If an important dimension of social history is the recognition of history as the prod-uct of multiple subjective perspectives rather than of an objective, unitary view, *Fox* takes that multiplicity as the departure point for its investigation of class conflict in a time of crisis (while demonstrating that even a notion such as "crisis" is class-specific).

Despite the polyphonic structure of the novel and the privileging of labour in the presentation of the conflict, Sweatman builds her explo-ration of labour's and management's reactions to the strike around the responses of a pair of upper-class cousins to their lives of luxury at such a critical time. Part of the luxury of being rich, *Fox* suggests, is having the choice of being oblivious to class, and the contrasting choices of Eleanor and Mary serve as the focal point of Sweatman's narrative collage. Eleanor, whose father has socialist sympathies, rejects this luxury and others; Mary, daughter of meat-packing mogul Sir Richard Trotter (who emphatically has no such sympathies), self-indulgently exercises it. As the two cousins go their separate ways, management and labour steer toward the inevitable collision.

Eleanor's involvement with her father's friend MacDougal, a bookstore owner, socialist proponent of the New Christianity, and a member of the strike committee, leads to her exposure to the hard-ship of workers and their families and her increasing sympathy with their cause.[127] Bored with a life of privilege that is also a life of lack of responsibility and control over her destiny, the naive Eleanor is moved by the passion and commitment she witnesses as she attends various rallies and speeches (featuring historical strike organizers such as George Armstrong and R.B. Russell) – a passion and com-mitment quite absent from her own life of ease. As Eleanor's involve-ment with McDougal increases, she comes to see herself as a double agent, uncomfortable with the soft, oblivious life of the rich but like-wise painfully conscious of her privilege and of her ignorance of the world of labour politics and working-class hardship. At the same time, in crossing the class divide, Eleanor is also given a sense of liberty that the patriarchal strictures of that privilege denied her. At least, unlike Mary, she reflects at one point, "I'm trying to leave myself behind" (*Fox* 154).

Mary, in contrast, is complacently inconvenienced by the strike and therefore peevishly unsympathetic to the cause of the strikers. Her fiancé, Drinkwater – a real estate developer and one of the principal organizers of the Committee of 1000 (an *ad hoc* cluster of the upper class banding together to protect their interests in an atmosphere of increasing turbulence and class strife) – is the ideological antithesis of Eleanor's MacDougal. Mary's narrow self-absorption is high-lighted during the strike when she is sent by her father to convince the family's cook to return to work and is repulsed by the poverty in which she lives. Stifling her naive rehearsed plea – "let's mend the fabric of society, come back to work, we'll pay you fairly" (135) – she is silently rebuffed by the sorority of immigrant women gathered there and firmly escorted out the door. Insulated from concern over any other's welfare but her own, Mary looks at Drinkwater and sees the future, and "she sees, that it is *good*" (81), whereas Eleanor, having been awakened to both class and gender inequity, "sees the future. *And it is missing*" (84). Here, as elsewhere, Sweatman reworks Biblical passages to highlight the New Christianity's social gospel but also the elite's lack of Christian concern for working people.

Given that the Winnipeg General Strike was largely an expression of the discontent of working-class immigrants, however, one might question the appropriateness of centring a novel about the strike on two upper-class women from the ethnic majority. This is especially pertinent since, as Reinhold Kramer notes, Sweatman's position is admittedly analogous to Eleanor's: her grandfather belonged to the Citizens' Committee, and her wealthy and prominent family are pri-marily supporters of the Liberals.[128] Yet, as Sweatman develops the cousins' romantic involvements to provide insight into the two sides' preparations for the coming showdown, that juxtapositioning is highly unfavourable to the elite. The resolve of the Committee of 1000 – who served during the strike "as capital's watchdog in its moment of crisis"[129] – is presented with a definite strain of irony, suggesting that their commitment to maintaining order is merely euphemistic language for maintaining an employment environment conducive to high profits. "The War," as Sir Rodney reflects, "was a terrible tragedy, lord knows. But it was a great boon for business" (74). The Committee are loath to let the good times go, and as they gather to coordinate their response they insist on their anonymity, which the narrator ironically presents as selfless civic service: "They don't like publicity. They want peace, and prosperity. Their only desire is for a quiet family life, and fairly liquid assets" (114).

The Committee's willingness to go to work themselves to ensure that essential services are maintained, and the formation of *ad hoc* vigilante squads or "Specials," are expressed as manifestations of a patriotic commitment to public order rather than, as Sweatman implies, a repressive affront to labour's right to collective action, reasonable pay, and acceptable working conditions. This is particularly highlighted by the firing of the regular police, sympathetic to the workers' cause, and the introduction of the Specials, who can be counted on to look out for the interests of the establishment. Sir Rodney's caution to Drinkwater reverberates with irony: "These disturbances only serve to magnify the differences between classes. Fragments of the community organized wholly for their own benefit. Then, once they gain power, they want to dictate what is right for the rest of us. And they frighten the politicians into going along with it" (77). The uncompromising position of the establishment is summarized by an agent of the Dominion censor, who observes to McDougal that the "people are damned cattle and you know it. We intend to drive them, to herd them as we wish" (24).

In contrast to such a self-serving, repressive response, the strike organizers display a quiet integrity and determination to defend the rights of the people, though there is a concomitant flurry of socialist rhetoric and oratorical flourishes that are most likely beyond the grasp of the people themselves. Scenes of McDougal musing over principles of social reform, the strikers' wives collectively striving to feed the workers' families during the strike, and the quiet (if somewhat ambivalent) determination of the workers as they walk out on strike are rendered without the irony that dogs the portrait of the Citizens' Committee.

That Sweatman's presentation of the conflict is clearly slanted in favour of labour can be seen by way of comparison with W.L. Morton's account in his seminal *Manitoba: A History*. Morton's description strives for a sense of balance that Sweatman, despite her use of multiple perspectives, is not willing to accord the conflict. Morton describes the formation of the Citizens' Committee as the "natural reply" provoked by the general strike and as "the spontaneous rising of the general community to repel the threat to its existence." The attempt to maintain services and the use of the special constables to maintain order are presented as symmetrical with the efforts of the strikers: "The semi-provisional government of the Strike Committee was now faced – it is almost true to say challenged – by a similar government of the Citizens' Committee. The sporadic violence of strikers in attempting to police the striking by picketing and intimidation was now met by the similar roughness on the part of citizen squads keeping the streets and local stores open."[130] The contrast highlights the way in which one person's notion of historical balance

(read: neutrality and objectivity) in the eyes of another can amount
to a problematic neutralizing of differences and inappropriate apportioning of responsibility.

Though the multiplicity of perspectives in the novel prevents *Fox*
from being simply a polemical indictment of the elite, the novel
leaves little doubt that the burden of responsibility for the confrontation ultimately rests solidly on their shoulders. The contrast
between the cousins and the circles in which they travel is developed
against a background of growing violence expressive of the upper
class's determination to maintain their economic, cultural, and political advantage and of the workers' resolve to resist being exploited:
scenes of soldiers on horseback attacking crowds of workers, destroy-
ing the office of a socialist newspaper, and attacking ethnic clubs; the
Specials beating a worker spraying anti-business messages; the strikers' wives confronting and then beating truck drivers attempting to
deliver goods to a department store employing scab labour. Furthermore, this background of violence is fleshed out and explained
through vignettes and monologues that heighten the sense of a privileged elite and a deprived working class. "The cumulative effect of
the many such monologues articulated through the novel," as Daniel
Fischlin insightfully notes, "is to construct interiorities through
which events are mediated, rather than the other (more traditional)
way around."[131]

The "forces of capital and the State," as Lorne and Caroline Brown
argue, "united in a powerful combination to smash the Winnipeg
general strike at all costs," creating an atmosphere of hysteria over
the imminent prospect of a bloody Bolshevik revolution.[132] In *Fox*,
the response of the establishment, especially of the federal government, to the increasing labour strife in the city is depicted in similar
terms as fairly hysterical and xenophobic, punctuated by headlines
from the two main Winnipeg newspapers and the Citizen Committee's *Citizen*. When it seeks to resort to violence to contain the violence that its response to the strikers has elicited, the Committee finds
ready ideological bedfellows in the government and the media. The
federal government implements a draconian amendment to the
Immigration Act to allow for the deportation of *"Any person deemed
to be a revolutionary who was born outside of Canada, whether a British
subject or a naturalized Canadian"* (171), and the newspapers play
along with this xenophobic tune.

While the novel unsurprisingly culminates with the suppression
of the strike, Sweatman highlights the divisive outcome once again
through the contrast between the two cousins and provides an interesting juxtaposition of class privilege and gender subordination.

Mary, on a golf outing as the strike violence heightens, anticipates returning to the clubhouse for Chablis – "it's a damn good thing her father has been able to supply the clubhouse with ice during this irritating strike" (179) – and afterwards lets herself be seduced by Drinkwater, with whom she "conceive[s] the son and heir, their first born, conceived on the afternoon the Citizens' Specials ride through Market Square" (181). As the authorities are rounding up the strike leaders, Sir Rodney presents Drinkwater and Mary with a magnificent home directly across from his own, symbolizing Drinkwater's accession to the business elite and Mary's being secured within the patriarchal preserve.

In the meantime, when Eleanor visits McDougal's ransacked apartment, she herself is protected from retributive violence only because the cop watching the apartment has been told "that she'd probably turn up and to keep his hands off her" (190), from which he correctly deduces that she must be rich. After hearing the news of McDougal's release from prison, Eleanor, still in her wedding finery, waits outside Stony Mountain Penitentiary with the other women to greet McDougal, who unsurprisingly does not seem happy to see her. He underlines the xenophobic reaction of the government by grimly noting that only those organizers with a "z" in their names are to be deported. Meanwhile, their homes have been ransacked by the Specials in a violation whose description makes Sweatman's allegiance in the novel crystal clear: "The private letters are not private, the voices have been taken, their lives have been confiscated, and the intricate conversation, the dreams they have been telling one another in the night have become *evidence, a conspiracy.* Scattered" (187). Thus Mary bears witness to the upper class's repressive retention of its state of privilege, while Eleanor bears witness to the wreckage of the lives of the workers that repression entails.

The novel ends with a sharply paced, telegraphic presentation of the events of Bloody Saturday, with the mob of workers in the street confronting the show of force by the Specials and attacking a streetcar that tries to proceed down Main. Sweatman's account of Bloody Saturday accords with that of Doug Smith in *Let Us Rise! A History of the Manitoba Labour Movement*, one of the sources for *Fox*: "After the arrest of the strike leaders, those veterans who supported the strike held a silent parade of protest. Mounted police, on horseback, made four charges through the parade, on the fourth charge firing into the crowd and killing two strikers. Then hundreds of the special police descended on the strikers, attacking them with clubs and revolvers. By evening the city was an armed camp controlled by the Citizens' Committee and its private army."[133] In Sweatman's version,

The Royal North-West Mounted Police charge a crowd of civilians,
21 June 1919.

the police likewise act rather than react, and she dramatizes the
slaughter of the innocent by highlighting the death of Stevie, a young
boy who has been running messages for the organizers during the
strike and who is shot in the face and killed. Once again, a comparison with Morton is instructive, as his account of Bloody Saturday is
a little more favourable to the authorities. In Morton's account, the
police responded to a demonstration after six of the leaders were
released on bail and the crowd resisted the first attempt to clear the
street: "In a second charge the Police, in serious danger of being
overwhelmed and killed, fired into the crowded street. One man was
killed and an unknown number wounded, one of whom died of a
gangrened wound."[134]

Progress, as the saying goes, is always only progress for some, and
the effect of *Fox* is to highlight that the attempt of the elite to safe-
guard their profit margin in the wake of the postwar economic
decline obviously came at the expense of a working class sorely in
need of better conditions. What *Fox* suggests more generally, however, is the deep-rooted fear of labour agitation on the part of the
political and economic establishment in Canada between the wars
and its willingness to dispense with democratic niceties in order to
contain one of the most substantial challenges from the left in the
nation's history.[135] This political critique, however, is somewhat
blunted by Sweatman's choice of protagonist; as Kramer rightly
observes, a "materialist might argue that by focussing on Eleanor's
political development, Sweatman inoculates the reader against more

fundamental systematic change."[136] The polyphonic structure and subversive politics of the novel, however, serve to minimize the ideological and perspectival disadvantages of such a choice. Sweatman avoids easy inversions as a revisionist strategy and tempers her portrait of the clash through her dialogic narrative collage and her emphasizing of how the strike was not just about class conflict but about ethnicity and gender as well. Indeed, through its portrait of a patriarchal, Anglocentric power structure asserting its authority during an upsurge of popular discontent, the novel highlights once again how central the legacy of colonialism has been to the building of the nation.

This consciousness of the inter-war period as one of the most significant eras of Canadian history in terms of class relations is also reflected in Heather Robertson's *Lily* (1986), though the tone of the novel is almost diametrically opposite that of *Fox*. In this second volume of *The King Years* trilogy, Robertson treats constitutional and party politics, "Willie" Mackenzie King's growing obsession with spiritualism, and the (dis)organization of the Communist party with systematic irreverence and presents historical episodes such as the 1919 Kirkland Lake miners' strike, the Beauharnois scandal, and the 1935 on-to-Ottawa trek in a thoroughly comic spirit. While *Lily* chronicles a fairly pivotal and serious time in Canada's history and like *Fox* examines the fascistic reaction to a very real and substantial consolidation of the left, Robertson's portrait is far from serious, and the novel comes closer instead to a giddy political farce, with Mr "Double Life" himself, Mackenzie King, setting the tone.[137] *Lily* is social history at its most panoramic and thorough in its turning over of historical stones, but without the revisionist earnestness that typically characterizes such a project.

The novel is subtitled "a rhapsody in red" because it chronicles the bog Irish Ottawa valley heroine Lily Coolican's growing involvement with the cause of the left and more specifically with the Communist Party. As in *Willie*, the first volume of the trilogy, Lily, King's fictional former mistress, provides in her diary an alternative, satiric history – in this installment the history of Canada, King, and chaos between the wars. Lily's principal romantic interest in this volume is Comrade Esselwein, a Jewish Russian emigré and friend of Trotsky who is revealed to be the RCMP agent John Leopold (a historical figure who infiltrated the party to monitor Bolshevik activity from 1920 to 1928 and was the key witness in the 1931 trial of eight party members, including Tim Buck). Lily's "romance" with both Esselwein and Communism provides the backbone for what is a fairly sprawling history, one that is certainly closer to a circus than a pageant.

Responsible for this carnival atmosphere is the fundamentally paradoxical result of the government's surveillance of labour agitation, around which much of the narrative revolves: the left is so disorganized that its activities must be sustained through the participation of undercover agents in the service of a government that paranoiacally overestimates the left's strength and support. From the Kirkland Lake miners' strike, the incident that initiates Lily's involvement with both Esselwein and the labour movement, to the on-to-Ottawa trek, which Esselwein is assigned to foment, Robertson presents the labour movement as quite hopelessly disorganized and ideologically convoluted. Their "actions" consistently have no result, the opposite result, or descend into farce. Esselwein organizes the miners' strike in Kirkland Lake (which occurs just as the general strike in Winnipeg ends), but the subsequent dictatorship of the proletariat fizzles amidst a flurry of ideological hair-splitting and practical incompetence. The brief rein of the Revolutionary Kirkland Lake Soviet culminates with the miners, in the company of Lily and the Prince of Wales (AWOL from a Royal tour), storming the "Alamo" of mining baron Harry Oakes, only to find Oakes and his co-defender, RCMP constable Dempster, "sound asleep in a litter of empty bottles" (*Lily* 38).[138] This episode sets the stage for a synoptic overview of working-class militancy between the wars, involving an impressive ensemble cast.[139]

Most contemporary historical novels, like most social history, represent a challenge to the political establishment's version of history, and *Lily* focuses on a form of authority central to labour history in Canada: the RCMP. Since the end of World War I, as Lorne and Caroline Brown note, the RCMP have had a long history not just of policing but of actively suppressing labour dissent.[140] While this history is a key focus of *Lily*, Robertson chooses to present Esselwein's monitoring and destabilization of the Communist party more as comedy than as political intrigue. A year after the strike, Esselwein returns a hero to Kirkland Lake, his flippant and parodic treatment of political ideology contrasting with the earnestness of his reports on the Party's activities. When Esselwein attends the formative convention in a Guelph barn in 1921, his levity, spontaneity, and revolutionary activity put him at odds with his earnest but ineffectual comrades. Despite the ideological paralysis and revolutionary passivity of his comrades in response to Esselwein's proactive energy, Esselwein's report to his superiors presents the party as ideologically unified and determined, systematically organized, and drawing on broad support.[141] "The truth," however, as Lily observes, "was that, without Esselwein's cash, the Communist Party of Canada would likely have collapsed completely. The masses had not rushed to the

Red Flag, possibly because the Party remained so secret nobody could find it" (69).

Robertson presents party members as hopelessly confused ideologues paralyzed by their own internal nitpicking and ideological bickering and by the delayed and hopelessly distanced guidance of the Comintern in Russia.[142] At a meeting in Toronto, Esselwein provides a scathing review of some of the founding members: "Spector the Soothsayer paws through his pamphlets, searching desperately for omens and revelations. Comrade Custance broods over Lenin, capturing Lenin's infuriating irascibility without a shred of his insight, and Chairman Macdonald, who believes everything he reads, is totally confused by the dialectic, which demands he believe two completely opposite things at once. What is to be done?" (72).[143] After he has been exposed as a fascist spy and his friend Trotsky has been purged, Esselwein succinctly summarizes the ironic outcome of his activities: "Six years of my life I spend subverting the Communist Party of Canada, and what do I find? They do the job better without me!" (127).

If Robertson's revisionist history throws light on a suppressed class conflict, it is less than flattering to the left, unlike in *Fox*. After witnessing the violent suppression of the 1931 Estevan miners' strike, Lily is galvanized to become a member of the party. She joins a political study group in Winnipeg and later becomes a cell member, but her idealism is doused by the cryptic organization and ideological obfuscation of the party: "We had no idea who belonged to other cells, or if there were other cells, although Ken encouraged us to think they were springing up like dragon's teeth. Communism was a state of mind, and the Party was an act of faith that somewhere out there, someone was doing something. It was a lot like Methodism, only the meetings were more interesting" (202). Lily's facetious accounts of the party, like Esselwein's, suggest that if the left missed its opportunity to make its mark on history, it has only itself to blame.

The greater irony, pointing to a more serious implication underlying the novel, is that such inaction comes at a time when, after the Depression has set in, concerted action could provide the critical mass for a revolution (at least if Lily is to be believed). As the government reels from a series of scandals, Lily reflects that it is "collapsing all by itself, Edmonton is already occupied by an army of unemployed. A couple of thousand men could simply walk into the banks, the legislature and the radio stations, sit down, and that would be that" (266). Essentially, there is a sense throughout the book that this was the left's missed opportunity.[144] This comes through particularly in Lily's exasperation over her comrades' inability to grasp the inappropriateness of their ideological hair-splitting to the situation in Canada and the real possibility of taking power; as she tells her friend Annie Buller (a Communist activist jailed for a year for her alleged involvement in the Estevan riot): "Annie, we are at the Finland Station. *Where is the train?*" (300). The crowning touch on this sense of futility is Esselwein's admission at the end of the novel that he has been the recipient of the secret reports Lily has been faithfully despatching for the party and that he is himself a double agent, "the shortest man in the Mounted Police, the only Jew, and, as far as I know, the first Bolshevik" (322).[145] At times, *Lily*'s sustained, giddy satire seems uncomfortably lacking in seriousness, but that effect is, in part, the result of Robertson applying that charge to the left.

If *Lily* is about a time of considerable popular support for the left, it is also about a time of considerable flirtation with the extreme right. As a consequence of *Lily*'s somewhat dizzying satirical history, however, it is hard to tell whether the left's incompetence, in light of the authorities' repressive and hysterical reaction to labour militancy, is to be taken more seriously or less. The reaction of the authorities certainly has violent consequences: miners "disappear" and are murdered in the wake of the Kirkland Lake strike, the protest at Estevan is met with force that results in casualties, and the on-to-Ottawa trek is brought to a violent halt in Regina. Furthermore, the RCMP is implicated in attempts on the part of the far right (who see Willie as sympathetic to the reds) to set up a quasi-fascist military dictatorship involving key (and historical) political figures such as Bill Herridge and Governor-General Byng.

This seems like heady stuff, but the RCMP and the fascist conspirators against Willie are described with the same carnivalesque tone as is the left. In the thick of the conspiracy is RCMP Superintendent of Intelligence Smythe, an anti-Semitic crypto-fascist who distributes copies of "the infamous pamphlet, *The Protocols of the Wise Men of Zion* ... to all cabinet ministers and members of the press gallery" (70) and gives Esselwein the tasks of proving that Willie is a Bolshevik and recruiting Lily to assassinate him. It is to please Smythe that Esselwein fabricates the Communist threat, "creating the impression that, while still young and disorganized, the Communist Party is a seething ferment of invisible agitation" (69). Later, Esselwein is assigned to investigate the Ku Klux Klan in Alberta and the premier, John Brownlee; in his persona as Baron Wittgenstein, Esselwein assumes that "his extremism would be taken for what it was, a script in a melodrama, but at RCMP headquarters, his paranoia is not only taken seriously, it is exaggerated" (217). The end result of the subversion of the Party is to help it flourish; it grows from a few hundred members during

Esselwein's early involvement to "hundreds of thousands of supporters, maybe a million" (322). Nonetheless, as Lily observes to Esselwein, "You cops have done all right out of the Red Menace" (322); the ultimate goal of the RCMP, ironically, is not so much to stamp out Communism as to cultivate it in order to consolidate and extend their own importance and power.[146]

What is seen from the right as a necessary assertion of order at a time of political instability, the novel presents as a fundamental threat to democracy. Smythe's hysterical scare-mongering is depicted as galvanizing "The New Democracy," a right-wing conspiracy to form a one-party system at the time of Willie's constitutional confrontation with Governor-General Byng in 1926 over the latter's interference in domestic politics. Herridge proposes to Lily the assassination of Willie, after which the "army will move in, Bungo [Byng] will declare a state of 'apprehended insurrection,' I think that's the phrase, invoke the War Measures Act, and we're home free" (109). The conspirators' attempts are frustrated, however, by the politically wily if somewhat oblivious Willie, whose actions are in turn presented as politically and morally dubious. "Operation Fat Boy" is forestalled when Willie resigns over Byng's refusal to allow him to dissolve his government (a dissolution Byng then allows to Willie's Conservative opponent Meighen), Byng is disgraced and recalled, and "New Democracy vanished like a pipe dream" (119). The conspiracy rears its ugly head later, however, at the time of the on-to-Ottawa trek, which Esselwein has been assigned to organize because, he speculates, it will provide a pretext for the government of R.B. Bennett to declare martial law and thus head off the putsch, which instead grinds to a halt when Byng dies of a heart attack.[147] Despite its humour, the novel does take a revisionist stance typical of social history, in that it exposes rather than acquiesces to the anti-democratic machinations of those in power.

The portrait of the right complements the portrait of the left in contributing to *Lily*'s presentation of the inter-war years as a politically volatile era, a veritable ideological hall of mirrors, though in Robertson's hands this volatility leans more towards farce than towards documentary realism. Robertson's compendious novel certainly makes history hum, unearthing (and certainly elaborating upon) the maze of political and class subplots of the time. Those who don't know their history, Marx says, are destined to repeat it – as farce. Robertson, however, seems to know her history and seems quite determined to repeat it as farce: what emerges is not, as in *Fox*, the picture of Marx's class struggle so much as a Keystone Kops political history. Robertson brushes history against the funny bone as much as against the grain, and it seems fair to question whether her democratic apportioning of satire in the novel has the effect of defusing class tensions and understating the political and ideological differences and violence of the time. Though the establishment bears the brunt of the irony in *Lily*, as it does in *Fox*, Robertson's stylistic and narrative choices likewise diffuse that political critique, underlining the delicate balance that stressing considerations of class in the historical novel requires.

"Where do any of us come from in this cold country?" asks Naomi rhetorically in Kogawa's *Obasan*. "We come from our untold tales that wait for their telling."[148] If the diversification of interests in the historical novel is any indication, the time for the telling of untold tales has come. The last thirty years have seen a raft of historical novels that write women, workers, immigrants, and minorities into Canadian history against the grain of a heritage of colonialism that slanted history very much in favor of an Anglocentric, male power structure.

The unearthing of suppressed histories, however, can be seen as a threat to the narrative of unity that for many historians and non-academics is necessary for a healthy nationalism, which should emphasize the smooth complexion of Canadian nation-building more than the warts. In *Who Killed Canadian History?*, J.L. Granatstein expresses the reservations of many historians about the revisionist orientation of social history. Citing *History of the Canadian Peoples* as an example, Granatstein laments the tendency of social history to distort the narrative of the Canadian past because it is filtered through limited identitarian lenses: "Their aim was to use history, or their version of it, to cure white males of their sense of superiority"; the result is that history graduates "know little about their own country's history."[149] While Granatstein emphasizes the importance of not airbrushing Canadian history, he argues that in this atmosphere there is a tendency to hyperbolize (and even distort) the atrocities of the past: "We should know about the appalling episodes in our past, and we should try to learn from them. But to pretend that Canada has been and remains a monstrous regime with blood-stained hands, to suggest that Canadian history is one of brutal expropriation, genocidal behaviour, and rampant racism, simply does not wash."[150]

Granatstein's account of social history, however, is itself hyperbolic, and what he problematically downplays, in his diatribe against it, is that the subversive tendencies of social history have emerged in part to counterbalance the traditional tendency to hyperbolize Canada as a peaceful, equitable nation. In his desire for "what the schools and the nation need: a history that puts Canada up front,"[151] Granatstein elides what so much social history and historical novels like *Away*, *Disappearing Moon Café*, and *Fox* emphasize: that putting

"Canada up front" requires a recognition, rather than a suppression, of the sometimes collaborative, sometimes compromising, sometimes competing forces involved in the negotiation of just what "Canada" means. Social history has emerged largely from the recognition that there is an established edifice of Canadian history that needs to be questioned, and Granatstein's fear-mongering about public ignorance of Canadian history falls short of sufficient justification for continuing to prop it up.

These novels suggest, rather, that the key to stability, as Leon Litvack argues, is negotiating the acceptance rather than the subordination of difference and tying questions of culture and ethnicity back to Canada's colonial heritage: "For many postcolonial societies, including Canada, the present is struggling out of a past heavily laden with cultural baggage and is attempting to construct a future. The cultural encounter between the center and the margin must function on a level where difference is accepted on an egalitarian basis. The initiation of cross-cultural dialogue has the potential to put an end to the apparently endless human history of conquest and annihilation justified by the myth of group 'purity,' and thus serve as the basis on which the postcolonial world can be creatively stabilized."[152] Indeed, an important part of that struggling out of the past is to put Canada up front in a much more critical and subversive fashion; thus one of the most important "sites" of the contemporary historical novel in Canada is that of the nation itself.

NATIONAL ALLEGORIES

"A nation," observes F.H. Underhill in *The Image of Confederation*, "is a body of men who have done great things together in the past and who hope to do great things together in the future."[153] In the past, the historical novel has certainly played a role in the cultivation of the kind of political and cultural nationalism that such an assumption of collective accomplishment implies. Herbert Butterfield argues that the historical novel has a kind of nationalist agency because it "cannot help reminding men of their heritage in the soil. It is often born of a kind of patriotism; it can scarcely avoid always being the inspiration of it. In this way it becomes itself a power in history, an impulse to fine feeling, and a source of more of the action and heroism which it describes. The historical novel itself becomes a maker of history."[154] Emblematic of a unitary national destiny, then, the historical novel compels readers to emulate the patriotic sentiments and accomplishments of its heroes as standard-bearers of that destiny. This is no less true in Canada, where historical fiction was a ubiquitous genre in the nineteenth century and played a significant part in the construction of a particularly Anglocentric notion of nationhood, as novels like Gilbert Parker's *The Seats of the Mighty* and, to a lesser degree, William Kirby's *The Golden Dog* reflect.

Such a nationalist agency, however, has been redefined in both contemporary theory and the contemporary historical novel. At a time when the representational qualities of both literature and historical discourse are being explicitly thematized and questioned in historical fiction, it is no surprise that the allegorizing of nation is likewise being substantially refigured. National cultures, Stuart Hall argues, "are discursive entities" that help to "construct identities by producing meanings about 'the nation' with which we can *identify*." National histories are one form in which national culture conveys "the narrative of the nation," providing "a set of stories, images, landscapes, scenarios, historical events, national symbols, and rituals which stand for, or *represent*, the shared experiences, sorrows, and triumphs and disasters which give meaning to the nation."[155] As narratives of the emergence of "imagined communities,"[156] national histories, the work of Hayden White suggests, are not mimetic narratives of a shared national past, but allegories. They present historical events as analogous to "some form with which we have already become familiar in our literary culture."[157] They make use of figurative devices, explanatory patterns, and strategies of emplotment that are necessarily tropological, as narratives of national emergence such as Arthur M. Lower's *Colony to Nation* or Donald Creighton's Laurentian thesis of the development of Canada in *The Empire of the St. Lawrence* exemplify.

Allegory, too, has been substantially reconceived. The questioning of correspondence theories of representation and the shifting views of historical and literary discourse, as numerous theorists of allegory argue, paved the way for a resurgence of allegory in the late twentieth century. Theresa Kelley notes that post-Renaissance allegory, rather than declining in the face of the force of "the standard-bearers of modernity: empiricism, historiography, realism (in the modern sense), and plain, rational speech," instead has survived "by making border raids on the very categories that have been presented as its contraries: realism, mimesis, empiricism, and history. The claim that allegory should be set apart from history and realism has for too long masked the degree to which all three terms are implicated in questions about knowing and representability that permeate modern culture."[158] A notion important to this reconceptualizing of historical discourse as allegorical is Northrop Frye's insight that "all commentary is allegorical interpretation, an attaching of ideas to the structure of poetic imagery";[159] criticism, in this sense, is not a description or a crystallization of the original but a symbolic reworking of it. In historical fiction, this allegorizing effect is doubled, as we "read" historical novelists "reading" history.[160]

As allegories, contemporary historical novels for the most part are more likely to dissent from the discourse of national culture, either by reworking the presentation of history to diminish its function as national allegory, by allegorizing national icons in a less flattering light, or by drawing attention to the use of allegory in the cause of colonial discourse or a hegemonic national culture. Some of the most interesting works of contemporary historical fiction, however, are those that consciously employ the language of allegory in the process of addressing the interpenetration, rather than separation, of allegory, history, and realism. Drawing on the work of Maureen Quilligan, Brian McHale argues that at the heart of allegory is an ontological tension: "allegory projects a world and erases it in the same gesture, inducing a flicker between presence and absence of this world, between tropological reality and 'literal' reality – reality in the *literal* sense of 'words on the page.' For what this flicker foregrounds above all is the *textuality* of the text."[161] McHale's description of allegory is eminently applicable to historiography and historical fiction, both of which display (if less prominently than formal allegory) such an ontological flicker between the presence of the past and its tropological representation. In other words, whereas at times historical fiction, like historical scholarship, "makes it sound as if history ... were doing the talking," it alternately reminds us that somebody is giving voice to it.[162]

The ontological flicker McHale describes is compounded when the novelists themselves consciously draw attention to the operation of allegorical discourse, emphasizing how important the movement between the literal and the figurative is in the construction of historical reality. Susan Swan's carnivalesque use of allegorical conventions in *The Biggest Modern Woman of the World* has drawn a good deal of critical attention, particularly as a device for postcolonial commentary on national discourse, and a similar, if less dramatic, concern with the writing of history at the level of allegory can be seen in Heather Robertson's *Willie* (the first volume of *The King Years* trilogy) and Wayne Johnston's *The Colony of Unrequited Dreams*.

As the critical commentary on the novel reflects, *The Biggest Modern Woman of the World* (1983) openly invites allegorical readings along postcolonial, postmodern, and feminist lines. At the same time, however, it cultivates a wariness of allegorical representation, especially through its play with figures of nation. Stephen Slemon argues that many writers in postcolonial cultures have given the allegory – a dominant mode of colonial discourse – an interventionist, anticolonial slant, and he cites Swan's novel as a Canadian example of this postcolonial impulse.[163] As most critics have observed, the principal characters of *The Biggest Modern Woman of the World* all take on allegorical overtones, not just because of their different nationalities, but because of Swan's blatant, parodic exploitation of the discourse of national allegory.

The self-consciously representative quality of the characterization and dialogue along national lines highlights and undermines the use of allegory as a textual device for reinforcing national identity. When Swan's protagonist Anna decides to leave Nova Scotia to pursue the showbiz life in New York, her occasional outbursts in response to the Yankees' ignorance about Canada subversively deploy Canadian stereotypes. During her first meeting with her employer, P.T. Barnum, for instance, she assures him that the "cold mummifies agents of disease, rendering the majority of people in the Canadas harmless" (*The Biggest Modern Woman* 69). The flip-side of this parody of misconceptions of Canada is a fairly systematic satire of the ruthless, democratic individualism of the Americans and its obverse, the celebration of free enterprise: "Fame," Anna upbraids Barnum, "that's all you Yankees think about. You're a nation of adolescent boys who want to show our parents in the old country you're important" (155). Anna's contesting of American cultural and political imperialism and her puncturing of Canadian stereotypes – both those held by Americans of Canadians and of Canadians by themselves – is carried off in a parodically allegorical fashion, oscillating between historical mimesis and a self-reflexive, comparative nationalism.

In her characterization of Anna, Swan exploits allegory's energy for political commentary and satire but avoids fixing Anna as an allegorical emblem herself. Though Anna often represents stereotypical Canadian "nation-states," so to speak – the Yankee baiter, for instance, or the self-effacing conciliator – and assesses the various allegorical positions her suitors propose to her, ultimately she is not reducible to any of them. This resistance is especially important given that such allegorical strategies have been a significant part of the arsenal of patriarchal and colonial discourse. In this respect, having Anna meet and be courted by the Canadian giant Angus McAskill (a departure from the historical Anna Swan's biography) is an important strategy on Swan's part. The presence of Angus prevents Anna from becoming a kind of allegorical representation of the nation, a kind of figurative totality, representing Canada and the stereotypical Canadian course of self-effacement and reticence. Indeed, Anna counters Angus's patriarchal assumption, after they make love, that they will be married, as she wants "to be a show-biz personality – not a rural drudge" (58).

That Anna's alternative suitor, Martin Bates, is American is of course key to the allegorical course of *The Biggest Modern Woman*. As with Angus, Swan reworks the historical Bates to suit her allegorical purposes in the novel: Martin's obsession with giantism and his desire to propagate a superhuman species of giants, *Americanus*, fuels his attraction to Anna, an allegorizing of the doctrine of manifest destiny, with patriarchal overtones. Swan presents in Martin an imperialist desire to appropriate Canada, which comes through particularly in their troupe's shipboard performance of "Olympian Love Call," which stages Anna's resistance to Martin's expropriative overtures in the form of an erotic, territorialized national allegory. She aspires to subdue him, but throughout the novel she consistently falls short of her goal and grows increasingly disillusioned with her role. Their rocky marriage, during which Anna chafes at the role of diplomatic helpmeet, is symbolic of Canada's hand-wringing over its complicity with its aggressive southern partner and provides a particularly good example of the oscillation in the novel between mimetic representation and a parodic, anti-representational foregrounding of allegorical significance.

For the most part, the feminist and nationalist implications of the novel as allegory are hard to separate. This is explicitly reflected when Anna laments, "I feel I am acting out America's relationship to the Canadas. Martin is the imperial ogre while I play the role of genteel mate who believes that if everyone is well-mannered, we can inhabit a peaceable kingdom. That is the national dream of the Canadas, isn't it? A civilized garden where lions lie down with doves. I did not see the difference until I married Martin. We possess no fantasies of conquest and domination. Indeed, to be from the Canadas is to feel as women feel – cut off from the base of power" (273–4). Anna's reluctance toward playing the role of conciliator quite clearly echoes Canada's reservations about being associated with its expansionist neighbour to the south, and it provides a particularly succinct illustration of Swan's ability to synchronize nationalist and feminist implications in the novel.

The representation of Anna's tumultous relationship with Martin points to the importance of Quilligan's redefinition of allegory as polysemous rather than simply doubly semantic, which shifts the emphasis "away from our traditional insistence on allegory's distinction between word said and meaning meant, to the simultaneity of signifying multiple meaning."[164] The allegory in *The Biggest Modern*

Woman, as the diverse criticism on the novel suggests, is not reducible to figures of nationhood because Anna's chafing at her celebrity and her objectification clearly have implications that may or may not be compatible with the image of Canada as the passive object of imperialist designs. Smaro Kamboureli stresses the feminist dimensions of the novel, arguing that it is Anna's very modernity that alienates her, that her "freakishness lies not so much in her gigantic proportions as in her 'modern' desire to assert her femaleness in a world dominated by Victorian men and mores."[165] Christopher Gittings examines the novel's "textualization of allegory and carnival as tropological spaces where postmodernism and post-colonialism work together to break down master narratives of Canadian colonial subjectivity."[166]

If anything, *The Biggest Modern Woman* warns against the dangers of national allegories and underlines their use in colonial and imperial discourse, suggesting that while they may be deployed for post-colonial, counter-discursive practices, they carry their own dangers. Hall's observation that the assertion of national unity is an exercise of power is certainly applicable to national allegories: "Instead of thinking of national cultures as unified, we should think of them as constituting a *discursive device* which represents difference as unity or identity. They are cross-cut by deep internal divisions and differences, and 'unified' only through the exercise of different forms of cultural power."[167] A particular danger is the ready co-optation of allegory within a patriarchal discourse that territorializes the nation as woman and totalizes national identity in competitive masculine terms. Swan instead parodically deflates such allegorical discourse throughout the novel, employing it to highlight various political and cultural courses and relationships but ultimately without allegorically totalizing Canada itself.

In focusing on a relatively unknown historical figure, *The Biggest Modern Woman* subverts a principal tendency of national allegories, which usually operate by focusing on figures and episodes seen as pivotal in shaping national destiny and identity. In contrast, Robertson's *Willie,* like Johnston's *Colony,* subverts the national allegory from within that convention. With the exception of Sir John A. himself, no politician has been associated with the course of Canada for as long as William Lyon Mackenzie King, and in *Willie* (1983) Robertson begins her satirical three-part anatomy of that association. Slemon argues in "Post-colonial Allegory" that "the extent to which we are able to see history as language, as discourse, as a way of seeing, or as a code of recognition is also the extent to which we are able to destabilise history's fixity, its givenness, and open it up to the transformative power of imaginative revision."[168] In exploring King's exile from power during the First World War and the political landscape in Ottawa at the time, *Willie* explicitly adopts the language of allegory to spoof King's tendency towards allegorizing his own role in history and to subject that role to a highly subversive revision.

Playing on King's obsession with Arthurian romance and his alternately messianic and melodramatic self-presentation, Robertson structures this first installment of her fictionalized biography of King as a romance. In romance, as Frye observes, "the virtuous heroes and beautiful heroines represent the ideals and the villains the threats to their ascendancy."[169] In the course of the novel, Robertson puts a feminist spin on this moral triangle, with Lily Coolican being courted by two suitors, Talbot Papineau, the Galahadian knight who goes off to fight in the First World War, and none other than King as the representative of the forces of (political) evil. With Talbot being the grandson of Louis-Joseph Papineau and Willie being the grandson of William Lyon Mackenzie, the two figures work as doubles: two grandsons of republican rebels who are potential heirs to the aging Liberal leader, Wilfrid Laurier. The fictional Lily, then, is used to bring together and to contrast the fortunes of two non-fictional characters and, within the loose and parodic framework of the romance, to provide an alternative history of the era.

The form of the narrative underlines its status as a subversive response to King's public image as a premier statesman. After Willie's death, Lily, who has had a long involvement (and secret, short-lived marriage) with him, is asked to look over his diary, which is being considered for publication. She is unsurprised to find that it is thoroughly self-serving, "a work of fiction, a political pilgrim's progress, justifying the ways of Willie to man, or at least to Willie, and those of us fortunate enough to be among the Good need fear no blame. The crucial pages are blank or excised with a razor blade, Willie acting, true to form, as his own mythologist" (*Willie* 10). The published version is to present only Willie's public face, in an act of convenient selection and omission. The resulting emphasis underlines the rhetorical character of historical documents, as the picture presented is of "a good man whose chronic hypocrisy could be taken as evidence of political genius, a humble man who summed up his political creed on the eve of the Second World War with the phrase: 'I may not have accomplished much, but think what I have prevented!'" (11). Lily reflects that "[a]nything that contradicts this portrait will be omitted" (11), including her, but she too has kept a diary, one which reveals the private side of Willie and quite a different version of his role in history.

The narrative develops in fairly chronological fashion, with Lily's first-person entries combined with omniscient narration, entries from King's diary, and letters between Lily and Talbot. Thus, within the overall structure of the romance, the novel is pseudo-documentary in form, openly intertextual, and continually irreverent. Allegorical postcolonial texts, Slemon argues, foreground "that historical material must be *read*, and read in *adjacency* to a fictional re-enactment of it." They thus require readers to have a binocular vision that foregrounds historical material's "secondary or conditional nature, its link to fictionality."[170] Lily's subversion of King's self-monumentalization certainly seems to approximate this strategy, in which "the binocular lens of allegory refocuses our concept of history as fixed monument into a concept of history as the creation of a discursive practice, and in doing so it opens history, fiction's 'other,' to the possibility of transformation."[171]

The romance provides *Willie* with the structure for such a transformation, and Lily, as romantic heroine, navigates the usual poles of peril and promise. A recurrent theme in romance is "the sexual barrier,"[172] and in *Willie* Papineau's privileged background and his joining the army present the requisite obstacles to his union with the working-class Lily, while Willie hovers ominously in the background. The romance framework and the history mesh quite nicely, the former providing the scaffolding for a wealth of historical material but also providing the dominant tropes for a parodic reworking of that material which questions the postcolonial nationalism so often associated with that era.

This is particularly the case with the profile of King that emerges in the novel. Not only are his notorious eccentricities dramatized, but the effects of his political machinations are highlighted through the moralized and melodramatic discourse of the romance, especially its "strongly enforced code of conduct" and the "suggestion of allegorical significance" that it imparts to the characterization.[173] Lily says of Willie's inability to destroy his diary, for instance: "It was his first love, wife and mother, the magic mirror to which, at the end of every day, he put the fateful question and received the same reassuring reply: every banality a profundity, every truism a parable, a temple of words as false as the fake ruins he constructed out of stolen stones at Kingsmere, a masterpiece of delusion." The voice of the diaries is serpentine, "soft and seductive, a tantalyzing, confidential voice singing a love song of pain and paranoia, a hymn to hatred, the long, pitiable lament of a passionate man unable to love" (11). In short, instead of playing the part of emerging champion of Canadian independence, in *Willie* King is to play the melodramatic villain.

William Lyon Mackenzie King (centre) with Archie Dennison (left)
and John D. Rockefeller (right) while studying industrial relations under
the auspices of the Rockefeller foundation.

Willie is presented in this role in characteristically ambivalent
terms: calculating yet gullible, idealistic yet petty, populist yet condescending and racist, messianic and self-doubting all at the same
time. The effects of Willie's machinations are particularly evident in
his involvement with J.D. "Junior" Rockefeller, whom he tries to
impress with his ideas about capitalism and labour relations. The
sinister aspect of Willie appropriate to the romance in this regard is
that he believes quite firmly that he is a friend of labour, vowing to
himself that he will refuse an offer of work from Rockefeller "if it
means any dirty work or a betrayal of the working man" (68). However, in the course of his association with Rockefeller, Willie serves
to give him a populist sheen and helps paper over the tensions

created by the murder of striking miners and their families at a Rockefeller-owned coal mine in Colorado. Both men absurdly dressed as miners, Junior delivers a prevaricating speech (written by Willie) to convince the workers that the Rockefellers are not profiting off their labour, and Willie manages to convince them of Junior's solidarity with their cause, enough to swing their vote in favour of a company union.[174] Like Johnston's protagonist Smallwood, Willie has a remarkable ability to construct a favourable self-image in the face of contradictory evidence, but he is much more successful and much less sympathetic in doing so.

Robertson's self-conscious, parodic treatment of allegory is particularly evident in her use of the figurative repertoire of Arthurian romance to cast Willie's Liberal careerism in an extremely unflattering light. Willie constantly mythologizes himself, glossing over contradictions. Backtracking on his initial support of conscription towards the end of the war, for instance, Willie revises his self-image as Laurier's lone supporter in his anti-conscription stand: "one man, one loyal colleague stands fast by his side, Sir Galahad by the aged Arthur, fighting the good fight against the forces of reaction, true to the death" (307). For a Galahad, however, Willie is not above political intrigue, having decided to "warn Laurier of the dangers in offering Major Papineau a seat in the House of Commons" (245) because of his militarist views and Tory leanings. When his mother tells him of Papineau's death in battle at Passchendaele, Willie calls it "a tragic loss" but to himself exults: "just King and Laurier alone, against the Forces of Evil, they'll sweep the country, already the crowds are flocking to see Laurier, Laurier and King, the old man and the young heir, triumphant together under the banner of Liberalism" (321). Willie falls conspicuously short of the behavioural ideals of Arthurian romance, the source of his transformation into hero being not moral and mystical power but hypocrisy and self-delusion. By highlighting this distance, Robertson contests the self-approval implicit in King's self-allegorization.

Though Talbot Papineau is likewise motivated by political ambition, his fate dramatizes the price at which Canada achieved its distinction during the war. As *Willie* progresses, Talbot emerges as the archetypal postcolonial nationalist hero, the Canadian who chafes against the colonial domination represented by the British high command, as reflected, for instance, by Neil Macrae in Hugh MacLennan's *Barometer Rising*. Initially, Talbot volunteers out of a naive sense of adventure and nationalism but quickly realizes that in the army he will be bored and unappreciated, once again subject as a colonial "to the condescending arrogance that so enraged him at Oxford" (104).

Once he is overseas, his idealism further deteriorates. His letters to Lily (which are abridged and adapted versions of the historical Papineau's letters in the National Archives) give a sense both of the horrors of the conflict and of the political and financial machinations behind it, particularly between the British and the Canadians and, in Canada, between the Tories and the Grits. A number of the letters describe life in the trenches, his participation in attacks, and the gruesome injuries and deaths of his comrades, in a fashion reminiscent of Findley's *The Wars*.[175]

Though Talbot is genuinely heroic and nationalist, particularly in comparison with Willie, he grows increasingly disenchanted with the war effort. Writing to Lily from the front he evokes the by-now stereotypical reading of the conflict, the idea that, in "the trenches of France and Flanders," as Arthur Lower put it, "the spirit of Canadian nationalism was born"[176]; the losses of Canadians, Talbot speculates, "may be the birth pangs of our nationality" (144).[177] Talbot's nationalism, however, is bound up with his political ambition, and for a time he abandons his regiment, though reluctantly, when offered a post in the War Records Office in London. The opportunity brings Talbot under the sway of Sir Max Aitken, and under Aitken's influence Talbot's politics initially turn militaristic, as he leans toward a belief in military control of the government. But Talbot comes to recognize the political liability of his association with such a prominent Tory, and, while planning the assault on Vimy Ridge, realizes that the British commanders are less interested in winning the war than in seizing the opportunity it presents to win promotion; in his resentment of the British Army he "is a *Patriote* after all" (280) like his famous grandfather.

Talbot's ultimate disgust with politics and his willingness to throw in his lot with the common soldier by rejoining his regiment at the front, leading to his death at Passchendaele, provide *Willie* with "the *anagnorisis* or discovery, the recognition of the hero" that Frye sees as the outcome of the "complete form of the romance."[178] Yet, while Talbot puts his life on the line at the front, Willie, emblematic of political expediency and hypocrisy, self-servingly vacillates over enlisting and thus survives to claim Lily after Talbot's death, denying *Willie* the happy ending – the celebration of "fecundity, freedom and survival" – typical of romance.[179]

The contrasting political courses that Talbot and Willie represent are mirrored in their treatment of Lily. As the recipient of Talbot's letters, Lily takes the place of Beatrice Fox, a young Philadelphia woman with whom the historical Talbot Papineau struck up an increasingly intimate acquaintance by correspondence from the

Talbot Mercer Papineau, officer in the Princess Patricia's
Canadian Light Infantry, with his dog Bobs.

front.[180] Though characterized by a wavering devotion, the tone of
these letters is courtly, platonic, and Romantic, and they fit nicely
within *Willie*'s romance framework. But Robertson's intertextual dialogue with Papineau's letters lacks the scathing satire aimed at King's
Arthurian predilection and implicitly presents Talbot as closer to the
Arthurian ideal: "Every woman has an instinct of affection for a
soldier just as a soldier wishes to have the love of a woman. Women
at home exaggerate the courage and qualities of a man who is fighting
and will create Galahads from ordinary clay" (211).

Alternating between longing for and alienation from the world he
has left behind as he reacts to his war experiences, Talbot vacillates
between such detached platonism, a more flippant flirtatiousness, and
a passionate willingness to commit to Lily. As a result, Lily entertains

doubts about their relationship and furthermore is conscious of the effects of class divisions, particularly because of the disapproval of Talbot's mother, Caroline. Their relationship does advance beyond the platonic when Lily visits Talbot in London at the time of the assault on Vimy, but after Talbot's death Caroline attempts to assuage Lily's grief by describing him as "a ladies' man" who "enjoyed the game of courtship too much to give it up" (326). Though the sincerity of his attachment to Lily is implicitly questioned in the novel, Talbot certainly behaves towards her in a strikingly different manner than Willie, in whom any idealism is conspicuously missing or hypocritically distorted.

First of all, Willie's villainy – as appropriate to the romance – has pronounced sexual dimensions, and he treats sex, like politics, in the moralized language of allegory. He is presented as a sexually frustrated puritan with violent rape fantasies who has an Oedipally close relationship with his dying mother while shamefully visiting prostitutes and, in his diary, recording the money spent as "Wasted." Willie's treatment of Lily, who comes to Kingsmere to type his book *Industry and Humanity* for him, underlines this villainy. He voyeuristically steals a pair of silk underwear and later tries to rape her after she insults his mother. Willie is at first penitent, but then accuses Lily of having "deliberately *flaunted* yourself in front of me ... like the Whore of Babylon, to distract me from my purpose in life. You have thrown yourself at me, and attempted to seduce me ... and drag me down into a slough of vile concupiscence" (229). Though he subsequently apologizes, the aura of virtue he asserts for himself is further undercut when Lily discovers that he has syphilis. Along with scenes in which Lily plays dominatrix while taking on the role of Willie's mother, *Willie* provides a view of King as a man whose sexuality was as complicated, ambivalent, and offbeat as his politics. If a central theme in romance is "the maintaining of the integrity of the innocent world against the assault of experience," it is Lily who needs to put up a defense – despite Willie's hypocritical protestations to the contrary.[181]

Robertson's wartime profile of Willie in the form of a parodic romance is buttressed by her parodic abridging, extending, and revising of King's diary in the National Archives.[182] In this fashion, *Willie* certainly shows how allegory, in Slemon's terms, can be used to draw attention to history as discourse and to open it up to a postcolonial transformation. In one chapter, for instance, Robertson presents what is ostensibly a series of entries from the diary for the last days of 1916; while much of the entries is verbatim, with some material omitted or rearranged for narrative convenience and emphasis, Robertson reworks and adds to the entries to insert the fictional Lily into King's life.

Elsewhere, however, Robertson's parodic "responding" to King's self-presentation is much more subversive, underlining the sexual and political hypocrisy lurking beneath the self-image that King presents in his diaries. Robertson reworks a series of entries from early 1917 as narrative segments describing Willie's love and concern for his dying mother, and though most of the details are consistent, she renders the scene somewhat melodramatically and caps it off with a midnight visit to a prostitute. (Her "invention" on this score, incidentally, is not without precedent, as C.P. Stacey suggests that King was accustomed to making such nocturnal excursions at this time.[183]) Her parodic reworking of historical sources provides a revisionist take on King's wartime activities but also makes readers aware of the implications of the forms that are evoked in historical accounts. Robertson's intent in *Willie* (and, indeed, in the trilogy as a whole) is to demythologize King, and she accomplishes this by subversively highlighting the allegorical self-inflation of a prominent figure's "record" of his activities.

Presenting an uncomplimentary view of such a public figure, however, even such an ambivalently notorious (and notoriously ambivalent) figure as King, unsurprisingly raises other historiographical issues, particularly about historical consensus and respect for "the historical record." Robertson observes in her acknowledgments that *Willie* "is based on real people and events but the story, the dialogue and the characterizations are completely fictional" (n.p.). However, her dialogic engagement of the historical record shows little interest in sustaining the distinction between what is real and what is fictional or between what is part of the historical record and what is not. This earned her the ire of Granatstein, who took Robertson to task in an interview on CBC Radio after the publication of *Willie*, accusing her of "distorting history without the justification ... of a greater artistic purpose" and objecting to the rape scene: "King's life and records are quite interesting enough without her doing this."[184]

Granatstein's point about King's life and records is a compelling one because his life, if anybody's, seems ready-made for fictional treatment without much touching up, though part of the problem, as Robertson responded, is that historians "leave out all the good bits."[185] At the same time, Granatstein's objections are intended to maintain a firm distinction between historical truth and allegorical truth; for him, the invented material is not appropriate because those things did not happen. For Robertson, however, such material is consistent with her subversive counter-allegorizing of King, as she emphasizes in responding to Granatstein's charges: "all you're asking the reader to do is to re-imagine history. It's a game. I call it suspension of belief.

During the course of the book you suspend your belief in the historical record and look at it again in terms of a more mythological point of view."[186] Thus Robertson sees the attempted rape of Lily as a metaphor for "that psychic and moral violence which the political system imposes on people" – a violence that is emphasized by the sexual, cultural, and class tensions that Lily witnesses in Ottawa.[187] *Willie* essentially reworks and extends the historical record to parodically remythologize King as a representative of the manipulation, exploitation, and sexism that permeated wartime politics in Canada.

Certainly, the novel provides a self-conscious example of White's model of historical narrative as a symbolic discourse that "likens" a series of historical events to a familiar literary form. Robertson is willing to take liberties in her use of the materials of history to buttress a particular allegorical history, in which King's machinations are "likened" to those of the romance villain. For Robertson, the question becomes whether those fabrications are consistent with the form in which she figures those events and whether the form itself is an appropriate choice, rather than whether they correspond to the historical record as the textual residue of those events.

One wonders, however, whether Robertson would offer the same defence as Findley, who said of his portrait of the Duke and Duchess of Windsor in *Famous Last Words*: "Nothing that any of the people do in the book that is *in fact* fictitious even remotely oversteps the boundaries of possibility," though to make one's point sometimes "involves heightening or underlining characters' traits."[188] As a metaphoric truth, Robertson's invention carries with it an incendiary literal implication. Such an addition, furthermore, marks a departure point from postmodern historiography, in which historians "have little of the imaginative freedom exercised by writers of fiction because we are in the business of the retrospective emplotment of historical events and narratives. While the historical account is a figurative exercise in the sense of being a product of the literary imagination, its relativism remains limited by the nature of the evidence."[189] *Willie* thus provides an enlightening example of the delicate equilibrium between historical material and narrative form, as well as of the allegorical resonance that emerges from writers' choices of both.

The principal effect of these choices is that *Willie*, as a socially revisionist allegorizing of Canada during World War I, dissents from rather than contributes to a celebratory narrative of national emergence. As a romance, it is clearly a modern romance and thus belongs to a genre that tends, according to Gillian Beer, not to remake the world "in the image of desire" but to resolve it "into images of dread. The function of romance in our own time may well prove to have been not wish-fulfilment but exorcism."[190] Rather than chronicling the forging of an independent, robust, anticolonial nationalism in the crucible of World War I, Robertson's *Willie* combines the allegorical patterns of the romance with the intertextual subversions of historiographical metafiction to present a much more complicated and much less complimentary picture of the Canada that emerges from the war. The death of Talbot and the ascendancy of Willie suggest that it is, instead, a Canada compromised by internal divisions, political machination, and economic exploitation, whose potential has been sacrificed to imperial interests.

Wayne Johnston's *The Colony of Unrequited Dreams* (1998) similarly explores the self-allegorizing, self-mythologizing tendencies of a notable political figure, Newfoundland's first premier, Joey Smallwood. Unlike *Willie*, and perhaps more like Wiebe's *The Scorched-Wood People*, *Colony* highlights the national aspirations submerged within larger narratives of national development. The novel serves as a reminder that Newfoundland, which has been absorbed into Confederation as a region or sub-region of Canada, has a much longer history as a separate colony and nation. In that respect, Johnston is concerned with a nation as it was and might have been. Emphasizing the legacy of colonialism and the significance of class and gender to the making and writing of history, *The Colony of Unrequited Dreams*, like *Willie*, focuses on the relationship between a key figure of nationalist aspiration and a fictional amour to address the construction of nationhood in allegorical terms.

The key text for Johnston's *Colony* is Frost's famous poem, "The Road Not Taken." The novel explores the effects of thwarted destiny, dramatizing the underlying question of what might have been, both in the private history of Smallwood and in the public history of Newfoundland. For the most part grounded in Smallwood's political biography, *Colony* traces the career of the champion of Confederation from his school days to the whirlwind of failed industrialization after the triumph of the pro-Confederation side and Smallwood's accession to the position of premier. Johnston's primary innovation is that he invents for Smallwood, as does Robertson for King, a lifelong romantic interest whose fortunes are thoroughly (and likewise subversively) bound up with his. Sheilagh Fielding is both Smallwood's one true love and his nemesis, and due to the constraints of class and patriarchal assumptions, as well as to the aftershocks of colonialism, their union is never realized. Thus their destiny is thwarted in a fashion that mirrors the fate of Newfoundland, whose potential for self-reliance and political independence is also never realized, and for much the same reasons. For its principal protagonists and for

Newfoundland as a whole, *Colony*, then, is an allegorical meditation on "the road not taken."

The majority of the novel is taken up with Smallwood's first-hand account of his political career, a narrative that is very much in the spirit of one of Johnston's key sources, Richard Gwyn's very readable *Small-wood: The Unlikely Revolutionary*. Like Gwyn, Johnston displays a certain satiric admiration for Smallwood's tenacity and his determined championing of Newfoundland and of the poor, while happily exploiting Smallwood's potential as a parodic Horatio Alger. Johnston's Smallwood is a wonderfully ambivalent comic figure, on the one hand displaying a remarkably dogged commitment to make a name for himself and for Newfoundland, and on the other hand being incredibly gauche, gullible, manipulative, and capable of talking the ears off a statue. As Johnston himself might put it, adverse circumstances that would have deterred a better man had little effect on Smallwood. Smallwood's ambivalence, however, goes deeper than this, as Johnston provides a kind of political and emotional archaeology of the man that underlines the exploitative power relations that have shaped the history of the island as a whole. Johnston depicts Smallwood both as mock-heroic champion of Newfoundland and as a man who, warped by his mission to save Newfoundland from the legacy of its past, is a carrier of the pathogens of its history. An important issue in the novel, as a result, is to which allegorical course the novel ultimately leans.

Johnston's Smallwood gives new meaning to the term "underdog." At the heart of *Colony* is Smallwood's struggle to overcome the daunting obstacles of geopolitical circumstance, class, and malnutrition. The symbol that hangs (both literally and figuratively) over Smallwood in the book is "the boot" – the wooden boot with the name "Smallwood" emblazoned on it that hangs at the entrance to the Narrows below St John's Signal Hill and, in a smaller version, outside his grandfather's boot store and factory on Water Street. Johnston exploits this literal sign (which did indeed hang outside Smallwood's grandfather's store) as a figurative sign of the station in life towards which Smallwood can reasonably be expected to gravitate. It is the image that hovers over him as he rebounds from life's setbacks, alone in the belief that he will make something of himself. Only after the victory of Confederation does Smallwood go out to the Narrows and take down the boot (shot full of holes by resentful anti-confederates), a gesture that signals his confidence that, finally, the boot no longer beckons.

It is, however, a long, agonizing, and largely farcical struggle to reach that point, and Johnston walks a fine line in constructing Smallwood's ambivalent memoir. The history of Smallwood's accomplishments

Water Street, St John's, in the late 1880s.
On the left hangs "the boot"

prior to Confederation is highly comic, particularly because of
Smallwood's complete lack of reticence and inability to be deterred,
embarrassed, or convinced that he is wrong. At the same time, however, his efforts highlight a background of intense political conflict
and economic and cultural deprivation, particularly of the Newfoundland working class and rural poor. Though Smallwood is the
central figure of the novel, in many ways Newfoundland itself is the
protagonist, and through Smallwood Johnston emphasizes the ele-
mental, class-bound, and poverty-stricken conditions in which those
below "the quality" eke out an existence. Perhaps Smallwood's most
formative experience is a stint as a reporter on the sealing ship *S.S.
Newfoundland*, which is caught in a bitter storm with a watch of men
still out on the ice. Turned away by Abram Kean, the captain of
another sealing ship, who was "too miserly to offer those men the
safety of his ship and sent them off to find his son's ship rather than
have them sit on his, eating his provisions and using up his coal and
oil" (*Colony* 114), the men are subsequently found, in the novel's most

striking moment, frozen in a series of poses, "a strange statuary of the dead" (107). The experience galvanizes Smallwood in his resistance to the exploitation of the merchant class, a determination that shapes the course of his foray into politics.[191]

In the early stages of his career, Smallwood's populism verges on the absurd. He is swept up by the rhetoric of socialism, which he masochistically practices in the most adverse circumstances. After a less-than-esteemed tenure in New York, Smallwood realizes that his allegiances lie with Newfoundland, and it is only upon his return that his political fortunes take a turn (though the pace of that turn is glacial rather than meteoric). Despite the comedy and ignominy of Smallwood's socialist career, back in Newfoundland he demonstrates a firm commitment to improving the lot of the poor. Johnston depicts his efforts at union organization as fairly Herculean (at least in intent, since the scarecrow Smallwood is a loose fit in the Herculean mould). His march across Newfoundland in the cause of unionizing the railway section men is certainly a heroic feat but also one in which the less-than-ninety-eight-pound, emaciated Smallwood cuts an absurd figure. Likewise, he journeys to remote outposts to unionize fishermen most of whom "had never heard of unions, had not the faintest idea what a union was or what difference it would make to their lives if they belonged to one" (359). As misplaced and absurd as Smallwood's crusades may seem to be, however, they display his populism and his commitment to Newfoundland.

If Newfoundland after colonialism continues to reflect the impact of colonial domination, an important reflection of that heritage is the prominence in St John's society of Anglophiles dismissive of Newfoundland. Smallwood's role as working-class underdog is sharpened by his subjection, and occasional resistance, to their condescension. For instance, Reeves, Smallwood's patronizing headmaster at Bishop Feild, provides his charges with a thoroughly colonial education and for good measure makes them draw a map of England at the start of every history class. Newfoundland he dismisses as a repository for the dregs of British civilization: "The worst of our lot comes over here, inbreeds for several hundred years and the end-product is a hundred thousand Newfoundlanders with Smallwood at the bottom of the barrel" (36). Though Smallwood engages in a certain postcolonial clowning and goading of Reeves, the latter's condescension has debilitating and persistent effects. Smallwood later tries to reverse this psychological colonization by repeatedly drawing the map of Newfoundland, something he "needn't have bothered doing, since England had been so early imprinted on my brain that no amount of drawing other maps could supplant it" (89–90).

Smallwood's shrewd forebearance and occasional subversions in response to such treatment are certainly intended to elicit sympathy and identification, underlining his belief in himself and in New-foundland and his unwillingness to accept subordination for either.

Smallwood's relationship with the quality – that is, the elite – who dominate the Liberal Party is equally calculating, though harder on the pride, and further underlines the class dimensions of Johnston's allegorizing of Smallwood's career. Smallwood recognizes the party as the only viable alternative to a doomed socialism and, for a man with "a pink past" (274), the only avenue to power. His Liberal mentor, Sir Richard Squires, correctly diagnoses that Smallwood is more interested in power than in his socialist ideal of selfless service of the people. Though the two become associates, Smallwood is allowed to visit Squires only after the quality have left, "as if class were determined by nature and I would no more presume to be his equal or be offended by his behaviour towards me than I would mind his pointing out that I was five foot six" (272). Smallwood's apprenticeship is hard to distinguish from humiliation, especially when he slavishly prepares the constituency of Humber prior to an election only to have Squires decide to run in it himself. Smallwood even puts his life on the line by helping Squires to escape a drunken mob that storms Government House at the height of Squires's corrupt administration. All of these details are drawn from the historical Smallwood's biography, but Johnston's portrayal of them is clearly tailored to underline the class barriers to Smallwood's advancement in the party. Smallwood's nemeses ultimately bring out in him his pride in Newfoundland and his resentment of those whose colonial stewardship has hamstrung its potential.

With the referendum on the island's future looming, Smallwood sees in Confederation the chance to make his mark and to represent the working class and the poor: "I recalled, too, Sir Richard's assessment of socialism as the 'politics of poverty' and therefore the only means of gaining power that was open to a man like me. I fancied I had at last found the version of socialism that Newfoundlanders might accept – confederation with a country that some thought of as a social welfare state. I would do what no politician in Newfoundland had ever done. I would make as my constituency, not the merchants or the hordes who voted as the merchants told them to, but the poor who were greater than the others in number if in nothing else" (433). With Confederation a particularly unpopular option in St John's, where union with Canada threatens to upset the merchants' monopoly, Smallwood's populist groundwork in the outports, where association with the nascent welfare state of Canada at least holds out the hope of some material improvement, serves to swing the second ballot in favour of Confederation. Smallwood – succinctly described in a review of the novel as "Newfoundland's anti-Bolivar" – gets his revenge by coming to power as premier, completing his protracted rags-to-riches advancement.[192]

As White emphasizes, part of what makes historical discourse ultimately allegorical is that the emplotment of historical developments is necessarily selective and ideological. While it is hard to call Johnston's portrait of Smallwood favourably selective up to this point, that it is so becomes clearer through the portrait of Smallwood in power. Johnston sympathetically shows in Smallwood, despite his triumph, the personification of Newfoundland's inferiority complex, the continuation of its colonial cringe, and the continuation of its economic, cultural, political, and psychological dependence as part of the Canadian confederation.

The effects of this cringe are particularly dramatized in Smallwood's disastrous drive to industrialize, during which he is bilked left, right, and centre by consultants, investors, and industrialists, who take advantage of his eagerness to improve the lot of Newfoundlanders.[193] In uncritically trusting his dubious Latvian director of industrial development, Alfred Valdmanis, and in denouncing any naysayers, Smallwood displays the lingering effects of a deference and insecurity honed by colonialism and class subordination: "I was infatuated, not so much with Valdmanis, as with the man he was impersonating, who had all those qualities that I felt the lack of in myself – worldliness, sophistication, business savvy, education, culture, taste, refinement" (514). Smallwood is depicted, for all his political shrewdness, as being gullible and easily impressed by credentials, his inferiority complex making him an easy mark.

Even in chronicling the setbacks of this stage of Smallwood's career, however, Johnston reads the historical Smallwood's record if not altogether favourably then at least conspicuously selectively, underplaying some of the more egregious and acrimonious failures of his regime, those which place his role as champion of Newfoundland in substantial doubt. Admittedly, the fictional Smallwood's career is narrated for the most part by Smallwood himself, but in the face of his willingness to detail both the achievements and setbacks of the early part of his career, the latter part of the novel is conspicuous for the general absence of details which seriously qualify his rags-to-riches account (something about which the historical Smallwood showed less reticence; indeed, an entire chapter of his I Chose Canada is devoted to chronicling his own failures).

For instance, Richard Gwyn argues that Joey Smallwood once in power turned Newfoundland into his personal fiefdom, something that Johnston's Smallwood concedes but more by way of summary than through dramatized episodes; the latter notes that, shortly after his being elected, he "was already ruling the province with such an iron fist that most people were afraid to speak out against me" but excuses himself on the grounds that he is following in the footsteps of his predecessors, that "it was legitimized by tradition as far as I was concerned" (497). Likewise, he refers, in a proleptic moment, to one of the more divisive programs of his career, the resettlement of outport communities in the 1960s and 70s, but again the glimpse is a passing one. Finally, not mentioned at all is the premier's intervention in a loggers' strike in 1959, during which, according to Gwyn, he introduced "the most punitive anti-labour legislation of any postwar Canadian government other than that of Duplessis" and betrayed his populist background (in contrast, Joey Smallwood devoted a chapter of I Chose Canada to defending his actions during the strike).[194] It may well be that the proximity and controversial nature of the post-Confederation history made discretion the better part of valour for Johnston, but this underscores rather than qualifies the idea that the allegorizing of history is always the product of ideological choices.

Johnston's Smallwood does concede that the road taken has not provided the salvation of Newfoundland for which he had hoped, but even in this recognition Johnston highlights Smallwood's devotion to Newfoundland: "I did not solve the paradox of Newfoundland or fathom the effect on me of its particular beauty. It stirred in me, as all great things did, a longing to accomplish or create something commensurate with it. I thought Confederation might be it, but I was wrong" (552). Smallwood confesses that this determination has warped him, made him prone to grandiose schemes and to a selfish clinging to power. Thus, for all his advancements, Smallwood's real objectives are ultimately thwarted, and the populism of the early stages of the narrative has been thoroughly compromised.

This allegorical course is fortified by the toll Smallwood's determination takes on his personal life, and particularly on his relationship with Fielding, which provides a mirror image of his political failures. Throughout the novel, Smallwood and Fielding are fated to cross paths again and again in an elaborate dance of attraction and enmity, oscillating between intimate near misses and acrimonious splits. Though unrequited and therefore potentially pathetic, their romance provides the novel with a comic heart that certainly distinguishes it from Robertson's more scathing treatment of King in *The King Years*. By virtue of a series of misunderstandings, grounded in mistaken assumptions and withheld information, Smallwood misreads Fielding throughout the novel and fails to consolidate their mutual attraction. Through their ambivalent relationship, Johnston dramatizes the personal costs of the class and colonial hegemony that shapes the politically obsessive Smallwood's devotion to making it above all else.

The complicated comic intrigue at the root of their frustrated romance dramatizes the effects of class and gender prejudices. Having allowed Smallwood to labour under the assumption that she wrote the letter that prompts his departure from Bishop Feild, Fielding much later reveals that the letter was sent by her class-conscious father after she blamed her pregnancy on Smallwood. Fielding's options are constrained by assumptions about both class and gender, as she knows that her father would not insist on marriage with Smallwood, as he would with the real father, Smallwood's upper-class nemesis Prowse. This circumstance is behind her divided, enigmatic response to Smallwood's overtures and shapes their ill-fated relationship for the rest of the novel. While uncertainty about Fielding's devotion to Prowse serves to prevent Smallwood from more openly and sincerely declaring himself throughout the novel, what distracts Smallwood more is his devotion to politics; he is not willing to let even Fielding get in the way of his desire to succeed and to help Newfoundland. As Fielding makes him realize at the end of the novel, had he known the truth when he proposed marriage to Fielding during his stay in New York, he undoubtedly, because of his political ambitions, would have cut and run all the same.

Behind their rivalry, furthermore, is a reversal of fortunes, as Smallwood is a particularly unpromising member of the lower middle class and Fielding is from the quality. In the novel he clearly overachieves while she is reduced to the fate that otherwise might have awaited him: she contracts tuberculosis and almost dies, works as a hack journalist with unrealized aspirations to be a writer, and is a chronic alcoholic with a reputation for being promiscuous. Fielding is quite clearly the more thwarted of the two, and the frustrations of her life fuel her bitter, satiric commentary on Newfoundland politics and history. Her writing as a journalist serves as a counterpoint to the narrative of Smallwood's political advancement, and her parodic history of Newfoundland, *Fielding's Condensed History of Newfoundland*, constitutes her revenge on a history that has cramped her style. Fielding spends a life of bitter estrangement, both from her children and from Smallwood, with whom the mistaken assumptions about the letter set off a nasty game of hide and seek that takes the form

of both private and public confrontations. Her bitter, often impene-
trably ironic undermining of Smallwood in her satirical newspaper
column, "Field Day," and her dissipated, secluded lifestyle provide
for Smallwood an enigma, the unravelling of which is almost as
important as his mission to save Newfoundland.

Johnston's fictional romantic subplot is played out in a clever dialogue with the historical circumstances of Smallwood's political
career. In developing their relationship, Johnston plays with details
and episodes from the historical Smallwood's life, inserting Fielding
into significant historical "gaps" and interstices.[195] Despite Fielding's
satiric subversion of Smallwood, Johnston's insertion of her into his
life story ultimately serves to humanize him, an effect particularly
evident in the ending of the novel, which consolidates the parallels
between Smallwood's thwarted relationship with Fielding and the
trajectory of his political career.

Smallwood's unravelling of the secret, which punctuates the gradual realization of his political ambitions and his subsequent disillu-
sionment, paves the way for a comic reconciliation that mirrors his
relationship with Newfoundland: "Our one moment, our one point
of intersection, had just come and gone. We had for years been moving
closer together and from now on we would move apart" (542). Upon
learning of Fielding's hidden past, despite displaying the unqualified
personal concern that he has up to this point avoided, Smallwood
recognizes that he nonetheless would have sacrificed the personal for
the political, even though she had loved him and "I had loved her,
I had at least once in my life been capable of that, able to escape my
self long enough to love. Suddenly, the unacknowledged sorrows
and blunders of my life surged up in me all at once" (550). Thus the
romantic subplot of *Colony* is very much an anatomy of repression
in the service of political advancement, but with a far more hopeful
and conciliatory outcome than in *The King Years*. Fielding's satiric
treatment of Smallwood, a projection of her romantic rejection, gives
way to a genuine sentiment that, unfortunately, is hard to credit
given the overwhelming accumulation of irony in the book, even in
light of the resolution of Fielding's frustrations.

The allegorical function of this subplot is made clear through
Fielding's own observations on Confederation, which openly echo
"The Road Not Taken" in considering what might have been for
herself and Smallwood and what might have been for Newfoundland. The potential of nationhood for the latter is destined to remain
the *"question that has been there from the start, unasked, unanswered,
unacknowledged,"* and *"will still be there"* (493–4). Johnston ends the
novel with a confessional "Field Day" entry from 1959, after Fielding's

reconciliation with Smallwood, in which Fielding explicitly pairs her fate with Newfoundland's:

We have joined a nation that we do not know, a nation that does not know us.

The river of what might have been still runs and there will never come a time when we do not hear it.

My life for forty years was a pair of rivers, the river that might have been beside the one that was. (560)

At the end of *The Colony of Unrequited Dreams*, however, both protagonists confront the fact of their history. Whatever dreams they might have had, in the wake of colonial mismanagement and exploitation, of class hegemony, of patriarchal restriction, and of the perversions of political ambition, are destined to be unrequited. However, in a tribute that Smallwood pays to Fielding, Johnston suggests that a union of Smallwood and Fielding, a modifying of Smallwood's political pragmatism and selfish drive by Fielding's artistic and self-sacrificing nature, might have produced a different outcome.[196] Thus Johnston's portrait of Fielding is a significant (and humanizing) technique in his rewriting of Smallwood's story as a comic, but also somewhat elegiac, national allegory – not of Canada, but of the other river, Newfoundland.

Allegory in its classic form, Deborah Madsen observes, is perceived as a mode that "subordinates the formal features of the text to preconceived intellectual structures and a didactic purpose." Although "the relationship between the literal surface of the narrative and its conceptual dimensions" may be different in modern allegories, she argues, "the way in which meaning is generated by the text remains basically the same."[197] Beneath the literal surface of a representation of historical developments in historical discourse and historical fiction, then, is a preconceived and didactic conception of the meaning of those developments. In this respect, Johnston's allegorizing of history, though less than reverent, is not particularly self-conscious. While there is a certain amount of satire of Smallwood's self-allegorization – his association of himself with the fortunes of Newfoundland – *Colony* ultimately adheres to, perhaps more than it subverts, those allegorical conventions in order to provide a more serious consideration of the fate of a nation. However, such a national allegory nonetheless disrupts the notion of Canada as a national totality and serves as a vivid reminder of how nation is always subject to the flux of history – to political, social, economic, and cultural forces – and is not a natural, organic formation. *Colony*, like Wiebe's novels of the NorthWest, emphasizes how nation, instead, is the product of an ongoing negotiation between its constituent parts.

Robertson's *Willie* and Johnston's *The Colony of Unrequited Dreams*, like *The Biggest Modern Woman of the World*, reflect the potential of the historical novel for subverting, rather than subscribing to, allegories of nation. Rather than constructing characters as earnest emblems of historical forces in the shaping of national destiny, they approach much more irreverently the tendency of their characters to see themselves as such. They reflect a much more sceptical attitude toward allegory as an accomplice of official, and predominantly masculine, history – indeed, it is no coincidence that the subversive forces in all three novels are women. These novels instead use allegory for more critical and postcolonial purposes, disrupting the unilateral semiotic correspondence on which it can rely and suggesting instead that the narrative of nation is subject to multiple readings.

However, while all three novels exploit the symbolic energies of allegory, there are significant differences in the degree of displacement of historical mimesis, the degree to which that allegorical discourse is foregrounded and scrutinized. In various contemporary hybridized forms of fiction, Kelley argues, "allegory authorizes 'meta-commentary' and improvisation; it may also harden into automaton figures with a strong hermeneutic grip on the means and ends of their production."[198] Where Swan's *The Biggest Modern Woman of the World* adopts a much more provisional and deconstructive approach to allegory and foregrounds its use as a nationalist strategy, Robertson's *Willie* subversively spoofs King's predilection for it, and Johnston's *Colony* portrays Smallwood's nationalism in a manner that teases at the edges of allegorical discourse and only slightly and playfully undermines its "hermeneutic grip."

If historical discourse functions as an allegorical representation of past events, what, then, are the implications of Johnston's relatively sustained mimesis compared to Swan's self-conscious and critical spoofing of national allegory? Madsen argues that allegory establishes not a single, circumscribed narrative encoding but an infinitely recessive hermeneutic process: "To use a well-worn phrase: every decoding is another encoding, as the allegorical narrative alludes to an elusive meaning situated in a prior encoding."[199] The ensuing "quest for unmediated vision … leads ever deeper into mediation and textuality" and "away from mimesis but it does not locate us 'at the furthest possible remove from historiography,'" as Paul de Man argues. "Instead, allegory situates itself at two removes from history as it writes about the writing of a transcendental discourse."[200] Thus allegory is an effective form not for encoding a transcendent, objective past but for developing historiographical commentary. As Madsen sees it, allegory's ambivalent capacity "to mythologize, on the one hand, and then to deconstruct its own mythology, on the other," makes it a key strategy for intervening "in the most crucial debates that have shaped the course of the New World's destiny."[201] *The Biggest Modern Woman*, as a thoroughly carnivalesque metafiction, much more than the other two novels foregrounds this ambivalence and exploits its historiographical potential. Nonetheless, all three novels use allegory to highlight the centrality of nation as a site of historical contestation.

The novels surveyed in this chapter, like social history in general, raise a central question: if history is not a unified, singular narrative but the product of a variety of perspectives that are not necessarily mutually compatible, what happens to the role of history as the foundation of a sense of nationhood? Such is clearly the anxiety of Granatstein's *Who Killed Canadian History?*. For Granatstein, social history clearly marks the loss of a consensus that he sees as both indispensable and achievable: "If written and taught properly, history is not myth or chauvinism, just as national history is not perfervid nationalism; rather, history and nationalism are about understanding this country's past, and how the past has made our present and is shaping our future. Moreover, I believe that the past can unite us without its being censored, made inoffensive to this group or that, or white-washed to cover up the sins of our forefathers."[202]

The converse of this anxiety is the repudiation of nationalist achievement inherent in or common to the embrace of the principle "There is no document of civilization which is not at the same time a document of barbarism." Granatstein is certainly resistant to the critique "that history was written by a small group of privileged white men to be read by others like themselves" and whose "interests understandably turned to war and political developments in which their peers participated and whose perspective they adopted."[203] "Our civilization and culture," insists Granatstein, "*is* Western, and there is no reason we should be ashamed of it or not wish to teach our students about it."[204]

These novels, however, suggest that there's more to the historical picture than meets Granatstein's eye and that "our civilization and culture" are undergoing constant renovation. Contrary to the argument that with no "vision, no national goals, no explicit sense of coexisting for some purpose," pluralism "ceases to have a cause" and the result is "mosaic madness,"[205] these novels suggest that part of the problem of Canadian history has been the imposition of "*a* cause" and the subordination of pluralism. From First Nations to colony to nation, Canadian history consists of a series of sites open for reconstruction, and most contemporary novelists, as this chapter shows, are undertaking that reconstruction in a substantially revisionist, and

not just supplementary, historical spirit. A valid postcolonial reconceptualization of the past, these texts suggest, must address the
dynamics of race, ethnicity, class, region, gender, and sexuality that
colonial renderings of Canadian history have suppressed or distorted. That these concerns continue to play such a substantial role
in the fiction of the last decade is a testament to the need for social
history and to the vitality of the fund of material it offers.

This reconstruction, moreover, is a matter not just of politics and
thematics, but of aesthetics as well. If the contemporary historical
novel reflects the inclination toward the telling of untold tales (of
natives, immigrants, minorities, workers, and women), the telling
itself has changed. Brushing history against the grain requires a
revision of technique. The wave of historical writing over the last
three decades has made clear that there are many untold, marginalized, or sanitized stories in Canadian history. But these novels also
reflect the sense that the new history cannot be told in the same old
way: as a realistic narrative told as if by authoritative eyewitnesses
to history. If the history of Canada, a history traditionally preoccupied with the public accomplishments of men of European descent,
has been intruded upon by those previously left out of that narrative,
then the unitary discourse of historical fiction has been subject to a
similar intrusion.

3 The Content of the Form: Textual Strategies

"The problem is to make the story."[1] The opening of Rudy Wiebe's seminal story "Where is the Voice Coming From?" serves as a coda for contemporary Canadian writers' preoccupation with literary form and historical reconstruction. Striving to "make" the story of Cree warrior Almighty Voice's death in the Minechinass Hills during a siege by police in 1897, Wiebe's narrator pores over the residual fragments of the incident – documents, artifacts, and photographs – and muses about the non-factual accretions, the inconsistencies, and the physical deterioration that pose difficulties to objective historical reconstruction. This contemplation of the evidence, which foregrounds the research that precedes that reconstruction, grinds to a halt when the narrator is confronted by the striking contradiction between the description of Almighty Voice in the official Award Proclamation and his appearance in a photograph. Faced with such fundamental incompatability, the narrator concedes the impossibility of objectivity and his implication in the narrative itself: "I am no longer *spectator* of what *has* happened or what *may* happen: I am become *element* in what is happening at this very moment."[2] The narrative then shifts to a mimetic description of the moment of Almighty Voice's death, but the story ends with the narrator confessing that he describes Almighty Voice's death chant as "a wordless cry" because "I do not, of course, understand the Cree myself."[3]

In its juxtapositioning of historical representation and anti-representational foregrounding of perspective, language, and the construction of history, Wiebe's story is an emblematic contemplation of "the content of the form" of historical fiction. This phrase – the title of a collection of essays by Hayden White that address "the problem of the relation between narrative discourse and historical representation"[4] – nicely encapsulates the aims of this chapter because it draws attention to the meaning of *how* we write history – that is, to the content that is implicit in historiographical forms. As White observes, "narrative is not merely a neutral discursive form that may or may not be used to represent real events in their aspect as developmental processes but rather entails ontological and epistemic choices with distinct ideological and even specifically political implications."[5]

Like many historians, contemporary novelists have recognized that the assumptions that shape how history is written are as problematic as those that shape what history is to be written about. Novelists, however, have had a freer hand in translating this recognition into narrative practice. Thus contemporary historical fiction reflects an experimentation with form, a search for ways of avoiding the perils of the assumptions about representation, rationality, contingency, reality, and writing that govern traditional history and the historical novel. The result is that the unitary, authoritative, realistic voice of the historical novel in Canada has been fractured, mongrelized, and in many cases subverted through a discursive interplay that challenges the authority of official history and brushes the form of history against the grain. The split that Michel de Certau sees in historiography is even more visible in the writing of historical fiction: "One type of history ponders what is comprehensible and what are the conditions of understanding; the other claims to reencounter lived experience, exhumed by virtue of a knowledge of the past."[6]

In this respect, contemporary Canadian historical novels undeniably reflect the influence of postmodern poetics. Various devices in these texts serve to draw attention to the construction of the text and to history itself as a construct. Postmodern historiographic metafiction, as Linda Hutcheon has dubbed texts that employ these strategies, is "both self-consciously fictional but also overtly concerned with the acts (and consequences) of the reading and writing of history as well as fiction. In other words, the aesthetic and the social, the present and the past, are not separable discourses."[7] Most of the texts under study here are discursively heterogeneous, employing different narrative registers, frame stories, and narrative self-reflexiveness or interdiscursivity, rather than the cohesive, authoritative voice of traditional historical fiction. Many of them are characterized by a fragmentation (as opposed to a unity) of perspective, mirrored in a fragmentation of the narrative itself.

Such techniques foreground the illusoriness of an objective, unified, detached view of history. Furthermore, that discursive heterogeneity often serves to highlight the intertextual nature of both history and fiction, drawing attention to the fact that narratives are necessarily made up of other discourses. The interplay between those different discourses, moreover, is a significant, typically postmodern strategy in most of these texts. Finally, this discursive heterogeneity is tied to a shift in attitude: the breaking of the traditionally unitary voice of historical accounts is mirrored by a subversive and often parodic response to the exclusions of official history, a carnivalization of history that underpins contemporary Canadian historical fiction's preoccupation with the content of the form of history.

The aim of this chapter, then, is to explore some key textual strategies in these novels and the implications of these strategies for the representation of history. Coming after the previous section's emphasis on historical sites, the preoccupation with novelistic form and textual strategies in this part of the book might suggest a questionable split between content and form. Rather, as the title of the chapter serves to underline, the democratization of historical interests and the increasing formal innovation in the historical novel in Canada are thoroughly interpenetrating developments. While it is possible to have the one without the other, most of the texts under discussion here reflect that the two have tended to go hand in hand. If contemporary Canadian historical novels reflect a revisioning of history and of Canadian history, they do so both in what they are about and in how they are written, and the following chapter is intended to explore some prominent patterns in the latter and how they shape the former. Rather than providing an exhaustive taxonomy of textual strategies, it provides selected examples intended to illustrate a more general shift in novelistic representations of history. Indeed, the fact that many of these novels could be discussed under all of these headings suggests a significant degree of convergence in both political and aesthetic aims.

METAHISTORY AND METAFICTION

As Linda Hutcheon's discussion of historiographical metafiction in *The Canadian Postmodern* suggests, many of these historical novels are specific kinds of postmodern texts, extending the prevalent self-reflexiveness about literary practice to considerations about the writing of history. According to Patricia Waugh, metafiction, as one kind of postmodernism, "converts what it sees as the negative values of outworn literary conventions into the basis of a potentially constructive social criticism." Rather than suggesting an exhaustion of literary realism, metafiction "suggests, in fact, that there may be as much to learn from setting the mirror of art up to its own linguistic or representational structures as from directly setting it up to a hypothetical 'human nature' that somehow exists as an essence outside historical systems of articulation."[8] Historiographical metafictions extend that potential to representations of the past. A significant aspect of the shift in historiography and in fiction has been a movement from an obsession with presenting a "picture" to a preoccupation with the discursive and representational conventions of such a presentation. Thus it is no surprise that contemporary fiction about history and historical subjects has increasingly directed its attention towards historiographical methodology, increasingly representing the past not "as it really was" but as it is being constructed by some interpreting agent.

The shift in emphasis, in Hutcheon's terms, is from representing history as product to representing it as process; historiographical metafiction thematizes or allegorizes "the act of *enonciation*, the interaction of textual production and reception, of writing and reading."[9] Such a shift implies a number of concerns on the part of contemporary novelists writing of history: the scepticism about objectively representing the past, the recognition of the mediation of the past in historiography and fictional discourse, and the struggle to find an appropriate form for addressing historical and historiographical issues. Key strategies for addressing these concerns in contemporary Canadian novels include foregrounding the act of researching and writing history and/or providing surrogates of the reader and underlining the act of selection, interpretation, and construction behind representations of the past.

In most of the novels in this study, metahistorical tropes and techniques provide the opportunity for extensive thematic and discursive engagement with issues of historical perspective, interpretation, and representation. Timothy Findley's *The Wars* and Daphne Marlatt's *Ana Historic* – both by now canonical examples of historiographical metafiction – provide a good background for examining how the writing of history is foregrounded in two lesser-known texts, Heather Robertson's *Igor: A Novel of Intrigue* and Wayne Johnston's *The Colony of Unrequited Dreams*. Despite their revisionist stances toward received wisdom about particular aspects of Canadian history and the role of the figure of the researcher/historian in their narratives, the four novels are ultimately extremely diverse in their attitudes towards the past, their representative strategies, and their aesthetic qualities. At the same time, all four novels, in a typically metafictive manner, explore the dotted line between history as process and history as product.

Findley's *The Wars* (1977) has been widely and rightly recognized as a ground-breaking historical novel in Canada because of its deheroicizing of the traditionally heroicized role of Canadians in World War I, but more so because of the metafictional strategies that Findley deploys in the novel to denaturalize the presentation of history. Rather than realistically and chronologically charting Robert Ross's childhood experiences, his volunteering for and preparation to go to war, and his experiences at the front, the narrative of *The Wars* instead mimes the process of researching Robert's story. Findley achieves this by situating readers as "you" the researcher who observes Robert's family photographs in the archives, conducts interviews with those who cared for Robert during his convalescences in England, and pieces together the fragments of his story. Findley's narrative strategies, as most critics have noted, emphasize that the past is not immediately available to the reader/researcher, but must be reconstructed through a process that is analogous to the construction of fiction itself.

Historical research is reliant, of course, on a variety of sources, and the narrative of *The Wars* inscribes an encounter with different traces of the past, while at the same time raising questions about their ability to provide access to the past. Photographs, as Lorraine York has underscored, figure prominently in the archival framework of *The Wars* and raise questions about that access. They provide images that at once evoke a historical context and atmosphere, and yet are static, requiring interpretation, a reading beyond the frame, and a consciousness of the effect of freezing and framing. While Findley's use of photographs helps to foreground the process of historical reconstruction, it is also tied to his concern with the preservation of life; as York persuasively argues, photographs thus play an important, positive role in the researcher's "fixing of the past in order to celebrate it" and serve as "a type of surrogate memory."[10]

Likewise, in a fashion typical of postmodern fiction, the transcripts of interviews with Juliet D'Orsey and Marian Turner serve both as contributions to Robert's story and as metafictional comments on historical reconstruction, in each case helping to develop the novel's central themes. They provide access to parts of Robert's story, but they also mime the historiographical act of interviewing and of reading sources in a fashion that foregrounds both the tension between fact and fiction and the role of perspective and mediation in constructing accounts of the past. Findley's use of transcripts highlights how the story is not just there but must be found, constructed from scraps of evidence. The interviews, furthermore, are occasionally disrupted by anti-mimetic intrusions that undermine the narrative as a progressive, chronological, linear unfolding of events and figure a more appropriately historiographical vision. Here the outcome is known, but the pieces must be put back together through a process that is fragmentary, overlapping, interpretive, and non-linear. The result of Findley's "faking and unmasking a historical record," as Simone Vauthier argues, is distinctly ambivalent: "Through the demystification of his pseudo-account, he seeks to ascribe a certain kind of truth to fiction, even as he is reminded, and reminds us, of its limits." He forces readers to "both suspend belief and acknowledge the artifice, both see through the layers of illusion to the verbal nature of the events and respond to the novel as if it were life."[11]

Where the traditional historical novel functions by creating the illusion of time travel, historiographical metafictions such as *The Wars* constantly remind us that such transport must always be vicarious. Findley's narrative strategies in *The Wars*, rather than providing the illusion of a complete, transparent, chronological representation of the past, provide the illusion of an incomplete, non-linear, interpretive, historiographical reconstruction. However, despite the self-consciousness the novel displays about representing the past, such strategies nonetheless raise the question of the ontological status of that reconstruction itself. Does such a narrative shift serve to trouble or to authenticate the novel as a reliable reading of an obviously controversial figure?

The issue is a complex one, particularly because so much of the narrative is not metafictively situated; the metafictional research framework recurs throughout the narrative but is far from consistently deployed. Most of Robert's life is conveyed through unattributed third-person narration typical of historical fiction. It combines segments of historical overview with limited-omniscient chronicling of Robert's experiences. Even in these segments, there are occasional metafictional interruptions that remind the reader that Robert's story is being reconstructed from the vantage point of the present, some sixty years later, but such interruptions are fairly rare. Some parts of *The Wars* have the historiographical authority and resonance of a novel like Raddall's *His Majesty's Yankees*, a painting of the big historical picture. Such an assertion of authority can, of course, be attributed to the researcher, just like the historiographical interpolations, but both serve to contribute to the impression that we "have" Robert's story. Furthermore, those occasions on which the authority of the narrative is openly questioned – such as the admission that at the time of the shooting of Private Cassles "the mythology is muddled" – implicitly verify the rest of the narrative, just as the narrative's consistent interpellation of a "you" finding the story suggests an inevitability to those findings.[12]

Echoing White, Hutcheon has emphasized that writing history and historical fiction is a political act, the imposition of a formal coherence that has ideological implications, and that the "creator or discerner of that formal coherence is in a position of power too – power over facts, clearly, but also power over readers."[13] The troubling question *The Wars* raises, then, is whether the ultimate effect of the metafictive, historiographical structure of the novel is to undermine or at least question the authority of the text as a reconstruction of the "history" of Robert Ross, or whether it simply defers the representational authority assumed by historical realism to the level of historiographical mimesis, suggesting that this version is the inevitable result of researching the story.

The former interpretation emphasizes the ambiguity and subjectivity of historical reconstruction – "Out of these you make what you can, knowing that one thing leads to another"[14] – and empowers the reader. As Diana Brydon puts it, "Robert's story exists only in the narrator's retelling; as soon as we attempt to re-tell it ourselves it becomes yet another story."[15] The latter interpretation suggests that the reader, though actively engaged in the research, will nonetheless come to the necessary conclusion or the same story. Frank Davey, for instance, argues that the novel unmistakably projects a "real" behind the process and the layers of narrative it entails and ultimately "attempts to divert the reader from awareness of the constructedness of the text and its characters."[16] That this is not an easy question to answer shows the ambiguity of Findley's work as a writer. As Evelyn Cobley argues about *The Wars*, while Findley's aims are obviously humanist ones and while he believes in the importance of the power of representation, his narrative practice is quite postmodernist and certainly raises questions about the nature of artistic production.[17] Findley wants to tell his story and foreground the telling too, and while he deftly manages the balance, the ultimate effect is undeniably ambivalent.

If scepticism about traditional historiography along epistemological, political, and gender lines necessitates a new approach to the form of history, Daphne Marlatt's *Ana Historic*, perhaps more than any other "historic" fiction in Canada, has responded to the challenge. In *Ana Historic*, the research motif is much more than metafictively dramatized; indeed, the whole notion of historical research is held up to the light as part of Marlatt's feminist deconstruction of the concept of history and the limitations of historical research in a patriarchal society. The Anansi edition of *Ana Historic* nicely captures the novel's foregrounding of historiography: over a background that juxtaposes a modern map of Vancouver and an archival photo of Gastown, a hand holds a photo (presumably of Annie's mother, Ina), illustrating the researcher's interaction with sources and the intervention of the personal in the historical. Annie's narrative essentially

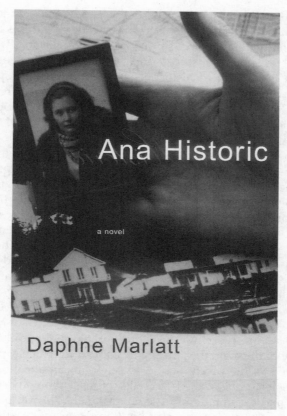

Cover of House of Anansi edition of *Ana Historic*.
"step inside the picture and open it up"

charts her opting-out of a masculinist academic history, recognizing the patriarchal attitudes and assumptions inscribed in its subject matter, its methodology, and its form. Marlatt's novel, as a result, is clearly historiographical rather than historical. As most analyses of the novel underline, Annie's efforts to write the story of Mrs Richards, who has been marginalized in a patriarchically defined history and thus effaced, are highly self-conscious in a way that raises feminist issues about subjectivity, narrative, and historiography.

As Annie's project departs from traditional history, she likewise increasingly opts out of being her husband's sexual and historical subordinate. He would, no doubt, she speculates, disapprove of her lack of regard for the boundaries of traditional phallocentric notions of history: "but this is nothing, i imagine him saying. meaning unreadable.

because this nothing is a place he doesn't recognize, cut loose from history and its relentless progress towards some end. this is undefined territory, unaccountable. and so on edge" (*Ana Historic* 81). Annie's entry into "undefined territory" subverts the masculine containment inherent in the notion of historical objectivity and appropriates for feminist purposes the recognition that the past is never represented on its own terms but for purposes that are very much defined according to values of the present, which in *Ana Historic* involve Annie's ongoing redefinition of her social and sexual identities.

This "opening up" of the picture of history, as Marlene Goldman and Manina Jones, among others, have noted, is effected particularly through the metafictionality and intertextuality of the narrative. As Annie struggles to write for Mrs Richards a larger role than she is given by history, segments of narrative describing Mrs Richards's arrival in Gastown, her adjustment to her new environment, and her experiences as a teacher and a widowed woman in a frontier logging town are interwoven with snippets of buoyant, almost giddy masculine episodes and descriptions from various sources that are on occasion identified in the narrative: local papers like *The Moodyville Tickler* and *The Mainland Guardian*, histories of logging including M. Allerdale Grainger's *Woodsmen of the West*, and various histories of Vancouver. For the most part, these intertexts are situated dialogically and ironically. They underscore the patriarchal context in which Mrs Richards is positioned as the pretty widowed schoolmarm and highlight the gushing, testosterone-soaked discourse of masculine physical accomplishment and exploitation of the environment. "Annie's reading of historical materials in *Ana Historic*," Jones argues, "disturbs the conventions that *prevent* her from speaking, the constructs that situate 'woman's place' in history as a fixed and unchangeable position of silence."[18]

Although these intertexts are foregrounded in a way that suggests a distinction between fictional narrative and "historical" or nonfictional intertexts, Annie's writing of Mrs Richards's story subverts any such distinction and reveals the patriarchal assumptions underpinning it. Marlatt's presentation of Annie's research is particularly important in this regard because the boundary between Annie's research and her writing is consistently blurred. Her narrative of Mrs Richards's life in Gastown is interrupted, compromised, even put under erasure by her reflections on her own historiographical practice, her attempt to write Mrs Richards's (ongoing) past without reinscribing her into the patriarchal order that banished her to the margins of history in the first place. "In accordance with the postmodern tactic of contesting discourses which are simultaneously invoked," says Goldman, Annie "does not attempt to do without history-making, although she rejects history as it has been fashioned."[19]

Furthermore, the degree to which Annie is working from sources is rendered highly ambiguous. There are references to Ana's journal in the archives, but Marlatt's description collapses Ana's writing with Annie's, much as Annie has been collapsing the distinction between herself and Ina: "they think her journal suspect at the archives. 'inauthentic,' fictional possibly, contrived later by a daughter who imagined (how ahistoric) her way into the unspoken world of her mother's girlhood" (30). Due to a circular thinking that it is a priority of women's history to open up, the journal, because it is private, is not deemed historical: "a document yes, but not history. you mean it's not factual" (31). The subsequent lines, "what is fact? (f)act, the f stop of act. a still photo in the ongoing cinerama" (31), provide an important reflection on how history presents itself as capturing the past, just as a photograph supposedly captures the present.

In a parodic "research" moment, Annie presents herself looking over Ana's shoulder as she writes, speculating about Ana's anxieties about representation: "what is she editing out and for whom? besides herself? it is herself there though she writes 'the' eye and not 'my.' objective out there and real (possibly) to others. she is thinking about those possible others leaning over her shoulder as she writes. or does she strive only to capture in words a real she feels beyond her?" (46). This highlighting of the importance of imaginative projection in writing out of a patriarchally selective past is further underscored by Marlatt's acknowledgment that only the most passing references to Mrs Richards as a teacher in Gastown and her marriage to Ben Springer are from "documented" sources. Thus an important strategy for Marlatt is the very dialogic way in which she treats historical intertexts and blurs the line between those intertexts and fictionalized ones, between present narrative and narrative of the past. In this fashion *Ana Historic* dissolves traditional ontological and epistemological boundaries between fiction and truth, and past and present, breaking the hegemony of such notions on constructions of women's subjectivity. "this is a work of fiction," Marlatt writes in her acknowledgments; "historical personages have been fictionalized to possible and/or purely imaginary lengths" (n.p.).

The implications of the length to which historical personages have been fictionalized, and thus the significance of *Ana Historic* as a historiographic novel, are most evident in the ending that Annie constructs for Mrs Richards. When Annie meets Zoe, the direction of her historical narrative becomes more closely tied up with the fate of her own story. Annie becomes particularly frustrated as she realizes that the "end" that history has in store for Ana is a conventional marriage to Ben Springer. Instead, she considers for her the alternative of a life in a Gastown hotel and the possibility of a lesbian relationship with Vancouver's first madam, Birdie Stewart. When Ana chooses that alternative, Annie laments that such a choice renders her ahistoric, her married, heterosexual status having provided the ground for her being "recorded" by history. Though initially Annie reverts to the conventional insistence on the division between fictional characters and historical figures, her reflection on the fate of Ina – broken down by the demands of a patriarchal system in a (for her) foreign country – prompts her to reject the hegemony of the (f)actual and to break out of the historiographical, narrative, and sexual boundaries that constrain her. The liberation through a lesbian relationship that she has projected for Ana she ultimately decides to opt for herself.

This does not, however, render the portrait of Ana an anachronistic projection of Annie's desires, but supports the possibility of a lesbian relationship as an alternative to patriarchal, heterosexual relationships. Marlatt argues in "Self-Representation and Fictionalysis" that the imaginary is a necessary part of a life story: "Every poet knows it is, just as i know that in inventing a life for Mrs. Richards, i as Annie (and Annie isn't me though she may be one of the selves i could be) invented a historical leak, a hole in the sieve of fact that let the shadow of a possibility leak through into full-blown life. History is not the dead and gone, it lives on in us in the way it shapes our thought and especially our thought about what is possible. Mrs. Richards is a historical leak for the possibility of a lesbian life in Victorian British Columbia."[20] Thus in *Ana Historic* "researcher" and historical subject merge in a narrative that assumes the freedom of imaginative projection to be not only a justifiable option but indeed a necessary corrective to the marginalization and patriarchal inscription of women in a linear, phallocentric, male history.

Though most Canadian historical novels published more recently than *The Wars* and *Ana Historic* reflect some sort of metafictional self-consciousness, generally they do so in a much more muted and less overtly postmodern way than those novels and other predecessors like Susan Swan's *The Biggest Modern Woman of the World* and Wiebe's *The Temptations of Big Bear*. True, the fragmented, non-linear, and occasionally self-reflexive narrative of Sky Lee's *Disappearing Moon Café* is reminiscent of *Ana Historic*, and the multiple perspectives of Margaret Sweatman's *Fox* – which, Reinhold Kramer argues, "'relines' what were formerly prose documents" – bring to mind Wiebe's dialogic strategies in *Big Bear*.[21] But, for the most part, the intextextual and metafictional elements of more recent historical novels, as Robertson's *Igor* and Johnston's *The Colony of Unrequited Dreams* illustrate, are less overt and disruptive, more submerged within the fictional worlds of the texts.

If *The Wars* wavers somewhat uncertainly between its moving (re)construction of a harrowing historical era and its self-consciousness about the process of that reconstruction, Robertson's *Igor* (1989), the final volume of her *The King Years* trilogy, shows no such hesitation. Like the trilogy as a whole, it abounds with prominent Canadian historical figures and addresses some of the principal episodes of a particular era, in this case the post-war initiation of the Cold War. However, its relative lack of self-consciousness in presenting those episodes highlights, by comparison, the degree to which *The Wars* owns up to its fictional practice. The focal point of *Igor* is the defection of cipher clerk Igor Gouzenko from the Soviet embassy in 1945 with documents pointing to the existence of an elaborate Soviet espionage network in North America. The novel is set in the early 1980s with Ronald Reagan in power in America and Pierre Trudeau in power in Canada, the political atmosphere very much replaying the Gouzenko era, which is *Igor*'s primary concern. Like many historical novels, *Igor* uses a contemporary setting as the base for a sustained examination of an earlier era. Though in doing so it lacks *The Wars*' metafictional interrogation of historiographical practice, *Igor* nonetheless underlines the importance of research and, by extension, the effects of mediation and manipulation in the construction of a picture of history.

Igor has much in common with *The Wars* because of the motif of research that provides the momentum for the narrative and because both narratives pay as much attention to the researching of the past as to the past itself. *Igor*, however, lacks or rather popularizes the metafictional qualities of Findley's novel. Where *Willie* makes use of the framework and repertoire of the romance, *Igor* adopts the framework and conventions of the spy thriller. The trilogy's central figure, Lily Coolican, plays an important role in *Igor*, but the novel focuses primarily on American-born journalist and ex-hippie Jennie Hutchinson, daughter of an American atomic scientist who disappeared (presumed drowned) just before the Cuban missile crisis. Jennie is conscripted by David Garrard, an undercover CIA agent who suspects that her father is alive and well and living in Moscow, to help make a movie about Gouzenko. The narrative follows David's efforts to use Gouzenko and Jennie's father to revive Cold War tensions and Jennie's increasing scepticism about Gouzenko and other Cold War myths. With this as her premise, Robertson sets about rewriting the history of Canada's involvement in the Cold War, particularly through the novel's focus on the central and enigmatic figure of Gouzenko.

Jennie's efforts to gather information on Gouzenko take her on a hermeneutic path at once typical of the thriller but also obviously historiographical. The narrative largely consists of Jennie's engagement with a series of sources: various documents on and interviews with figures involved with Cold War politics and specifically with Gouzenko, including the Royal Commission,[22] King's memoirs, and Julius and Ethel Rosenberg's jail-house letters. Jennie's research efforts are complemented by Garrard, whose interviews with various figures and tapping of Jennie's and Lily's conversations impart a sense of intrigue and menace to the story but also some variety to the presentation of historical material. The research motif contributes to the conventional vector of the spy thriller, which is the unearthing of the "real" story, but principally Jennie's efforts provide Robertson a vehicle for commenting on the Gouzenko myth. In adopting the form of the spy thriller, Robertson concentrates on the contemporary framework of Jennie's sleuthing and does not, as in the first two volumes, provide a vivid depiction of a past era. All the same, the figure of Gouzenko is at the centre of a complex and pivotal era in Canadian history, and, just as in the previous two volumes of the trilogy, Robertson explores the political machinations of the time in considerable detail.

As the most notable figure, Gouzenko is portrayed in an unflattering light, to say the least, as Robertson chops the pedestal (largely of his own making) from under his feet. When Jennie interviews Gouzenko for the movie, she finds him paranoid and self-aggrandizing, arguing that the RCMP is saturated with Soviet spies, whom the suppression of his documents is intended to protect. His obsession with himself and his contribution, and his paranoia about retribution, are legendary. However, while the profile of Igor is constructed through Jennie's investigation and consultation of sources, that consultation is not anti-mimetic, as it is in Wiebe's story or Findley's and Marlatt's novels, but principally the pretext for revisionist history. The story of Gouzenko's defection is fleshed out by Jennie's consultation of Gouzenko's Governor-General-Award-winning novel, *Fall of a Titan*, which she dismisses as unreadable, and his ghost-written autobiography, *This Was My Choice*. Conversations with a reporter from *The Toronto Star* and with Chester Frowde, the *Ottawa Citizen* night editor who first turned Gouzenko away, put Gouzenko's defection in a less flattering light: "Gouzenko," Jennie summarizes, "was a one-man media event" (*Igor* 103). This research leads Jennie to the conclusion that Gouzenko did not have the documents when he went to the paper and may, indeed, not be whom he claims to be. Thus Jennie's consultation of sources, almost all of which are historical, synthesizes and interprets a wide range of historical material, allowing Robertson to represent the Gouzenko affair and subject it to a less heroizing treatment.

Robertson's objective goes beyond demythologizing Gouzenko personally. Jennie's research leads her to scrutinize the government's treatment of the Gouzenko affair, and through her findings Canada's role as America's Cold-War sidekick is roundly criticized. When Jennie is informed that Gouzenko's documents at the National Archives were reviewed in 1976 and restricted, she also discovers from the archivist that the commission reviewed not the original documents but presumably the translations. Jennie's reflections on the ambiguity about the documents' authenticity allow Robertson to present the commission's activities as parallel to those of the House Committee on Unamerican Activities during McCarthyism: "The people arrested and interrogated were not told of any charge against them, many of them had no legal counsel and were never shown the evidence that incriminated them. Most of the evidence was verbal testimony by Gouzenko himself, the people he accused and other witnesses" (91).

Jennie also reads the Royal Commission report, noting the discrepancies between Gouzenko's story and the evidence and remarking on the commission's willingness to "change the evidence to suit Gouzenko's story, rather than questioning the story!" (93). Jennie then editorializes on the relative innocence and lack of secrecy of the implicated spies, again evoking the spectre of McCarthy: "The 'secrets' they gave, if in fact they did, were insignificant. On the witness stand they were badgered with incriminating questions about their 'Communist sympathies.' If they refused to confess to being Communists, they were accused of being 'furtive, secretive and evasive.' Any way you lose. McCarthyism was made in Canada, and Canada has no Fifth Amendment" (93).

When the transcripts of evidence given at the inquiry are released (Gouzenko's documents remaining private), Jennie reflects that Gouzenko's testimony reads like a spy thriller and that the two judges who heard his testimony *in camera* bought it all very deferentially: "From then on everything is simple: Gouzenko is telling the truth, the people he accuses are lying" (142). Through the breathless pace of the thriller, Robertson emphasizes the government's role in the construction of a Cold-War consensus or (to appropriately take a phrase from Edward Herman and Noam Chomsky) the manufacturing of consent, with the Soviets metamorphosing overnight from allies to enemies.[23] At this point in the novel, the narrative cuts between sources with few or no narratorial interludes, Robertson's priority obviously being to develop her revisionist reading of the case. The pace and structure of the novel are reminiscent of one of Robertson's key sources for the book, John Sawatsky's oral history *Gouzenko: The Untold Story*, which consists of interviews with those who knew Gouzenko and/or were involved in the affair. The testimony is not arranged in blocks but in alternating snippets to provide a kind of chronological narrative, filling in the details from different points of view. Robertson's strategy of miming research, moving from voice to voice to present the story, very much echoes Sawatsky's decision to present *Gouzenko* as an oral history that is very much a patchwork of voices, brief accounts focused on particular stages of Gouzenko's story. At least some of *Igor*, then, reads like a condensation of sections of *Gouzenko*.

Chomsky, indeed, would probably like this book because Jennie's investigation develops into a reading of the Gouzenko affair as a cover for an American conspiracy, engineered by the CIA and British intelligence, to monopolize nuclear science in a post-war redrawing of alliances. Jennie's consultation of King's diaries plays an important role in the development of this theory. Thanks to King's obsessive and meticulous documenting of events, times, and meetings, Jennie discovers that the implications of Gouzenko's defection were processed at such a speed that the Undersecretary for External Affairs, Norman Robertson, must have known beforehand what Gouzenko had with him: "only moments after Igor's interrogation ends, Norman Robertson is able to give the Prime Minister an alarming account detailing the vast scope of Soviet espionage in North America," whereas "the documents took months to decipher, translate and interpret" (119). The effect of this account was to panic King out of his desire to sustain amicable Soviet-Canadian relations and into alerting the Americans and the British to the spy scare; Gouzenko's defection was intended to provide a cover for the fact that both had been spying on the Soviets. The pot, at times, boileth over,[24] but beneath the novel's thick intrigue is Robertson's serious intent to read post-war Canadian history against the grain.

This she does with aplomb, as *Igor* then proceeds to give the Gouzenko myth one more turn of the screw. Lily develops the hypothesis that the Soviets essentially staged Gouzenko's defection, a theory that is further developed when Lily and Jennie go to interview John Knox Buchanan, a retired diplomat writing a book debunking "the myth that Canada became a world power at a time when Canada became an American puppet" (222). The Russians, it is suggested, knew about the bomb (and therefore couldn't "steal" its secrets) and staged the Gouzenko affair to spread the conviction that they did

Igor Gouzenko on TV (detail).
"If Igor didn't exist he would have to be invented"

have the bomb, to prevent a triumphant and expansionist America from flexing its post-war nuclear muscle in the direction of Russia.

This possibility raises the spectre that, as Jennie reflects, it was "all unnecessary – the barbed wire, the ID badges, the FBI, the interrogations, the fear, the silence, McCarthy, the Cold War, the Rosenbergs, all those ruined lives" (225). The suggestion ultimately turns the Gouzenko myth completely on its head, giving a double spin to the cliché about Gouzenko that, "if Igor didn't exist he would have to be invented" (31). Ultimately, then, Jennie's implication in David Garrard's plot – which is to use Gouzenko one more time to keep Canada on side – and her desire to protect her father provide a fairly flimsy narrative skeleton on which to hang a lot of history and with which to turn the traditional politics of the Gouzenko affair upside down.

Though research is used in both novels to provide an earnestly intended rereading of significant eras in Canadian history, the differences between the role of research in *Igor* and the role of research in *The Wars* are pronounced. Findley's narrative draws attention to the process of historiographical construction in a way that highlights the function of selection, interpretation, and re-presentation, how the past is ideologically mediated in the process of research. Findley treats his sources as texts, questioning the relation between the trace of the past and the past itself, foregrounding and playing with the research process and with the distinction between fact and fiction. In *Igor* the same process is subordinated to the provision of a revisionist history that itself is not obviously subjected to scepticism. Robertson moves her narrative through a series of sources as part of the hermeneutic mission of her protagonist, representing the conveying of information as the obtaining of information and creating the illusion that what Jennie finds is the "real" story beneath the accepted public myth.

While Robertson is unapologetic about playing fast and loose with historical detail in the trilogy and raises the reader's consciousness about the ideological nature of received history, *Igor* ultimately lacks the historiographical and metafictional impact of *The Wars* and subordinates the metafictive potential of the novel to the thriller's demand for intrigue and a relentless narrative pace. Given Robertson's accomplished career as a journalist, it would be disingenuous to criticize her style for being journalistic; her priority is to tell a good story and to pack a lot of information into it, and the novel's historical revisionism is not intended gratuitously. But it might be argued that the research framework in the novel itself is a little obsessive and prevents her from telling a good story, a shortcoming compounded by a certain glibness of style and love of the wisecrack; *Igor* reads, indeed, like E.L. Doctorow's *The Book of Daniel* as revised by Groucho Marx. Findley's treatment of research is part of a clear concern with the content of the form, while research in Robertson's novel throws the emphasis on story – both that of Gouzenko-era Cold-War intrigue and that of Jennie's detective work in revisiting that era. In that respect, *Igor* represents perhaps the most popularized and naturalized example of the historical novel's foregrounding of the writing of history.

The Wars, *Ana Historic*, and *Igor* are to varying degrees historiographic, drawing attention to the process of historical research and (re)construction and underlining the biases that shape the history produced by that process. In that respect, they all make use of parodic structures, which serve, as Martin Kuester observes, to res-ituate historical material and the points of view they necessarily inscribe in a new textual environment.[25] While this structure charac-terizes all historical writing, Kuester argues, contemporary historical novels in Canada tend towards a largely revisionist and postcolonial parodic "repetition."[26] Whereas for the three previous novels such a parodic structure is largely achieved through the foregrounding of research, Wayne Johnston's *The Colony of Unrequited Dreams* achieves similar effects and addresses similar issues by being, essentially, a parodic history. In a satiric style somewhat reminiscent of *Igor*, Johnston comically presents the narrative of Newfoundland history as a struggle of contesting voices and as a symbolic but nonetheless determining influence in the lives of his protagonists.

If the boot hangs over the story of Smallwood's political career, what hangs over the novel as a whole is "the book," D.W. Prowse's monumental *A History of Newfoundland*, a narrative that Smallwood hopes to see himself enter as a historical agent and an accomplishment he hopes to repeat as a chronicler of the story of Newfoundland. Johnston facetiously conveys Smallwood's uncritical admiration of Prowse's *History*: "To me, it was as if the *History* contained, not a record of the past, but the past itself, distilled, compacted to such density that I could barely lift it" (*Colony of Unrequited Dreams* 46).[27] The latter is a swipe at Prowse's prolixity and historiographical obsessiveness (in his preface to the second edition, Prowse beams that it gives him the opportunity "to record the advance and pros-perity of the Colony during the past year"[28]). This obsessiveness is subsequently underlined when Smallwood is taken to visit the esteemed historian by his grandson Prowse, only to discover that the herculean historiographical labours of the elder Prowse have left the esteemed historian quite bonkers and a family embarrassment. Toiling under the delusion that he is still working on the first edition of the *History*, a work long completed, he fills thousands of pages with illegible writing, "as if he had advanced in his art to the point of inscrutability and now was writing for no one but himself" (49). The termination of the ideal of historiographical comprehensiveness, Johnston playfully suggests, is madness, pathological solipsism.

If *The Wars*, *Ana Historic*, and *Igor* foreground the production of history, especially through their focus on research, the role of Prowse's *History* in *Colony* foregrounds the effect of the finished product. Beyond inspiring Smallwood to ride to the rescue of Newfoundland by providing a chronicle of exploitation, "the book" also plays a piv-otal role in the shaping of Smallwood's personal and romantic

A

HISTORY OF NEWFOUNDLAND

FROM THE

English, Colonial, and Foreign Records

BY

D. W. PROWSE, Q.C.

Judge of the Central District Court of Newfoundland

WITH A PREFATORY NOTE BY EDMUND GOSSE

*WITH THIRTY-FOUR COLLOTYPES, OVER THREE HUNDRED TEXT
ILLUSTRATIONS, AND NUMEROUS MAPS*

London

MACMILLAN AND CO.

AND NEW YORK

1895

Title page of "the book"; D.W. Prowse's
A History of Newfoundland.

relationships. Prowse's *History* is the text from whose title page the individual letters are cut that make up the note precipitating Smallwood's departure from Bishop Feild and his lifelong ambivalence towards Sheilagh Fielding. Though Fielding blames her pregnancy on Smallwood, Fielding's father cuts the letters out of his copy of the *History* because he senses that the younger Prowse has hurt his daughter in some way and thus "there would have been a certain symmetry in choosing that book" (549). If both Smallwood and Fielding are battling the legacy of history, "the book" quite literally is accessory in complicating their lives. It symbolizes the intrusive presence of the narrative of the past, the cumulation of class hegemony and colonial subordination that overdetermines the circumstances in which Smallwood and Fielding encounter each other, and ultimately prevents them from realizing their mutual attraction. Thus, by being at the heart of the key intrigue in the novel, "the book" suggests the malevolent, divisive effects of history in a class-bound, colonized society.[29]

"The book" is also the narrative that Fielding parodies in her own history of Newfoundland, excerpts from which serve to counterpoint the sequences of Smallwood's autobiographical narrative. In this fashion, Prowse's *History* makes its principal contribution to what can be seen as *Colony's* postcolonial and metahistorical objectives. Fielding provides an outlet for the parodic voice that is the principal mode of Johnston's writing, evident particularly in the madcap father figures of *The Story of Bobby O'Malley*, *The Divine Ryans*, and *Human Amusements*. In *Colony*, that voice provides a crucial corrective to colonial history and Smallwood's political history. Fielding, in short, tells the story of Newfoundland and the story of Smallwood (a distinction the latter might not be inclined to make) with tongue firmly planted in cheek, both in "Field Day," her "satirical columns, so irony-laden you could not pin down her politics" (259), and in her satiric *Fielding's Condensed History of Newfoundland*.

Fielding cites Prowse's history as the dreaded precursor to her own, and her striving against it amounts to a historiographical variation on Harold Bloom's "anxiety of influence," in which every "poet is caught up in a dialectical relationship ... with another poet or poets."[30] In contrast with the reverent Smallwood, Fielding engages with Prowse in a kind of Bloomian strife, reflecting the anxiety of displacing such a formidable precursor: "That BOOK! Had we departed from this world ignorant of its existence we should have been happier than we expect to be when the final curtain falls. Little comfort is it now that upon the publication of our History all memory of his will from the minds of the reading public be erased. If not from mine. No, never from mine, unless one of the balms of heaven be amnesia" (406). With her obsessive irony, Fielding allows Johnston to play parodic historian, subverting the colonial and class biases of what might seem the pathological history of Newfoundland, a history of harshness, destitution, and crass, brutal exploitation.

Fielding underlines this history not by agreeing with Prowse's history, which dramatizes the effects of these biases, but by reversing its terms. In this respect, Fielding's writing echoes the impetus for Smallwood's – the sense that Newfoundland has never been governed in the interest of the people – although that intent is couched in a sharp and at times impenetrable thicket of irony. Moreover, given the crippling effect that that history has had on Fielding's own life, her parodic interventions amount to a kind of satiric revenge. This dimension of Fielding's *History* is evident, for instance, in her inclusion of a florid introduction by Sir Richard Squires (mimicking the verbosity of Prowse's history), for which Fielding later ironically thanks him: "We can think of no one more appropriate, or by whose kindness we could be more flattered, than Sir Richard to commend to the public a book that his record in office has inspired us to write and whose virtues, if any there be, are animated by his own" (505). (Translation: such a satiric history is made possible by the corrupt, exploitative, and hypocritical behaviour of the likes of Sir Richard.) Thus does the *History* allow Fielding (and by extension Johnston) to exact a certain amount of postcolonial justice on the figures who have dominated Newfoundland's past.

In the hilarious entries to the *History*, Fielding, through consistent ironic inversion and understatement, dramatizes England's harmful indifference to Newfoundland, the exploitative incompetence of the colonial elite, and the brutal self-interest of the merchant class. A good example of her satiric approach is the chapter entitled "Treworgie's Reign of Terror," in which Fielding parodically recounts the reformist efforts of John Treworgie, governor of Newfoundland in the mid-seventeenth century (during the reign of Cromwell) from the point of view of the fishing merchants. Prowse writes that amidst "the dreary record of wrong and oppression, Treworgie's seven years administration is the one bright spot in our history."[31] In Fielding's version, during Treworgie's reign, settlers (those who live in Newfoundland all year round) "are allotted better fishing grounds and are exempted from 'unfair' punishment by the admirals" (147), the captains of fishing boats travelling to the fishery every summer in the service of West Country merchants. Josiah Child, representing the merchants, travels to England after the restoration of the monarchy to have these injustices corrected. The efforts of the settlers to survive are portrayed as depriving the merchants of their rightful spoils, and after Child's appeal the king "is convinced that the only way to stop the exploitation of the merchants by the settlers is to depopulate the island" (149).[32]

Throughout the early chapters of Fielding's *History*, the merchants and England are implicitly depicted as effectively conspiring against any attempt to establish a sense of permanence and domestic commitment in Newfoundland. When England concedes the northeastern third of Newfoundland to the French in the Treaty of Utrecht, Fielding observes that "England can be excused for this so-called blunder, for the only people who advise against it are the settlers who have lived on the shore for years and are to be supplanted by the French, and so can hardly be expected to give an honest estimation of its worth" (169). In Fielding's version, the history of Newfoundland is a long, heroic struggle on the part of the merchant class and their supporters in the English court to resist exploitation at the hands of wily, manipulative fishermen, Catholics, and other devious upstarts. The real flavour of the merchants' behaviour, however, shows through clearly at times, such as when Fielding cites a history of Newfoundland written by the colony's chief justice in 1793, which "sets forth the thesis that England has for three hundred years been exploiting Newfoundland" (209). Fielding facetiously dismisses (and implicitly applauds) such a conclusion as the attempt of a "peevish crank ... to get back at some West Country merchants who, he said, 'are so miserly that, were I to allow it, they would be constantly contesting in my court some Newfoundlander's right to breathe their air'" (209–10).

What lies under Fielding's history is a crippling history of colonial negligence, of resistance to settlement and any form of political autonomy, and of repressive economic exploitation, dramatized all the more through Fielding's hyperbolic inversions. Fielding lauds the presence in the early 1800s of a "non-elected, governor-appointed Senate-like council consisting of six clear-sighted Protestant opponents of self-rule, with absolute powers of veto" (294), who successfully resist the diabolical reformist efforts of the newly established legislature: "What a debt is owed to these six men who stood alone against the enemies of Newfoundland, and whose only support consisted of the governor, the Colonial Office, the Privy Council, the British Parliament and the king of England. If not for them, the 1830s would have seen the Poor Relief Bill passed in spite of the opposition to it of the poor themselves, on whose behalf the merchants marched in protest through the streets" (295). Such parody underlines how history is governed by perspective and how perspective is governed by self-interest.

Through Fielding, Johnston also inscribes a scepticism about Newfoundland's relationship with Canada, both before and after joining Confederation. For example, Fielding observes of Newfoundland's attempt to effect a reciprocity treaty with the United States in 1889 – a move vetoed by the British after Canada complained – that Newfoundland's unilateral action "was clearly in contravention of Clause 6(b) of the British North America Act, which states that 'the interests of one part of British North America may not be sacrificed to those of another except when the phrase "one part of British North America" is defined as "Newfoundland"'" (489). Though Johnston's satire draws attention to the ideological filtering of history, through Fielding's parody he implicitly asserts, unlike more postmodern historiographical novelists, the "real" history of Newfoundland.

This is also the case with "Field Day," which provides Johnston with a vehicle for a parodic and more critical account of Smallwood's career and the political scene in modern Newfoundland. Fielding is far more satiric and cutting than Smallwood tends to be either towards himself or his political colleagues, a good example being the ironic account of Sir Richard Squires's near-lynching by a drunken mob, which instead is presented as a revival of the bygone custom of the Nones, a playful "chase involving the entire population" (327). Fielding's commentary, both in her capacity as journalist and in her personal relationship with Smallwood, provides a more critical perspective on him that serves as an important corrective to his, if not self-aggrandizing, at least not particularly self-critical, autobiographical narrative. For instance, she says of his support of confederation in "Field Day" that "Smallwood does not really want Confederation. He has come out in favour of it only because he believes this is the best way of ensuring its defeat. He is our truest patriot" (442).

Once Smallwood is in power, Fielding continues to take him down a peg, despite the proof of his success and his inclination toward dictatorial behaviour. Responding to Smallwood's optimism that Newfoundland "can be one of the great small nations of the earth" (513) and his habitual use of the construction "great small" to hyperbolize Newfoundland's promise (in appropriately relative terms), Fielding writes that in "one of the great small hours of the morning, it occurred to me that our forests were among the great small woods in the world, as is our premier one of the great Smallwoods in the world, not to mention one of the great small Smallwoods in the world" (514). Thus, if there is a certain amount of censoring or selectivity to Johnston's presentation of the historical Smallwood, the character of Fielding at least turns a more critical and satirical eye on the history that is presented.

This critical position, however, is modified by the way in which it is grounded in the fictive situation of *Colony*. Fielding's career as Swiftian chronicler of Newfoundland politics and history, it is progressively revealed, has been a function of her bitterness over her thwarted life, a connection that is signalled by her relative silence after her reconciliation with Smallwood. Through romantic intrigue and acerbic satire, Johnston dramatizes the distorting effect of a history that needs contesting. With her rewriting of Newfoundland's history by parodying Prowse, her parodic subversion of Smallwood's career, and the literal and metaphoric influence of "the book" in her own life, Fielding's role in the novel is very much to do unto history what history has done unto her. If the path of her life has been thwarted by history, she does her best throughout the novel to thwart history in turn, though the question remains whether she is ultimately more thwarted than thwarting.

Her reconciliation with Smallwood takes some of the lustre off her career as guerilla historian, but she nonetheless serves the purpose of repeating Newfoundland history with a difference. While *The Colony of Unrequited Dreams* is much more lighthearted and less anti-mimetic in its engagement with the writing of history than are *The Wars* and *Ana Historic*, it nonetheless serves similar purposes: to foreground the constructed and ideological nature of historical accounts; to illustrate the impact of history on the lives of individuals; and to underline how historiographical assumptions affect the shape of the narrative that is taken to be a story mirroring the past.

In *Deconstructing History*, Alun Munslow argues that deconstructive historians, self-conscious about their own practice, seek out "that which is present in the text that runs against the grain of what, at first blush, it appears to assert" and illuminate "that which is avoided and suppressed as well as that which is openly de-legitimised and denied" in historical writing.[33] While writing history is still possible, "the way in which history is interpreted and reported as a narrative is of primary importance to the acquisition and character of our historical knowledge."[34] Deconstructive history thus highlights that the implicit effect of historical discourse's illusory unity and authority is to suppress dissent and to hide the machinery of the production of history. Likewise, most contemporary historical novels in Canada strive to demythologize history, either by stepping into the picture and opening it up, like *The Wars* and *Ana Historic*, or by creating its revisionist, parodic double, as do *Igor* and *The Colony of Unrequited Dreams*. If for empiricist historians history is a given, all of these novels look this gift horse in the mouth.

Yet the differences between the latter novels and the former suggest a movement away from a more radically historiographical form. Less prevalent in the last decade or so has been what Jones has theorized as the "documentary-collage," a technique "that self-consciously transcribes documents into the literary text, registering them as 'outside' writings that recognize both as taken from a spatial or temporal 'elsewhere' and as participating in a historical-referential discourse of 'non-fiction.' The works both invoke and undermine the oppositions between categories such as textual/referential, intratextual/extratextual, literary/non-literary, or fiction/non-fiction, and thus stage a kind of documentary dialogue. The document ... is foregrounded as a strategic site of contending readings."[35] While it would be too much to argue that this relative shift marks a departure from the formal experimentation of the 1970s and early 80s and a realist retrenchment in the commodity-conscious 1990s, it would not be out of order to say that Canadian historical novels have become less experimental rather than more.

TALKING BOOKS: ORALITY AND HISTORY

"Writing created history," observes Walter Ong in his seminal study *Orality and Literacy*.[36] For Ong, historical consciousness is the product of literate cultures, and in *Orality and Literacy* he stresses the consequent differences between literate cultures and what he calls primary oral cultures. History, as a form of thinking about and conveying a sense of the past, is an extension of Ong's thesis that, without writing, "the literate mind would not and could not think as it does ... More than any other single invention, writing has transformed human consciousness."[37] Ong's anatomy of this transformation is somewhat ambivalent; he argues, on the one hand, that writing has made possible most of the intellectual, cultural, and scientific accomplishments of human civilization[38] and, on the other hand, that, as a "technologizing of the word," writing "is a particularly pre-emptive and imperialist activity that tends to assimilate other things to itself."[39]

Ong's insight that literacy has profoundly shaped modern cultures and is a formative influence on (rather than an ancillary medium of) history is shared by many contemporary Canadian novelists. If their narrative strategies are any indication, however, they seem more concerned with writing's complicity with various forms of hegemony than with its potential for various forms of accomplishment. This anxiety about literacy is a reflection of a number of things: the association of writing with the larger apparatus of imperialism and its role in Canadian history; the contemporary anxiety in both critical theory and literary practice about writing, closure, and objectification (as opposed to the contingency, flexibility, and performativity associated with oral forms); the association of writing with the closure of official history, in which historiography and historical documents become the Word of the authoritative version of the book of History; and the association of writing with an alienating modern, technological society.

Reflecting these concerns, many contemporary historical novels in Canada make use of devices that inscribe a tension between the oral and the written or counteract the apparent fixity, closure, and finality of the written through the use of oral conventions or through frame narratives that subsume the written within the oral. As with Ong's study, however, these attempts to recover the oral from beneath the palimpsest of literacy run the risk of establishing a questionable binary relationship between a privileged but primitivized orality and a literacy that is constructed as at once imperialistic and historically inevitable and desirable.

The tension between the oral and the written has been a particular concern of Rudy Wiebe's work, and *The Temptations of Big Bear* dramatizes a number of Ong's insights. Oral peoples, Ong maintains, consider words to have sacred and magical properties, a potency that "is clearly tied in, at least unconsciously, with their sense of the word as necessarily spoken, sounded, and hence power-driven." In contrast, words in literate societies "tend rather to be assimilated to things, 'out there' on a flat surface. Such 'things' are not so readily associated with magic, for they are not actions, but are in a radical sense dead, though subject to dynamic resurrection."[40] This somewhat problematic contrast between orality as dynamic and metaphysical, and literacy as objectifying and de-animating, is certainly reflected in Wiebe's novel. Big Bear's voice in particular is a sign of spiritual presence and majesty, whereas writing is predominantly a secular, mundane, objectified instrument of European colonization.

Another key idea in *Orality and Literacy* is that, unlike writing, oral speech involves a sense of immediacy and authenticity: "By contrast with natural, oral speech, writing is completely artificial. There is no way to write 'naturally.' Oral speech is fully natural to human beings in the sense that every human being in every culture who is not physiologically or psychologically impaired learns to talk."[41] Wiebe's novel certainly highlights the artifice of writing rather than its potential, suggesting that, compared to oral speech, it fosters an alienation, a sense of absence that creates a distance between the word and the source, thus giving rise to the potential for slippage or for an imperialist rewriting of the spoken. The dangers of such a distance are illustrated by the transformation of Treaty Six between the time it is signed with Governor Morris and the time that the band receives its copy, from which many of the "sweet" promises have been excised. The spoken word, by contrast, is very much bound up with its speaker, not just because of the physical presence of the speaker, but also because of the honour and responsibility that go with speaking. Orality thus is contingent, contextual, and interpersonal. The written word, in contrast, is portrayed as implacable, impersonal, monologic, and of questionable integrity. For instance, Big Bear observes of a Battleford newspaper critical of his reluctance to sign the treaty that as "long as a paper is there it speaks words whenever you want it to, and they are always the same and people believe words they hear too often."[42]

Ong subsequently qualifies this apparent critique of writing by clarifying that it is a compliment, though he does sustain the impression that writing is nonetheless more conventional, more constructed than speech: "Like other artificial creations and indeed more than any other, it is utterly invaluable and indeed essential for the realization of fuller, interior, human potentials. Technologies are not mere exterior aids but also interior transformations of consciousness, and never more than when they affect the word."[43] Somewhat similarly, *The Temptations of Big Bear*, for all its reservations about literacy, ultimately is a literate response to the request that Big Bear makes at the end of his trial: "I ask the court to print my words and scatter them among White People. That is my defence!"[44] That the contrast between orality and literacy in the novel is, of course, developed in writing creates the same sort of tension that Ong both explores and is plagued by in *Orality and Literacy* and that occurs in a number of other Canadian historical novels.

Orality's allure of authenticity is also important. Ong, for instance, qualifies his portrait of orality by noting that spoken words "do not themselves transmit an extramental world of presence as through transparent glass," but he nonetheless reflects a tendency to see writing as somehow more semiotic than speech.[45] He questions the Saussurian characterization of words as signs, arguing that this view of words, which is most prominent in "typographic and electronic cultures," tends "to reduce all sensation and indeed all human experience to visual analogues."[46] Running through *Orality and Literacy* is the implicit suggestion that orality is a kind of prelapsarian state. Ong's tendency to privilege orality as authentic, Terry Goldie argues, is symptomatic of a binaristic response to indigenous cultures, because the "split between literate and non-literate is often used as the defining point for an absolute division between white self and indigene Other."[47] Goldie contends that in Ong's account orality "represents a different order of consciousness, one which makes the indigene so clearly Other, something far more alien than simply an older, a more primitive, a more sexual, a more violent society."[48]

Furthermore, the tendency to naturalize speech in Ong's work, as well as in literary works like Wiebe's that seek to effect a fictional accommodation with the indigene, reflects "a desire for an alienation from self, an alienation which is impossible to fulfil."[49] As a result, these texts have a somewhat masochistic relation to writing: "In what would seem an impossible paradox for works which write about orality, most white texts describe writing as failing when it tries to encapsulate orality, apparently because of the inadequacy of its Ongian imperialism in the face of a vast epistemological chasm."[50] Orality, then, is clearly part of the "temptation" side of the ambivalent response of whites to indigenes that Goldie dissects in *Fear and*

Temptation, and he argues that implicit in Ong's view of orality is a primitivist desire for a state of pre-technological innocence and ultimately "a belief in a metaphysical presence."[51] Thus, while Ong's study serves as a profound reminder of how literacy is not just taken for granted but has been almost imperialistically naturalized as a discursive and ideological order, it also raises profound questions about how, from within that order, literate people view orality.

These questions are dramatized in many contemporary Canadian historical novels through narrative strategies that reflect substantial reservations about literacy and suggest a desire for recovery of the oral. If many Canadian novelists are making use of metafictive devices to foreground various aspects of the writing of history, the development of oral frame narratives can be seen as a particular kind of metahistorical strategy, one that draws attention to the troublesome association of writing and history. Jack Hodgins's *The Invention of the World*, Guy Vanderhaeghe's *The Englishman's Boy*, Wiebe's *The Scorched-Wood People*, and John Steffler's *The Afterlife of George Cartwright* in very different ways make use of oral frameworks and conventions to foreground concerns with orality, literacy, and history.

Hodgins's much-analyzed *The Invention of the World* (1977) bears revisiting in this context because of its explicit concern with oral historiography and its self-conscious, parodic depiction of the oral historian. Principally regarded as one of the most notable and successful importations of magic realist strategies into Canadian fiction, *The Invention of the World* is also a work of historical fiction, one that more humorously but no less productively explores the relationship between writing and speech in the recording of the past. Though its lack of the public figures and events characteristic of the historical novel may seem to distance it from the genre, Hodgins's novel does revolve around a fictional religious colony that gestures to a number of historical colonies whose colourful stories are a distinctive part of the history of Vancouver Island. Hodgins's narrative strategies in the novel, furthermore, certainly affiliate it with historiographic metafictional novels, particularly those that explore the relationship between the oral and the written.

The novel's concern with oral history is an offshoot of how Hodgins has chosen to tell his history "slant." Hodgins researched some historical colonies on Vancouver Island, particularly the Aquarian Foundation run by the charismatic Brother XII, but obviously decided against writing a traditional historical novel. In an interview, Hodgins notes that he originally intended to write about Brother XII but "discovered very early in my attempt at research that people didn't want to talk about it. So I couldn't get very far if I wanted to be faithful to fact."[52] Instead (according to W.J. Keith, as a result of reading a dubiously non-fictional account of the foundation by the brother of Brother XII[53]), Hodgins sets mythic discourse within a parodic and historiographical framework that problematizes both myth and history while at the same time acknowledging their force and importance.

If historical fiction enacts a kind of Bloomian anxiety of influence, *The Invention of the World*, it might be argued, amounts to a parodic Bloomian struggle between Hodgins's original vision of the book as a historical novel and the metafictional form that it ultimately took. In that sense, the figure of the obsessive chronicler Strabo Becker can be seen as Hodgins's parodic double (an appropriate effect in a novel filled with doubles). Through Becker, Hodgins parodies and foregrounds the limitations of the traditional historical novel and raises important concerns about historiography in general and oral history in particular, thematizing the unreliability of historical discourse and the mediating, distorting presence of the historian.

Becker, as ferryman, is a kind of parodic Charon, but he is also named after a Celtic historian and geographer interested in Druidic culture, an affiliation that underlines his role as a figure of the historian and writer pursuing the aim of getting at the story.[54] Becker is presented as an obsessive gatherer and chronicler, which can be seen as a humorous self-reflection of Hodgins as he might have been, writing a straightforward historical novel: "this man has pretensions. He has chosen to nest on a certain piece of this world and to make a few years of its history his own. The debris of that history is around him and he will reel it all in, he will store it in his head, he will control it; there will be no need, eventually, for anything else to exist; all of it will be inside, all of it will belong only to him. Becker wants to be God" (*Invention of the World* x). In this respect, one can see a parallel between the messianic pretensions of colony founder Donal Keneally and those of Becker – and, by extension, of the historian and novelist.

Through Becker, Hodgins signals the impossibility of getting at the real story (whether mythic, historical, or a combination of the two) and furthermore signals the perversity of the desire to do so. Hodgins's portrait of Becker as historian emphasizes that the oral is far from a guarantee of metaphysical presence or historical truth. At the beginning of the novel, Becker reflects that he "knows only this much: that the tale which exists somewhere at the centre of his gathered hoard, in the confusion of tales and lies and protests and legends and exaggerations, has a certain agreed-upon beginning" (xi). The sense of certainty suggested here, however limited, is contradicted by subsequent assertions and disclaimers. In short, Becker is not consistent in his attitude towards the truth. More importantly, however, the idea that there is a tale at the centre of the uncertainty is increasingly undermined.

As the narrator of "The Eden Swindle," which provides the story of the exodus of Keneally and his people from Ireland and the establishment of the colony, Becker prefaces his account with an image of the historian providing history through synthesis: *"Trust me or not, believe what you want, by now the story exists without us in air. I am not its creator, nor is any one man; I did not invent it, only gathered its shreds and fragments together from the half-aware conversations of people around me, from the tales and hints and gossip and whispered threats and elaborate curses that float in the air like dust"* (69). He then proceeds to narrate the story with a general sense of coherence and mythic resonance, occasionally punctuated by phrases that inject a note of uncertainty such as "They say" and "We have no way of knowing."

Though such reflections suggest that Becker has a firm grasp of the limits of historical knowledge and the real, that he can separate the historical wheat from the mythical chaff, Hodgins undermines the reliability of Becker's account by inserting obvious inconsistencies that are never reconciled. For instance, despite the fact that he is conveying an account of it, Becker observes of Keneally's destruction of his counterfeit god machine (an icon he has devised to impress the people of Carrighdoun) that the "memory of that day was never mentioned by any of them to another and was not even passed on to the following generations" and that with the death of the youngest child present, "the final trace of the day's memory was completely erased" (100). Likewise, Daniel Doherty's nephew – who is left behind to take the blame for the murder of a landlord killed for money to fund the exodus to Canada – writes a letter on the eve of his execution cursing Keneally, and Becker relays the contents even as he notes that the letter was burned by the jailor without even being opened. These "deliberate reminders of the essential deceptiveness of fiction" suggest that there is more of "invention" in Becker's account than he would care to admit.[55] The messianic Becker achieves a god-like omniscience through his possession of such knowledge, but that omniscience is foregrounded and subverted as the novel progresses.

The reflexive strategies of historiographical metafiction are turned toward oral history most openly in the "Scrapbook" section of *Invention*. Here Hodgins foregrounds and parodies historical fiction's intertextual dialogue with sources. As a book of scraps, of sources, this part of the novel gestures towards Becker's belief that one can piece together the fragments to get the story, upholding oral history's aim of preserving the past in the form of recordings of personal and private discourse. But the scraps in Becker's book are less "scraps" in the sense of fragments that contribute to the constitution of a unified, true story than "scraps" in the sense of competing attitudes to the past, skirmishes about what that story should be or whether the truth can be reached. The contingency, selectivity, unreliability, and subjectivity of historical memory is made clear from the divergence of opinion, the reluctance to comment, the sense of hyperbole, and the dismissal by some sources of other sources quoted in the scrapbook section. This historiographical mêleé highlights the way in which a source is not an unproblematic repository of the past and also highlights the importance of Becker as the agent organizing the story through his research. *The Invention of the World* thus dramatizes that oral history, as Elizabeth Tonkin cautions, "is not intrinsically more or less likely to be accurate than a written document."[56]

While some of Becker's sources confirm the mythic status of Keneally's stories, some debunk such an interpretation. Others even refuse to participate, such as Henry Burke, whose long and vehement rejection of Becker's overtures emphasizes the impact and limitations of the process of gathering information, underlining how the novel is in many ways about how Becker is *not* getting the story. Furthermore, the sources he does interview are by no means reliable. People will "do anything that comes into their stupid heads to get attention, anything at all, and I know what I'm talking about" (214), Edward Guthrie cautions Becker; then, after advising Becker that he's "a fool and more than a fool if you believe one word anybody tells you about that Keneally," he says, "listen to this, I won't bullshit you, it's the truth" (207). The scrapbook ends on a similar note of uncertainty, when Virginia Newman likewise counsels Becker, "You're wasting your time with all this, because the best you can hope for is ignorance and prejudice. None of us will ever know what really went on it that place" (216). Becker's scrapbook thus provides a good illustration of Hodgins's ambivalence towards historiography and representation, as these scraps are on one level a way of telling the story itself, a mimesis of the diverse, opinionated fragments out of which a history must be constructed, and on another level illustrate how the story that emerges from these fragments cannot be told, or at least cannot be trusted as the straight goods.

Hodgins distances the novel, however, from explicitly postmodern fiction such as that of Robert Kroetsch, arguing "I never write about anything that I don't want people to believe quite literally" and insisting that he is "not playing games with words," that is, not trying to trick or manipulate his readers.[57] He observes that a certain element of that kind of literary intellectualizing went into the writing of *Invention* but "had to be pushed aside in favour of the story teller's *instincts* and *intuitions*."[58] At the same time, Hodgins's foregrounding of oral historiography seems fairly compatible with Alan Munslow's description of deconstructionist history: "the deconstructive consciousness does not reject rationality or reason *per se*, but instead suggests that its exercise does not always result in rightness or will lead to truth. The deconstructive position does not reject historical reality but questions our access to it, our apprehension of it and, therefore, its meaning."[59]

Becker's exertions as oral historian, furthermore, are not only a failed attempt at attaining a god-like historiographic omniscience; they are also constructed as perverse and almost parasitic. As a former resident of the colony tells him, "It's an awful thing you're doing, digging up other people's pasts, rooting around in dirt like an old hog" (176). Just how awful is underlined in "The Wolves of Lycaon." In this section, Becker's series of interviews with Lily Hayworth foregrounds the mechanism of research, the ambivalent relationship between researcher and source, and the ambiguous relationship between source and story. Oral history, Stephen Caunce insists, "is a two-way process, giving something to a contributor as well as the researcher, and requiring something from the collector as well as the contributor." However, an occupational hazard of oral historians is that they run the risk of colonizing "the history they uncover": "The tape recorder should not be used to set oral historians apart as a group with special skills, and so promote the process of takeover. If they act as friends and enablers they can help the possessors of the original knowledge to realise the significance of their own wealth and help prevent these vast new historical territories becoming the exclusive possessions and empires of remote scholars."[60] "The Wolves of Lycaon" foregrounds Becker's obsession with the story, his almost necrophilic pursuit of the past, and his inability, ultimately, to get it.

Lily's self-consciousness as a historical source highlights some of the limitations of oral history, especially the effect of the intrusion of the historian or researcher. Her reflections on her account underline the unreliability of oral history and the principle that objects change their behaviour under scrutiny: "I just talk like me until I start talking into this machine and start thinking about what I'm saying, and then it doesn't sound like me talking any more. Maybe it's because I can see it, laid out on a page, when you get at it with that typewriter of yours. Then I think, maybe that's the way I talked *then*, maybe people don't talk the same way all their lives any more than they look the same way all their lives" (251). The presence of Becker and his recording machine creates in her an almost paralyzing self-consciousness, while at the same time she is tickled by "the way that little thing is gathering me up" (261). Even though she recognizes that she could lie and Becker would not know the difference, the fact that she is being recorded prompts her to tell the truth: "It already unsettles me enough to think that after I'm gone that tape is capable of telling this stuff over and over again without me here to explain it or correct it, so I'd never be able to stand it, thinking this was an out-and-out lie recorded on it forever" (261). One effect of the oral historian's transcription, then, is to fix and frame the account, taking it out of context, out of the possibility of dialogue, supplementation, explanation. Tonkin argues that a common fallacy hold by literate people, resulting from the transcription of oral narratives, is that oral tellers are "talking books."[61]

Lily's reservations here bring to mind Ong's arguments that writing, particularly print, not only decontextualizes and objectifies words, but in doing so also intensifies individualism and private ownership: "By removing words from the world of sound where they had first had their origin in active human interchange and relegating them definitively to visual surface, and by otherwise exploiting visual space for the management of knowledge, print encouraged human beings to think of their own interior conscious and unconscious resources as more and more thing-like, impersonal and religiously neutral. Print encouraged the mind to sense that its possessions were held in some sort of inert mental space."[62] Following Ong, it can be argued that Becker's personal obsession with Keneally's history provides a fictional and historiographical demonstration of the shift from communal interchange to private introspection in literate societies.

Lily's imagery suggests that Becker's historiographical activities of taping, editing, and transcribing are parasitic and the equivalent of the fates measuring and cutting human lives. She repeatedly portrays Becker as a spider, pulling threads of narrative or sucking the juices out of those he interviews. Hodgins underlines this parasitism when Lily, still plagued by Becker during her illness, points out the selfish, voyeuristic quality of Becker's labours: "Don't you ever talk about yourself, Becker, don't you ever give anything of yourself away? Or are you only like your little black box, pulling in all the world and giving it back nothing more than itself?" (275). To her surprise, however, Lily discovers that although the tape "had pulled it out of her and gathered it up, she hadn't been left without. She'd been left with it all ... Your own life, stored in a pulpy brain, its own souvenir" (274). Though this suggests that being interviewed has helped Lily consolidate her memory of the past, the section ends on an ambiguous note that undermines any thought that what Lily has told Becker is the truth. As she sits in the house, hearing the ghost of Keneally rummaging around below, Lily resists alerting Becker, who has essentially been rubbing her nose in the dirt of the past: "She would tell him, instead, about the wolves of Lycaon. It wasn't much, but it was as close, now, as she dared to come, and for a while it would make him suspect there was meaning after all in her vision. Not that she had any intention, ever, of commenting on its truth" (284).

If Becker's lust for the past is both messianic and ghoulish, at the end of the novel he does, like Wade Powers and Maggie Kyle, come to terms with his search. During the trip to Ireland described in "The Pilgrimage," Becker is still eager to find some "revelations," some signs of the presence of the mythic, some confirmation of the story he has put together. Yet, as he completes the circle of Keneally's life by scattering his ashes on the hill, he concedes the uncertainty of his knowledge of the past by observing that myth, "like all the past, real or imaginary, must be acknowledged ... Even if it's not believed. In fact, especially when it's not believed. When you begin to disbelieve in Keneally you can begin to believe in yourself" (314). This observation prefigures Maggie's subsequent search for her home in the north and her return to her colony, which represents a kind of accommodation with rather than enslavement to the past.

Likewise, on the flight home, Becker scribbles in his notebook further words of wisdom that underline some of the novel's key themes: "*Words only nibble at reality, don't really touch it, can't really burn through to it. Symbols not much better. If words won't do, and symbols fail, maybe only the instinct, some kind of spiritual sense, can come close. All we can trust. Maybe all our lives that instinct is in us, trying to translate the fake material world we seem to experience back into pre-Eden truth, but we learn early not to listen. Instead, we accept the swindle, eat it whole*" (319–20). While such an observation seems to undercut the validity of his enterprise, it underlines a strain of idealism in the novel and also provides a reflection on Keneally's messianism and Maggie's attempts to make more of life than it handed her in the first place.

That Becker has gained such wisdom about his role is reflected in his comments at the beginning of "Second Growth," which he calls a "true story" despite all its hyperbole and magic realist elements. These comments recall the opening to "The Eden Swindle" and signal Becker's concession of the ultimate elusiveness of the story: "*Believe what you want, trust me or not, this story exists independent of both of us.*

Donal Keneally is dead. His story has returned to the air where I found it, it will never belong to me, for all my gathering and hoarding" (339). Thus through Becker, as a parodic double of the historian and the historical novelist, Hodgins conveys his recognition of the impossibility, not of telling the story, but of telling the true story.

Hodgins thus foregrounds the problematic relationship between the oral and the written and suggests that writing transforms and distorts the oral. However, he does not use the figure of the oral historian to suggest that the spoken word is any more reliable than the written, and he is as sceptical about the validity of oral history as he is about literacy's ability to capture it. In this respect *The Invention of the World* differs from *The Englishman's Boy*, *The Scorched-Wood People*, and *The Afterlife of George Cartwright*, which likewise foreground the problems of literacy and history by inscribing oral cultural frames and/or oral narrators. The relationship between the oral and the written in all three novels is much more uneasy than in *The Invention of the World*, a tension which has everything to do with the fact that the oral cultures they address are those of native people.

If *The Englishman's Boy* deals with the same cultural conflicts and the same era in the history of the West as *The Temptations of Big Bear*, it also raises similar concerns about the relationship between the oral and the written, particularly through the relationship between the various levels of narrative in the novel. Harry Vincent's narrative is a retrospective view, chronicling Harry's experiences in Hollywood some thirty years later, after his return to Saskatoon. Harry's narrative in turn "contains" Shorty's story, which is conveyed to Harry verbally. The segments of Shorty's narrative, however, which alternate in contrapuntal fashion with segments of Harry's first-person narrative, are presented as a third-person-omniscient narration, describing Shorty's arrival in Fort Benton, his journey north in the company of the wolfers, and his involvement in the Cypress Hills Massacre.

The source of this very literate and literary narrative, in which Vanderhaeghe creates a strong sense of verisimilitude and immediacy and makes use of an elaborate figurative repertoire, is generally ambiguous. Occasional stylistically colloquial focalizations from the perspective of the Englishman's boy approximate a first-person narration consistent with Shorty's lingo and help establish the connection between the two characters. Otherwise, that this is the story that Shorty tells Harry can be deduced from occasional connections between Shorty's comments and the Englishman's boy's reflections. It can also be deduced from the sequence at the ranch house during which Shorty is described telling the story, since it is Shorty narrating rather than Shorty's narration as such that is represented: "He knew exactly what he wanted to say and would frequently request me to read back to him what I had written in my shorthand notes" (*Englishman's Boy* 204). Thus Shorty's story is presented predominantly in the detached voice of third-person historical realism rather than as an explicitly subjective and oral account.

The rhetorical and artistic purposes of such a strategy seem fairly evident. That narrative voice balances Harry's first-person narrative and also permits Vanderhaeghe a stylistic freedom that depicting the Englishman's boy's history consistently in Shorty's pithy, colloquial register (wonderfully rich and concise though it is) would not. The strategy, however, provides an interesting study in alternative deconstructionist approaches to history. Shorty's story is narrated in a fashion that generally effaces the origin and the subjectivity of the account and furthermore contrasts it with Damon Ira Chance's openly distorting and imperialist reading of it in his film. This suggests that Harry at least, and presumably Vanderhaeghe as well, wants Shorty's version to ring true. Nonetheless, the foregrounding of perspectives on history in the novel, particularly because of the implicit contrast between this version and Chance's reactionary revisionism in his rewriting of Shorty's story in his film *Besieged*, draws attention to history as the site of competing constructions of the past. The narrative's bypassing of Shorty as the source of this history and the transformation of oral testimony into a written account thus create a tension between the illusion of immediate access to the past and the foregrounding of history as the site of ideological struggle.

In a similar vein, Harry's "transcription" of Shorty's account raises questions of appropriation that are central to Vanderhaeghe's critique of the Hollywood machine, which is addressed in the next chapter. But through the story that frames Harry's and Shorty's stories Vanderhaeghe also raises concerns about colonial appropriation very similar to those raised by *Big Bear*. Those two narratives are "contained" within the telling of Fine Man and Broken Horn's making off with the wolfers' horses at the opening of *The Englishman's Boy* and their triumphant return to their camp at the end of the novel. These framing segments are narrated from within an ostensibly indigenous discourse reminiscent of Wiebe's novel. Like Wiebe, Vanderhaeghe strives to simulate the perspective and cultural assumptions of his native characters rather than subscribing to the traditional Western's depiction of the Indian as incomprehensibly, incoherently barbaric. Nonetheless, these sections are presented through an authoritative, detached, third-person-omniscient narration and not evidently subjectivized as the perspective of a particular character, raising reservations similar to those that have been voiced about Wiebe's novel.

Thus the frame story of *The Englishman's Boy* likewise potentially represents a questionable containment of Assiniboine culture within the discourse of a white writer, particularly because the concerns of the framing segments overlap with those of the narratives for which they serve as bookends. Fine Man seeks to honour Strong Bull, a holy man who has been discredited because he has taken to drawing pictures of his people with the white man's "drawing sticks" so that "the grandchildren will recognize us" when "they pass into the Mystery World" (331). This concern with textual recording and memory runs throughout the rest of the book, and its colouring of the ending of the novel raises interesting questions about the relationship between orality and literacy. Indeed, Shorty, reluctant to give Harry the Indians that Chance wants for his epic Western, compares writing to imprisonment: "I'd guess you lock a wild Indian up between the covers of a book, same thing is going to befall him. He's going to die" (145). Furthermore, the focus on Strong Bull's drawing provides a somewhat ambivalent ending: Fine Man's triumph over the wolfers is modified by Strong Bull's somewhat ominous vision of change, which includes the increasing influence of whites, the disappearance of animals, and the diminishing of tribal memory.

However, given the subversion of the imperialism of the Western that Harry's and Shorty's narratives effect, it is important to stress how the frame story serves to subvert the usual ending of the Western (in which the whites are victorious and the Indians vanquished) and to resist the perspectival closure typical of the Western, in which the "possibility of sympathetic identification with the Indians is simply ruled out by the point-of-view conventions; the spectator is unwittingly sutured into a colonialist perspective."[63] In Vanderhaeghe's novel, the whites' narratives are instead contained within the story of a successful coup on the part of the two Assiniboine and of the realization of Fine Man's power dream. Thus, while it might be tempting to read Vanderhaeghe's use of the frame story as appropriative artifice, as a yoking of the oral for the purposes of the literate that repeats the colonization it seeks to decry, such a reading, I think, unproductively effaces what literacy paradoxically requires: making use of literate strategies to dramatize the negative effects of a literate culture. In its engagement with colonialism and the writing of history, then, *The Englishman's Boy* illustrates what a significant and complicated consideration orality is in the writer's choice of narrative strategies, with one hand taking back in terms of deconstructive efficacy what it gives with the other.

The same might be said of John Steffler's *The Afterlife of George Cartwright* (1992), a novel about the experiences in Labrador of eighteenth-century explorer George Cartwright. One hundred and seventy years after his death in 1819, the spectral Cartwright still haunts (and hunts) the fields of Nottinghamshire. Though time still passes, Cartwright himself is no longer subject to the flux of history. For him, "the past and the present are elusive background phenomena, subject to occasional capture"; that is, he is able "at times to tune in a detail from either the past or the ongoing course of time and, by concentrating on it, become witness to some event in the affairs of the dead or the living" (*Afterlife* 3). As the title of the novel hints, *Afterlife* is narrated by Cartwright from beyond the grave, suspending the rationalist expectations of empiricist historiography and problematizing the narrative as a written history.

This, however, is a familiar technique, having been employed in Wiebe's *The Scorched-Wood People*, and an exploration of Wiebe's treatment of the conflict between orality and literacy through this device provides a useful point of comparison with *Afterlife*. Wiebe's account of the rise and fall of the Métis nation is narrated in the voice of the Métis bard Pierre Falcon, a controversial strategy that, as W.J. Keith rightly observes, is "the crucial aesthetic issue in the novel."[64] Falcon, as a Métis, is unsurprisingly sympathetic to Riel and to the fate of the Métis nation.[65] He thus provides "a representation of the spirit of all the Métis," and his account is "less a meticulous account of what happened than a comprehensive presentation of what the Métis see as having happened."[66] As a celebrated Métis bard, furthermore, Falcon brings oral conventions and an oral sensibility to the story of Riel and the Métis, highlighting, as in *Big Bear*, the cultural and political differences that underscore the relationship between orality and literacy. As Tonkin argues, "oracy implies skilled production, and its messages are transmitted through artistic means. An oral testimony cannot be treated only as the repository of facts and errors of fact."[67] Thus oral strategies help to realign history with artistry rather than science.

These motives, of course, are complicated by the fact that Falcon is not a realistic choice as narrator, having died in 1876 before many of the events he narrates transpired, most notably the second Métis uprising. Wiebe thus recruits him as a spectral narrator, singing of Riel from beyond the grave. This seems appropriate since the historical Falcon's song about McDougall, "the Misfortunes of an Unlucky 'King,'" the last he composed, was printed in the first issue of the provisional government's newspaper, *The New Nation*, and was considered "'la Marseillaise' of the Métis" during the second uprising – so in that sense Falcon was there in spirit.[68] Nonetheless, such a strategy obviously demands a certain suspension of disbelief from the reader, and if George Woodcock's reaction is any indication, that cooperation is not always going to be forthcoming; in his review of the novel, Woodcock complains that "the idea of his [Falcon's] continuing as a spectral narrator strains one's credence to the wrenching point."[69] Yet it is quite obviously Wiebe's intention to test credence in the novel, and the choice of Falcon seems very consistent with Wiebe's religious, political, and historiographical intentions.

Falcon's presiding from beyond the grave gives an important historical (and historiographical) scope to the novel and a certain continuity to the whole history of the Métis nation's struggle for self-determination as a people. Historiographically, Falcon's spectral status justifies access to events, explaining the presence of a fairly complete inventory of historical evidence and other capacities of an omniscient narrator, but it also accounts for the interpretation of that evidence from a perspective sympathetic to Riel and the Métis. Beyond this familiar historiographical function, Falcon's spectral status allows Wiebe to imbue his narrative with a definite anachronistic scope. As Coral Ann Howells nicely puts it, Falcon's story "is bound by historical inevitability, for it is told after the future has already happened."[70] Falcon knows what's coming, and there are all sorts of analepses and prolepses that project an aura of inevitability, repetition, and tragedy onto the story. However, though there are parts of the narrative in which Falcon is looking back at events from a hundred years later, conscious of the subsequent fate of the Métis, this anachronistic position is marked by a resistance to historical closure rather than by a confirmation of it; Falcon underlines the persistence of Métis identity and the legacy of Riel, reminding readers that the book of history has by no means been closed on the Métis.

That Falcon's narration, however, is not a homogeneous, consistent, "oral" one complicates things. As various critics have observed, beyond the issue of the credibility of a spectral narrator, the very heterogeneity and omniscience of Falcon's narration raises doubts about the success of the technique.[71] As narrator, Falcon vanishes and reappears in a fashion that is not likely to strike readers as particularly spectral. Furthermore, while many passages are clearly tied to his perspective, much of the narrative sounds like that of the revisionist, historically informed Rudy Wiebe presenting his "take" on the Riel "rebellions." Especially in the wake of Big Bear, however, it is unwise to think that this is the work of a writer who has forgotten who is doing the talking, but clearly an effect of Wiebe's interest in dialogism and his resistance to a "straight" fictional history. In approaching the story of Riel, Wiebe does not juxtapose different discourses as starkly as in the earlier novel, but neither does he thoroughly submerge that heteroglossia within Falcon's monologic perspective (as would easily have been possible).[72]

Embedded in the novel, Penny van Toorn argues, is a hierarchy of voices characterized by a series of significant struggles or relationships.[73] The most important relationship in this hierarchy is, of course, Wiebe's presentation of Riel. Having Falcon as narrator clearly provides a crucial mediating voice between the writer and Riel; this way, whatever support or critique of Riel the novel provides can, in theory, be attributed to Falcon rather than Wiebe. Such a sense of attribution, however, is quite rare in the novel. Furthermore, as van Toorn argues, Wiebe's voice dominates this hierarchy and stands in an obviously advantageous position when situating Riel's voice dialogically within the novel's panoply of voices: "Wiebe supports Riel's political cause but cannot condone his lapses into physical violence. Wiebe therefore puts two distinct languages into the mouth of his protagonist: a language of peace and love which enjoys Wiebe's full authorial endorsement, and a language of hatred and violence against which Wiebe levels his condemnation."[74] Certainly there is merit to van Toorn's argument that the end result, as in *Big Bear*, is that this heteroglossia is recuperated into a monologic, Mennonite, pacifist vision.[75] Yet, despite the presence of Falcon as narrative repository, the array of voices and the general reticence of the narrator put the reader in the similar position of having to assess the merits of the various voices, to recognize embedded in those voices the different world views and political necessities coming into conflict.

Of more considerable importance is the tension between orality and literacy that *The Scorched-Wood People* enacts perhaps even more problematically than *The Temptations of Big Bear*. Through Falcon, as through Big Bear, Wiebe suggests the substantial distance between an oral culture and a literate culture, but the account of the rise and fall of a primarily oral culture takes a very literary form. On the one hand, this is no surprise; *The Scorched-Wood People* is a novel, after all. Clearly it seems ingenuous to fault Wiebe for a failure of verisimilitude or credibility in his construction of Falcon as narrator. It is intended as a narrative innovation that presumes the suspension of realistic expectations and obviously permits an important historical omniscience, but a mystical rather than empirical one.

On the other hand, however, Wiebe's flouting of realism in his choice of an oral framework for the novel raises some troubling questions. Through Falcon as narrator, Wiebe emphasizes the difference in historical perspective and the continuity of memory between the Métis and the literate, European culture increasingly encroaching upon them. Nonetheless, there is a certain discursive tension between what we might assume to be the "voice" of Pierre Falcon – as suggested by Wiebe's representation of his voice (those instances in which Falcon seems to be speaking in a very personal manner) and by the language of the historical Pierre Falcon's songs – and the fundamentally literate historiographical consciousness that prevails in so much of the narrative. For instance, a strange effect is created when Wiebe interrupts the scene in which Falcon sings his ballad of King MuckDougall to have Falcon narrate Riel's interview with the dying Governor Mactavish. Falcon, who has been interacting with his audience in a fashion typical of the oral storyteller or bard, is suddenly called upon to assume the voice of the omniscient historical narrator, an interlude that highlights the jarring contrast between Falcon's disparate functions.

That this contrast is an effect not only of tone but also of capability is evident in Falcon's assessment of Macdonald's decision about Riel's fate: "I know of no historian who has commented on this to say the least strange legal distinction that the men who shot and killed Canadian soldiers only *intended* to wage war while Riel, whom no witness had ever seen with anything more than a cross or a pen in his hand, that he and he alone had actually waged war" (*Scorched-Wood People* 316–17). The passage suggests the "tremendous store of historical, psychological and other knowledge which can go into sophisticated narrative and characterization today" that Ong argues is a product of literacy, of "technologies of the word [that] do not merely store what we know [but] style what we know in ways which made it quite inaccessible and unthinkable in an oral culture."[76] The elaborate phrasing and the assumption of historiographical comprehensiveness seem out of place coming from an oral Métis bard; their very literacy does more than "stretch the credence."

The oral and the literate, in short, coexist uneasily in Falcon's narration, which is problematic given how they are at the forefront of the political and cultural clashes the narrative describes. Written words, as in *Big Bear*, are associated with finality, inflexible rationalism, and violence. Literacy – particularly but not exclusively that of the bureaucratic apparatus of colonization – is associated with finality, closure, and monologism, and is effectively alien to the Métis world, even to the highly literate and articulate Riel. Thus the choice of Falcon as narrator and his self-conscious reflections on the form of his art serve to destabilize the novel as a written account of history. Falcon makes numerous references to how oral imperatives limit his ability to chronicle the fate of the Métis nation and, in short, suggests that he is unable to be the narrator of the narrative over which he presides. The key passage reflecting this paradox follows Riel's description of his epiphany – his vision of his mission for his people – in St Patrick's cathedral in New York. In a lament that very much underlines the importance of the oral framework in contributing to the contemporary implications of the novel, Falcon explains that he has presented Riel's experience in Riel's own words because his prayers for a vision of a song for Riel have not been answered. He denies his ability to celebrate Riel's achievement in traditional oral form and yet implicitly underlines the persistence and importance of Riel's achievement in sustaining Métis identity through the troubles of the ensuing century (140–1).

The questioning of Falcon's status as narrator underlines, furthermore, the centrality of Wiebe's narrative strategy to what is perhaps the key theme of the novel: the importance of faith. While it seems banal to say that it takes an act of faith to accept Falcon as narrator, such an act of faith takes on greater significance in a narrative in which belief is constantly at issue: belief in the Catholic church, belief in Riel as a prophet, belief in the possibility of a Métis nation. As the Métis put their belief on the line to defend Batoche, Falcon reflects on Riel's encouragement of his people to make their own decisions, determine their own destiny, even if it means rejecting the authority of the priests; in doing so, Falcon quite clearly dramatizes the issue of his own narration:

how can I sing this sad, last act of our people when I found my greatest strength at the altar of our merciful Lord in St. Francois Xavier and when I died was buried with the full blessing of Holy Mother Church and every priest within two days' travel? The word and understanding is very near you: you need no revelation from beyond the grave; as our Jesus said when he was on earth, if you will not believe what is already discernible on earth, then neither will you believe that which comes extraordinarily from beyond.

The word and understanding are ancient: if with all your hearts you truly seek God, you will surely find him. (284)

Here Falcon reflects on the importance of the power of belief in assessing the significance of Riel, the religious and political self-determination of the Métis, and the validity of Falcon's narration of the history of the Métis nation. In this respect, Falcon's exhortations, an expression of his values as a Métis bard, underline what Marie Vautier sees as a very postcolonial resistance, implicit in the renewed emphasis on storytelling, to the rationalist and empiricist conventions of Eurocentric historiography.[77]

Yet it is ultimately a compromised resistance, as the Biblical resonances of the passage suggest. Van Toorn argues that while "Falcon's immersion in the Métis life-world acknowledges the cultural and historical relativity of all human truths," Wiebe essentially deploys him to convey an ultimately ahistorical truth: "When Falcon speaks from ground-level, Wiebe implicitly concedes that human constructions of meaning are always provisional, products of ongoing historical processes of social struggle and communal discovery. Yet through the posthumous, extra-historical voice of Falcon, Wiebe can imaginatively transcend the perceptual limitations of all who remain bound within the contingent historical world, where truth can only be discovered dialogically. Falcon's post-historical omniscience, his view from beyond the grave, works rhetorically to dehistoricize, and hence authorize, truths which Wiebe believes to be absolute and eternal."[78]

Furthermore, if belief is one way of reconciling Falcon as narrator to the narrative that he presides over, the oral and the literate still coexist uneasily, and "the word" (however ancient) that prevails in the novel is the written word. Literacy ultimately wins out, determining the terms in which a decolonizing revisionist history of the West must take place, not only through the narrative voice that dominates the novel – that of a literate modern historian – but also through Riel's own obsession with recording his people's history in words: "who would hear them if he did not speak, did not write, write?" (80). To this degree, The Scorched-Wood People more than The Temptations of Big Bear accords with Ong's appreciation of literacy, with the idea that "without writing, human consciousness cannot achieve its fuller potentials, cannot produce other beautiful and powerful creations. In this sense, orality needs to produce and is destined to produce writing."[79] Ong's characterization of oral cultures pining for literacy is problematic to say the least, and Goldie critiques it as reflective of a "historicist sensibility" that "assesses non-writing as transitional, not essential."[80] But for Riel in Wiebe's novel, literacy is less an attraction than a necessity, a defense against a numerically superior and imperialistic literate culture's efforts to quash his people. This concession to literacy in The Scorched-Wood People is perhaps consistent with the tragic tenor of the novel as a whole, which like Big Bear records the inevitable overwhelming of an oral culture.

However, the enacting of that inevitability within a written narrative – which, as Ong argues, represents a displacement and refiguring of oral consciousness – that is ostensibly that of a celebrated Métis bard creates an inescapable ironic tension in the novel.[81] Much as Wiebe makes use of narrative tactics to reflect (to use van Toorn's key phrase) "the historicity of the word" and of racial, political, and religious identity, that historicity is figured through a writing of the oral. The novel thus exemplifies what Ong sees to be the paradox of literate critiques of literacy: "Once the word is technologized, there is no effective way to criticize what technology has done with it without the aid of the highest technology available. Moreover, the new technology is not merely used to convey the critique: in fact, it brought the critique into existence."[82] Thus it can be argued that in *The Scorched-Wood People* Wiebe provides a fundamentally (though far from fatally) paradoxical defense of orality. In his depiction of a literate culture's conquest of a substantially oral culture, he problematically appropriates Falcon as a figure of the oral only to displace him, to use him as the vehicle for a fairly monologic and thoroughly literate revisionist history of the rise and fall of the Métis nation.

Steffler's use of a spectral narrator in *The Afterlife of George Cartwright* is certainly reminiscent of Falcon's role in *The Scorched-Wood People*, but Steffler employs the device to very different postcolonial and historiographical ends. Providing Cartwright with an ambiguous, solitary "afterlife" affords the narrative an omniscient perspective similar to that of Wiebe's novel: it is anachronistic, and for the most part the presence of the narrating subject is minimal. But because *Afterlife* is an autobiographical history rather than the history of a people, the spectre of Cartwright hovers over the narrative much more significantly than does Falcon in *The Scorched-Wood People*. By recruiting Cartwright as posthumous narrator and constructing a bigger picture around excerpts from the historical Cartwright's journal, Steffler draws attention to the selectivity of written history, providing an interesting but also troublesome revisionist portrait of Cartwright.

Though the spectral Cartwright has the ability to zero in on any point in time, he gravitates much more to the past than to the present, particularly to the events of his stays in Labrador. This preoccupation provides the pretext for a roughly chronological rendering of Cartwright's history – including his family's economic woes and his disaffection with his career in the military, which preface his embarking for Labrador. But it is also the result of Cartwright's experiences in and impact on Labrador, which he returns to obsessively out of a sense of lack of closure. Even in death he continues to write in his journal, hoping "that some insight, some as yet unthought thought or unremembered memory is needed to complete his life and allow him to get on with his death. He feels certain that where he is now cannot be the end" (61). This conveys the idea that Cartwright is a tormented soul, stuck in a sort of limbo – his "ghost haunt[ing] the English countryside until it gains an awareness of its own wrongdoings."[83]

The source of Cartwright's unease seems to be a sense of guilt over his past actions – a sense of guilt that sets the portrait of Cartwright apart from Wiebe's Franklin, Bowering's Vancouver, and Wharton's

Sexsmith. Cartwright's "afterlife" is steeped in regret: regret over the loss of his Labrador empire to an American privateer and the lack of achievement of his dreams (which leads him to "finish" his journal by recording what he planned to do as if it actually happened); regret over his failed relationship with his housekeeper/mistress, Mrs Selby, whose adultery he responds to with hypocritical and stern authority; regret over his wanton slaughtering of animals; and, most of all, regret over his decision to take a group of his Inuit friends to London – which leads to the death not only of almost the whole group but also of the rest of their community when Cartwright's lover Caubvick refuses to give up her smallpox-infested hair. Cartwright's spectral retrospective, in short, allows him to reconsider his actions, and his sense of torment suggests that they are found wanting.

In a manner reminiscent of Wiebe's *A Discovery of Strangers*, *Afterlife* questions the customarily celebrated colonial attributes through a subversive dialogue with verbatim excerpts from Cartwright's journal, in which those attributes are subject to less critical scrutiny. But, taking a page out of *The Scorched-Wood People*, Steffler has the spectral Cartwright himself conduct the retrospective assessment of his accomplishments and decisions. What gets emphasized instead of colonial achievement is the essential destructiveness of Cartwright's presence in Labrador. Cartwright's love of hunting serves as the most obvious manifestation of this destructiveness. He exhibits an almost primeval thirst for the hunt that goes well beyond what is necessary for providing for his little colony and in numerous instances engages in rampant slaughter, most notably when he comes upon a pool teeming with polar bears and wantonly shoots as many as he can.[84] His hawk, Kaumalak, serves as an extension of Cartwright's blood-thirstiness; he has "made her specialize in the business of slaughter" whereas in "the wild she would kill only enough to feed herself and her young." Looking back from his perch outside of time, he sees himself as infantile, prelapsarian, in his bestiality and wonders "Who, if not God, is to blame for making monsters like me?" (268). Later, he laments "that I should have learned to worship instead of slaughter," because the "things we most love to kill we ought to worship most passionately" (284). Unlike Falcon, who is a relatively passive narrative repository, Cartwright, in his position as narrator, is posthumously forced to reconsider his identity.

Cartwright's meditations on his treatment of Mrs Selby are likewise tinged with remorse, not just because of the questionable justice of his dismissal of her, but also because of the justice of her criticisms of his imperial loyalty. An incredibly repressed presence in the historical Cartwright's journal, Mrs Selby is recruited by Steffler to exact a fictional, dialogic revenge.[85] One of Cartwright's principal failings in Mrs Selby's eyes is that Cartwright clings to an English sense of order in establishing and maintaining his empire in Labrador, despite his disaffection with the military for undervaluing him and overlooking him for promotion. Instead, as Mrs Selby encourages him, he would probably prosper by being more independent. "Your pious loyalty is neither honest nor handsome" (124), she admonishes him, emphasizing that being more genuinely self-interested would be more conducive to survival in such an isolated outpost of empire. Indeed, Cartwright's insistence and authority ultimately cost him his empire when he is stripped of his possessions by the privateer John Grimes and abandoned by most of his people in favor of the liberty that Grimes, in comparison with Cartwright, seems to represent.

Like Robertson's Lily and Johnston's Fielding, Mrs Selby questions the politics of a male historical figure and serves to subject his portrait to subversive scrutiny. In the process she highlights the self-serving selectivity and bias of autobiographical historical documents, emphasizing the omissions and distortions of written texts. Halfway through his narrative, Cartwright records in his journal that he has received "a most unexpected and shocking affront" – that Mrs Selby has been reading and writing in his journal – and warns her in writing "to remember your place" (157). After she ignores this admonition in the cause of "bring[ing] greater balance and truth to your account of events" (157), Cartwright confronts her verbally and insists, "stop tampering with my journal!" Mrs Selby, who finds nearly no mention of herself in the journal, retorts, "Mr. Cartwright, I want you to stop tampering with the truth!" (158) and points out the journal's omissions and self-serving interpretation of events. Thus Steffler employs Mrs Selby to open up Cartwright's journal (literally and figuratively) to dialogic scrutiny, emphasizing what lies outside the written and by extension what lies within and destabilizing the rigidity of Cartwright's colonial perspective.

Mrs Selby also questions Cartwright's attitude toward the Inuit. She is sceptical about his belief in his civilizing effect on them and openly objects to his exploitation of them through trade. In this respect, however, Cartwright is portrayed much more ambivalently than are Franklin, Vancouver, and Sexsmith in the other novels. Before meeting the Inuit, Cartwright displays a similar imperial megalomania; he hopes "to capture some, to convince them by force of his peaceful intentions, and, as a result, become famous as the man who led them out of their savage obscurity" (109). However, while he is often imperious and condescending, Cartwright is depicted as much more genuinely admiring of the Inuit and their ways. He takes

Caubvick as his lover and says of his friend Attuiock after his death, "I never loved a man more than him" (236).

Cartwright's attitude towards the Inuit comes closer, perhaps, to the kind of mediator Alan Lawson sees in the figure of the settler.[86] Before the initial contact, he reflects on "the idea of mating his culture and country to theirs, bringing the two continents into contact, with himself as the bridge," and he expends considerable effort to this end. Yet he finishes that same reflection with the thought that "[p]erhaps he could become their great leader" (102), and this sense of superiority and megolamania compromises the cultural exchanges between them. He is, in short, unable to let go of the primacy of English culture, and his stewardship of his Inuit charges ultimately proves fatal. Having exposed them to smallpox by taking them to London, Cartwright has the opportunity to allay the destructive effects of the trip by throwing Caubvick's hair into the sea. However, he balks at Caubvick's insistence that, in exchange, she come live with Cartwright and Mrs Selby, an ultimately fatal moment of timidity and guilt: "He wanted to handle her gently, not rob her of what little she had left" (21).

This cowardice provides the keenest sense of regret, as it is his most conspicuous – and most colonial – failing: "If I'd forgotten Marnham and married Caubvick, my estate would have been all of Labrador. My family would have been everything alive there. Even now those unclaimed kin clamour in my chest" (73). As Kathleen McConnell argues, initially the "interdependence of colonizer and colonized ... indicates an ambivalence, an uncertainty as to the source of authority" that goes beyond that binary opposition.[87] However, although Cartwright and Caubvick are aligned by "their desire to straddle boundaries," when Caubvick tries to move "from dominated to dominant ... the consequences are dire"; "Steffler's novel," McConnell concludes, "continues to project onto the perceived Other a positionality determined by the imperium long ago."[88]

Despite Steffler's dialogic subjection of Cartwright's journal to postcolonial revision, for the most part the device of the spectral retrospection renders the novel susceptible to Tony Tremblay's critique of it as "a combination of redress and reparation expressed as a revisionist historiography borne of remorse."[89] *Afterlife*'s presentation of Cartwright not as triumphant explorer but as guilt-ridden wanderer in limbo suggests that, although Cartwright went to Labrador and behaved, to a great degree, like the typical imperial invader, at least he felt bad about it afterward. This impression is bolstered by the spectral Cartwright's occasional visits to the present, with whose weak, lethargic inhabitants he is less than impressed. He sees them as the "bastard offspring" (251) of his inventor brother Edmund, whose schemes were generally aimed at making life easier – with the result that the present generation is, in Cartwright's eyes, feeble and even undeserving of life. This very Nietzschean contempt for the weak, which stands in contrast to Cartwright's own robust love of life and striving to survive under hostile conditions, is not particularly ironized in these segments, suggesting that, whatever his shortcomings, Cartwright at least was no layabout.

Perhaps the most interesting aspect of Cartwright's afterlife, however, and that which has the most troublesome implications for Steffler's postcolonial questioning of literate historiography and representation of the oral culture of the Inuit, is Cartwright's departure from that afterlife. At the end of the novel, Cartwright relives the scene at the pool, and this time he is caught and eaten by a bear; he "feels no pain, feels instead the satisfaction of feeding a fierce hunger" (293). This fate reverses the outcome of the earlier scene and can be taken as compensating for his penchant for unrestrained slaughter. Peter Jaeger, looking at the novel's ecological implications, argues that "Steffler's writing proclaims the idea that consciousness-raising will affect social change by creating an emblematic character who gains freedom through awareness."[90]

More important, however, the scene repeats Attuiock's earlier description of being eaten by the bear-spirit Torngarsoak as part of the process of his becoming an *angakok* or shaman (137–8). Attuiock is reconstituted after the arrival of his *torngak*, a white owl, and he then completes the ritual of becoming an *angakok* by successfully eluding his predecessor. Cartwright's vision seems to be compensatory, penance for his destructive attitude toward the land – remedying scarcity of game "due to breaches of traditional observances" being an important part of the role of Inuit shamen.[91] As the bear eats him, "as more of him vanishes, a feast of new beauty appears. Small ferns and mosses curly as hair spring from the cracks in the rock where he was sitting." The effect of being devoured, which often precedes being introduced to the secrets of healing in shamanistic initiation,[92] is to erase Cartwright from the scene and return it to its prior state: "The bear's white head is a wide pointed brush, moving from side to side, painting him out, painting the river, the glittering trees in" (293).

Cartwright's spirit, in short, appears to be delivered from a guilt-ridden purgatory in a mystical, penitent apotheosis that mirrors Inuit shamanistic initiation. The spectral frame of *The Afterlife of George Cartwright*, it might be argued, strives for a syncretic, postcolonial revision of the fate of the historical George Cartwright. The novel intertextually exploits the voice of the historical Cartwright to express regret for the effects of colonialism. By compelling Cartwright to keep writing until he achieves a state of penitent self-awareness, Steffler suggests not so much that writing is purgative but that it reflects a state of impurity. In the form of the ending, the novel inscribes the desire to reverse history, to paint the colonizer out of the scene both figuratively as well as literally. That such a desire is figured in the terms of an oral culture that has been erased through the intervention of the colonizer, however, is a paradox that resonates strongly and renders the fictional Cartwright's remorseful and compensatory departure a particularly ironic one. Whereas in *The Scorched-Wood People* the spectral narrator is the site at which the oral problematically gives way to the literate, in Steffler's novel the literate problematically gives way to the oral, evoking a desire for transculturation that is highly uneasy.

All four novels, and others, in various ways suggest that it is a perilous task to write the oral. Yet the difference between *The Invention of the World* and the novels by Vanderhaeghe, Wiebe, and Steffler reflects how that task is complicated both by the legacy of colonialism and by the politics of cultural negotiation that that legacy has made a necessity in a settler-invader society. As *The Scorched-Wood People* and *The Afterlife of George Cartwright* demonstrate, the use of oral frameworks and the effort to convey a sense of the dynamic, provisional, and immediate experience of orality and oral cultures can be symptomatic of a postmodern nostalgia for a kind of prelapsarian oral state prior to the alienating advent of literacy and its appropriative association with authority – particularly authority over the past. Yet all of these writers are too conversant with the accomplishments of literacy to openly strive for such an Edenic resonance, and in the case of Hodgins's novel the illusoriness of such an objective is quite blatantly conveyed. Nonetheless, these four novels share the sense that writing is a "technologizing of the word" and that like most technologies it can have oppressive applications.

Their recognition of the hegemonic instrumentality of writing, however, does not translate into a desire to somehow be "out of" writing or into a self-defeating attempt to get back to orality, though Steffler's novel certainly leans in this direction. Rather, they represent an attempt, from within literacy, to understand and inscribe the limits of literacy, to imagine an outside, and thus to bring to readers' attention the limits and implications of a literacy previously taken for granted. In doing so, furthermore, they provide salient insights into the nature of historiography. They suggest the need for a contingent and contestable, rather than authoritative, historiography. They cultivate a more sceptical attitude toward the historical document (whether written or a transcription of the oral) and toward the reconstruction of the historical context, a reconstruction that is both necessary and elusive. Finally, they recognize that telling the story of the past is an exercise not just of power but of communal responsibility, one that is distorted in a literate society that materializes language, objectifies it, and renders it a potential possession – and does the same thing, in turn, to the story of the past. In this respect, they suggest how important it is to a settler-invader culture to come to terms with how the tension between orality and literacy has warped its history.

THE TRACE OF HISTORY IN MYTH / THE TRACE OF MYTH IN HISTORY

The use of oral conventions and frameworks in contemporary Canadian historical novels seems to suggest a resistance to the dominance of writing, rationality, and empiricist historiography – all features of an alienating modern, technological society. The prevalence of myth or mythologizing tendencies seems to suggest much the same. Many of these novels in various ways reinstate myth – as the residual trace of preindustrial, premodern, oral cultures and their knowledges – as a corrective or alternative to history and make use of mythical discourse to question realistic assumptions about historical time and causality. As part of a more general project to recover the energies and knowledge of oral cultures, the use of myth in these historical novels likewise raises concerns, as does the use of oral frameworks, about the potential construction of a cultural binary opposition, the privileging of an ostensibly more simple and primitive world view as a kind of nostalgic retreat from modernity. Yet, ultimately, as with the use of oral strategies, what these novels provide is a more sophisticated, though nonetheless somewhat ambivalent, relation to myth.

History and myth, like fact and fiction, have often been presented as binary opposites. Particularly within the empiricism that dominated nineteenth- and early twentieth-century historiography, history essentially has been seen as a scientific, factual, objective representation of the past, governed by a belief in historical causality, progression, and continuity. Myth, in contrast, has been largely associated with a poetic, prehistorical consciousness and seen as a symbolic discourse that stands in a figurative rather than representational or mimetic relationship to reality. In this opposition, as Eli Wiesel argues, history has been the privileged term: "Myths imply morality or immorality, whereas history calls for objectivity. Myths take sides;

history remains neutral. Myths display passion; history is opposed to anything resembling passion. Its only contact with passion is the readiness to record it as it does anything else."[93] As a form of cultural discourse, myth, viewed from within a rigid, empiricist historiography, is closer to fantasy and entertainment than to the provision of knowledge.

Such a dichotomy has long had its critics, and in the first half of the twentieth century there has been, as Mircea Eliade notes, a significant shift in scholarship from the treatment of myth as fiction and fable to a treatment of myth, as in its archaic understanding, as a true story, "a story that is a most precious possession because it is sacred, exemplary, significant."[94] Much structuralist anthropology suggests that myth and history are merely different kinds of culturally conditioned knowledges that reflect different attitudes towards time. This distinction, for Eliade, is premised on a difference between history as grounded in profane, chronological time and myth as grounded in "a 'sacred' Time at once primordial and indefinitely recoverable."[95] The difference between the two kinds of knowledge, ultimately, is that historical memory is the preservation of that which is transient and mutable, whereas mythical memory is the preservation of absolute, essential knowledge and is necessarily metaphysical: "It is the experience of the sacred – that is, an encounter with a trans-human reality – which gives birth to the idea that something *really exists*, that hence there are absolute values capable of guiding man and giving a meaning to human existence."[96]

In *The Myth of the Eternal Return*, Eliade argues that mythic ritual enacts a return to a primordial state, to a time outside of linear history. The eternal return resides in "the repetition of an archetypal gesture," a gesture that acknowledges "the cyclical structure of time, which is regenerated at each new 'birth' on whatever plane. This eternal return reveals an ontology uncontaminated by time and becoming."[97] Mythic consciousness, in what Eliade describes as primitive societies, is profoundly antihistorical since "the primitive, by conferring a cyclic direction upon time, annuls its irreversability … In a certain sense, it is even possible to say that nothing new happens in the world, for everything is but the repetition of the same primordial archetypes."[98] Therefore, "through the initiation of archetypes and the repetition of paradigmatic structures," myth enacts "an implicit abolition of profane time, of duration, of 'history.'"[99]

This conception of myth, of course, has had a profound influence on twentieth-century Western literature. The prevalent formalism of literary modernism, as many critics have observed, can be attributed in part to a desire to escape history, to transform events that transpire in historical time into paradigmatic, universal, timeless prototypes or into autonomous, spatialized aesthetic objects. These objectives subsequently have been criticized as a retreat from historical and political responsibility and engagement (a charge that too often, and wrongly, has been applied to modernism as a totality). Myth has played a central role in this formalist turn of modernism, both by providing an archive of archetypal figures and stories through which to give literature an ostensibly universal resonance and by providing an aesthetic and discursive model for texts seeking such a resonance.[100] The use of myth, like the use of oral frameworks, suggests writers' nostalgia for a prelapsarian world.

Contemporary theorists and writers, however, have increasingly undermined both the distinction between history and myth and the ahistorical modernist notion of universality, exposing historiography's subjective, fictionalizing, and mythologizing qualities. Historians, of course, have often been accused of mythologizing their subjects; Eliade, for one, points out that, ironically, mythical thought "more than anywhere else ... survives in historiography!"[101] In the terms of empiricist historiography, however, such a tendency has been seen as just bad history, the product of rhetorical excess and a lack of necessary historical objectivity. Contemporary theorizing of historiography, however, has more substantially undermined the distinction by questioning the mimetic viability of historical discourse and underlining the continuities between fiction and history. Because we are not eyewitnesses to the past, Munslow argues, we deploy narratives that serve both as "a surrogate for the past and as a medium of exchange in our active engagement with it. History is thus a class of literature."[102] In short, the traditional oppositions between truth and fantasy, history and myth, fact and fiction are grounded in a problematic metaphysics of realism that both contemporary theory and contemporary fiction have profoundly troubled.

Despite its inscribing of scepticism about modernist literary practices, however, contemporary fiction has by no means abandoned myth as the product of a discredited mysticism and a problematic ahistoricism. Indeed, myth persists as a presence in contemporary literature, including historical fiction, but often with a postmodern difference. It is marked by a more contingent and more historicized attitude toward myth. Monika Fludernik points out that one "of the most noticeable developments in recent fiction, particularly in what is here called historiographical metafiction, seems to be the reinvention of myth as a viable attitude in relation to the past."[103] Historical fiction has always raised interesting questions about the relationship between myth and history because the genre provides for a curious alchemy of the historical and the fictional, in which historical figures are often given mythological resonance, as in, for instance, Scott's seminal *Waverley*. Contemporary historical novels, however, have more substantially complicated the distinction between myth and history by consciously rendering historical material within mythic frameworks or by putting mythic discourse and historical discourse in dialogic interaction, thus foregrounding the relation between the two and muddying the waters that supposedly separate them.

As Claude Levi-Strauss has observed, "in our own societies, history has replaced mythology and fulfils the same function" of ensuring that "the future will remain faithful to the present and to the past."[104] One of the most obvious signs of this continuity is how historical novels give a mythical resonance to the depiction of historical events. For Eliade, "the foremost function of myth is to reveal the exemplary models for all human rites and all significant human activities," those "primordial 'stories' that have constituted [people] existentially."[105] For all that the post-Enlightenment West is increasingly secular and rationalist, that mythologizing impulse has not been eradicated, especially as indicated by its continuing centrality to literature. This remains the case even with self-conscious historical fiction such as Findley's *The Wars* – which has been seen as a mythic novel, though one that runs counter to the conventional mythologizing of the soldier-hero renowned for his military accomplishments and for his courage and fortitude in battle.[106] Though Robert Ross can be seen as displaying all of these attributes, he does so largely outside of or indeed against the terms of a military establishment that is constructed as essentially insane and apocalyptic. If *The Wars* is a narrative both of Robert's experiences in the war and of the researching of that life, an important aim that unites the war narrative with the historiographical metafiction is the novel's valuing of life.

Throughout *The Wars*, Robert is mythologized not as a military standard-bearer but as a fighter "against despair" and an agent of preservation. Robert repeatedly is positioned as having to alleviate the destructive effects on animals of irrational human behaviour, and his sympathy for and affiliation with the natural world is sustained throughout the novel. The war essentially puts Robert in a position where he must choose between life and what he sees as the forces of death: the military establishment that has precipitated the carnage. The killing of Captain Leather signals the extent of Robert's recognition of the military establishment as inimical to the preservation of life. Preservation is also at the heart of the novel's historiographical concerns. At the end of the novel, when the researcher sees Robert's and Rowena's breath in the photograph at the archives, Findley suggests that the act of attempting to reconstruct and to understand the past is in itself a kind of preservation and a resistance to despair; in that sense, the reader/researcher is invited to extend Robert's mission by revivifying his story. As Eliade observes, both "historical" societies – those that feel the need to record "their own acts for the use of their successors" – and "primitive" societies, which do not feel this need, require a periodic regeneration that reveals nonetheless a shared anxiety about the "irreversibility of events" associated with historical consciousness.[107] In this light, *The Wars* can be seen as serving such an archetypal function, since it certainly reflects an anxiety about the apocalyptic militarism of modern nations and suggests the need for a decidedly pacifist social renewal.

But what kind of preservation does a novel like *The Wars* achieve? Is it the spatializing preservation of much modernist literature, in which Eliade sees "a revolt against historical time, the desire to attain to other temporal rhythms than that in which we are condemned to live and work"?[108] Eliade argues that the effect of reading a novel is similar to the effect of listening to a myth in a traditional society; "in both cases alike, one 'escapes' from historical and personal time and is submerged in a time that is fabulous and trans-historical."[109] Eliade obviously has a particular model of the novel in mind, and in a novel like *The Wars* that ontological effect is frustrated by the intensity and detail of the historical situation it depicts as well as by the postmodern historiographical devices that prevent such an escapist immersion. Thus the modernist deployment of myth to achieve an ahistorical, archetypal resonance is submerged in *The Wars* within a self-conscious postmodern framework that dramatizes the need to engage with history. The result is a profound tension between two substantially different attitudes towards history. *The Wars* certainly seems to illustrate Hutcheon's observation that, despite the "continuity between the modernist and the postmodernist," the "self-consciousness of art *as art*" of the latter is part of an engagement with, rather than a disengagement from, "the social and historical world."[110] *The Wars* in some ways retains the exemplary resonance of myth and its modernist avatars (and, for that matter, of much history) but foregrounds the role of readers in constructing such a reading.

In *Myth and Reality*, Eliade points to myth's persistence in modern literature as something "desacralized or simply camouflaged under 'profane' forms" and to how the novel in particular "has taken the place of the recitation of myths in traditional and popular societies."[111] Traditionally, Vautier argues, myths, as prior, essential, and superior stories, have been employed in literary texts "to enhance an ordinary story and keep the paradigmatic original story alive in a contemporary form."[112] Thus, it can be argued, they mark a contemporary example of the "eternal return" of the primordial. If the narrative of *The Wars* takes on the resonance of myth, in Michael Ondaatje's *In the Skin of a Lion*, a prior myth gives resonance to the narrative. *In the Skin of a Lion* provides an interesting example of how postmodern texts deploying myth to underpin representations of the past walk a fine line between historicizing and dehistoricizing the contexts they depict.

Myths, of course, very often have historical precedents, though those precedents have receded with time and the stories themselves have taken on the sense of timelessness, grandeur, and ahistoricity traditionally associated with myth. This is true of *The Epic of Gilgamesh*, on which *In the Skin of a Lion* is consciously modelled. Gilgamesh was probably a historical Sumerian king but has persisted through time as the kind of larger-than-life figure that populates folk myth.[113] What is interesting in the context of a discussion of contemporary historical fiction, however, is what the relationship of the Gilgamesh myth to the portrait of labour relations and class struggle in modern Toronto suggests about Ondaatje's intentions in the novel. According to Vautier, myths characteristically have been seen as "immutable, universal stories ... that are frequently recuperated in epigonic, fictional renditions of the original myths" and sometimes "employed as teleological and transhistorical master narratives in literature."[114] In contrast, what she calls (after Margery Fee) New World Myth "works against traditional assumptions about the universality and transhistoricity of myth."[115] In New World Myth, myth "exchanges its traditional function as transhistorical master narrative ... for a function characterized by postmodern indeterminacy, complex postcolonial attitudes, a questioning of history, and a developing self-consciousness that creates provisional and relative identities."[116]

Vautier's contrast between different deployments of myth is useful for highlighting some key tensions in *In the Skin of a Lion*, since the echoes of *The Epic of Gilgamesh* have a somewhat paradoxical effect in a novel that deflects attention to a historically marginalized community and subverts the notion of history as a record of achievement of prominent public individuals. As Gordon Gamlin and Carol Beran have observed, the Babylonian epic clearly provides the model for many of the scenes in *In the Skin of a Lion*, evoking many of the themes that Ondaatje's novel develops, and the parallels between Gilgamesh and Ondaatje's hero Patrick Lewis are sustained throughout the novel.[117] Ondaatje's deployment of a mythological intertext is worth exploring further because it raises the key issue of whether this is a case of the "eternal return" of the original or a repetition with a difference.

In the Skin of a Lion, like *The Epic of Gilgamesh*, revolves around the central character's response to the death of a loved friend. In the epic, Enkidu challenges the unmatchable strength of Gilgamesh. Though Gilgamesh defeats Enkidu, he is impressed with the latter's strength and the two become fast friends, a friendship that is paralleled by the relationship between Patrick and Alice Gull. Together Gilgamesh and Enkidu journey to the Land of the Cedars to challenge Humbaba, the giant guardian of the forest, a quest that is fuelled by Gilgamesh's desire to combat evil but also to consolidate his reputation. When the two confront Humbaba, he appeals to Gilgamesh for compassion, and Enkidu counsels Gilgamesh not to be deceived, just as Alice warns Patrick against humanizing the rich: "Compassion forgives too much. You could forgive the worst man. You forgive him and nothing changes" (*In the Skin of a Lion*, 123). Gilgamesh is swayed, and the two slay Humbaba, bringing upon themselves the wrath of the gods. When Gilgamesh then spurns Ishtar, the goddess of war, she sends the Bull of Heaven to destroy him, and when he and Enkidu kill the bull, Enlil, the highest of all gods, decrees that Enkidu must die. Thus Enkidu's involvement in Gilgamesh's violent activities leads to his own death, in the same way that Patrick is very much implicated in the death of Alice as a result of their battling the evils of capitalism.

After the death of Enkidu, Gilgamesh, in despair and grief, resolves to "wander through the wilderness in the skin of a lion" in search of Utnapishtim, a Noah-like figure who has discovered the secret of everlasting life.[118] Patrick, in a similar state, travels to Muskoka to do justice to the memory of Alice by bombing the hotel. Gilgamesh travels through the mountain of Mishu and reaches the garden of the gods, where he meets Siduri, maker of wine, who initially bars her gate against him but overcomes her suspicion, advising him against his search for everlasting life and urging him to appreciate the life he has. This scene is echoed in Ondaatje's novel when Patrick encounters the blind Elizabeth in "The Garden of the Blind" and, after he tells her of the bombing, she counsels him, "Don't resent your life" (170). Siduri also directs Gilgamesh to Urshanabi, the ferryman who takes him across the waters of death to Utnapishtim. After he tells Gilgamesh the story of his surviving the flood, Utnapishtim puts Gilgamesh's desire for everlasting life to the test by challenging Gilgamesh to "prevail against sleep for six days and seven nights," but Gilgamesh instead sleeps the entire time.[119]

Thus Gilgamesh's journey to Utnapishtim provides the background to Patrick's journey north to bomb the hotel; Gilgamesh's desire for immortality in the wake of Enkidu's death is echoed in Patrick's feeling "removed from any context of the world" (172) and in his desire to be "unhistorical" after the death of Alice.

Patrick's attack on the waterworks parallels the fate of Gilgamesh after he leaves the garden of the gods. Utnapishtim gives Gilgamesh a last opportunity to achieve eternal life: he describes to him "a plant that grows underwater" and counsels him that, if he succeeds in finding it, "then your hands will hold that which restores his lost youth to a man."[120] In order to achieve his goal, Gilgamesh "opened the sluices so that a sweet-water current might carry him out to the deepest channel; he tied heavy stones to his feet and they dragged him down to the water-bed." Gilgamesh finds the plant, cuts free the stone "and the sea carried him and threw him to the shore."[121] In *In the Skin of a Lion*, Patrick's infiltration of a different kind of "plant" obviously follows a similar strategy: Patrick, Caravaggio, and Giannetta commandeer the yacht *The Annalisa* to approach the waterworks, and Patrick jettisons his battery lamp and air tank after he is sucked into the intake pipe of the plant, thus achieving his objective of getting inside.

In the epic, however, Gilgamesh loses his prize when he stops to bathe in a pool and a serpent rises out of the water and snatches it away. This development certainly puts the climactic exchange between Rowland Harris and Patrick in an interesting light, as it is Harris who frustrates Patrick's aim to blow up the plant. Gilgamesh fails to achieve everlasting life, but he nonetheless fulfills his destiny, which is to gain wisdom and to be a king who rules wisely. Consequently, it might be argued that Patrick likewise fails in his ahistorical, revolutionary goal but comes to understand his humanity, his complicity in abuses of power, his very location in history. As Beran observes of Gilgamesh, "the loss of his comrade, his period of mourning, and his learning the secrets of the great Flood turn him from a wild, strong youth into a responsible ruler. The definition of the hero changes from the man of sheer physical strength to the man with special knowledge of the human condition, of death and survival, as expressed in Enkidu's death and the story of the Flood," which Gilgamesh is told by Utnapishtim.[122] Thus *In the Skin of a Lion* shares with the Gilgamesh epic a concern with the responsible exercise of power, a grieving over the death of a beloved friend that precipitates a quest for a way to be outside of historical existence, and a reaching of knowledge that effects a reconciliation to one's place, and to one's social responsibility, in the historical world.

The effects of such a parallel, however, are quite ambivalent. On the one hand, the novel questions the ahistoricism of revolutionary action and, especially in its construction of Patrick as bestial, suggests the dangers of the desire to effect social change through revolutionary violence. In that sense, it could be argued that Ondaatje uses his mythic subtext not to suggest the repetition of an ahistorical pattern, but to reinscribe the importance of being historically and socially situated. However, despite the sense of community cultivated by Ondaatje's interweaving of multiple narratives, the parallels between Gilgamesh and Patrick to a great degree reinstate Patrick's importance as the central protagonist and underline the narrative's interest in his quest and in his movement from his flirtation with an ahistorical anarchism to his acceptance of a historicized humanism.

Such a narrative scheme seems comfortable in the bourgeois novelistic tradition of focusing on the development of the individual, as well as in Avrom Fleishman's humanist characterization of the historical novel. While emphasizing the importance of the "rich factuality of history," Fleishman nonetheless implies a view of historical consistency rather than change: "The esthetic function of historical fiction is to lift the contemplation of the past above both the present and the past, to see it in its universal character, freed of the urgency of historical engagement. The reflection from the present to the past is completed when the historical novelist reaches not the present from which he began but the constants of human experience in history – however these may appear to him in his time and place."[123] In this respect, *In the Skin of a Lion* retains something of the hierarchical structure that Vautier sees New World Myth as challenging: "Instead of having traditional myths come down from the heights to enhance an ordinary story and keep the paradigmatic original story alive in a contemporary form, the narrators of New World Myth novels ... emphasize what has frequently been dismissed as local colour or *des histoires de village*."[124] In the case of *In the Skin of a Lion*, however, it might be argued, particularly through the focus on Patrick, that that sense of community and local context is ultimately displaced and rendered incidental, or at least secondary, within the repetition of an archetypal pattern.

The problematic relation to myth of *The Wars* and *In the Skin of a Lion* can be seen by way of comparison with Hodgins's *The Invention of the World*. Hodgins's novel much more openly stages an interrogation of mythic discourse, rather than investing historical material with mythological significance or more or less submerging myth as a kind of intertextual scaffolding. *The Invention of the World* not only evokes mythological subtexts against which readers are to consider the significance of what happens in the novel, but also clearly raises questions about how we read myth and how we read it into the present. Hodgins develops this interrogation not only through his treatment of the central myth of Donal Keneally, but also through the reactions of Keneally's contemporaries and of the latter-day colonists who have inherited his mythic legacy.

Hodgins draws on Celtic and Biblical tradition to give a mythic resonance to Keneally's character, but almost from the beginning he also uses various strategies to question and undermine that mythic status.[125] The circumstances of Keneally's birth certainly give him the requisite mythic genealogy: his mother claims Brian Boru, who drove the Vikings out of Ireland, as an ancestor; Keneally's birth is predicted by the ghost of Catherine ni Houlihan; his mother is mounted, according to witness Grania Flynn, by "a monstrous black bull" (*Invention of the World* 71); and then after his birth she is swallowed by the earth. As Robert Lecker observes, Keneally's origins echo the bull figure of Donnataurus in the Tain Bó Cuailnge story and also the legend of Taurus-Europa.[126] The sense of destiny that is characteristically attached to such mythical progeny is fortified by allusions on the part of the inhabitants of Carrighdoun to various heroes from Celtic legend such as Finn MacCool and Cuchulain, along with Brian Boru. The evocation of such figures initially positions Keneally as a liberator, but his gargantuan appetite for food and sex, his inclination towards mischief rather than work, and his murder of his good twin reveal Keneally to be disinclined to use his powers to benefit the people.

Keneally's ascendancy to the position of leader of the colony, as a number of critics have observed, underlines his status as a failed hero and false messiah.[127] Keneally aligns himself with historical figures like Charles Stewart Parnell and Michael Davitt by leading Carrighdoun's resistance against a less-than-despotic landlord; however, his confronting of the bailiff threatens to bring the wrath of the authorities down on the farmers' heads, and rather than celebrating his victory they insist that he take responsibility. In the account of Keneally's subsequent clash with the bailiff, what is first presented as "a mighty battle" that has been recounted down through generations, gradually assuming the larger-than-life proportions of myth, is somewhat undercut as Becker concedes that the "truth was simpler." However, Becker still gives a certain mythic aura to the account of their fight, especially through his observation that the wounded bailiff left "a trail of blood behind him that scorched the grass and melted stones" (88). Keneally is rewarded for his defiance by being escorted out of the village, and is already seen more as a trouble-maker than as a hero, his mythic status compromised.

In hiding from the authorities, Keneally has an epiphany, the revelation of his life plans, that leads to his exploratory trip to North America and ultimately to his establishment of the colony. Keneally's efforts to complete his mission, however, reveal him to be a messianic and megalomaniacal charlatan, while sustaining the ambivalence towards myth and belief that characterizes the whole description of his history. Keneally's attempts to lure converts to his cause are patently manipulative, an instance of "the invented world of imitation truth and false magic" that is opposed in the novel, Cecilia Fink argues, to "the created world of transcendent truth."[128] This manipulation is signalled particularly by Keneally's iconoclastic destruction and enslavement of his God machine (bringing to mind Noah's cheesy magic tricks in Findley's *Not Wanted on the Voyage*). The cause of Keneally's ascendancy, the onset of fear in Carrighdoun during the Year of the Mist is itself mythic, (a materializing of the emotional that is reminiscent of the deluge of Macondo in *One Hundred Years of Solitude* and signals *Invention*'s affinities with magic realism). Keneally starts calling himself The Father and uses magic to keep his followers pacified and enthralled. His dedicatory speech for the colony underlines his ascendancy, as he positions himself in a long line of saviours from the Bible, Irish history, and Celtic legend, giving himself a mythical legacy that by this point in the narrative is fully ironic.

If an important dimension of mythic figures is their exemplary value, Keneally's behaviour represents a perversion of the examples he narcissistically cites. The story of the colony itself is the story of Keneally's betrayal of his leadership role. Under Keneally, the colony becomes in many ways a miniature of a colonized Ireland. According to Lily, the inhabitants acquiesce to Keneally's messianic pantomime out of an elaborate mix of fear, gratitude for delivery, and a lack of self-esteem that Keneally happily sustains. Keneally's browbeating and bullying of his charges, his sexual promiscuity and exploitation of the women in the colony, and the suspicion that he murdered his first wife and her lover echo the behaviour of the charismatic leader of the Aquarian Foundation and underline the authoritarian control that so often accompanies such charisma.[129]

Keneally's behaviour leads to the subsequent ironic reversal of the heroic narrative to which he aspires. When he is finally confronted by Paddy O'Mahoney, he responds very much in the same manner as did the bailiff in Carrighdoun, and in resisting his authority Paddy usurps Keneally's role as defiant liberator in the same terms, most notably by killing Keneally's dog. At this point, Keneally himself has finally succumbed to the disease of fear that he had exploited for so long in his charges. By virtue of this comic reduction of Keneally's defeat of the bailiff, Fink argues, "legend becomes reality, reality becomes myth, and myth is finally levelled to simple historical fact," a typically magic realist "movement across the myth/reality distinction."[130] Thus Hodgins obviously draws on the power of myth to give resonance to Keneally's character, but that mythic resonance is undercut both through the portrayal of Keneally as false messiah and through the deliberate ambiguity, and parodic deflation, of his mythic status.

That ambiguity, however, is part of the legacy of the myth of Keneally, and just as important to *Invention* is what others, most notably Maggie and Becker, do with that legacy. As Becker observes of Keneally, "As long as he was out there, unreckoned with, unlabelled, he was a fascination and a threat. You couldn't be sure how much reality to grant him. Evil is always like that. Even after it's destroyed itself right in front of your face, you still aren't sure if it was something to be scared of or not" (306). An important part of Maggie's role in the novel is her wrestling with the very question of "how much reality to grant" the story of Keneally, and the conclusion she reaches is just as central to Hodgins's treatment of myth as is that story itself.

As critics have noted, Maggie's life is a parodic replay of Keneally's: born in a way of the earth (she hides from her parents underneath her house), she escapes the oppressive world of her family in the north and heads south, where she comes to be viewed as an uppity country girl, a logger's whore trying to climb the social ladder. As a beautiful woman trying to buck the system, Maggie is as much a part of the public domain as is Keneally, and their fates are thoroughly intertwined. At the beginning of the novel, it is divulged that she has a preposterous, secret scheme, a desire to rise above her constricting social circumstances, "to rise somehow until she could see right down into the centre of things. Nothing less. But let the people who scoffed find that out about her and there was no telling what they'd have to say about it" (13). Maggie's ambition obviously parallels Keneally's, and because of it she is, like Keneally, very much a central figure in the public imagination of the island.

In establishing the Revelations Trailer Park – a kind of residual colony in which she strives to undo the damage caused by Keneally – Maggie denies her own needs and cultivates an atmosphere of dependency similar to that of Keneally's reign. She gives refuge to those who have been psychically damaged by Keneally, particularly Madmother Thomas, and in a more positive and caring way presides over the inhabitants, who, like their predecessors in the original colony, are seen as loonies and are socially ostracized. However, while serving as custodian in such a fashion gives her a sense of purpose and contentment, it also in some ways renders her a prisoner of the myth. Hodgins emphasizes the weight of this legacy, and the dialectic of Maggie's engagement with it, when Maggie first moves into the house that previously belonged to Keneally: "It was her house now, she'd created it out of an ugly old abandoned monster, it inhabited her as certainly as she inhabited it" (43).

For most of the novel, Maggie's mission is constructed as a repetition of Keneally's perverted, messianic leadership. The eccentric Julius Champney sees her ambitions as misguided and idealistic, a lack of acceptance of the world, and in the process makes the connection with myth explicit: "She ought to relax enough to enjoy her special state in a world of people who lacked much of those things. But she had her ridiculous plans, she insisted on *rising*, she insisted on *seeing*, as if she believed still, that there was somewhere, ultimately, to go, something to see that would make some real sense of it all. You'd think she was that girl in the fairy tale, that mermaid, dreaming of legs" (230). Maggie becomes consumed by a sense of failure, her unhappiness a public spectacle relished by island residents. In Ireland, however, she experiences a kind of epiphany, reminiscent of Keneally's earlier divine realization of his mission. Compelled by Lily's will to return Keneally's remains to Carrighdoun, perhaps as a kind of exorcism, Maggie feels the presence of magic, which implicitly confirms the reality of the myth and suggests the possibility of realizing her own ambitions. She reflects on her persistent instinct to climb: "She would trust it, follow it, she would climb – my God, she thought, she would soar – until she was able to understand all there was to understand about the universe and be all that she was capable of being" (293). As she moves closer to Keneally's origins, her reflections take on a somewhat messianic tone that connects her both to Keneally as false prophet and Becker as omniscient historian.

When one tries to soar, Wade Powers fears, there is always the possibility of crashing, and this is, indeed, what happens on their return to Vancouver Island. Maggie, prompted by her epiphany on the hilltop, decides to return to her own origins in the north of the island. She searches out the house in which she was born, only to find that it has been occupied by young hippie squatters. The outcome of her quest suggests that her epiphany has been somewhat misguided, reflecting a belief in the importance of the past, of origins, of history, that is consistently undercut in the novel. This defeat, however, paves the way for Maggie's ultimate victory. Maggie does go back to her colony, but with her messianic pretensions substantially chastened: "Well, she could handle it, she couldn't heal them all by herself or cancel that monster's damage alone, but she would do what she could" (335). Furthermore, her marriage to Wade puts an end to the lack of fulfilment both characters have felt throughout the narrative, giving the novel a comic triumph and the sense of personal and social resolution that goes along with it.

What this resolution suggests, it can be argued, is not, as Lecker maintains, that Hodgins "mocks the assumption that self identity can only be found by returning to the past, to ancestral stories, or to visions of departed ghosts."[131] Instead, *The Invention of the World* suggests that the force of myth and history must be acknowledged, whether or not one believes them to be true, but also that one must not be a slave to the past at the expense of the present. Indeed, Hodgins feels that "myth is closer to reality than history. While history is a collection of the facts, myth is the soul that surrounds those facts."[132] Becker's description of the Bible during his interviews with Lily thus serves as a kind of *mise-en-abyme* for the novel: "A strange story, he said, if you'd read it. It has two beginnings. The first, a single chapter, would have us all made in the image of God, perfect spiritual creatures. Then someone else came along, started it all over again, and had us all made out of clay. The rest of the story shows a lot of people trying to get back to that first beginning, back before the mist and the clay. You get all the way up to nearly the end of the book before you meet the man who knows how to manage it" (244). However, instead of a Second Coming, with Maggie as the new messiah, Hodgins presents the final section of *Invention* as a "Second Growth," a more indigenous and indeed postcolonial image that frames the relation between past and present in a much more complex fashion. The title suggests that the present grows out of the humus of the past, is nurtured but far from constrained or overshadowed by it.

Hodgins's use of myth in the novel suggests that we shape our identity not by denying the weight of the past nor by being captives to it. Becker's *mise-en-abyme*, as part of Hodgins's parodic use of myth, presents the story of Maggie not as exemplary of the process of "eternal return" nor simply as a subversive rewriting of a prior story, but as an illustration of the complex washing of the past into the present. Hodgins suggests that the past necessarily takes a mythological form, and while it might not be possible to completely demythologize that past, it is certainly possible to achieve some kind of accommodation with it that resists the inheritance of a hegemonic mythology.

The differing functions of myth in *The Wars*, *In the Skin of a Lion*, and *The Invention of the World* provide a good background for appreciating perhaps the most interesting contemporary novel dealing with myth, Jane Urquhart's *Away*, in which the tension between the specificity and temporality of the historical and the ahistoricity and archetypicality of the mythical is likewise at issue. In "Myth and History," Wiesel, writing of the destructive power of myth in the history of the Jews, observes that "there is myth in history just as there is history in myth" and concludes that "in the Jewish tradition the opposite of history is not myth. The opposite of history is forget-fulness."[133] Wiesel's comments about the complex relationship between history and myth have a lot of resonance for *Away*. Like *The Invention of the World* and, to a lesser degree, *In the Skin of a Lion*, *Away* provides a valuable contribution to this complicating of the distinction between history and myth because of its lyrical style, its poetic structure, and its foregrounding of the complex relationship between the magical and the real, the mythic and the historical.

Away involves a complex interplay between the continuity, causal-ity, and progression traditionally associated with a historical con-sciousness and the poetic, magical, iterative qualities traditionally associated with myth. To a degree, *Away* provides the kind of histor-ical verisimilitude typical of the historical novel, but the narrative is also filled with remarkable, magical episodes and events, and is marked throughout by the presence of the supernatural. *Away* raises questions about history without sharing historiographical metafic-tion's discursive and generic self-consciousness. As a historical novel, however, *Away* does have definite affinities with magic realism, in which "the supernatural is not a simple or obvious matter, but it is an ordinary matter, an everyday occurrence – admitted, accepted, and integrated into the rationality and materiality of literary realism."[134]

Though magic realism is typically associated with Latin American writers such as Alejo Carpentier, Carlos Fuentes, Isabel Allende, and Gabriel Garcia Marquez, the term has gained a broader applicability, including, as Stephen Slemon observes, in English Canada, where it provides interesting possibilities "within the context of English-Canadian literary culture and *its* specific engagement with postcolo-niality."[135] Furthermore, magic realist texts, because of their integra-tion of the supernatural into the real, provide an important site for negotiating between the mythic and the historical, as novels such as Marquez's *One Hundred Years of Solitude*, Salman Rushdie's *Midnight's Children*, and Angela Carter's *Nights at the Circus* testify.

Magic realism "often facilitates the fusion, or coexistence, of pos-sible worlds, spaces, systems that would be irreconcilable in other modes of fiction."[136] *Away*, like other magic realist texts, illustrates the possibilities of the mode for representing the interplay between myth and history. It seamlessly combines the verisimilitude and plausibility typical of the historical novel with the spectral and magical, constructing a fairly detailed historical context while retaining a sense of the fantastic, the spectral, and the primordial typical of myth. While the novel reflects the chronological progression typical of the historical novel, the main structural devices and thematic motifs of the book frame the historical progression of the narrative in a mythic pattern and give it a lyrical tone and an archetypal resonance.

To begin with, *Away,* like *In the Skin of a Lion*, is explicitly grounded in an oral framework: as Esther O'Malley prepares to lay down to die, her last act is "to give shape to one hundred and forty years" (*Away* 21) by remembering the family story told to her by her grandmother Eileen. Esther's "whispering in the dark" (21) of the story of her great-grandmother Mary and her grandmother Eileen comprises the bulk of the novel and creates a link across five generations. Running through Esther's tale is a series of metamorphoses (Ovid being the novel's resident muse) that have marked the lives of Mary and Eileen and also her own life. Indeed, the oral frame itself constructs the genealogy of Esther's own metamorphosis: at the beginning of the novel, Esther recalls a conversation at age twelve, in which Eileen warns her of the dangers of metamorphoses and of changing names; the story Eileen tells Esther will reveal her to be Esther's grandmother, prefiguring the revelation at the end of the novel that her mother, Deirdre, raised as her uncle Liam's child, is Eileen's daughter: "I am speaking of the kind of name change that turns you into someone else altogether, someone other than who you are, the change that takes you off to somewhere else" (9).

These metamorphoses are variations on the state of being "away," and the occurrence of this state in successive generations gives the novel a strong sense of mythic repetition. At the beginning of Esther's tale, her great-grandmother Mary pulls a drowned sailor from the sea off Rathlin Island and thence is transformed, present but absent, there but not there, haunted by the drowned sailor "from an other world island" (8). Though the people of Rathlin Island hope to salvage her (and preserve themselves) by marrying her to Brian O'Malley, she vows, paradoxically, "I will be your wife but I will not be your wife" (57). In Upper Canada, Mary (her name changed to Moira) stays true to her word. She leaves Brian and their children and goes to live by the shore of Lake Moira to be close to her spectral lover, and her frozen body is returned to the family seven years later by Exodus Crow.

Mary's enchantment by the drowned man is replayed in Eileen's infatuation with Aidan Lanighan. Descriptions of Aidan echo the image of the drowned man, and Eileen's feeling of familiarity with him suggests the continuing presence of the daemon lover: "There's something in me that remembers you from somewhere ... How could I know you this well?" (290–1). While such overt echoes of Mary's fate project an air of the spectral over Eileen's relationship with Aidan, her enchantment, though romantic like Mary's, is very much wrapped up with her embrace of Irish nationalism and her belief in Aidan as the focus of Irish revolutionary hopes in Canada. Thus, when she is repudiated by Aidan after the assassination of D'Arcy McGee and after the revelation that Aidan has been acting as McGee's spy, she realizes that she has been under a spell, has essentially been "away": "So this is what it is to be away, her mother's voice told her. You are never present where you stand ... Your flag- stones are a series of dark lakes that you scour, and the light that touches and alters them sends you unspeakable messages. Waves arch like mantles over everything that burns. Each corner is a secret and your history is a lie" (345).

From the beginning, *Away* establishes in the history of the women of the O'Malley family a characteristically mythic sense of repetition and the presence of the supernatural: "They were plagued by reve- nants. Men, landscapes, states of mind went away and came back again. Over the years, over the decades. There was always water involved, exaggerated youth or exaggerated age. Afterwards there was absence. That is the way it was for the women of this family. It was part of their destiny" (3). Thus the dominant force in the O'Malley family history is a kind of destined repetition, the inevita- ble presence of romantic enchantment, which is given supernatural and archetypal overtones and resonates with Eliade's idea of the "eternal return": "In this family all young girls are the same young girl and all old ladies are the same old lady" (325).

This sense of destiny and the pattern of enchantment are repeated in Esther's own life when a fisherman – whose "dark curls, his pale hand and his bright green eye" (354) echo Mary's drowned sailor and Aidan – takes refuge from a storm in her house on Loughbreeze Beach. The pattern, however, is repeated with a difference, as Esther "was told a story at twelve that calmed her down and put her in her place" (3). Esther takes Eileen's advice "never to go away" (9), which sets up a tension between change and stability that runs through the book. Eileen's intention is to convince Esther of the advantages of stability, and Esther benefits by being able to recognize the familiar (and familial) pattern when it appears in her own life: "It was his swimming to her land, the storm, his journey over beach stones that mattered. The unpredictability of his arrivals and the certainty of his departures. Between his visits, when she found herself waiting, she knew it was for a kind of completion – his absence from, not his presence in her life." Winter puts an end to his visits and "Esther stayed alone on the land" (354).

However, although Esther's life as a result is less tumultuous than Mary's or Eileen's, she has no children and therefore no audience for her family history. In this respect, how the O'Malley family saga is framed raises concerns about historical consciousness and cultural continuity. As Esther tells her story to an empty house, she sees herself as the repository and conduit of oral culture: "Esther lying still in her sleigh-bed feels like an Irish poet from a medieval, bardic school. She is aware that those men and women lay in their window-less cells for days, composing and then memorizing thousands of lines, their heads wrapped in tartan cloths, stones resting on their stomachs. Esther has neither rocks nor plaids with her in this bed but shares with the old ones a focused desire. Nothing should escape" (133). The frame story serves to disrupt the chronological progression of the narrative and to provide it with a certain didactic urgency, thus giving *Away* an oral quality more typical of myth than of historical narrative. More significantly, it also foregrounds the relationship between the oral tradition and historical memory (not least of all because the story will die with Esther as the last descendant of the O'Malley line) and underlines the importance of preservation and continuity in the face of change and disintegration.

Another important element of *Away* that contributes to the novel's blending of the historical with the fantastic and the poetic is Urquhart's use of the parts of an Irish triad to structure the narrative: "The three most short-lived traces: the trace of a bird on a branch, the trace of a fish on a pool, and the trace of a man on a woman" (n.p.). While the relatively detailed and specific historical events that characterize the historical novel indeed provide the larger canvas for the O'Malley family saga, the section titles give a metaphoric cast to each stage of the family history and effect a kind of narrative containment of the historical within the personal, the poetic, and the mythical. To put it in Eliade's terms, the events of profane, chronological, historical time are contained within a structure shaped by the repetition of events of primordial time.

The first section, "A Fish on a Pool," concentrates on Mary's enchantment by the drowned sailor and her marriage to Brian O'Malley and concludes with the family's coming emigration to Canada, though the broader background to the dilemma of Mary's being "away" is the exploitation of Ireland by the English, the great famine of the 1860s, and the massive, forced exodus of a substantial proportion of the population of Ireland. The title of the section refers obviously to Mary's attraction to the sea, her discovery of the drowned sailor, and her subsequent transformation – the fish being, as Libby Birch observes, a common form taken by "the hidden tribes of the *Tuatha de Dannan*" in Celtic mythology.[137]

It also refers to Mary's encounter with Osbert Sedgewick, whose passionate collecting of natural specimens is symbolic of his exploitative, if well-intentioned, relationship with his tenants and of his obliviousness to the lives and suffering of the Irish peasantry. When Mary encounters Osbert taking specimens from tidal pools and implicitly criticizes his disturbance of nature, Osbert is shaken by Mary's spectral air and the effrontery of her suggestion. Echoing the Celtic tradition that "one received wisdom at the water's edge," Osbert is haunted by his encounter with Mary and is compelled to leave off his collecting.[138] He is even prompted to ensure that the family is included in the list of those to emigrate to Canada to alleviate the suffering caused by the famine; Osbert insists to his brother Granville that there is "this light in her ... and it must not be put out" (122). Thus Mary leaves her "trace" on Osbert – so much so that ultimately he follows the family to Canada. As Mary's encounters with the dead sailor and with Osbert reflect, her "personal fortunes" are certainly shaped by the larger historical context of the famine, but that dire and realistic sociopolitical situation, in an ontological blending typical of magic realism, occupies the same space in the narrative as the mythical, archetypal situation of the woman who is "away."

The title of the second section, "A Bird on a Branch," foregrounds the mythic and uncanny, as it gestures to Exodus Crow and to Eileen, both of whom have prophetic abilities and project a certain sense of destiny onto the family's fortunes over the course of the rest of the narrative. As a young girl, Eileen, who has inherited something of her mother's prophetic ability and mystical aura, spends much of her time in a willow tree beside the O'Malleys' cabin. She foresees, for instance, the coming of Exodus just before he arrives with the frozen body of Mary in tow, as well as the later arrival of Osbert Sedgewick. Exodus, as his family name suggests, serves as a spiritual guide and messenger for the O'Malleys since he has been instructed by Mary to tell her story to her children, specifically to Liam, who, he says, because he "will move forward and make the change, *must* hear the story" (175). Exodus contributes to the mythic quality of the story because he recognizes in Mary a mutually shared quality of *manitou*, "the spirit that is everywhere" (176), but also because his message from Mary and the advice he gives the family confirm a sense of foreordination. Liam indeed does go ahead to make "the change," becoming a successful landowner and capitalist, and freeing the family from a history of poverty. However, he makes the change by selling the family's land grant to Osbert, who seizes on the possibility, which "the crow" reveals to Eileen, of gold on the property. The sale brings upon the family, as Exodus warns, "the curse of the mines," a desecration of landscape for profit that, by the time of Esther's narrative, has reached a crescendo.

Thus, while the middle section of the novel portrays the struggle of Irish immigrants to forge a living on the less-than-fertile Canadian Shield and the struggle over sustaining or jettisoning an Irish identity in a new land, arching over its historical realism is a sense of destiny and of supernatural powers governing the fate of the O'Malley family. Here Celtic mythology, in which the Sidhe often take the form of birds, merges with the trickster tradition so important in Ojibway and other native cultures in an ironic and postcolonial syncretism that Brenda Cooper argues is a key aspect of magic realism: "Magical realist writers strive towards incorporating indigenous knowledge in new terms, in order to interrogate tradition and to herald change." The return to indigenous traditions, including myths, requires a certain ironic distancing to avoid the perils of cultural nationalism, which is inimical to "one of magical realism's defining features – its hybridity that contests boundaries and violates them."[139]

The title of the final section, "The Trace of a Man on a Woman," suggests the romantic priorities of the narrative of Eileen's relationship with Aidan Lanighan, but the romance is very much bound up with the broader fabric of Irish-Catholic nationalism and Fenian agitation in Canada and the reaction to D'Arcy McGee's "betrayal" of the cause. Eileen falls for Aidan as he "dances" the hopes and aspirations of the Irish Catholics at the Seaman's Inn in Port Hope and later follows him to Montreal, where she insists on participating in the patriot cause by concealing a pistol that Aidan intends to take as "a precaution" (323) when going to hear D'Arcy McGee speak in Parliament. By giving the pistol to Aidan's cohort Patrick, Eileen serves as unsuspecting accessory to the assassination of McGee and foils Aidan's attempt to prevent it. Thus, when McGee is shot, Aidan accuses Eileen of killing him, of being in "some kind of dream … some kind of goddamed otherworld island" (343).

The spell (both romantic and political) is broken. "His dance was not a petition to McGee," Eileen realizes; "it was an expression – an affirmation – of partnership. Whenever Aidan danced, the voice of D'Arcy McGee had been present, dancing with him in the room" (343). The departure of Aidan echoes the departure of Mary's daemon lover, and Eileen returns home to Port Hope in a similarly enigmatic, spectral state, telling Liam, "I've given up on outer words … I live on an otherworld island" (346). Thus Eileen's participation in the politics of a pivotal historical era – the struggle for cultural cohesion and political consensus at the time of Confederation – ultimately leads to a repetition of the mythic pattern that governs the history of the women of the O'Malley family. The relatively brief "trace" of Aidan on Eileen marks her for the rest of her life: "I can't, you see," she tells Esther, "get the face of a certain young man out of my mind" (351).

Away thus provides a fictional demonstration of Levi-Strauss's observation that "the gap which exists in our mind to some extent between mythology and history can probably be breached by studying histories which are conceived as not at all separated from but as a continuation of mythology."[140] Such significant historical contexts as the great famine, the grim crossing of the Atlantic in the immigrant ships, Confederation, and the Fenian agitation leading up to the death of D'Arcy McGee provide the background, but also a great deal of resonance and significance, to a family saga that is very much grounded in Irish popular beliefs and shaped by the repetitive pattern and supernatural influence typical of myth. Because of the structural importance of myth in *Away* and because of how the novel dramatizes the metamorphoses of cultural heritage and inherited mythology in a new environment, it is very compelling to read it in light of Vautier's postcolonial articulation of myth in historical fiction. Though *Away* lacks the narrative self-consciousness of the novels around which Vautier builds her definition of New World Myth, it nonetheless to a degree displays the kind of postcolonial transformation of the function and resonance of myth that she describes.

New World Myth, in contrast with the use of myth as positive paradigm, articulates itself "against that out of which it originates" and "introduces not only a notion of flexibility but also a social, political, historical, and temporal component into the traditional concept of myth as something immutable, eternal, and, especially, transhistorical. The term itself is oxymoronic; it deliberately introduces a historical dimension into traditional notions of mythic universality."[141] Vautier argues, furthermore, that New World Myth blurs the boundaries between fiction, history, and myth and, therefore, that to the catalogue of postmodern paradoxes "we may now add the concept of 'myth' as comforting *and* disquieting, structuring *and* decentring, old *and* traditional, and new *and* generative."[142] While *Away* may not be postmodern, such a description certainly captures the effects of its very ambivalent use of myth.

New World Myth, moreover, is notably historiographic, "concerned with both epistemological uncertainty and the need to know, … intent on imaginatively reclaiming the past while flaunting its awareness of the processes involved in this act."[143] While such flaunting is

Thomas D'Arcy McGee.

notably absent in *Away*, this effect nonetheless is achieved through
the complex relationship, centred on the figure of D'Arcy McGee,
between the personal and the political, the mythic and the historical.
Urquhart presents McGee almost exclusively from the ideologically
overdetermined perspective of Irish patriots and refrains from providing a more conclusive portrayal of his assassination. These choices
put historical concerns at the service of mythical ones, but do so in a
way that raises questions about the relation between history and myth.

For instance, though Eileen sustains her resentment of McGee,
later, talking to Esther, she concedes that she "should be grateful to
D'Arcy McGee for something ... He put me in my place" (350). This
somewhat enigmatic reference to the revelation of her state of being
both romantically and politically "away" serves, to a certain degree,
to contain McGee's role in the novel, restricting him to providing a
trace of history on the O'Malley family myth, in which a transhistorical

pattern is repeated once again. However, McGee leaves his mark all the same, particularly because Esther (thanks to Eileen's experiences) is to learn the virtues of stability. Likewise, the somewhat oblique presentation of the assassination, which merely suggests by association that "the man called Patrick" (335) is responsible, throws the emphasis on Eileen's participation in revolutionary politics and the fetishized, romanticized nationalism that leads to her romantic, cultural, and political alienation. In this respect, McGee's presence in the novel as the epicentre of debates over the place of Irish immigrants in the new dominion contributes to the kind of historicizing effect that Vautier sees in New World Myth. The novel sets up a dialectic between myth and history and, unlike *In the Skin of a Lion*, reveals the operation of historical consciousness impinging on and alleviating the inevitability of a mythic paradigm; it thus historicizes without inscribing the teleological inevitability of historicism or the rationalism of empiricist historiography.

Urquhart's *Away* thus provides a moving illustration of Wiesel's adage that the "opposite of history is not myth" but "forgetfulness." As a historical novel, *Away* lacks the discursive heterogeneity and interrogativeness typical of the historiographical metafiction so prevalent in recent English-Canadian literature. Instead, its blending of historical realism and the marvellous provides a more seamless and less openly dialogic, but no less effective, postcolonial historicizing of myth. *Away* thus provides a good illustration of Cooper's argument that magic realism involves "seeing with a third eye," especially in its treatment of time: "Time itself is hybrid. Magical realist time tries to be neither the linear time of history, nor the circular time of myth" but occupies a liminal position between them.[144]

In *Away*, Urquhart weaves a powerfully lyrical, magical, and historically detailed narrative that underlines not only the importance of a consciousness of the past, but also an appreciation of the mythic patterns within which the past comes down to us – not just in the oral tradition but in contemporary popular culture as well. The novel thus demonstrates that what we think of as history and what we think of as myth are not neatly separable, as empiricist historiography would have it, but are interpenetrating aspects of our perception of the past. It illustrates how both the personal and the political are suffused with mythological resonance but also emphasizes the importance of resisting the iterative, metaphysical momentum of that mythology in order to open it up to historical change. Like Hodgins, Urquhart's attitude towards myth suggests the importance of a third way between myth and history, particularly within a postcolonial context in which the possibility of returning to a prelapsarian, precolonial condition is a dangerous illusion.

Mythologizing historical events has been a central and controversial element of the traditional historical novel, which is often seen as trading historical accuracy for popular appeal. Indeed, turning events that transpire in profane, chronological time into myth, Eliade contends, is characteristic of the popular imagination. He argues that, instead of wishful thinking, this transformation of events from the specific and historical to the archetypal and categorical is required to ensure their persistence in popular memory.[145] Thus the "memory of the collectivity is antihistorical" because, as it transforms historically specific events into archetypes, "it annuls all their historical and personal peculiarities."[146] Such a formulation of the relation between myth and history suggests that a form like the historical novel is fundamentally paradoxical because its mythologizing and aestheticizing effect is ultimately ahistorical and thus works against the depiction of "historical and personal peculiarities."

The use of mythology in contemporary historical novels, however, illustrates the empiricist and rationalist assumptions behind the contention that the historical novel is an oxymoron. Novels like *The Wars*, *In the Skin of a Lion*, *The Invention of the World*, and *Away* reflect a much more complex engagement with myth's archetypal function and its relation to history. To varying degrees, they caution against the seduction of the eternal return and inscribe instead an appreciation for historical specificity and context without reinscribing a slavish historicism or a sense of authoritative empiricism. In this sense, all of these novels resist the allure of myth as a retreat from history – a recurrent feature of literary modernism – but without returning to history as a retreat from myth – a recurrent feature of modern historiography.

The problem with retreating from history into myth, as critiques of this impulse in modernism tend to emphasize, is that it usually marks a disengagement from historical and political change. One of the attractions of myth, Eliade argues, is that suffering in the profane and "historical" world is made more palatable by recuperation of it into mythic patterns, which give it meaning and therefore make it more tolerable and provide a sense of hope or at least resignation.[147] This is, of course, a very modernist longing. The regeneration fundamental to mythic structures, he maintains, renders history more tolerable because it is the time in which "an entire cosmic cycle" or "a single cycle nearing its end" is to be played out.[148] But, as Eliade asks at the end of *The Myth of the Eternal Return*, how is one to deal with the terrors of history without such consolation? It is a significant question, and, unfortunately, Eliade's fear of nihilism in the face of those terrors leads him to answer it with a somewhat sophistic reassertion of the need for God, and faith in God, as a kind of guarantee of human freedom.[149]

Contemporary Canadian historical novels, on the other hand, tend to eschew such a metaphysical reliance and resist the temptation to retreat from the terrors of history. Instead they tend to rework myth precisely to provoke greater contemplation of and engagement with history, particularly by dissolving the boundaries between history and myth. Historians, as Tonkin observes, "have labelled as 'myth' what seem unrealistic ways of representing the past, but it can sometimes be shown that mythic structures encode history, that is they register actual happenings or significant changes. 'Realism', on the other hand, is an equally culture-bound judgment of likelihood."[150]

If both myth and realism (which most empiricist historians assume their history to be) are culturally determined modes of representing the past, the important achievement of these novels is that they prompt us to consider more closely the advantages and disadvantages of those modes, rather than adopting the passive position cultivated by the opposition between history as a scientific description of the past and myth as a fabulous and fictional rendering of it. These novels use mythological discourse to render history in a fashion more palatable to the public memory but also to inscribe a resistance to the decontextualizing, ahistorical effects of myth both in its traditional manifestation and in its modernist avatar. At the same time, these novelists use mythical codes to disturb the allure of historicism and to provide a reminder that just as myth may contain the trace of history, history is also always shot through with the trace of myth.

Myth is thus deployed, like oral frameworks and conventions, to question the assumptions of empiricist historiography and recover the energies of premodern and precolonial cultures. Along with historiographical parody and metafictional strategies that disrupt the cohesiveness and authority of historical mimesis, these strategies illustrate how the shift in "the content of the form" of contemporary Canadian historical novels has signalled a distinct break with a historical realism that comfortably coexisted with an empiricist historiography. With their generic heterogeneity, narratorial self-reflexivity, foregrounded intertextuality, and suspicion of historiography and literacy, these novels have substantially departed from the historical novel's traditional ideals of unity and historical authenticity. All in all, these strategies, combined with the resistance to official history reflected in these novels' postcolonial revisionism and emphasis on social history, have substantially carnivalized the historical novel in Canada. If history has characteristically been figured as a pageant, a glorious procession of the historically noteworthy, in these novels historical pageantry has given way to the popular, heterogeneous, material, and marginal spirit of carnival.

As Bakhtin, the principal theorist of the carnivalesque, describes it in *Rabelais and His World*, the carnivalesque in literature represents a return to a marginalized folk culture as well as a questioning of official culture, subverting its spirit of seriousness and authority. Bakhtin describes "the culture of folk humor" in the Middle Ages as essentially subversive and argues that carnival forms "were sharply distinct from the serious official, ecclesiastical, feudal, and political cult forms and ceremonials. They offered a completely different, non-official, extraecclesiastical and extrapolitical aspect of the world, of man, and of human relations; they built a second world and a second life outside officialdom."[151] Postmodern fiction, Brian McHale argues, reworks a literal carnival context that is absent from contemporary society, compensating "for this loss of the carnival context by incorporating carnival, or some surrogate for carnival, at the level of the projected world."[152] "Carnivalized literature," therefore, "is heterogeneous and flagrantly 'indecorous,' interweaving disparate styles and registers. Where the official genres are typically unitary, both generically and ontologically, projecting a single fictional world, carnivalized literature interrupts the text's ontological 'horizon' with a multiplicity of inserted genres."[153]

Bakhtin's notion of the carnivalesque finds expression in contemporary fiction's engagement with history in its resistance to official "representations of pastness"[154] and its disruption of the single world that traditional historiography seeks to project – good examples being Rushdie's *Midnight's Children*, Carter's *Nights at the Circus*, and Swan's *The Biggest Modern of the World*. Obviously, none of the historical novels under scrutiny in this study fits the description of carnivalized literature so well as Swan's novel. Of the more recent fiction, only *Disappearing Moon Café* and *Fox* approach the carnivalesque qualities of *The Biggest Modern Woman* or Bowering's *Burning Water*. At the same time, most of these novels, in their more iconoclastic and irreverent treatment of historical figures and in their intertextual and parodic approach to the past, nonetheless seem to partake of the carnivalesque spirit. The anti-authoritarian, inventive, heterogeneous, and liberating spirit of the carnivalesque is generally evident in contemporary historical fiction's movement away from monologic historical discourse, from historical precision and authenticity, and from a reverent or respectful attitude towards the past.

However, although the work of Bakhtin has proved tremendously influential in contemporary conceptions of the novel, his celebration of carnival has not been without its critics, and criticism of his work in turn has important implications for the carnivalesque tendencies of the historical novel in Canada. Numerous commentators on Bakhtin have pointed out his excessively utopian portrait of the communal energies of the carnivalesque; the ambivalence of the market, which provides the context for the carnival, as a site of division and commerce as well as cultural subversion; and, perhaps most important, the fact that carnival is an officially sanctioned release of potentially revolutionary energy.[155] Recognizing that the novel is, and always has been, a commodity, a product of the market, qualifies the degree to which carnivalesque strategies in the historical novel amount to a subversion of official history and suggests that the form stands in a much more ambivalent and ultimately less irreverent relation to that official culture. Indeed, in the culture of our own times, at least for some critics, the lines between official culture, the marketplace, and subversive representations have become increasingly indistinct. The blurring of these divisions has profound implications and is, therefore, the subject with which the final chapter of this book is concerned.

4 Speculating in Fiction: Commodity Culture and the Crisis of Historicity

Contemporary English-Canadian historical novels, as the two previous chapters illustrate, exhibit a pronounced scepticism towards established beliefs in progress, reality, and history, as part of the "incredulity toward metanarratives" that Jean-Francois Lyotard sees as definitive of postmodernism. The novels surveyed thus far not only reflect an expansion and contesting of what counts as history, but also foreground the machinery of historical representation – setting historiography and literary representation in the limelight beside, rather than concealing them behind, the picture of history. What the self-consciousness and self-referentiality of most of the textual strategies explored in the previous chapter underline, moreover, is these novelists' recognition of how historical inquiry and historical representation are by definition shaped by contemporary standards and concerns.

As E.H. Carr argues, "we can view the past, and achieve our understanding of the past, only through the eyes of the present"; thus, for Carr, the "function of the historian is neither to love the past nor to emancipate himself from the past, but to master and understand it as the key to the understanding of the present."[1] For Michel de Certau, this influence is even more profound: "history endlessly finds the present in its object and the past in its practice. Inhabited by the uncanniness that it seeks, history imposes its law upon the faraway places that it conquers when it fosters the illusion that it is bringing them back to life."[2] The last chapter of this book, "Speculating in Fiction," explores the temporal duality of these novels – that is, how they remain submerged in the present while training a periscope on the past, representing the past in order to engage with the postmodern present and particularly with the capitalist ethic that has shaped it. It examines the ambivalent fashion in which contemporary historical novels "speculate" in history, on the one hand inscribing an uncertainty and scepticism about historiographical practice and commodity culture and on the other hand speculatively "investing" in history as the raw material for the production of marketable fiction.

How does the contemporary historical novel find "the present in its object" and what kind of present does it find? Cultural production in Canada, as elsewhere, has been shaped by undeniable and profound economic, social, political, and cultural developments, the litany of which is familiar from a proliferation of discussions of postmodernity. They include the increasing ascendancy of an ostensibly free market economy and of international corporations; the spread of technologies of communication, most notably television, video, and the computer; and the movement towards an ostensibly post-ideological age in the wake of the end of the Cold War and the erstwhile "triumph" of capitalism, in which differences will ultimately be eradicated through inclusion in an international market economy. One of the effects of these various developments, according to Fredric Jameson, is that we live in a time of "the enfeeblement of historicity" and that historicity is in "crisis."[3] Indeed, "the concept of the postmodern," Jameson argues, can best be grasped "as an attempt to think the present historically in an age that has forgotten how to think historically in the first place."[4]

Cultural production in postmodernity, particularly because of the influence of spatializing technologies like video, television, and computers, argues Jameson, is characterized by a sense of depthlessness. This sense of depthlessness is fortified by the intertextuality and self-consciousness of postmodern cultural production, which amounts for Jameson to a "reshuffling of fragments of preexistent texts, the building blocks of older cultural and social production, in some new and heightened bricolage: metabooks which cannibalize other books, metatexts which collate bits of other texts – such is the logic of postmodernism in general."[5] Furthermore, postmodern thought has undermined traditional representation and aesthetics and may itself "be more *thoroughly* aestheticising than any previous body of thought."[6]

The potential consequence of contemporary theory and culture's questioning of notions of the real, of history, of art is a displacing of the ground upon which political contestation might take place. Thus, for critics such as Jameson, Terry Eagleton, Aijaz Ahmad, and others, postmodern cultural production is in many ways decadent and complicit with contemporary consumer culture.[7] Critics such as Linda Hutcheon, Brian McHale, and Patricia Waugh, however, see greater potential for political and social critique in postmodernist cultural production. They make a persuasive case that much of that production – while it may undercut established notions of history, subjectivity, and reality that make oppositional critique possible – shifts the grounds for contestation from the level of product to the level of process. Waugh argues that literary postmodernism does not dissolve but rather rescues "the possibility of coherent subjectivity, historical significance and ethical stability by re-examining rather than refuting their foundations in modern thought and representation."[8] Rather than abandoning the metaphysical underpinnings of traditional notions of morality, subjectivity, and reality, postmodern art and theory have underlined the importance of opening them up to greater scrutiny and to a more provisional, contingent, and situational politics.

What, then, are the implications of writing historical fiction in such a commodifying, depoliticizing, and dehistoricizing age, in which, as David Harvey puts it, it "is difficult to maintain any sense of historical continuity in the face of all the flux and ephemerality of flexible accumulation"?[9] Given the anti-foundational tendencies of postmodernism, the position of a cultural product like the historical novel, which in so many ways relies on an appreciation of the past, is particularly perilous. Jameson argues that the undermining of a sense of historicity within postmodernity has stripped the historical novel of its customary function. The historical novel developed, he argues, as a projection of the emergence of the middle class, "as that class sought to project its own vision of its past and its future and to articulate its social and collective project in a temporal narrative."[10] Within postmodernity, however, the traditional historical novel has essentially become obsolete because "we no longer tell ourselves our history in that fashion, but also because we no longer experience it in that way, and, indeed, perhaps no longer experience it at all."[11] In short, just as the rise of the historical novel accompanied the rise of a sense of historicity, the decline of historicity in the postmodern era has precipitated the decline of the historical novel.

If a weakening of the sense of historicity is a necessary concomitant of postmodernity, in what light does that put the present flourishing of the historical novel in Canada? Does that make it an elegiac phenomenon, the swan song of a literary genre that has lost its bearings? Or is it exemplary of a paradoxical postmodern "speculation," representing the past in a self-consciously "speculative" fashion (rather than according to the principle of objectively reconstructing the past in fiction), while nonetheless "speculatively" investing in the past by exploiting it as material in the creation of a product? The novels examined in this chapter – Jane Urquhart's *Away*, Michael Ondaatje's *In the Skin of a Lion*, Thomas Wharton's *Icefields*, Susan Swan's *The Biggest Modern of the World*, and Guy Vanderhaeghe's *The Englishman's Boy* – suggest that historical novelists have found new bearings that often (in a common postmodern ambivalence) point in conflicting directions.

If frame stories can be useful devices for disrupting the illusion of a recreated past and for commenting on historiographical and fictional assumptions, they can also provide a significant dual temporality. Through frame stories, writers can explore the effects of the present on the past but also exploit a representation of the past to comment on the conditions of the present. This is certainly the case in Urquhart's *Away*. The device of the frame story helps to give shape to the past, but through it Urquhart also extends her engagement with questions of cultural heritage and history quite openly to the present, which *Away* depicts as endangering the legacy of the past. A persistent motif throughout the frame story is that of erosion and excavation, both literal and figurative. Urquhart gives to the idea of "unearthing" a rich and dramatic series of resonances – historical, cultural, ecological, and industrial – as she emphasizes the intimate relationship between history and landscape. What emerges, as a result, is a powerful comment on the economic priorities of the new (that is, postmodern) dominion.

One of the common features of magic realism, with which *Away* clearly has affiliations, is, as Jameson observes, "the articulated superposition of whole layers of the past within the present."[12] That superposition is very much allegorized through Esther's reflections in the novel's frame story. Buried in the landscape of Loughbreeze Beach are fragments of the past, and archaeological imagery is used repeatedly to punctuate Esther's consciousness of the past in the world around her: "Under the sand of the peninsula that reaches out into the lake there exist rooms whose wallpaper depicts bridges, willows, and streams – the scenery of a foreign land. Under the water at the end of a germinating jetty there are pilings clothed in seaweed that remember the search for a white sail and a pale hand" (*Away* 19). However, the stories that preserve the past are slipping. In an image reminiscent of the plague of insomnia in *One Hundred Years of Solitude*, Esther stores messages around the house and tapes stories to the furniture. She tries, like Marquez's Jose Arcadio Buendia, to fix meaning in a state of semantic dissolution, in her case a dissolution of the connection of the present to the past.

Her narrative is her last stand against this slippage: "She wants to reconstruct the pastures and meadows that have fallen into absence – the disassembled architecture, the great dark belly of an immigrant ship, a pioneer standing inland stunned by the forest, a farmer moving through the beams of light that fill his barn" (21). As the last in her family line, however, Esther has no audience. Her story, therefore, as Sheila Ross argues, "is a lamentation for a lost mythology," but *Away* itself "is an enactment of its revitalization."[13] In this regard, *Away* reflects an important, and postmodern, dimension of magic realism as a literary mode, its "impulse to reestablish contact with traditions temporarily eclipsed by the mimetic constraints of nineteenth- and twentieth-century realism."[14]

The erosion of tradition is not simply the result of the passage of time, but also the result of industrial activity. In the background of Esther's narrative swan song is the relentless operation of a limestone quarry (the curse of the mines realized), and through her descriptions of mining Urquhart connects her historical concerns with a critique of contemporary economic activity. Whereas the rest of the narrative inscribes a sense of the cumulative power of history and the mythic patterns with which it is interlaced, the frame story, by focusing on the destruction of landscape, emphasizes that the accumulated past is nonetheless susceptible to erosion.

The mining in the frame story is associated not with a recovery of the past but with the destruction of memory: "in Eileen's world abandoned structures decomposed, sinking back into the landscape from which they had sprung. In Esther's lifetime she has seen architecture die violently. It has been demolished, burned, ripped apart, or buried. Nothing reclaims it" (135). "Esther's regenerative story," as Anne Compton observes, "is the antithesis of the industrial process that converts landscape into cement."[15] This industrial activity undermines the efforts at preservation or remembering that Esther's narrative – and by implication Urquhart's – represents: "Esther thinks of the million-year-old fossils that decorate these stones and how the limestone record of their extermination has brought about the demise of her own landscape, the enormous hole in the earth, the blanket of concrete dwellings that is obliterating the villages she knew as a child" (20–1).

The men on the night shift of the cement company are clearly allegorized; they are figures of violence and historical ignorance, working in darkness, never bending "to the quarry floor to rescue a fossil released by dynamite" (237). Their activity takes on political overtones, as they are described as being "out of step with the rhythms of the rest of the world" and "represent the most dangerous kind of shape changers: those who cannot see, because of darkness, beyond the gesture of the moment" (238). Coming at the beginning of the final section of the novel, before Eileen's romantic and political involvement with Aidan, this image provides a preface to the revolutionary activity of Aidan's patriot acquaintances and to Eileen's naive participation. It suggests the destructive nature of a static, inflexible adherence to nationalist mythology, but it also suggests the implications of blindness and an expedient fixation on the present in contemporary society.

Indeed, the final image of the novel makes a larger association between the cement company as a representative of industrial activity, capitalism, and the loss of historical consciousness, as the work of the night crew breaks the silence in the wake of Esther's death: "Now the land itself fragments, moves away from piers in boats named after brief histories towards other waters, other shores. No lamps at all are lit tonight in the empty house on Loughbreeze Beach. The men at the quarry, angered by something they don't quite understand, set their jaws and shift the gears of their equipment with grim forcefulness. Under the glare of artificial light the fossilized narratives of ancient migrations are crushed into powder. The scream of the machinery intensifies" (356). That the boats pulling up to the company pier to receive the limestone – the commodified residue of "landscape and fossils" (352) – are named *Sir John A. Macdonald* and *The New Dominion* consolidates the parallels between the two eras.[16] Thus *Away* conducts a cultural and political archaeology of the nation and makes a lyrical appeal for the preservation of historical memory.

It also fearfully dramatizes the contribution of an obsession with production and consumption to "the enfeeblement of historicity," most immediately because of its effect on landscape: "The traces of wounds left behind by industry are permanent. Fragile architecture abandoned by settlers is not" (11). In this sense, the traces of one disruption – the famine and the ensuing migration that brought Esther's great-grandparents to Upper Canada – are threatened by another. Both the nineteenth-century sequences and the twentieth-century narrative that frames them illustrate the dangers of historical myopia, an expedient and fetishized preoccupation with the immediate, which in our own times has taken the form of the apotheosis of the market and the uncritical acceptance of productivity as the index of a nation's vitality and importance.

In this fashion, *Away* provides a synoptic assessment of the state of the dominion – from the literal "new dominion" at the time of Confederation to the "new dominion" of our present global capitalist era. In this respect, Urquhart's linking of precapitalist modes of subsistence to modern colonial and capitalist modes of production represents a typically magic realist reaching back beyond modernity to put into question some of its more inimical effects. Speaking of writers in Western Canada, at a time when Urquhart had yet to establish her reputation as a novelist, Geoff Hancock observed that magic realism "may recover truths that have been degraded by the onslaught of commercial activity, environmental pollution, and a decline of the ideal which the New World once promised."[17] Looking at *Away* in light of this comment, what is particularly compelling about the novel is that it both participates in that process of recovery and dramatizes the degradation that has rendered that recovery such a pressing need.

Away is somewhat exceptional in that it achieves its temporal dualism and comments on the present through the juxtaposition that Esther's narrative affords, rather than through the overtly metahistorical self-consciousness of *The Wars* and *Ana Historic* or the proleptic, subversive anachronism of, say, *Burning Water* and *The Biggest Modern Woman of the World*. Nonetheless, its allegorical engagement with the degradation of the environment in contemporary capitalist society demonstrates that historical fiction can be a highly effective means of contemporary political, social, and cultural critique.

Historical fiction can also, however, be a retrograde aestheticizing of the past – a superficial, popular image with merely the allure of the bygone – and this is no less the case in a postmodern era in which aesthetic practices have become increasingly compromised by and bound up with commodity culture. As David Bennett argues, "the high ground from which modernism's 'culture' asserted its critical distance from bourgeois society" has been eradicated by "the postwar culture industry's integration of aesthetic and intellectual production into commodity production in general."[18] The duality of a cultural product like the historical novel becomes troublesome in a culture in which the border between making the past aesthetically pleasing and converting the past into a consumable commodity becomes increasingly blurred. The relationship between the politics and aesthetics of the contemporary historical novel's representation of history is thus a crucial dimension of its postmodern ambivalence.

Aesthetic concerns and historiographical considerations in the historical novel, as theoretical discussions of the genre reflect, have always stood in uneasy equilibrium. In his 1850 essay *On the Historical Novel* novelist and theorist Alessandro Manzoni bemoaned the conflicting complaints of critics of the genre, some of whom objected to the historical inaccuracy resulting from the lack of distinction between fact and invention and others who complained that distinguishing "factual truth from invention … destroys the unity that is the vital condition of this or any other work of art."[19] Somewhat ironically, the historical novel has been praised as capable of presenting the past more vividly and authentically precisely because of its use of novelistic strategies that help fortify a sense of historical verisimilitude, of lived historical experience. At the same time, that immediacy often comes at the cost of historical precision, in the sense that aesthetic choices override historiographical ones.

This uneasy balance, however, becomes more precarious within a postmodernity that exhibits definite aestheticizing, dehistoricizing, and depoliticizing tendencies. For Jameson, postmodernism is no less ahistorical than modernism; the interest in the past in postmodern culture does not amount to a return to history but involves simply "incorporating the 'raw material' of history and leaving its function out, a kind of flattening and appropriation"; in this "new and original historical situation … we are condemned to seek History by way of our own pop images and simulacra of that history, which itself remains forever out of reach."[20] In contrast, Hal Foster argues that an appropriate label for much contemporary cultural production is what he calls the "anti-aesthetic"; in this model, in short, postmodernism contests the aestheticizing inclinations of modernism. The "anti-aesthetic" questions "the very notion of the aesthetic" and the autonomy, ahistoricity, and purposelessness attributed to it in modernism. The "anti-aesthetic," like postmodernism, "marks a cultural position on the present," can question the place of the aesthetic in contemporary culture, and is amenable to "forms that deny the idea of a privileged aesthetic realm."[21]

"Anti-aesthetic" or renewed, redoubled aestheticism? The answer, as with most answers about postmodernism, is not likely to be one or the other but rather both. In an increasingly self-conscious literary culture, Canadian novelists often exhibit their awareness of the dangers of "using" and aestheticizing history. Nonetheless, they are necessarily engaged in doing so, and as that culture is also a relentlessly consumerist one, aestheticizing history tilts easily and precariously into commodifying history, making it readily consumable rather than cultivating a historical consciousness or an engagement with how history is constructed. Thus in contemporary historical novels the aesthetic and the historical jostle for position as they always have, but with a significant – and decidedly political – difference. Two novels that provide an interesting illustration of this ambivalence, in different contexts but in quite similar fashion, are Michael Ondaatje's *In the Skin of a Lion* and Thomas Wharton's *Icefields*.

The public debate over Ondaatje's portrait of the historical Count Laszlo de Almasy in *The English Patient*, which has been interpreted by some as romanticizing fascism, shows how the intersection between history, aesthetics, and politics is a busy one and far from easy to navigate. *In the Skin of a Lion* provides material for similar controversy. The novel has been widely appreciated as a *tour de force* of historiographical metafiction, providing insights into historiography, fiction, politics, humanism, art, love, and capitalism in ways that blur their edges, and is certainly one of the aesthetically richest works in Canadian literature. However, as with *The English Patient*, the relation between the aesthetic and the political in the novel has led to a great deal of debate, problematizing or at least modifying an otherwise appreciative reception. In this sense, *In the Skin of a Lion*'s treatment of history showcases a key problem of postmodernism, which draws, Mike Featherstone argues, "on tendencies in consumer culture which favour the aestheticization of life, ... with the goal of life an endless pursuit of new experiences, values and vocabularies" – tendencies that may "lead to nihilism and social disintegration" but "may just as possibly lead to mutually expected self-restraint and respect for the other."[22] This ambivalence can be seen in the uneasy balance between the novel's emphasis on class conflict and its aestheticizing of experience.

At first glance, the politics of *In the Skin of a Lion* seem pretty clear. As E.L. Doctorow's *Ragtime* does for New England, *In the Skin of a Lion* portrays Toronto during a phase of capitalist expansion and provides a critical portrait of the treatment of labour. The entrepreneurial Ambrose Small, flagbearer of "bare-knuckle capitalism" (*In the Skin of a Lion* 57), exemplifies the aggressive, speculative economic order displacing the inherited, genteel privilege of the old monied class. Small succeeds by emulating those he seeks to displace, not only signalling the transition from a culture of entitlement, but also shattering the illusion of the benevolence of the wealthy, his "blatant capitalism [clarifying] the gulf between the rich and the starving" (59). Ondaatje uses the lacuna of the historical Small's disappearance to provide the context in which Patrick meets Clara Dickens and develops his rivalry with Small for Clara's affection, a rivalry that confirms Small's ambivalent ruthlessness, his rags-to-riches rapaciousness.[23] The ambivalent Small is a brazen representative of the Janus-face of capitalist modernity, whose social, cultural, and architectural excess is underpinned by a ruthless exploitation of labour. Clara and Patrick seem to appreciate Small's ascendancy and the threat it represents to the financial establishment, but when Patrick discovers and confronts him, Small first sets him on fire and then tosses a Molotov cocktail at him – bare-knuckle and more.

Patrick's main partner on this ideological dance card, however, is Rowland Harris, who represents capitalism with a human face and puts Patrick's political determination to the test. Through Harris, Ondaatje presents the emergence of modern Toronto as the reconfiguration of space within what is essentially a capitalist narrative, a narrative in which the workers are subsumed, given no agency. When Alice falls off the bridge during the construction of the Bloor St Viaduct, Harris reflects (echoing Shelley's *Frankenstein*), "This [the viaduct] was his first child and it had already become a murderer" (31). In doing so, he overlooks the workers who have perished during the construction because these, in the logic of capitalism, would be "natural" deaths. Harris is thus initially presented as a representative of a capitalist order whose mapping out of its designs on the urban space of Toronto is realized through the exploitation of labour.

That sense of exploitation, however, is increasingly obscured after the demise of Alice, who warns Patrick against a temptation to humanize the rich and urges him to "name the enemy and destroy their power. Start with their luxuries – their select clubs, their summer mansions" (124–5). Though sceptical of Alice's ideological appeals, Patrick fulfils her desire for "thunder" with his bombing of the Muskoka hotel after her death. The climax to the novel, however, substantially reworks the class polarities and antigonisms that Alice so vividly presents to Patrick. When Patrick infiltrates the waterworks to confront Harris over the lives lost during its construction, Harris is figured as Scheherazade, knowing "he had to survive until early morning" (237) and succeeding by talking Patrick to sleep.

Harris portrays himself as a small fish in the pond of capitalism and suggests that it is Patrick's rejection of power that allows "the bland fools – the politicians and press and mayors and their advisers – [to] become the spokesmen for the age" (238). Moreover, he forces Patrick to recognize his own responsibility in the death of Alice. Conversely, Harris recognizes the visionary heroism and achievement of Patrick's penetration of the plant. Thus, when Patrick falls asleep without detonating the explosives, Harris cites the line from the Gilgamesh epic and has Patrick's wounds tended to, instead of having him arrested. Class conflict appears to give way to reconciliation. What we are to make of this change in fortunes is perhaps the key question of *In the Skin of a Lion*. Is this a positive endorsement of Patrick's choice of the human over ideology? And, in that case, is his attack on the Muskoka hotel in contrast a misguided act of violence to be disowned? Or are we to see Patrick's failure to act as a negative capitulation, brought about because Patrick has been undermined by the weaknesses anticipated earlier by Alice (his susceptibility to Harris's self-justification, his guilt over Alice's death, his ultimate allegiance to humanism over revolutionary politics)?

The frame narrative at the end of the novel complicates these questions. Ondaatje places the sequence in which Patrick infiltrates the waterworks between the call from Clara and his departure for Marmora with Hana. At the end of the prior sequence, Patrick is asleep at the waterworks, and afterwards Hana rouses Patrick before they start on their trip, suggesting that the sequence has been a dream; at the same time, however, the frame narrative refers to Patrick's "good arm" (243), which suggests that the aborted attack has actually occurred. The ambiguity is, I think, quite intentional: frame narrative and framed narrative overlap, their edges disrupted, their ontological status put in limbo, a strategy that imparts to the reader the responsibility for writing the ending to the novel. Given the importance of the waterworks sequence to the politics of the novel, however, such indeterminacy can seem like an abdication of responsibility and definitely contributes to uncertainty about Ondaatje's political stance. Patrick's confrontation with Harris is the culmination of intense class conflict and violence throughout the novel, and presenting the outcome of that struggle in such an ambiguous fashion creates a serious tension between the aesthetic and political merits of having an open ending and the political merits of delivering an unambiguous denunciation of the evils of modern capitalism.

Like the ambiguity of the climax, the lush aestheticism of the narrative as a whole, it has been argued, functions to dissipate or compromise the novel's political energies. Throughout the novel, Ondaatje's depiction of labour, the dangers of labour, and labour agitation is highly aestheticized, merging violence, exertion, exploitation, and beauty in highly problematic ways. Nicholas Temelcoff, for instance, is presented as a kind of daredevil aerialist of the construction world as he works on the Bloor St Viaduct: "He knows his position in the air as if he is mercury slipping across a map" (35). Yet the arduousness and hazards of his work are subsequently underlined when he tells Alice of his injuries and his near escape during an accident similar to one that left his predecessor cut in two. Likewise, Patrick's father Hazen is portrayed as a "wizard" of explosives working for logging and mining companies, able to move "a log into precisely the location he said it would go, exploding a half-ton of shale" (15), but is killed in a cave-in in a feldspar mine because the "company had tried to go too deep and the section above him collapsed" (74).

Panorama. Victoria Park Pumping Station.
"This was choreography in 1930"

For the working class, artistry comes at a cost – an idea nicely captured in a brief description of the waitress at the diner Patrick frequents, who "through years of habit, had reduced to a minimum the action of pouring coffee or flipping an egg. He could spot the oil burns on her wrists, the permanent grimace in her eye from the smoke" (111).

Perhaps the most telling passage in this respect, however, is Patrick's reflection on the dyers taking a smoke break from their work in the tanneries: "Their bodies standing there tired, only the heads white. If he were an artist he would have painted them but that was false celebration. What did it mean in the end to look aesthetically plumaged on this October day in the east end of the city five hundred yards from Front Street? What would the painting tell?" (130). In a narrative passage typical of the "self-consuming" quality of much self-reflexive postmodern fiction, Ondaatje goes on to relate the arduousness, toxicity, and exploitation of their occupation.[24] The passage concisely captures how the working class is paradoxically depicted throughout the novel: everything is at once "aesthetically plumaged" but also politically charged.

Neither are such descriptions restricted to the lives of workers. For instance, whereas Harris is presented as oblivious overseer during the bridge construction, Ondaatje's images of the building of Harris's lavish waterworks, in contrast, repeatedly emphasize construction not as a narrative of labour exploitation but as artistry, performance: "This was choreography in 1930" (111). As a result of the obsession with sensual experience in the novel, Frank Davey argues, "the sensuous becomes a bridge between classes: A text which has appeared to offer indignation at the disparities of a capitalist society becomes one which charitably views both entrepreneur and workman equally as potential artists."[25]

Ultimately, Patrick's detente with Harris and the obsession with the aesthetic shift the emphasis from a dramatization of class dialectics to a more humanized and less polarized vision of the relation between capital and labour. The politics of *In the Skin of a Lion*, consequently, have been a matter of some debate. Christian Bök argues that the novel subscribes ambivalently to social reform, portraying "political idealism with a kind of nostalgic sympathy" but ultimately "as an obstacle to political reform."[26] Fotios Sarris observes that *In the Skin of a Lion* aims "to humanize history and consequently its corollary, ideology," but also "suggests that such a history militates against radical, revolutionary action."[27] The key here is the novel's central image, taken from a description of one of Alice's plays: "Each person had their moment when they assumed the skins of wild animals, when they took responsibility for the story" (157). Sarris concludes that "Ondaatje may be suggesting – anomalous as it may be nowadays – that the novelist should strive to be a spokesman for his age, that the writing of a novel should be a political act, one of those moments of assuming the skins of wild animals"; for Sarris, Ondaatje does this by illuminating and humanizing what is behind official history.[28]

Is the point, then, pens, not bombs? As Alice herself says of her agit-prop performance, "You reach people through metaphor" (123). Or should we simply respect the fact that Ondaatje has written a profoundly complex and thought-provoking novel that raises readers' consciousness about capitalist exploitation of workers and leave it at that? That seems to be Ondaatje's desire: "Novels that give you the right way to do things," he observes, "I just don't trust any more. The problem of what does someone like Patrick do, what does someone like Temelcoff do. That's so closely bound with character – human character, as opposed to politically correct behaviour."[29]

Through its open-ended, fragmentary style, the novel certainly leans towards what Roland Barthes calls the writerly novel, which positions the reader as primary producer of meaning. "Just as Patrick rejects the power and finality of a destructive blow," Gordon Gamlin maintains, "Ondaatje surrenders the authority of a closed narrative system."[30] Susan Spearey likewise sees the novel's indeterminacy as a virtue. She argues that the novel resists reinscribing the kinds of narrative, political, and historical models that it questions and "espouses no explicit political or ideological agenda which would harness it to a framework privileging linear historical time."[31] The fragmented narrative and emphasis on spatialized images, furthermore, provide "a model for a more open reading of texts and of history."[32] The novel clearly signals an awareness of its rejection of a realist, teleological, fictional history – "*Only the best art can order the chaotic tumble of events. Only the best can realign chaos to suggest both the chaos and order it will become*" – and in the very structure and pacing of the novel Ondaatje takes his own advice: "Meander if you want to get to town" (146).

But whose town? Patrick Lewis's or Rowland Harris's? While the two main representatives of individual and civic capitalism in the novel, Small and Harris, come, like Patrick, from humble backgrounds and are constructed as being outside the social and financial elite, they nonetheless are part of the capitalist machine that grinds down the workers. That the distinctions between Patrick – who labours in Harris's projects and participates in revolutionary actions – and figures like Harris and Small are undermined as the novel progresses is one of the intentions but also one of the problems of *In the Skin of a Lion*.[33] A recurrent critique of postmodernist fiction is that its self-reflexive rejection of artistic and political foundationalism simply repeats the apolitical aestheticism of much modernism, and *In the Skin of a Lion* is certainly susceptible to such a critique. The politics of the writerly novel in this case rest in uneasy equilibrium with the politics of writing a history of working-class immigrants and class conflict, bringing to mind Jameson's observation that postmodern texts "flatten" our sense of history. Ultimately, however, *In the Skin of a Lion* demonstrates how anti-foundationalism is not necessarily apolitical: while Ondaatje resists grounding the dialectical energies of the novel on political or moral absolutes, his characteristic oscillation between beauty and violence produces both a commodified, aesthetically pleasing history and a powerful critique of the forces of capitalism.

The already substantial debate over the politics of *In the Skin of a Lion* provides a good comparison point for an exploration of Wharton's *Icefields*, whose fragmentary narrative, lyrical style, and generic affiliations echo Ondaatje's novel. The most compelling parallel between the two, however, is that they both look at capitalism's reconfiguring of space at the moment of Canada's emerging modernity – *In the Skin of a Lion* in an urban context and *Icefields* in terms of the Canadian "wilderness." *Icefields* traces, through a series of stages, the fixing of Jasper National Park as park, that is, not so much as wilderness preserve but as commodified, picturesque natural resource to be exploited through tourism. If *In the Skin of a Lion* charts the reconfiguration of urban space according to the designs of capitalism, Wharton, focusing particularly on the development of the Columbia icefields, does the same for natural space, with a much more tangible proleptic vision. Like *In the Skin of a Lion*, *Icefields* develops a critique of capitalism that threatens to be compromised by its aestheticizing of the historical context through which that critique is developed.

As in Ondaatje's novel, resistance to capitalist development is central to *Icefields*, which focuses on the opposition between guide Frank Trask and the man he saves at the beginning of the novel, Edward Byrne. When Byrne falls down a crevasse on the Arcturus Glacier off the Columbia icefields during an 1898 expedition of the Royal Geographic Society, he sees, through the play of light in the crevasse, the figure of an angel large enough "to surround and enfold him in its wings" (*Icefields* 12). He becomes obsessed with the glacier, and his protective behaviour towards it and his enigmatic vigil as he waits for the angel to emerge pits him against Trask's efforts to develop the area into a tourist attraction.

Like many historical novelists, Wharton reworks historical sources to give prominence to his fictional protagonists. He changes the details and the chronology of the actual expeditions, in which, for one thing, Edward Byrne did not participate because he is a creation of Wharton's.[34] Wharton takes an accident from Hugh Stutfield and Norman Collie's 1897 expedition in the Banff area and moves it to the Athabasca valley a year later, introducing Byrne and Trask as the principals involved. In the original incident, C.S. Thompson (who is briefly mentioned in *Icefields*) fell into a crevasse near the summit of what was thought by expedition members to be Mount Murchison and required a hasty extrication "from the awkward position he was in, for he could not move and was almost upside down, jammed between the two opposing sides of the crevasse."[35] The somewhat dramatic account of the rescue certainly supplied some of the details for Wharton's scene, but there is no sign of an angel, and Thompson's experience, unlike Byrne's, was less than epiphanic.[36] Wharton obviously found the moment more than worthy of record (or at least of remixing), and his reworking of the historical expeditions is obviously orchestrated to introduce, in dramatic fashion, the two figures who are pitted against each other throughout the rest of the narrative: Trask and Byrne.

The Royal Geographical Society expedition is the preamble to the claiming and commodification of the mountains, and Byrne's participation dramatizes the conflicting inclinations of the scientist towards a colonizing appropriation on the one hand and towards a more creative, artistic, even metaphysical inquisitiveness on the other. The former tendency is certainly, at least to some degree, exhibited by Byrne's colleagues. Their expedition is intended to prove or disprove the legend of Mount Brown – which has *"been on every map in the empire for sixty years as the highest on this continent"* (18) – and in that sense repeats Sexsmith's inclination to colonize the territory.[37] In the novel, Stutfield exhibits the proprietary impulses of the scientific explorer when he observes of the icefield that they "are probably the first human beings ever to see it. Definitely to have traversed it" (50). Wharton gives their discovery a sense of wonder that ties it somewhat ironically to Miranda's "brave new world" speech in *The Tempest*, as he observes: "Collie had not found his mountain. He had stumbled upon a new world" (49).[38] The irony, however, as in *The Tempest*, is that the world is not new.

In contrast with such appropriative urges, Byrne's discovery of the angel fills him with a very metaphysical wonder, though for that very reason the reticent Byrne keeps that discovery to himself. The angel is obviously problematic for Byrne as a man of science, and, as he records later on in his journal, he resists the temptation to relate his experience to his colleagues at the Royal Society: *"And now, in this cathedral of skepticism and science, I found myself unwilling to speak of it. In fact I panicked for a moment when the thought occurred to me that I had not only imagined the figure in the crevasse, but that the entire expedition was only a fantasy of mine, a hallucination"* (59). Were he to mention it, he fears, his colleagues would deny he had even been on the expedition. (Given that Byrne is a fictional character, Wharton's reflection on the rigidity of scientific rationalism is marked by a certain self-reflexive, ironic humour as well.)

Byrne becomes an enigmatic figure, obsessed with charting the regression of the glacier, keeping the object of his quest to himself, but having a meticulous regard and concern for the glacier that for everybody else clearly goes beyond the scientific. He reads Sexsmith's book, intrigued by Sexsmith's reticence about the icefields, speculating that, "like me, he encountered something that he dared not set down in his memoirs" (181). Scientific control struggles with spiritual awe: Byrne responds to the Victorian geologist John Tyndall's musing that imagination might be "an energy *locked like latent heat in ancient inorganic nature*" by wondering *"was it a power that overflowed from some unseen source, pressing inexorably forward to enclose and reshape the world?"* (169). What motivates Byrne all the same is the spirit of scientific inquiry: *"The possibility of a spiritual entity trapped, frozen, in ice. Enmeshed somehow in physical forces, immobilized, and thus rendered physical and solid itself ... And when it melted out of the ice, would it then just sublimate back into metaphysical space, leaving human time and scientific measurement behind?"* (171). As Ronald Clark notes, many Victorian mountaineers were geologists, "men whose daily life and thought brought them into full and unavoidable contact with the awful problems posed by the revelations of this science which was then eating so deeply into many men's accepted beliefs."[39] In the figure of Byrne, Wharton illustrates this ongoing negotiation between the empirical and the metaphysical, but also inscribes an appreciation for a Romantic response to the sublimity of nature.[40]

This internal struggle is set against Byrne's struggle with Trask over the development of the icefields, and Wharton's portrait of their mutual antagonism clearly has implications for the commodification rampant in contemporary society. Trask is loosely modelled on the Brewster family, who played a pivotal role in opening up the Rockies, including the icefields, to tourism; they promoted excursions to the Columbia icefields first by pack-horse and later by bus and snowmobile, and also operated the Athabasca Chalet, which preceded the present Columbia Icefield Chalet.[41] The Romantic Byrne becomes an impediment for Trask as the latter seizes on the commercial possibilities of the Athabasca valley and the icefields. The friendly rivalry that develops between the two dramatizes a more fundamental – and strikingly contemporary – tension between preservation and development.[42]

When Byrne returns, ten years after the expedition, Trask, now part owner of a chalet near the glacier, speculates that Byrne might prove useful in promoting the icefields. Byrne's aloofness – the legacy of his preoccupation with his discovery – makes him a "romantic figure to those who keep to the immaculate lawns that girdle the chalet and go no further," and Trask considers the possibility that Byrne's narrow escape could "be turned into a profitable curiosity. The man who was trapped in the jaws of icy death. The *icy* jaws of death might be better" (66). Trask, with his pitch-man's sensibility, epitomizes the instrumentalist and exploitative thinking of an emerging consumer society, but Byrne is clearly not of the same mind. *"It might work,"* Trask muses. *"If he wasn't such a stiff-necked bastard"* (66). Indeed, Trask and Byrne subsequently clash when Byrne's warning of a glacial moraine, with a core of glacial ice, running through the location of Trask's proposed hot springs is verified, causing the planned railroad to be diverted and Trask's hot springs to be relocated. "No more icy surprises" (89), Trask icily requests of Byrne, implicitly objecting to the effrontery of science (and nature) in getting in the way of progress.

If the development of the mountains represents progress, Wharton clearly underlines, like Ondaatje, that progress comes at a cost. The establishment of the boundaries of the park in 1907 is ultimately an act of exclusion: "*Within the boundaries of this new preserve, hunting, trapping, and unauthorized settlement are prohibited*" (61). For most of the original inhabitants, including the native people of whom Byrne hears from Sara, this means expulsion because only "those who had sanctioned business within the boundaries ... were allowed to remain" (74). The power to sanction, of course, resides largely in the hands of white politicians and businessmen, part of the larger political and financial apparatus of a burgeoning federation. The human costs of development are also poignantly reflected in a scene (one of a number reminiscent of *In the Skin of a Lion*) in which Byrne tends to a dying immigrant railroad worker pinned to a rock face by a spike through his hand. What Wharton likewise emphasizes, if in a more low-key fashion than Ondaatje, is how national development takes place in the interests of the political and financial elite and on the backs of those positioned as others in a young, muscular, Anglocentric Canada.

In *Postmodernism*, Jameson argues that consumerism as a culture functions by effacing the politics and dynamics of production and by reifying the product, which "somehow shuts us out even from a sympathetic participation, by imagination, in its production. It comes before us, no questions asked, as something we could not begin to imagine doing for ourselves."[43] In *Icefields*, however, the politics and dynamics of the transformation of the icefields into a commodity are very much foregrounded, particularly through the portrait of Trask. Trask's activities in the novel provide a good example of how the natural world is reinscribed, refigured, and packaged for "the tourist gaze."[44] "Tourists are semioticians," observe Chris Rojeck and John Urry (evoking Jonathan Culler), and Trask's management of the icefields certainly illustrates the potential effect of tourism, in which "the sign or marker is constitutive of the sight which, in a sense, cannot be 'seen' without the marker."[45] While Wharton is writing of an era in which tourism in the Rockies was in the process of becoming commercialized, it is also clear that his narrative is looking ahead to (and back from) a postmodern era in which, "with the extraordinary proliferation of images and signs in the last few decades, this economy of signs has swept across and overwhelmed the signs typically consumed by the traveller while away."[46]

Trask begins the process of commodifying the icefields with his guided walking tours to Arcturus glacier: "*We can take you above the clouds at a very reasonable charge, and let you touch a real glacier"* (101). When Byrne later takes up residence at the chalet, he is asked by Trask to write a "short primer on ice and glaciers" (195) for the tourists to accompany Trask's diorama of "Jasper and Environs." Typically digressing into profound philosophical and geological speculation as he starts to write, Byrne catches himself, realizing that "Trask wants his tourists to have the model, a brief explanatory text, and a view of the real thing. Prehistory will come alive for them, they will commemorate the moment by buying postcards, souvenirs, film for photographs" (197). Trask recognizes and exploits the fact that, as Jennifer Craik observes, "there is a good deal of self-delusion involved in the pursuit of tourist pleasure. Although tourists think they want authenticity, most want some degree of negotiated experiences which provide a tourist 'bubble' (a safe, controlled environment) out of which they can selectively step to 'sample' predictable forms of experiences."[47]

The conflict between Trask and Bynre intensifies after Byrne returns from the calamity of World War I. Trask is bent on pursuing development in the park in an atmosphere of burgeoning modernity: "Trask allows himself some cautious optimism. He has heard of a new wave of explorers massing out there in the cities. Families in automobiles who will glide through the mountains on smooth gleaming highways. Checking the names of glaciers in illustrated guidebooks. Gazing in awe at a world that is no longer invisible, no longer a blank space" (247). Amidst this optimism, the "only problem" is Byrne, who has built a shelter at the base of the glacier, having calculated the approximate time of the emergence of the angel, and is resistant to Trask's plans to conduct tours of the glacier and the icefields by ice-crawler. "Parks has agreed to it," says Trask, making the argument by now so familiar from countless development schemes pitting local workers against environmental activists: "Everybody but you wants this to happen, it'll make work for a lot of people" (249). When Byrne complains of the centuries-old trees Trask's men have cut down, Trask responds, "Ned, in this world the trees and rocks have to move, not the men," to which Byrne retorts, "That's not what you told Sara's people" (250). Thus Byrne, in referring to the expulsion that paved the way for the park, points out the double standards and ironies of Trask's expropriative development – that it reconfigures both human and natural resources, often quite violently, in the construction of a pristine wilderness preserve.

Toward the end of the novel, Trask's exploitation of the icefields reaches fairly giddy extremes, as Wharton engages in some parodic commentary not just on modern marketing, but also on the ascendancy of simulacra in our own times. Tourism of course provides a ready illustration of Jean Baudrillard's notion of the replacement of representation by simulation, "substituting signs of the real for the real itself."[48] "When the real is no longer what it used to be," argues Baudrillard, the result is "a proliferation of myths of origin and signs of reality; of second-hand truth, objectivity and authenticity. There is an escalation of the true, of the lived experience."[49]

In Trask, Wharton parodies the artifice of tourist promotion and the paradoxical desire for presence that it exploits. For instance, Trask builds a bus terminal, for the exterior of which "he envisions an igloo-style facade to go along with the 'little Arctic' motifs" of his other exhibits. "*A sunny pleasure dome with caves of ice!*" (253), he thinks, with a parodic echo of Coleridge. Trask even considers importing "penguins to swim in the melt pool at the terminus" (253), a sign that what matters is consumer spectacle rather than environmental authenticity and preservation. Finally, Trask writes in his brochure that "*the altitude and permanent snow of the Rockies has created an arctic landscape in miniature*" and that tourists therefore "*can now journey to these accessible 'polar regions' without leaving the comfort of your automobile. See a world that only a few brave explorers have seen!*" (253–4). Such an invitation to a kind of ersatz colonization is also obviously intended to link Trask to the figure of Sexsmith, both men serving as representatives of the colonizing mentality of their respective eras. Yet, despite all his intrusive development in the Athabasca valley, Trask assures Byrne that there will be no development on the glacier itself because "I want these people to feel like they're going back into the ice age. It's got to be *wild*" (256). The irony of Trask's transformation of the area into consumer experience is of course that it represents a travesty of the idea of wilderness, and what he seeks to offer instead is a very controlled, very packaged – in short, tamed – "wild."

The further irony, which is brought home by Byrne's scientific research, is that Trask's cash cow, the glacier, is slowly melting, "another joke at his expense in the country of illusion. That the ice should be disappearing at the same time that someone has finally found a use for it" (254). (When Voltaire dismissed Canada as "quelques arpents de neige" he obviously didn't know good real estate when he saw it.) But that Trask's instrumentalist mentality – his insistence that the wild must have "a use" – is ultimately tragic is particularly under-lined by the ironic reversal at the end of the novel: it is Trask, not Byrne, who witnesses the emergence of the angel from the glacier. Returning to the chalet after a conversation with Byrne up by the glacier, Trask loses his way, his guiding instincts dulled by his entre-preneurial obsessions. Finding himself at the foot of the glacier, he leans against a pinnacle of ice – "*Just like a folded wing*" (259). He rationalizes that the angel has probably been sculpted as a diversion by one of his construction crew, and though he does admit to himself that another (presumably more wondrous) possibility exists, it is "one that instinct tells him to keep to himself"; he assumes that "Byrne would tell him that what he saw could easily be explained as a natural phenomenon of ice erosion" (261). Thus, due to Trask's pragmatic common sense and Byrne's aloof rationalism, the moment of emergence that Byrne has been waiting for passes by untestified.

While Trask remains unchastened by wonder and committed to the path of commercial development, Wharton provides Byrne with a kind of surrogate epiphany that consolidates his role as Trask's foil and makes an important statement about perception of the natural environment. Byrne returns to Jasper to help Trask officially open the Glacier Tour, and as the crowd waits to board the ice-crawlers that will take them out onto the glacier, Byrne wanders to the terminus of the glacier and discovers a Venus' Slipper: "His scientific understanding contracts. Orchids do not grow here. Nothing grows here. The unceasing collision of ice and rock grinds away all life. Nothing can survive at the terminus" (273). The orchid serves as a replacement for the angel and shifts the focus from metaphysical wonder to natural wonder (or perhaps points to the former in the latter), something that has characterized Byrne's scientific sensibility and has been conspicuously missing in the pragmatic and entrepreneurial Trask. Wharton underlines this sense of wonder in the last line of the novel, as Byrne invites a Japanese alpinist, left behind by the tour, to see the orchid: "come with me ... I want to show you something rather extraordinary" (274).

While *Icefields* is a novel about the aestheticizing of the wilderness and of ice, the novel itself provides a lushly aesthetic rendering of the wilderness and more particularly of ice and the icefields, creating a certain tension with its political aims reminiscent of *In the Skin of a Lion*. Through the striking architectural, geological, and painterly descriptions that vivify the icefields throughout the novel, Wharton develops in detail what might be called a poetics of ice. For instance, as Byrne climbs an icefall, in the heat of the sun the "ice weakens, sloughs off its brittle outer skin, releasing itself into liquid all around him. He is climbing an emerging waterfall" (99). Byrne himself (as Wharton's scientific alter ego) displays a similar lyrical touch in his description of the terminus of the glacier in his notebooks: "*Stones, fragments of a lost continent, lie scattered in the dirty snow of the till plain. A shattered palette at my feet, the mad artist having just stalked away.*" In a style strikingly reminiscent of Ondaatje, Byrne concludes the image: "*The enchantment of these mute fragments is undeniable. The bewitching garden of signs*" (140–1). As with Ondaatje, such highly aestheticized descriptions raise important concerns. Tourism, of course, thrives by aestheticizing and commodifying nature (among other things), packaging it for ready consumption. Given that *Icefields* critically portrays Trask as engaged in aestheticizing ice in order to commodify it, an important question is whether Wharton might not be susceptible to the same critique.

Byrne's impressions of the icefields, however, in contrast with Trask's, are underscored by an almost metaphysical appreciation for the artistry of nature. Byrne, for instance, "reads the glacier's writing": "*Tiny fragments of hand quartz, frozen to the basal surface of the glacier, scar the limestone bedrock as the ice flows forward*" (143). Later, he watches the glacier buckle as it melts and "rears up a cathedral"; then, when "the sun breaks through cloud, the cathedral fills with light. The warmer air hollows it into a more baroque, flamboyant shape. Spires, archways, gargoyles begin to flow. Waterfalls set festive ice bells ringing" (161). If *Icefields* celebrates impressionistic, individual aesthetic experience, particularly through such perceptions on the part of Byrne, it at least does not, like *In the Skin of a Lion*, place that celebration in uneasy relation with collective, oppositional politics. Indeed, it can be argued that *Icefields* instead places that individual experience of nature in opposition to a commodified, staged, and ultimately ersatz one.

"Nature" itself, however, is a loaded term, and while that opposition suggests a binary division between a mediated and an unmediated experience of nature, even a Romantic appreciation of nature such as Byrne's is subject to mediation. Describing different forms of the tourist gaze, Urry observes that "the romantic gaze, which is much more obviously auratic, concerned with the elitist – and solitary – appreciation of magnificent scenery, an appreciation which requires considerable cultural capital," nonetheless contains "elements which we now can classify as postmodern." Indeed, the romantic gaze involves the internalizing of ideal representations "from postcards and guidebooks (and increasingly from TV programmes)," and even when people "cannot in fact 'see' the natural wonder in question they can still sense it, see it in their mind. And even when the object fails to live up to its representation it is the latter which will stay in people's minds, as what they have really 'seen.'"[50] Thus even the experience of the sublimity of nature, according to Urry, is mediated. Indeed, the mediation of nature can be seen in the scientific assumptions through which Byrne approaches his environment, and even the metaphysical surprise of seeing the angel, which is an affront to those assumptions, can be seen as the projection of a very European outlook onto an indigenous "spirit place" in the New World.

What *Icefields* suggests through the contrast between Byrne and Trask, however, is that not all mediation is necessarily equal. Byrne's appreciation of the icefields is ultimately that of the Romantic artist, Trask's ultimately that of the horse-trader. These may seem to be two sides of the same bourgeois perspective, but there is a substantial difference between sublimity and commercial tourism as transformative aesthetics. The important distinction between Byrne's experience of the icefields and Trask's, moreover, is that Byrne's approach is not interventionist like Trask's; he does not physically reshape the environment to suit his needs, however much his own assumptions shape the inscription of it in his writing.

Such an opposition is of no small importance in assessing the accomplishment of *Icefields*, since an unavoidable issue that the success of the novel raises is its own complicated status as commodity.[51] Jameson argues that an Archimedean critical position outside postmodern culture is unachievable since "we are *inside* the culture of the market and ... the inner dynamic of the culture of consumption is an infernal machine from which one does not escape by the taking of thought (or moralizing positions), an infinite propagation and replication of 'desire' that feeds on itself and has no outside and no fulfillment."[52] *Icefields* certainly provides a good example of that "inner dynamic" at work. The novel's popularity is due, at least in part, to the fact that it provides a novelistic image of the Rocky Mountains, easily the most commodified landscape in Canada, if not in the entire world. *Icefields* is clearly destined to become part of the packaging of the Rockies, one of many aesthetic frames through which consumers view and desire the mountains. Some readers will come to the mountains through Wharton's image of them just as most tourists come to the mountains initially through the framed and aestheticized images of the mountains in brochures, postcards, and coffee-table books. Thus a novel that dramatizes the manipulation and operation of "the tourist gaze" ironically is destined to serve as a popular channel for it.

Such a fate, however, does not amount to a neutralizing of the novel's politics. Admittedly, *Icefields*, with its very aestheticized critique of the commodifying of the wilderness, and *In the Skin of a Lion*, with its highly aestheticized presentation of class conflict, would seem to present themselves as perfect illustrations of Jameson's assertion of the inevitable complicity of postmodern cultural production with the consumer capitalist society within which it is produced. At the same time, *Icefields* and *In the Skin of a Lion* suggest the terms for a renewal of the historical novel, but on different grounds. These novels ultimately are "representations of pastness," and, however much those representations aestheticize the past and in the process complicate the political and cultural critiques that they develop, they nonetheless amount to something much more significant than a reshuffling of texts and a packaging of the past.

One of the pitfalls of arguing that it is impossible for postmodern art and literature to maintain a critical distance from late capitalist society because they are "within" that society, as does Jameson up to a point, is that it cultivates a sense of futility and a capitulating apoliticism. *Icefields* and *In the Skin of a Lion*, like so much contemporary historical fiction, are neither unreflexive mimetic representations of the past nor simply aestheticized, depthless "reshufflings" of texts. These novels show the importance of undercutting any binary formulations about the politics of cultural production in postmodernity and thus serve to contest the assumption that cultural production is either critical of or complicit with consumer capitalism. What they show, in fact, is that most contemporary historical novels are generally both, just to varying degrees. What they also show, moreover, is that many contemporary historical novels are at least openly trying to address that complicity by foregrounding and critiquing that culture through their representations of an erstwhile past.

This binocular vision, the simultaneous orientation towards the past and the present evident in *Away*, *In the Skin of a Lion*, and *Icefields*, is, of course, not new to the historical novel, in which the underlining of the past as the precondition of the present and the exploitation of the past to moralize about or justify the present have been recurrent elements. The historical novel also customarily presumes a degree of "previous historical knowledge generally acquired through the schoolbook history manuals devised for whatever legitimizing purpose by this or that national tradition" and enacts "a narrative dialectic" between that prior knowledge and the novel's presentation of that history.[53] But this semantic doubling and dialectic movement obviously become problematic in a cultural context in which the sense of historicity has been eroded and in which there is, at least according to Jameson, no familiar past to serve as precondition (and indeed very little interest in or understanding of such a historicist orientation). Taking *Ragtime* as an example, Jameson describes the crisis of the historical novel in the postmodern age, its loss of that dialectical function in an "aesthetic situation engendered by the disappearance of the historical referent."[54]

While it might be argued that a stylized, stereotypical, popular history has always prevailed (and is not just an offspring of postmodernity), Jameson's point is that with the anti-foundationalism of postmodern art and theory, that sense of depthlessness is no longer taken as a distortion of a "true" history. The crisis of historicity is the acceptance that there is no longer a true history by which something might be judged a distortion and that all history is necessarily stylized, cut off from its referent. He feels that the "historical novel can no longer set out to represent the historical past; it can only 'represent' our ideas and stereotypes about that past (which thereby at once becomes pop history)."[55] For Jameson, then, a genre reliant on historical "depth" loses its purchase in an era of depthlessness.

However, rather than signalling the death of the historical novel, Monika Fludernik suggests, this crisis of historicity might signal its rebirth. Different times require different forms, and Fludernik puts forth the compelling point that historiographic metafiction has inherited the place of the historical novel – it is the new historical novel for an age with a new sense of history. Historiographic metafiction's "departure from nineteenth-century models is due to a reconceptualization of the historical and of historiography as much as to a difference in fictional styles and techniques. Historiographic metafiction, from this perspective, appears to be simply the updated late-twentieth-century version of precisely the same genre (the historical novel) which has meanwhile adapted to twentieth-century conceptualizations of the novel and of the historical."[56]

In some contemporary historical novels, this adaptation involves an anachronistic concern both with the production of history and with history as a product. The "representation of pastness," in other words, is oriented towards how "pastness" is constructed in a commodity-conscious present. This is particularly evident in Susan Swan's *The Biggest Modern Woman of the World* and Guy Vanderhaeghe's *The Englishman's Boy*. The two novels provide an interesting and valuable contrast, as they both dovetail, in very different ways, concerns about the validity of historical representations and of historicity and about the commodification of history in an irredemiably capitalist age. If contemporary historical novels occupy the paradoxical position of being both of and about postmodernity – a culture characterized by scepticism about traditional history and by strong dehistoricizing and commidifying impulses – *The Biggest Modern Woman of the World* and *The Englishman's Boy* demonstrate how such an ambivalent position contributes to, rather than undermines, the continuing validity of the historical novel.

Swan's *The Biggest Modern Woman of the World*, much more than *The Englishman's Boy*, fits Fludernik's description of historiographic metafiction. Swan's novel is characterized by a sustained self-reflexiveness that recognizes and inscribes a sense of complicity with capitalist culture. Because it is clearly both postmodern and about postmodernity, *The Biggest Modern Woman* provides perhaps the most interesting illustration of the delicate equilibrium between critique and complicity in the speculative economy of late capitalism. The question of artistic complicity in consumer culture is of course complicated by historiographical considerations; at issue are not only the writer's relation to consumer culture, but also the writer's commodification of history. In this respect, *The Biggest Modern Woman* combines a feminist critique of capitalist speculation and the writing of history while at the same time raising concerns about postmodernist fiction's relation to the historical record and about proprietary rights to the past. Perhaps more than any other novel, *The Biggest Modern Woman* dramatizes the contemporary historical novel's "speculative" duality, its ambivalent "investment" in history.

The double semantics of *The Biggest Modern Woman* – its simultaneous focus on the late nineteenth century and the late twentieth century – is an effect of the self-reflexive portrait of Anna Swan's ambivalent relationship with North American commodity capitalism. As most critics have noted, the novel progressively contests, as part of its critique of Yankee-style capitalism, the objectification and commodification of Anna because of her size. By systematically exposing the exploitation of Anna, *The Biggest Modern Woman* makes a particularly postmodern contribution to the emphasis on gender relations in the representation of history, providing a succinct reminder that commodity culture is not an equal opportunity employer. Anna's fate in the masculinist economy of the spectacle is to be resolutely objectified.

As Marlene Goldman, Smaro Kamboureli, Theresa Heffernan, and others have noted, Swan depicts capitalist enterprise as part of a larger masculine order in which women are economically, intellectually, artistically, and sexually subordinated.[57] The men who control Anna's career consistently close off avenues of subjective expression and perpetuate her objectification and passivity in a patriarchal Victorian order. Anna, however, is a commodity in Swan's novel just as she is a commodity in P.T. Barnum's and Apollo Ingalls's eyes, and various formal elements in the novel inscribe a consciousness of that paradox. In conjunction with the novel's self-reflexive critique of the masculinist construction of Anna as an exhibit, *The Biggest Modern Woman* openly signals its own status as commodity, most conspicuously through the motif of the "spiel." The spiel, of course, is a verbal lure, calling consumers to an attraction and combining performance, rhetoric, and marketing. As she tells her story, Anna recurrently reflects on her tendency to lapse into spieling, the private voice recurrently returning to the public eye that has given shape to that life story. As Heffernan argues, the spiel foregrounds how "Anna's art (and by way of implication Swan's novel) is not 'true' or 'pure' but contaminated by interest."[58] The spiel as a commodified verbal performance thus stands as a metaphor for Swan's story of Anna.

The spiel, moreover, has historiographical implications as well, since Anna's story, in a typically postmodern doubling, is itself an extended spiel, a verbal self-presentation, a life story as exhibit. In her "Real Time Spiel" (which, because the second spiel it contains is set in 1977, anachronistically situates the narrating subject in "an ontologically ambiguous and liminal zone that straddles 1877 and 1977"[59]) Anna announces, "This is my final appearance and I promise to tell all. What really happened to the BIGGEST MODERN WOMAN OF THE WORLD in a never-before-revealed autobiography which contains testimonials and documents by friends and associates (from their perspective) of a Victorian lady who refused to be inconsequential" (*The Biggest Modern Woman* 2). This preamble obviously serves as a kind of narrative introduction, signalling the interplay between the form of the novel and its subject, but it also allows Susan Swan to foreground the status of her portrait of Anna Swan as a commodity, to signal her consciousness of *The Biggest Modern Woman*, in turn, as a commodification of history. Part of Swan's critique of consumer culture, in other words, is a self-conscious inscription of the perils of complicity that accompany participation (however critical) in that economy.

In this respect, the novel establishes an important ironic distance from traditional historical presentations of Anna's life. As Brian McHale observes, carnivalized genres such as Menippean satire and its heir, postmodernist fiction, are "official literature's dialectical antithesis and parodic double."[60] *The Biggest Modern Woman of the World* certainly stands in this relation to its historical precursors, most notably the Sunrise Trail Museum and Phyllis Blakeley's book on Swan and Angus McAskill, *Nova Scotia's Two Remarkable Giants.* Swan feels free to depart from the historical record at will, not only by providing the private life of a public figure (and allegorizing what an oxymoron that is), but also by providing speculative additions, preposterous additions, and open revisions to that historical record. Some of Swan's embellishments are plausible and restrained in the usual manner of the historical novel, such as her elaboration of scenes of Anna being pestered at school and of the malicious curiosity of her neighbours in Seville. Others, including numerous Rabelaisian scenes such as Anna's urinary confrontation with her childhood nemesis Hubert Belcourt, or the description of Queen Victoria parading through the arch of Anna's legs and pausing to inspect her drawers, strain any sense of historical authenticity a reader might be inclined to entertain. Finally, particularly by suturing the two halves of

Blakeley's book together, bringing Angus McAskill into Anna's orbit, Swan openly and consciously contradicts the historical record and reworks it to her narrative convenience.

The insights into history, gender, and postmodernism that the self-conscious, parodic narration affords *The Biggest Modern Woman* have received a generally positive critical reception. An interesting exception to this approval, however (somewhat reminiscent of J.L. Granatstein's objection to Heather Robertson's *Willie*), further complicates these issues of historical representation, commodification, and postmodernity. Linda Swan-Ryan, one of a number of Anna Swan's descendants who attended a reading by Susan Swan shortly after the novel was published, subsequently wrote a letter to *MacLean's* questioning Swan's assertion "of her divine prerogative as a writer to take the name of a real person and to subject that name to any flight of fantasy in which she might care to indulge."[61] Additionally, Goldman notes, Susan Swan "has received four letters from outraged elders of the giant Swan's family suggesting that the book be burned because, in their eyes, it is 'an inaccurate biography of their ancestor.'"[62]

In her disappointment that "the author felt that the true story of the giantess's life was not worthy of writing and thus making many more people aware of this part of our Nova Scotian heritage," Swan-Ryan displays a more traditional view of history that the novel is out to deflate.[63] Heffernan defends Swan by arguing that she "is sensitive to the potential conflict between her acknowledged desire to recover the history of women (or freaks or Nova Scotia) and her awareness of the impossibility of recovering a true history or a definitive story" through the way she contests both normalized and masculinized presentations of Anna's story.[64] But there are other material considerations of such historical representation that Heffernan's defense does not take into account. Swan-Ryan's objection indeed raises interesting and important issues of proprietary rights to history and the problem of exploitation, just as Swan's novel dramatizes important issues of proprietary rights to and exploitation of the fictional Anna.

In her preface to the novel, Susan Swan presumes a genealogical connection with Anna Swan, though "neither her descendants nor my relatives have enough information on our backgrounds to establish a connection"; the story has it, however, that "both branches of the families trace their way back to a Scandinavian ancestor" (n.p.). Swan-Ryan's tart response to this claim is that had Susan Swan "by accident of birth received a different surname, one can only speculate on who then would have been the focus of her mythical talent."[65] That a Nova Scotian descendant is questioning a Toronto writer's novelistic version of a part of that province's history is not to be summarily dismissed. It raises questions of the "local control" – both in familial terms and in regional terms – that is such a staple of the postmodern theory and poetics in which Swan's novel is thoroughly grounded.[66] Given the tension between the metropolitan context *out of which* Swan is writing and the "regional" or "provincial" context *of which* she is writing, the question becomes whether Swan's novel allegorizes a resistance to, or indeed enacts, a capitalist appropriation, exploitation, and commodification. Perhaps, in characteristic postmodernist fashion, the answer is "both."

If Swan self-consciously recognizes her narrative as compromised and complicit with the capitalist culture it satirizes, how then is it different from a history like Blakeley's, which, on the one hand, provides a less "fantastic" (and in that respect perhaps more acceptable) "true history of the giantess's life" but, on the other hand, at least in some ways objectifies Anna as historical curiosity? Blakeley's book serves to celebrate size and physical accomplishment, positioning Anna within the discourse of "the normals," with some "human interest" and social observation thrown in. In contrast, Swan highlights the alienating effects of such a celebration and explores Anna's private life, emphasizing the psychic, the emotional, and the sexual.

Swan's novel ultimately has a very different tone than Blakeley's somewhat glib and romanticizing popular synthesis of Anna's life, parodying some aspects of her presentation of the giants' legends. Swan's postmodern, postcolonial, and feminist allegory is obviously very different in emphasis from Blakeley's rags-to-riches success story: "So passed from the scene a woman who by accident of nature left a humble country home to tour the capitals of the world. Sought after by entrepreneurs, gazed at by millions, feted by royalty and finally fulfilled with a home and successful marriage, Anna remained throughout it all a gracious, charming woman of whom Nova Scotians can be proud."[67]

Swan's story, like Blakeley's history, commodifies Anna's story once again, but one big difference is that Swan presents Anna's history without historiographical pretense, quite deliberately and parodically undermining any sense that this is the "true story," and satirically portrays the process of commodification. The question remains, however, whether Swan could not have written a more traditional historical novel with greater fidelity to the historical record and more plausibility as a historical representation, one which raises the same issues but in a less "fantastic" fashion. Would such a fictionalization have been susceptible to the same kind of criticism?

Anna Swan with her husband, Captain Martin Van Buren Bates.
"gazed at by millions"

The answer is, presumably, that it would not have, but the question throws into relief what the novel accomplishes by virtue of being "fantastic" and by quite consciously *not* aspiring to the customary historicizing function of the historical novel. Instead, the novel's heterogeneous, self-conscious, parodic form deflects attention away from Anna as historical curiosity to the construction of history (and, for that matter, to the construction of curiosities). But is such historiographical imitation empty, a Jamesonian "reshuffling of texts"? Jameson argues that one result of the abolition of the referent in postmodern art and theory is that pastiche replaces parody. "Pastiche is, like parody," Jameson maintains, "the imitation of a peculiar or unique, idiosyncratic style, the wearing of a linguistic mask, speech in a dead language." The difference is that parody relies on a standard of normality, the "conviction that alongside the abnormal tongue you have momentarily borrowed, some healthy linguistic normality still exists," whereas pastiche "is a neutral practice of such mimicry, without any of parody's ulterior motives, amputated of the satiric impulse, devoid of laughter."[68] Allen Thiher argues that this is the dilemma of a contemporary, postmodern attitude to history that resists history's primacy as a discourse: "parody is always in a secondary position with regard to the 'historically real' and implies that history is a primary discourse through which we might have access to some real that allows the parody to stand out as an inversion, and not merely as the insane."[69]

The Biggest Modern Woman suggests, however, that behind postmodern indeterminacy one *can* find an ulterior motive, a satiric or critical impulse. Though Anna's spiel at the beginning of the novel positions her as author and editor of her life story, as presiding over this heterogeneous and dialogic account, the ending of the novel puts that control in doubt. The epilogue contains testimonials delivered after Anna's death, and her story contains documents to which she is unlikely to have had access; this raises the question of editorial control, of whether the posthumous gathering of Anna's life story has substantially reshaped the account. These uncertainties, Heffernan argues, "are undoubtedly the author's own intrusion and are meant to undermine Anna's authorial control of her narrative. This discrepancy, which greatly affects the plot and Anna's character, redefines history, not as the *real* facts available about Anna and which are employed in the novel as intertexts, but as the making of the fiction we read."[70] The indeterminacy of the novel's collation of documents, then, is not a matter of merely playing with words. Rather, it is a clever formal manifestation of important feminist themes like the constriction of artistic control and individual identity in a patriarchal society and furthermore draws attention to the construction of historical accounts and the values that shape them.

One answer to Swan-Ryan's objection, then, might be that Susan Swan obviously felt, in some respects, that "the true history" of Anna

Swan was worth writing but, like so many contemporary novelists writing about the past, had reservations about what a "true history" was. Thus, in writing about Anna Swan in the way she does, Susan Swan has these and other bigger fish to fry. At the same time, as Goldman argues, despite Swan's frustration that her critics fail to distinguish between fiction and non-fiction, their "confusion points to an important connection between history and fiction because the inability to 'recognize the difference' between the two, on one level, clarifies the absence of difference" – an absence that the novel itself dramatizes.[71]

Linda Swan-Ryan's defence of her ancestor echoes the objections of many critics to what is seen as postmodernist fiction's dangerously relativizing and destabilizing treatment of history. For many who uphold the integrity of the historical record in moral terms, Brian McHale observes, "history is the record of real human action and suffering, and it is not to be tampered with lightly; inventing apocryphal or fantastic and deliberately anachronistic versions of history is a betrayal of that record."[72] But, as novels like *The Biggest Modern Woman of the World*, *The Scorched-Wood People*, *Ana Historic*, and others demonstrate, there are compelling reasons for being sceptical about that record. The crisis of historiography is that "the reliability of the historical record in capturing experience," as McHale makes clear in his response, "is the last thing we can be sure of, and one of the thrusts of postmodernist revisionist history is to call into question the reliability of official history. The postmodernists fictionalize history, but by doing so they imply that history itself may be a form of fiction."[73]

Such anti-representational and relativizing strategies do not sit well with everybody. As McHale notes, Gerald Graff and others have raised important reservations about postmodern poetics, arguing that they have lost their critical edge and serve to support rather than contest the status quo. Consequently, "nowadays everything in our culture tends to deny reality and promote unreality, in the interests of maintaining high levels of consumption. It is no longer official reality which is coercive, but official *unreality*; and postmodernist fiction, instead of resisting this coercive unreality, acquiesces in it, or even *celebrates* it." In this respect, postmodernist fiction "is morally bad art."[74]

In response, McHale concedes that "'unreal reality' is a recurrent theme and object of representation in postmodernist fiction" – particularly of "postmodernism's revisionist approach to history and historical fiction, and of postmodernism's incorporation of television and cinematic representations as a level interposed between us and reality" – but not the only one.[75] The important point, however, is that much postmodernist fiction does resist this "coercive unreality" and furthermore suggests that the division between official reality and official unreality is not a firm one, a particularly significant point for historiography. The contemporary historical novel provides a good instance of how postmodern fiction about "unreal reality" has much to say, rather than simply providing the verbal equivalent of a hall of mirrors.

In this respect, the most significant novel since the appearance of *The Biggest Modern Woman of the World* is Guy Vanderhaeghe's *The Englishman's Boy*. Although it is predominantly a realistic novel, *The Englishman's Boy* is openly concerned with the place of history in postmodern culture and does exhibit some characteristically postmodern concerns, such as with the self-referentiality and narcissistic depthlessness of postmodern cultural production and the promotion of an unreal historical reality. Like *Away*, *The Englishman's Boy* suggests that the commercial imperatives of contemporary society, in this case as represented by Hollywood, contribute to an erosion of our appreciation of time and history. A key insight of Jameson's *Postmodernism* is that postmodernism is characterized by an emphasis on the visual and the spatial at the expense of the temporal; in "the new spatial logic of the simulacrum" the past becomes "a vast collection of images, a multitudinous photographic simulacrum."[76] With its emphasis on film and on a filmic treatment of history, *The Englishman's Boy* grapples with the implications of this shift and dramatizes the fate of history in the age of the moving image.

Vanderhaeghe's novel has much to recommend it as a lyrical, gripping allegory of colonial violence, as exemplified by his portrait of the Cypress Hills Massacre. Yet what makes the book even more complex and compelling is how that postcolonial narrative is layered with an exploration of a cultural colonization – rooted in the image and represented by Hollywood – that was consolidated during the twentieth century. In the novel, the individualistic, lawless but code-bound culture of the nineteenth-century frontier has been contained and commodified in the glamorous, hierarchic, capitalist culture of Hollywood early in the twentieth century. Vanderhaeghe's depiction of the production of Westerns emphasizes how Hollywood imperialistically contains, restricts, and distorts the subjects it celebrates in its representations. Through its juxtaposition of the two eras, *The Englishman's Boy* brings together issues of individual agency, historical accuracy, cultural colonization, and the relation between politics and aesthetics.

Vanderhaeghe's dramatizing of the metamorphosis and aestheticizing of frontier culture is part of a larger portrait of Hollywood's preoccupation with illusion, a preoccupation that creates a certain narrative self-reflexiveness in *The Englishman's Boy*. In contrast with the narrative of Shorty's participation in the Cypress Hills Massacre, the Hollywood sequences, because of the focus on film and on celebrity culture, more substantially foreground the constructed nature of artistic production and disrupt the sense of verisimilitude. Vanderhaeghe sets up this effect early in the novel with Harry's blunt opening, "History is calling it a day" (*The Englishman's Boy* 5), which is followed by his description of a carnival of anachronism, a scene in which the Holy Family mingles with Aztecs, Valley Forge veterans, and Elizabethan ladies-in-waiting; only subsequently is this collapsing of history contextualized as Harry's view out of the window of Damon Ira Chance's Hollywood studio.[77] This self-consciousness about representations of history is sustained throughout the novel's depictions of the megalomania, artifice, and luxury of Hollywood. Episodes such as the "Running W" (a notoriously cruel staged fall of horse and rider) that kills Wylie's brother, and Chance's party at which prostitutes masquerade as Hollywood leading ladies like Clara Bow, Gloria Swanson, and Lillian Gish, lend that part of the narrative an air of unreality that makes the nineteenth-century history seem authentic and substantial by comparison.

These elements of the novel inscribe a metafictional scepticism about the filmic machinery behind the Hollywood Western and create out of this era of cinematic modernism a familiar sense of postmodern vertigo, the infinite recession of the real behind a proliferation of signs. Vanderhaeghe's Hollywood evokes Baudrillard's "age of simulation," which "begins with a liquidation of all referentials – worse: by their artificial resurrection in systems of signs, which are a more ductile material than meaning."[78] The Hollywood in which Harry toils leaves the reader questioning what is real in a way that the sequences set in Whoop-up country do not, creating a sense of self-reflexivity that points to how Hollywood, as a maker of "unreal reality," has no equal.

The exploitative character of Hollywood's illusion-making is most prominently dramatized through Chance's attitude toward history and his imperialist appropriation of Shorty's story. Following the example of his idol, D.W. Griffith, Chance is attracted to history as cinematic material because he feels that its factuality appeals to the pragmatism of the viewing American public. For Chance, the medium of film, emblematic of the power of forward movement, is also emblematic of the American spirit. Evoking Frederick Jackson Turner's frontier thesis of American development, Chance lectures Harry: "The American spirit is a frontier spirit, restless, impatient of constraint, eager for a look over the next hill, the next peek around the bend in the river. The American destiny is *forward momentum*. What the old frontiersman called westering. What the American spirit required was an art form of forward momentum, an art form as bold and unbounded as the American spirit. A *westering* art form! It had to wait for motion pictures. The art form of *motion*!" (108).[79] Thus the imperialism underlying Chance's vision of the west is for Chance not only a fundamental part of the American character but also of cinema itself.

The making of *Besieged* displays the exploitative process of production behind the Hollywood illusion industry and amounts to a replication of colonial violence, with Chance and Fitz's attitudes echoing those of the belligerent and racist wolfers. Harry's description of Chance's mania for authentic detail in making preparations underlines the film's repetition of colonial plunder. Chance instructs his buyers to "fan out across the country, chequebooks in hand, to dun private collectors, to seduce destitute reservation Indians who might be persuaded to part with Grandpa's medicine bundle, coup stick, or eagle war bonnet for a pittance" (225). When Chance realizes that Shorty is unlikely to appreciate the "moment in the sun" the film will give him, he displays a characteristic Hollywood cynicism and opportunism by considering killing him off and getting publicity out of it in the bargain: "Not literally dead," he reassures Harry; "I was thinking more along the lines of an announcement of the great plainsman's passing – the timing would have to be nicely calculated" (207).

Chance's neocolonialism, however, is most evident in his vision for his epic, which is grounded in a self-exculpatory, racist triumphalism characteristic of the Western.[80] He subverts Shorty's unheroic, unflattering, and sobering account, replaying and compounding the violence of the massacre by seeking to portray it not just as heroic self-defense but as a fascistic allegory of the necessary victory of the strong over the weak. When Harry finishes the screenplay, Chance objects to it because it portrays the Assiniboine girl – who, according to Shorty, was gang-raped and left to die in the burning trading post – as a victim. This does not fit with Chance's vision, which, in language highly evocative of Nietzsche's *The Will to Power*, requires her to be "a sort of Indian Samson" (251) representing the complicity of the Assiniboine in their own destruction: "The weak wish the strong to be sentimental because they know it undermines their strength. But in the world we face at this moment, we must keep strong. Only the strong will survive" (252). The role of the girl must be changed, Chance orders, because the "enemy is never human" (256).

Chance's filmic interpretation of the massacre, furthermore, is a projection of his racist attitudes about the Hollywood and the America of his own time. Chance's era is marked by anti-Semitism, a hysteria over Bolshevism, and a concern over the mongrelizing of America by immigrants – an America in which, as Neil Gabler observes, "nativism and xenophobia were rampant."[81] In a Hollywood dominated by directors with European roots, many of them Jews, Chance sees himself as solely capable of appreciating the American character, and his Nietzschean reading of the Indian is repeatedly buttressed by parallels to Jews. At a time of the rise of fascism and after the success of Bolshevism in Russia, Chance argues that Americans, exhibiting that frontier spirit, must likewise be ruthless and strong, and not, like the Jews, make the mistake of being "sentimental and emotional" (296). In a mongrelized America where many have no memory of the struggle for the frontier, Chance sees his epic Western as an opportunity to "rewrite the history of the foreigner, erase completely those sentimental flowers of memory and light their minds with the glory of American lightning" (297), an almost religious vision of assimilation – with film as the means of conversion.

While Chance promotes film as a democratic and populist medium, his desire to use it to educate is demagogic and authoritarian. Waxing poetic on Griffith's Civil War epic *Birth of a Nation*, Chance veers dangerously close to a form of mind control in his vision of the power of film:

Images take root in your mind, hot and bright, like an image on a photo-plate. Once they etch themselves there, they can't be obliterated, can't be scratched out. They burn themselves in the mind. Because there's no arguing with pictures. You simply accept or reject them. What's up there on the screen moves too fast to permit analysis or argument. You can't control the flow of images the way you can control a book – by rereading a chapter, rereading a paragraph, rereading a sentence. A book invites argument, invites reconsideration, invites thought. A moving picture is beyond thought. Like feeling, it simply *is*. The principle of a book is persuasion; the principle of a movie is revelation. (107)

Chance intends to use film to "impress" his lesson on his audience and to discourage reflection – a demagogic approach to history that Harry later ties to overtly fascist figures such as Hitler and Mussolini.

Chance's belief in the power of intuition and impression is underpinned by an ultimately exploitative attitude toward history. He privileges a fidelity not to historical fact but to what he sees as the spirit of the past. "Facts are of the utmost importance," he says to Harry.

"If I can convince the audience the details are impeccably correct, who will dispute the interpretation? The truth of small things leads to confidence in the truth of large things" (230). Chance's attitude towards history thus provides a coercive inversion of Lukács's rejection of "the cult of facts" in the historical novel, in which what matters for Lukács is the integrity of the interpretation rather than the impeccable accuracy of the details.[82] History for Chance provides the placebo of fact but is ultimately the raw material for a vision of the past that is fascist, imperialist, and carefully commodified. Chance's version of "the truth of the large things," furthermore, is a self-serving, racist philosophy of history in which "every man is the servant of historical forces" but those "who familiarize themselves with the currents of the age to which they are confined" increase their chances of survival (103). Implicit in Chance's view of film and of the spirit of the age is his desire to be a big fish in those currents, increasing his chances of survival at the expense of others.

If Chance's imperialist appropriation of Shorty's story and his authoritarian philosophy of history draw attention to "the integrity of the interpretation," to questions of historical veracity, however, so do the contrapuntal narrative structure and historical perspective of *The Englishman's Boy* itself. The twentieth-century sequences, particularly those conveying Chance's attitude toward history, reflect a certain degree of the hyperrealism characteristic of much postmodern historiographical metafiction. The nineteenth-century sequences, which convey Shorty's story, come closer to the traditional model of the historical novel as "a tale, a piece of invention; only, it claims to be true to the life of the past."[83] The difference helps to buttress the validity of Shorty's relatively postcolonial version. However, if Chance seems to be tinkering with both the details and the spirit of Shorty's history to suit his own artistic and polemical purposes, it should be noted that Vanderhaeghe is tinkering as well. Vanderhaeghe's presentation (via Shorty) of the Cypress Hills Massacre in places conspicuously departs from the rough consensus among historians about the episode. The fate of the Assiniboine girl, for instance, is a considerable reworking of what historians suggest; according to Philip Goldring, there were four rape victims, rather than one, and there was no evidence of a body burned in the trading post.[84] The point, ultimately, is not that Shorty's version is true and Chance's is false, but that compared to Chance's interpretation (indirect as our perception of it may be), Shorty's version is much more compatible with the somewhat divided historical accounts of the incident.

The integrity and coherence of that account next to Chance's self-aggrandizing, imperialistic adaptation suggests Vanderhaeghe's resistance to complete historical relativism, that is, to recognizing both versions as equally rhetorical and constructed, as equally "fictive." Vanderhaeghe's priority seems not to be, like Wiebe's, "to get at the truth of things." Nonetheless, the novel does strive to establish a presumably more historically accurate, or at least more morally complex and palatable, version against which to highlight the fascism and racism of Chance's version. The difference between historical accuracy and moral complexity, of course, is a substantial one, and Vanderhaeghe's critique of Chance's promotion of an unreal historical reality raises larger questions about historiography and postmodernism's concern with illusion.

If we view postmodern, deconstructionist history as asserting historical representation to be completely arbitrary, relative, and textual, the difference between the two versions that the novel sustains would be undermined. Alun Munslow argues, however, that even within deconstructionist history "the historian is not a free agent, like a sculptor who can take the clay of evidence and shape it however he/she likes."[85] Drawing on Hayden White, Munslow argues that the "rejection of the correspondence theory does not mean that we are completely free to select any tropic-emplotment-argument-ideological configuration for the evidence, and then proceed to some ultimate historical version of literary deconstruction that allows any meaning to be imposed on the past while declaiming any responsibility for it." Rather, historical interpretation is shaped and restricted by the "recognition that there is a substantial degree of reciprocity between the mental prefigurative process and the evidence," which has "previously been interpreted and textualised by other historians." As a result, no historian "can work in ignorance of previous interpretations or emplotments of the archive."[86]

Vanderhaeghe ultimately approaches history much less as a free agent than Chance, and *The Englishman's Boy*, thought it has certain postmodern inclinations, ultimately charts a course closer to the traditional ideal of the historical novel. Through his portrait of Chance, Vanderhaeghe, in a fashion compatible with postmodern historiography, certainly draws attention to the political and rhetorical dimensions of the emplotment of history. At the same time, the creative liberties Vanderhaeghe takes in his novel suggest that, while he is not concerned with complete historical fidelity, he remains closer to Georg Iggers's model of "plausibility" than to the substantially "new creation" that Naomi Jacobs sees as characteristically postmodern.[87] Jacobs's characterization of contemporary historical novels as creative fictions in which historical material is revised and adapted at will applies more to novels like *The Biggest Modern Woman of the*

World and *Ana Historic* than to *The Englishman's Boy. The Englishman's Boy* ultimately inscribes a belief in the importance of historical consciousness, a resistance to a completely relativist recognition of history as fair game, as fodder for any narrative construction.

Moreover, the novel highlights the powerful dehistoricizing force of the visual media that are undeniably in the ascendant. *The English-man's Boy* contests not only Chance's exploitative and fascist approach to history, but also his valorizing of the image that is so much a part of the spirit of the age as he sees it. Vanderhaeghe's comments in a 1984 interview, which are reprised in *The Englishman's Boy* as part of Chance's praising of the power of film, suggest the importance, to him as a writer, of such a resistance: "Yes, I believe very strongly in print. Arguments in print can be examined again and again and again. You can live with them for years. Whereas television and radio and cinema primarily leave impressions. They persuade us by impressions rather than by analysis and logic. I often feel like I'm in a way like one of those highly specialized, nineteenth-century industrial workers who were destroyed by technological innovation. It seems to me that writers now are one of those dying species overwhelmed by technology."[88] It is hard not to see *The Englishman's Boy* as staging a contest of technologies, with Vanderhaeghe adapting a very nineteenth-century form (the historical novel) to contest the effects of a twentieth-century one (film), with the representative of the latter ultimately being denied the victory he presumes.

Vanderhaeghe's portrait of Chance is clearly intended to comment on the imperializing tendencies of contemporary Hollywood and of a consumer culture that objectifies and decontextualizes its raw material – historical and otherwise – for passive consumption by an audience that it actively seeks to homogenize. *The Englishman's Boy* poignantly illustrates how the Western has monopolized the public's knowledge of the history of North America in general and of native people in particular, but it also suggests that Hollywood's imperialism of the image has a much vaster reach. The relationship between power, capital, culture, and the image that *The Englishman's Boy* depicts in a very nascent state has become, by the time in which the book was written, much more consolidated. The irony of *The English-man's Boy*, of course, is that this splendid allegory resisting the commodification of history and cultural colonization in an increasingly global consumer culture is itself a consumer commodity, aestheticizing and packaging history for consumption by readers. The book, in other words, is *of* that culture just as (though it is not fair to say "as much as") it is *about* that culture.[89] For all that, however, *The English-man's Boy* demonstrates that to be of that culture does not neutralize one's ability to be critical of it.

Vanderhaeghe's novel is characteristic of the more muted self-consciousness of recent English-Canadian historical fiction, which the contrast with *The Biggest Modern Woman of the World* helps to highlight. While reflecting scepticism about the historical record and the production of history, historical novels published in Canada over the last two decades generally lack the postmodern experimentation and extreme revisionist and deconstructionist urges of much postmodern historical fiction – novels like D.M. Thomas's *The White Hotel*, Robert Coover's *The Public Burning*, and Leonard Cohen's *Beautiful Losers*, which is atypical of Canadian fiction in its sustained eschewal of historical mimesis. Instead, it seems fair to say that Ronald Hatch's assessment of 1986 still *more or less* applies: "For most Canadian historical novelists carrying on the search for narrative styles that would free them from the implicit determinism of realism, the sense of an arbitrary history holds little appeal. Instead, they look for different ways of presenting the past which leave intact a comprehensible movement forward in time, for narrative forms which force the reader to encounter that movement as he becomes aware of the elements of narrative and interpretation in all explanations of the past."[90]

A possible explanation for this relative conservatism is that most contemporary Canadian novelists have had the somewhat paradoxical dual task of making their history and questioning it too. Some Canadian historical novels have served the dialectical function that Jameson describes as typical of the genre: Parker's *The Seats of the Mighty*, Raddall's *His Majesty's Yankees*, and Wiebe's revisionist account of Riel in *The Scorched-Wood People* all play on readers' assumptions about the significance of pivotal developments in Canadian history. But most contemporary novelists have had to give a sense of depth to Canadian history while often dramatizing the sense of depthlessness that late capitalist culture cultivates. As much as Canadian novelists make use of various devices to question the place of historiography and historical consciousness in a postmodern era, they also exploit realist conventions to cultivate an acquaintance with that historical arena in the first place. The result, as novels such as *Away*, *In the Skin of a Lion*, *Icefields*, *The Biggest Modern Woman of the World*, and *The Englishman's Boy* illustrate, is a paradoxical, but at least in some respects critical, relationship with postmodernity. In different ways, these novels scrutinize and question the economic and cultural imperatives of postmodernity, and reflect the adaptability, versatility, and continuing relevance of the historical novel in a dehistoricizing postmodern age.

If history is a form of fiction, furthermore, that does not mean that it is cut from whole cloth (a metaphor that captures many historians' reservations about postmodern historiography). Rather, it is an emplotment and imaginative reworking of historical intertexts, of always-already textualized evidence and accounts of the past. Thus the crisis of historicity in postmodernity, it might be said, is not so much the complete repudiation of the historical record's ability to refer to the past, as it is the loss of interest in that record, the dwindling ability to see events in an extended historical perspective because of the emphasis on immediacy and consumption, rather than on historical understanding and heritage, in postmodernity. It is thus not so much that the past ceases to matter, but, as Fludernik argues, that the form in which it does has changed.

For Jameson, however, historical thinking in postmodern society has not vanished but has become commodified. Contemporary culture is "irredeemably historicist, in the bad sense of an omnipresent and indiscriminate appetite for dead styles and fashions." Thus "a certain caricature of historical thinking" persists.[91] The relation between caricature and commodification raises the question of whether destabilizing the integrity of the historical record and implying its ultimate fictionality, as these novels do to some extent, amounts to the historical bad faith Jameson describes. Postmodernism, Stuart Hall stresses, in many ways has the effect of strengthening local traditions but also serves to erode traditions and a sense of history: "The more social life becomes mediated by the global marketing of styles, places, and images, by international travel, and by globally networked media images and communications systems, the more identities become detached – disembedded – from specific times, places, histories, and traditions, and appear 'free-floating.'"[92] Consumerism, argues Hall, has the effect of disengaging identities from their specific contexts and essentially making them available as commodities, a process that clearly erodes or reshapes history.

An important question, then, is whether contemporary Canadian historical novels contribute to this decontextualizing effect. The novels in this study, however much they put the historical record and traditional historiography in question and transform the past into marketable aesthetic objects, certainly fall short of the very fetishized and dehistoricized transformation of the past that Jameson associates with postmodernism. Most, in short, are closer to the traditional historical novel or to parody than to pastiche. While they reflect a substantial measure of resistance to historicist and empiricist views of history, they are also conscious of the importance of resisting caricature and of cultivating an appreciation for, if not a teleological consciousness of historical development, at least a temporal perspective that extends beyond a commodified heritage moment. They cultivate a sense of history not as the passive consumption of a given past but as a more speculative and dialogic view of the past that takes in our modes of perception at the same time. They are simultaneously specular and speculative, like figures looking through a window whose view is obscured by the reflection of the interior in which they stand.

While there is no doubt that contemporary Canadian historical novelists are exploiting the allure of history, the temporal duality of their work nonetheless provides for a very discriminating and critical stance toward postmodern society rather than simply a collusion with it. These novels quite obviously dramatize a consciousness of how perceptions of the past are necessarily infected by the present – especially the insistent present of a dehistoricizing postmodernity. Yet they resist the notion that such presentism amounts to a form of advanced glaucoma, a thorough obscuring of historical vision by contemporaneity, and instead strive to keep in view what might have preceded and shaped that present.

Period Piece

As the previous chapter emphasizes, historical novels are marked by a duality as "period pieces": they serve to comment about the times *in which* they are written as well as about the times *of which* are they are written. Rather than detached, Olympian depictions of the past, that is, historical novels are historically situated representations with contemporary motivations and concerns. Much the same, of course, is true of *Speculative Fictions*, which, as a study of English-Canadian historical novels of the last three decades, has certainly been marked by current political, social, cultural, and critical developments. Thus the final segment of this study is a "Period Piece" not just because it offers some tentative conclusions about those novels, but also because those assessments necessarily have been shaped by the concerns of the present. These concerns include, in particular, debates over the viability of national frameworks as literary critical paradigms, over the vitality of Canadian history, and over the very viability of Canada as a nation-state.

The first of these concerns has the most direct bearing on *Speculative Fictions* because, despite all its scepticism about nation, the study has an undeniable national focus, resulting from the decision to concentrate on texts dealing primarily with Canadian history and from the emphasis on the shared tendencies in these texts' treatment of history. Such an approach may seem out of sync with the prevailing mood in Canadian literary studies, which, as Terry Goldie emphasizes in a stock-taking millennial issue of *Essays on Canadian Writing*, reflects a movement "away from assumptions of fields of knowledge to assumptions of methods of interpretation."[1] "Canadian literary criticism," as Renée Hulan argues in another contribution to the issue, "has been concerned less with differentiating boundaries around national literature than with trying to understand what happens along them. Most recent criticism shows that literature cannot be defined or circumscribed by national boundaries, imagined or otherwise," and has stressed instead "the in-betweenness of Canadian literary production."[2] Poststructuralist and postcolonial critical approaches and postmodern poetics – which tend to emphasize diversity, disunity, and plurality – have increasingly provided more popular and appropriate frameworks for dealing with the heterogeneity and "in-betweenness" of that literature, consolidating disenchantment with nation as a literary critical paradigm.

In light of this critical shift and the present diversity and cosmopolitanism of English-Canadian literature, why exclude from the discussion of these texts a consideration of historical novels of other nations or of Canadian novels dealing with history outside the borders of Canada, especially given *Speculative Fiction*'s emphasis on the postcolonial and the postmodern? These critical frameworks are certainly valid and, for that matter, not incompatible with the approach taken in this study. At the same time, however, the very cosmopolitanism of the culture in which postcolonialism, postmodernism, and poststructuralism have flourished warrants caution, since it can, as Stuart Hall observes of consumerism, have the effect of "disembedding" identities. As Elleke Boehmer for one has argued, criticism of postcolonial writing tends to concentrate, in a somewhat exclusive and distancing fashion, on the points of intersection between postmodernism and postcolonialism, minimizing the importance of the particular contexts behind those texts. In light of this, Boehmer asserts the importance of remembering that the postcolonial text "emerges out of the grit and rank specificity of a local culture or cultures, history or histories."[3] Within an ambivalent cultural globalization – one that is both liberating and imperializing – jettisoning nation as a focus of cultural study has its perils, and an increasing reaction to the privileging of cosmopolitanism, hybridity, and liminality in theorizing about postcolonial texts has been to return to the specificity of national or local cultures.

This is not to suggest that the orientation of *Speculative Fictions* is motivated by suspicion of poststructuralism and postcolonialism as potentially imperializing Western critical paradigms, a charge that runs the risk of diminishing the undeniable liberatory value of those frameworks (which obviously have had a substantial influence on the construction of history in this study). Rather, it is motivated by the belief that it is possible to retain a national framework without resurrecting the totalizing cultural and political nationalism to which much poststructuralist and postcolonial criticism has rightly reacted. *Speculative Fictions* is thus not an exercise in "differentiating boundaries around national literature" but an attempt to gauge the tendencies of a series of texts in relation to "the grit and rank specificity of a local culture or cultures, history or histories."

Dismissals of the notion of a distinctive Canadian culture or identity that have been shaped by poststructuralist and postcolonial unease about cultural authenticity and literary nationalism, furthermore, can come uncomfortably close to the increasingly frequent neoconservative arguments that Canada is culturally, politically, and historically unmoored and therefore should give itself up to the inexorable pull of the United States. While there are important differences in the motivation for those arguments, those differences provide little consolation if the end result is the same: an erosion of concern for the specific modalities of historical and cultural experience in Canada. Thus employing a national paradigm, in a self-conscious and self-critical fashion, may be preferable to seeing Canadian writing marginalized and/or decontextualized within global commodity culture and an unevenly internationalized literary criticism.

In a 1978 essay, Margaret Laurence contended that Canadians needed to "write out of what is truly ours in the face of an overwhelming cultural imperialism" coming from Britain and the United States, and – despite the various caveats it is tempting to add to it – that advice still seems valid.[4] Admittedly, the formulation "what is truly ours" is suggestive of cultural essentialism, and Laurence's warning conjures images of musk oxen drawn in defensive, circular formation – a vision of Canadian literature that is perhaps not as appropriate as it was in 1978. But if Canadian literature is presently more robust and less beleaguered than it was then, this is because "to write out of what is truly ours," in a more broadly defined and internationalized sense, has become more readily accepted, even taken for granted.

The conspicuous concern with history has played a great part in that development. This concern with history, however, has not been a monolithic and homogeneous phenomenon, and the interests, features, and strategies of the English-Canadian historical novels published over the last thirty years are extremely varied. To try to delineate recurring characteristics of the most recent of that fiction is thus to run the risk of an even more tenuous historical (and historicist) segmentation. At the same time, to do so helps to put in perspective the achievements of the earlier texts, to highlight the continuities and departures of the later, and in the process to give a broad view of the writing of history in contemporary English-Canadian novels.

What is most immediately obvious from this study, first of all, is that the history that matters continues to be a popular, social history. The commitment to social history evident in *Obasan, The Wars, The Temptations of Big Bear, The Biggest Modern Woman of the World*, and *Ana Historic* has been sustained in recent Canadian historical novels. For the most part, Jane Urquhart, Sky Lee, Rudy Wiebe, Margaret Sweatman, and others illuminate the lives of those who have been left out of or written over by official history: the Irish immigrants of *Away*, the residents of Vancouver's Chinatown in *Disappearing Moon Café*, the Tetsot'ine of *A Discovery of Strangers*, the working-class immigrants of *Fox*. Social history and its novelistic counterparts – *In the Skin of a Lion, Alias Grace, The King Years, Fox*, and others – do more than put flesh on the bones of official history. They suggest that what has been presented as the backbone of Canadian history is instead a narrative told by those in power in the interests of those in power, to assert an expedient order over the past.

As a consequence, where these novels do portray historically prominent figures and events, they tend to do so in a subversive and carnivalesque fashion. Robertson's Mackenzie King, Wiebe's Franklin, John Steffler's Cartwright, and Wayne Johnston's Smallwood are treated in a similar vein as Wiebe's Macdonald and George Bowering's Vancouver. Although Smallwood and Cartwright are presented somewhat sympathetically, these portraits are generally irreverent and iconoclastic, knocking prominent figures off pedestals often of their own documentary making, emphasizing the importance of opening up official history to discursive contestation. Furthermore, these subversive portraits tend to emphasize the effects of the actions of those public historical figures on the historically marginalized, particularly on aboriginal peoples, questioning the cost to others at which their prominence has been achieved.

These novels testify that social history has amounted to more than a brief swing of the pendulum away from the political and military history that prevailed before it. The anxiety this has occasioned, not just among traditional historians but also within the political and social establishment, is that the centrifugal force of such a swing threatens the very fulcrum of Canada and that what is needed is a return to a more traditional political history that will provide a unifying narrative for the nation. These novels, however, often stress what such an argument glosses over: that privileging unity tends to work in the favor of certain interests, contributing to the very kind of hegemony to which social history emerged as a reaction in the first place. This is a key insight highlighted, for instance, by the class conflicts in Sweatman's *Fox*, the political machinations of the elite in the name of nationalism in Robertson's *The King Years*, and the debates over ethnicity, religion, and nationalism in Urquhart's *Away*.

At the same time, calls for a unifying narrative are not without justification, especially given the tenuousness of historical conscious- ness and cultural identity in Canada. Since the official history to which social history reacts is much less prominent and established in Canada than in, say, the United States or Britain, it might be argued that subverting official history in Canada is like knocking on the walls of a house of cards, or, in the case of the historical novel, engaging in a subversive, dialectical dialogue with a conversational partner whose voice is hardly familiar or resounding to begin with. But such a defence is ultimately misleading. What the momentum of social history suggests – in its literary as well as historiographical manifestations – is a confidence in the vitality of Canadian history and a commitment to appreciating that vitality not by suppressing its variety and conflict but by underscoring them. Perhaps the lesson to be learned is that Canadian historiography does not have to swing like a pendulum and that it is possible to reconcile social history's concern with demographic plurality and historical minutiae with a desire to present the big historical picture of traditional history, with- out reviving the exclusions and hegemonic tendencies of the latter. At least some of these novels – *The King Years*, *Away*, *The Colony of Unrequited Dreams*, for instance – manage to strike such a balance.

Because of social history's challenging of various forms of authority, the commitment to it in these novels is also part of a larger postco- lonial renegotiation of Canadian history, Canadian culture, and Cana- dian identity. Novels such as *The Englishman's Boy*, *A Discovery of Strangers*, *Away*, and *Icefields* have extended the postcolonial engage- ment of novels like *Burning Water*, *Obasan*, and *Big Bear*, writing away from or against an official history that serves to consolidate the accomplishments of colonialism. For the most part, these fictions sug- gest that Canadian history is not the record of a collective past but a varied terrain that can be viewed through multiple perspectives and continues to be contested on many fronts. Their revisionism resides in a desire to provide fuller or different pictures of Canadian history, which necessarily involves exposing the inequities – particularly along racial, cultural, gender, and class lines – that colonial accounts of Canadian history both enshrined and submerged. It amounts, furthermore, to a definite repudiation of colonial and neo-colonial dismissals of the significance of Canadian history, dramatizing that

that history was less uneventful than the stereotype suggests and underscoring whose interests such a stereotype serves.

This repudiation, however, does not come as part of a postcolonial resistance that asserts a unified national history as a way of writing back to the colonial centre. Rather, it reflects a resistance simultaneously to the history of colonialism and to a national history that is potentially equally imperious. Most of the novels published in the 1990s reflect a scepticism about the role of nation and a sustained concern with particular places: Winnipeg in *Fox*, Labrador in *The Afterlife of George Cartwright*, southeastern Ontario in *Away*, the Rockies in *Icefields*, and The Rock in *The Colony of Unrequited Dreams*. They focus on different geographies and different temporalities – the circular time of the Tetsot'ine, the arrested development of Newfoundland nationalism, the liminal time between myth and history – with the result being a variety of disparate, if connectable, histories rather than constituent parts of a monolithic and synchronized national past. While *Away* provides a sustained examination of the ethnic and political negotiations required for a more hospitable new dominion, in most of these novels the nation is a marginal presence, often associated with oppressive or threatening political forces: the neo-colonial presence of Canada in *Colony*; the bullying, xenophobic, opportunistic federal government in *Fox* and *The King Years*.

The contestatory, postcolonial revisionism evident in these novels, however, is susceptible to criticism not only from the perspective of traditional historians, but perhaps more seriously from within the poststructuralist and postcolonial perspectives that so often inform such revisionism. This is perhaps the case even more with recent historical novels than with their earlier counterparts. First of all, particularly where Canadian historical novels address the history of colonialism and of native people, they run the risk – as evident in Wiebe's *A Discovery of Strangers* and Steffler's *The Afterlife of George Cartwright* – of becoming consolatory narratives compensating for the sins of official history. In representations of episodes in the history of colonialism, for instance, the explorer/discoverer is repeatedly depicted as a colonial bully and the savage/civilized dichotomy between the colonized and the colonizer is recurrently reversed. These strategies run the risk of reinforcing the binary opposition between the two and encouraging simplistic approaches to the legacy of colonialism, instead of a more nuanced understanding of that legacy and of what, therefore, is required to more effectively decolonize that history.

Afterlife's Cartwright does make some posthumous strides towards transculturation, which makes the novel more than an exercise in villainizing the colonizer. And Wiebe's *Discovery* is a sustained, dialogic attempt to re-view a chapter of the history of the exploration of the north through contending prisms, highlighting the imprint of culture on perceptions of the past. Nonetheless, these novels, along with Wharton's *Icefields*, lack the ideological nuances afforded by the self-reflexive, parodic approach to colonialism of, say, *Burning Water*, which emphasizes the complex, contemporary context of a settler-invader culture that necessarily informs an investigation of its history. The legacy of colonialism and the treatment of native people historically remains the most vexing aspect of the current obsession with history in Canadian literature, and it is more than likely that native writers in Canada before long will turn to the historical novel to provide their own perspectives on that legacy.

Another, related vulnerability of such postcolonial revisionism is that, in so far as it serves to "correct" official history, it implicitly or explicitly asserts a more authentic version – as is the case with *Discovery*, say, or *The Englishman's Boy*, or *Alias Grace* – a stance that jeopardizes its own contestation of the "truth" of official history or of reactionary revisionism. Such an assertion, obviously, has been questioned in much contemporary historiographical theory and in most of the historical novels of the 1970s and early 80s, but less so in the novels published since then. If postmodern historical fiction follows postmodern historiography's assumption that it is "probably best to view historical narratives as propositions about how we *might* represent a past reality, suggestions of *possible* correspondences rather than *the* correspondence," most of the novels published over the last fifteen years are less up-front about their hypothetical status.[5]

To be sure, recent Canadian historical fiction continues to foreground the intertextuality of history and to make use of metafictional commentary on historiography, oral frameworks and narrative strategies, mythic conventions, and carnivalesque discursive tactics. The continuation of this concern with "the content of the form" suggests an unabated wariness of scientific, mimetic, Western historiography and of realistic, objective historical fiction. At the same time, it is tempting to generalize about more recent novels that they are less experimental and carnivalesque than *Burning Water*, *Ana Historic*, *The Biggest Modern Woman*, *The Wars*, and *Big Bear*. While Sweatman's *Fox* and Lee's *Disappearing Moon Café* can be excepted, most recent texts are more accessible, less fragmented, and more concerned with conveying a coherent picture of history. The ontological and epistemological disruptions and stylistic innovations of the earlier texts are less in evidence, and the postmodern displacements and self-reflexiveness of novels like *Away*, *The Englishman's Boy*, *Alias Grace*, *Icefields*, and *The Colony of Unrequited Dreams* are ultimately more subtle and recuperable. These novels come across as less profoundly sceptical about historiography, less concerned with fracturing and interrogating retrospection, and largely, if somewhat ambivalently, rooted in historical verisimilitude and an engagement with (rather than abandonment or disruption of) the historical record.

That most recent Canadian historical novels are more subtle and less insistent about foregrounding the writing of history may be a sign of the times. That is, they may reflect the distance of the fiction of the 1990s, and the prevailing commodity-conscious literary culture, from the experimentalism and anti-establishmentarianism of the 60s and 70s (one aspect of postmodernity, it might be observed, giving way to another). Behind postmodernism, Mike Featherstone argues, is "the growth of a consumer culture and expansion in the number of specialists and intermediaries engaged in the production and circulation of symbolic goods" – and historical novels are undeniably part of that consumer culture.[6] This is not to suggest that writers like Urquhart, Johnston, Vanderhaeghe, and Wharton are more conservative and co-opted but rather that they are writing as part of a literary culture that is less supportive of experimentation and in which one of the principal imperatives is consumability.

The result, in short, is a much more accessible fiction, but a fiction in which the ambivalently "speculative" nature of writing about history nonetheless continues to be highlighted. As the previous chapter stresses, in a culture fixated on the present, the immediate, the transient, and in which "money and commodities are themselves the primary bearers of cultural codes" and "are entirely bound up with the circulation of capital," writing about history becomes doubly complicated.[7] In such a dehistoricizing culture, David Harvey observes, "tradition is now often preserved by being commodified and marketed as such. The search for roots ends up at worst being produced and marketed as an image, as a simulacrum or pastiche."[8] As a result, these novels, like their predecessors, are in the paradoxical position of raising questions about the aesthetics, politics, and ideology of writing history, while nonetheless using the past as raw material, transforming it into a textual commodity, but they are doing so in a climate of hyper-awareness of that process of commodification.

It is a fine balance, and the demands of writing historical fiction at a time of deep scepticism about historiography and wariness about commodifying the past are reflected in the subject matter and textual strategies of the novels themselves. The concern with the impact of capitalism and consumer society on the representation of history is perhaps even more prevalent in recent fiction, so much of which adopts an ironic and critical attitude towards capitalism and/or the writing of history – *Fox, Icefields, Away, The Englishman's Boy,* and *Colony,* for instance. At the same time, there are some important differences to be noted: while *Fox* and *Disappearing Moon Café* do foreground the construction of history and disrupt historical mimesis, the historical self-consciousness of most of the other texts is in some ways outweighed by the power of those stylistic and generic qualities that contribute to their popularity: the exploitation of the Western in *The Englishman's Boy,* of the thriller in *Igor,* the lyricism of *Icefields* and *Away,* the satire of *Colony.* These aesthetic imperatives threaten to overwhelm the historiographical commentary and dialogic interplay to which they nonetheless contribute, locating these novels farther from historiographical parody and closer to pastiche – an empty, dehistoricized simulation of the style of the past – than their forebears.

However, despite their relative lack of formal and ideological self-consciousness about the textual nature and rhetorical overdetermination of reconstructions of history, these novels retain a historical and political substance that makes them nonetheless productive and valuable. Revisionist history, I would argue, can be about more than itself. Self-consciousness is not the be-all and end-all of contemporary historical fiction's reconfigured relation to the past. Revisionist history is not simply specular – a hermetic, textual projection of its own presuppositions and discursive conventions onto the blank screen of history. It is both specular *and* speculative – using the past to mirror the present but also building a bridge back to the past by speculating about it on the basis of the residue of that historical "past reality" and reworking that residue in the context of a fictive situation. Though novels like *Icefields, Away,* and *Disappearing Moon Café* are less concerned with providing versions of significant historical episodes in dialogue with the historical record, this is certainly the case with novels such as *Discovery, Fox, The Afterlife of George Cartwright,* and even the less obviously intertextual *The Englishman's Boy.*

To point this out is not to reinshrine a historical empiricism that these novels for the most part undermine or question but to suggest that the past is not as remote or removed as much poststructuralist theory would have it. For all their foregrounding that it is not possible to write about what is in the past without writing about how one writes about the past, these texts for the most part convey that the past matters, that it has a material significance and does not simply amount to a disembodied, textual, referent-less archive, an anti-materialist perspective that we adopt at our peril. Vanderhaeghe's Harry Vincent says of the wolfers of *The Englishman's Boy* that they "cast longer shadows than I had any inkling of,"[9] and many of these novels reflect a similar concern with the reach of the shadows of the past.

In various ways, they acknowledge the importance of historical continuity and materiality, for instance in their authors' concerns with the palimpsest of place – Ondaatje, Urquhart, Wharton, and Vanderhaeghe are good examples – or in their reconfiguring of historicity: *Away*'s negotiation of a third way between history and myth, *The Englishman's Boy*'s upholding of individual agency in the face of imperializing historical forces, *Discovery*'s resistance to a Eurocentric, teleological, linear history. Nonetheless, what most of these texts emphasize, if less so than their predecessors, is that those shadows are "read" through interpretive conventions and ideological perspectives that are not innocent or objective but rather play a substantial role in how we construct narratives of the past and in what we do with those narratives.

What these texts resoundingly affirm, ultimately, is that, contrary to the stereotype, Canada has more than a little history. Certainly, the revolutions, civil wars, military conquest, and religious strife that punctuate the history of other nations such as the United States are conspicuously lacking. But as Mark Starowicz (producer of the television series *Canada: A People's History* and one of the contributors to the *Globe*'s "The Death of History" series) insightfully notes, "the absence of such things is not evidence of the absence of history." Rather, the fact that Canada "had every ingredient" for violent internicine conflict, such as "clashing religions, languages, races and contested land," and instead "mixed them into a complex, multipart quest for equilibrium" makes Canadian history "one of the most relevant histories in the global era."[10] Starowicz's assessment is a little hale, to be sure, but, in the global scheme of things, not without justification. What is debatable about it, however, is his characterization of the level of strife in Canadian history, not his characterization of that history's significance. Canadian history is interesting and does matter, as English-Canadian historical novels of the last thirty years amply illustrate.

And the historical fiction keeps on coming. Appearing during the writing of *Speculative Fictions* were *Broken Ground*, Jack Hodgins's novel of Canadians in France during World War I, and Fred Stenson's sweeping epic of the fur trade in the NorthWest, *The Trade*, and still to look forward to is George Elliott Clarke's forthcoming novel about two black men hung for murder in Fredericton in the 1940s, *George and Rue*. Timing, space, and the practical consideration of having at some point to come to a stop precluded these novels from consideration here, yet they testify all the same to the wealth of historical fiction, and the wealth of history, that Canada has to offer.[11]

Canadian history is dead. Long live Canadian history!

Notes

PREFACE

1 Atwood, *In Search of* Alias Grace, 15.
2 Robert Kroetsch, *Creation* (Toronto: New Press, 1970), 63. Kroetsch's writing before and since that observation, of course, has generally exhibited a card-carrying postmodernist's reservations about the "real."
3 See Duffy, *Sounding the Iceberg*, v, and Jameson, *Postmodernism*, 284.
4 Despite the reservations about historiography that the book expresses, if anything this project has sharpened my appreciation for the work that historians do.
5 See, for instance, Isabelle Allende's *The House of Spirits*, Salman Rushdie's *Midnight's Children*, and Gabriel Garcia Marquez's *One Hundred Years of Solitude*.
6 This is a consistent theme both of Thomas King's fiction and of his comments in interviews and articles on native identity and whites' perceptions of native people. In expressing his wariness of being mistaken for "an authentic Indian," for instance, King points out that the kind of Indian people would like to have is "some 19th century Native on a pinto pony in a teepee." Thomas King, interview by Jace Weaver, *Publisher's Weekly* 240, no. 10 (1993): 56.

CHAPTER ONE

1 Rudyard Griffiths, "Mistakes of the past," *The Globe & Mail*, 18 September 2000, A13. Griffiths is director of the Dominion Institute, a corporate-sponsored charity recently founded to promote a more traditional and conservative perspective on Canadian history.

2 "The death of history?" *The Globe & Mail*, 23 September 2000, A16.

3 This issue is addressed by Ray Conlogue in one of two contributions to the series, "Why do Canadians confuse this man with a car?" *The Globe & Mail*, 19 September 2000, R1.

4 Patrick Watson, "The death of history is bunk," *The Globe & Mail*, 22 September 2000, A17.

5 Wiebe made this point during a visit to my senior course on history, theory, and Canadian historical novels at the University of Alberta in June 1998. I'd like to extend my appreciation once again for his generosity in joining us for a vigorous, interesting, and enjoyable discussion.

6 Keith, *Epic Fiction*, 88.

7 The useful but contested notion of metanarratives comes, of course, from Jean-Francois Lyotard's definition of the postmodern as "incredulity toward metanarratives," which he sees as characterizing "the state of our culture following the transformations which, since the end of the nineteenth century, have altered the game rules for science, literature, and the arts." Lyotard views these transformations in terms of a "crisis of narratives" (*Postmodern Condition* xxiv, xxiii).

8 Fleishman, *English Historical Novel*, 3.

9 Lukács, *Historical Novel*, 46.

10 Conrad and Finkel, *History of the Canadian Peoples*, xiv.

11 The phrase comes, of course, from Anderson's *Imagined Communities: Reflections on the Origins and Spread of Nationalism*.

12 Bhabha, "DissemiNation," 300.

13 Joyce Appleby, Lynn Hunt, and Margaret Jacob suggest, in contrast, that social historians "did not oppose the standards of objectivity or the codes of professional discipline; they used those very standards to challenge the traditional interpretations which had excluded marginal or nonconforming historical groups" (*Telling the Truth* 200).

14 Scott, *Gender and the Politics of History*, 9.

15 de Certau, *Writing of History*, 30.

16 Manzoni, *On the Historical Novel*, 63.

17 White, *Content of the Form*, 26.

18 Butterfield, *Historical Novel*, 18.

19 Fleishman, *English Historical Novel*, 10.

20 Gossman, "History and Literature," 26.

21 Foucault, *Archaeology of Knowledge*, 7.

22 Barthes, "Historical Discourse," 154.
23 Derrida, *Of Grammatology*, 158.
24 Croce, *History as the Story of Liberty*, 19.
25 Carr, *What Is History?*, 10.
26 Elton, *Practice of History*, 9.
27 Ibid., 84.
28 Ibid., 56–7.
29 White, *Tropics of Discourse*, 102.
30 White, *Metahistory*, 30.
31 Ibid., 427.
32 de Certau, *Writing of History*, 11.
33 Foucault, *Archaeology of Knowledge*, 49.
34 Ibid., 46.
35 Foucault, "Order of Discourse," 52.
36 Foucault, *Archaeology of Knowledge*, 120.
37 Collingwood, *Idea of History*, 246.
38 Jacobs, *Character of Truth*, xiv.
39 McHale, *Postmodernist Fiction*, 87.
40 Hutcheon, *Canadian Postmodern*, 1.
41 Hughes, *Historical Romance*, 8.
42 Jones, *That Art of Difference*, 13.
43 Lukács, *Historical Novel*, 61.
44 Ibid., 63.
45 de Certau, *Writing of History*, 37.
46 Jacobs, *Character of Truth*, 75.
47 Bowering, *Burning Water*, 21.
48 Jacobs, *Character of Truth*, 75.
49 Lukács, *Historical Novel*, 39.
50 Ibid., 54.
51 Allemano, *Historical Portraits and Visions*, 51.
52 Jacobs, *Character of Truth*, 19.
53 McHale, *Postmodernist Fiction*, 16, 17.
54 Kuester, *Framing Truths*, 70.
55 Daphne Marlatt, "On *Ana Historic*: An Interview With Daphne Marlatt," interview by George Bowering, *Line* 13 (1989), 98.
56 White, *Tropics of Discourse*, 54–5.
57 Aristotle, *Poetics*, 1451b, 1–2, 6–7.
58 Fleishman, *English Historical Novel*, 8.
59 The phrase is the title of a collection of White's essays, *The Content of the Form: Narrative Discourse and Historical Representation*.
60 White, *Tropics of Discourse*, 84.
61 Ibid., 91.
62 Jameson, *Political Unconscious*, 58.

63 See White, *Metahistory*, 31.

64 White, "Value of Narrativity," 18.

65 See Ibid., 27.

66 As White observes in *Metahistory*, "the very claim to have discerned some kind of formal coherence in the historical record brings with it theories of the nature of the historical world and of historical knowledge itself which have ideological implications for attempts to understand 'the present,' however the present is defined" (21).

67 White, *Tropics of Discourse*, 88.

68 Polkinghorne, *Narrative Knowing*, 59.

69 Munslow, *Deconstructing History*, 68.

70 White, *Tropics of Discourse*, 85.

71 Instead, White laments, "when many contemporary historians speak of the 'art' of history, they seem to have in mind a conception of art that would admit little more than the nineteenth-century novel as a paradigm" (*Tropics of Discourse* 42).

72 Hutcheon, "History and/as Intertext," 176.

73 Lukács, *Historical Novel*, 303.

74 Rudy Wiebe, "On the Trail of Big Bear," in *Voice in the Land*, ed. Keith, 132–3.

75 One of the most controversial readings of Canadian historical figures has been the 1982 National Film Board production *The Kid Who Couldn't Miss*, whose presentation of World War I pilot Billy Bishop provoked a strong reaction from veterans' groups and various politicians. For a discussion of the controversy and for an interesting analysis of Bishop's memoir *Winged Warfare* and the reworking of Bishop's story in John Gray's play *Billy Bishop Goes to War* and *The Kid Who Couldn't Miss*, see M. Jeanne Yardley's "Unauthorized Re-Visions of the Billy Bishop Story," *Textual Studies in Canada* 3 (1993): 86–96.

76 For instance, Catherine Cundy notes that Rushdie was sued for libel by Indira Gandhi for suggesting in *Midnight's Children* that she hastened her husband's death by heart attack. Gandhi won the case, and Rushdie was obliged to remove the suggestion (*Salman Rushdie*, Manchester: Manchester UP, 1996, 37). Timothy Brennan argues that "the story of Indian nationalism is erased from the book that documents its sad outcome, and the most dramatic illustration of Rushdie's argument is an absence" (*Salman Rushdie and the Third World: Myths of the Nation*, Houndmills, Hampsh.: Macmillan, 1989, 84). For a brief account of the publication woes of Robert Coover's *The Public Burning*, see William H. Gass's introduction to the 1998 Grove Press edition of the novel (New York: Grove Press, 1998), xi–xviii.

77 Brennan makes this charge against Rushdie, for instance; see Ibid., 166.

78 Raddall conducted extensive research at the Public Archives of Nova Scotia, covered the ground of various locations at different times of the year, and relied on both contemporary accounts – principally *The Diary of Simeon Perkins 1766–1780* – and on histories such as John R. Brebner's *The Neutral Yankees of Nova Scotia* and Wilfred Kerr's *The Maritime Provinces of British North America*.

79 Qtd. in Donna Smyth, "Raddall's Desiring Machine: Narrative Strategies in the Historical Fiction," in *Time and Place: The Life and Works of Thomas H. Raddall*, ed. Alan R. Young (Fredericton: Acadiensis, 1991), 63.

80 Jameson, *Political Unconscious*, 82.

81 Kristeva, "Bounded Text," 41.

82 Ibid., 45.

83 Ibid., 55.

84 de Certau, *Writing of History*, 94.

85 LaCapra, *History, Politics, and the Novel*, 8.

86 Jacobs, *Character of Truth*, 1.

87 Bakhtin, *Dialogic Imagination*, 345.

88 Ibid., 355.

89 Ibid., 354.

90 LaCapra, *History and Criticism*, 36.

91 Kerby, *Narrative and the Self*, 4.

92 Polkinghorne, *Narrative Knowing*, 150.

93 Kerby, *Narrative and the Self*, 101.

94 Jacobs, *Character of Truth*, 33.

95 Ibid.

96 Kuester, *Framing Truths*, 148.

97 Bakhtin, *Dialogic Imagination*, 361; italics in original.

98 Derrida, *Of Grammatology*, 158.

99 See Appleby, Hunt, and Jacob, *Telling the Truth*, 236–7. "The move toward the most radically skeptical and relativist postmodern position," they argue, "inevitably leads to a cul-de-sac" (236). Postmodern history "often seems to consist of denunciations of history as it has been known rather than of new histories for present and hence future time. Periodic exercises in theory have an undeniably useful function as criticism of unself-conscious assumptions about art or history or science, but postmodernism cannot provide models for the future when it claims to refuse the entire idea of offering models for the future. In the final analysis, then, there can be no postmodern history" (236–7).

100 Iggers, *Historiography in the Twentieth Century*, 144.

101 Ibid., 145.

102 Appleby, Hunt, and Jacob, *Telling the Truth*, 250, 251.

103 See Stanley Fish, "Interpreting the *Variorum*," *Critical Inquiry* 2 (1976): 483.

104 de Certau, *Writing of History,* 30.

105 See, for instance, Munslow's overview *Deconstructing History,* which defends postmodern historiography, and Appleby, Hunt, and Jacob's *Telling the Truth About History* for a moderate critique.

106 Munslow, *Deconstructing History,* 166.

CHAPTER TWO

1 Young, *White Mythologies,* 20.

2 Rudy Wiebe, "On the Trail of Big Bear," in *Voice in the Land,* ed. Keith, 134.

3 McClintock, "The angel of progress," 257–8.

4 The phrase "the empire writes back," of course, is Salman Rushdie's and provides a key figure for postcolonial practice, as well as the title for Ashcroft, Griffiths, and Tiffin's Book *The Empire Writes Back: Theory and Practice in Post-colonial Literatures.*

5 Hutcheon, "'Circling the Downspout,'" 156.

6 Brydon, "Introduction: Reading Postcoloniality, Reading Canada," 2.

7 Lawson, "Postcolonial Theory," 20.

8 Boehmer, *Colonial & Postcolonial Literature,* 247.

9 Barker, Hulme, and Iversen, Introduction to *Colonial Discourse/Postcolonial Theory,* 10.

10 JanMohamed, "Economy of Manichean Allegory," 63.

11 Robertson, "Lust, Murder and 'Long Pig,'" 20.

12 Ashcroft, Griffiths, and Tiffin, *Empire Writes Back,* 34.

13 Kaltemback, "Explorations Into History," 85.

14 Wiebe's portrait of the expedition illustrates Olive Dickason's argument that First Nations peoples' role in post-contact history has been marginalized and represented Eurocentrically: "Far from being passive partners in European enterprises, as usually portrayed, they were active participants. Indeed, that participation was essential to European success." Thus, Dickason concludes, in "the most profound sense of the term, they are Canada's founding peoples" (*Canada's First Nations,* 2nd ed., Toronto: University of Toronto Press, 1997, xii).

15 Huggan, "Decolonizing the Map," 120.

16 As Michael Krans observes of the original expedition, because they "needed the struggle between themselves and the land, they felt no need to adapt themselves to it; because they viewed the land as formless, they felt free to impose upon it a colonial form" ("Writing for an Elsewhere" 78).

17 Ibid., 72. See Krans's essay for an extended discussion of the dynamics of the officers' mediation of their experiences in a colonially self-aggrandizing fashion: "while the expedition is entirely dependent

on the Indians, the explorers' desire to appear in control means that they must actively over-write some of the aspects of this relationship" (85). Krans contends, however, that this mediation does not simply reflect, as a New Historicist reading would have it, that the discourse of these officers remains hermetically sealed within their own cultural and ideological presuppositions but is the product of a more dialectical engagement with their new environment.

18 MacLaren, "Retaining Captaincy of the Soul," 88.
19 Richardson, *Arctic Ordeal*, 156.
20 Ibid., 157.
21 JanMohamed, "Manichean Allegory," 62.
22 Tremblay, "Piracy, Penance," 160.
23 Ibid., 164.
24 JanMohamed, "Manichean Allegory," 65.
25 Tremblay, "Piracy, Penance," 171.
26 Ibid., 170–1.
27 The importance of Wiebe's strategies in *Discovery* can best be seen through a brief comparison with Brian Moore's *Black Robe*, which chronicles the experiences of Jesuit priest Father Paul Laforgue in the early 1600s as he travels from Quebec under the command of Champlain to relieve a mission on the shores of Lake Superior. Moore describes being inspired by reading Francis Parkman's *The Jesuits in North America* and from there going on to read *The Jesuit Relations*, noting that "unlike the English, French, and Dutch traders and explorers, the Jesuits came to North America not for furs or conquest, but to save the souls of those whom they called 'the Savages'" (*Black Robe* viii). Moore's aim is ostensibly an anthropologically revisionist one, but unlike Wiebe's text, his narrative of Laforgue's experiences with his Algonkian guides and among the Hurons certainly privileges Laforgue's perspective. Furthermore, rather than postcolonial and counter-hegemonic in intent, it is very much in the humanist tradition of presenting contact as a tragic and balanced clash of cultures. The novel, Moore notes, shows that "the Indian belief in a world of night and in the power of dreams clashed with the Jesuits' preachments of Christianity and a paradise after death"; "each inspired in the other fear, hostility, and despair, which later would result in the destruction and abandonment of the Jesuit missions, and the conquest of the Huron people by the Iroquois, their deadly enemy" (ix). The effect of Moore's emphasis on Laforgue, as much as he sees his intent as a revisionist one (correcting a stereotype of the indigene), is to heroize his mission among the Hurons and equalize the situations of European and native.
28 JanMohamed, "Manichean Allegory," 65.
29 Lawson, "Postcolonial Theory," 25.

30 JanMohamed, "Manichean Allegory," 65.

31 Lobb, "Imagining History," 113.

32 Ibid., 120.

33 Vancouver, it would seem, died 12 May 1798 of a chronic malady in Petersham, England, and not at the hands of Menzies six years earlier.

34 Vautier, *New World Myth*, xv.

35 Ibid., xv-xvi.

36 Ibid., xvii.

37 Carnegie, *Saskatchewan and the Rocky Mountains*, 175.

38 Sexsmith's dream about the Knights of the Grail following Arthur to the West is presumably gesturing to some versions of the Grail legend in which Avalon is depicted as being located to the West, and Wharton may be playing on the theory that the Grail or its teachings were brought across the Atlantic to present-day Nova Scotia in the late fourteenth century. See John Matthews, *King Arthur and the Grail Quest* (London: Blandford, 1994), 142–4. This theory is put forth by Michael Bradley in *The Holy Grail Across the Atlantic* (Toronto: Hounslow Press, 1989) and by Andrew Sinclair in *The Sword and the Grail* (New York: Crown Publishing, 1993).

39 William Shakespeare, *The Tempest*, III.II.86–8.

40 *The Tempest* has proved to be a popular text for such postcolonial reworkings. See Diana Brydon's article "Re-Writing *The Tempest*," *World Literature Written in English* 23, no. 1 (1984): 75–88.

41 Lawson, "Postcolonial Theory," 25.

42 van Toorn, *Rudy Wiebe*, 140.

43 Rudy Wiebe, "In the West, Sir John A. is a Bastard and Riel a Saint. Ever Ask Why?," in *Voice in the Land*, ed. Keith, 209–11.

44 Such an interpretation is far from universal, particularly among eastern historians. For at least one contrasting view, witness Desmond Morton's summary of the conflict in his introduction to *The Queen V. Louis Riel*: "Certainly it is the Riel version of government policy in the North-West which occupies the history books. A generation which faces the genuine dilemmas as well as the rhetoric of aboriginal rights and native claims should have more sympathy for the difficulties which confronted Macdonald and his colleagues" (Introduction to *The Queen V. Louis Riel*, Toronto: University of Toronto Press, 1974, xxx).

45 van Toorn, *Rudy Wiebe*, 150.

46 Wiebe was attracted to Big Bear because of the divided reactions people had to him, and it is an attraction that has proven to be resilient. He co-wrote the screenplay for and participated in the production of a 1999 film treatment of the novel and collaborated on *Stolen Life* with Big Bear's granddaughter Yvonne Johnson.

47 See Hutcheon's chapter on historiographical metafiction in *The Canadian Postmodern*, 61–77.

48 Wiebe's emphasis in *Big Bear* can be usefully measured by way of comparison with Peter Such's *Riverrun*, a novel published in the same year, which charts the decimation of the last surviving band of Beothuks through disease and violence on the part of white settlers in Newfoundland in the early 1800s. Such's novel certainly addresses many of the same themes as *The Temptations of Big Bear*, but the novel's narrative strategies, despite Such's use of intertexts and competing perspectives, are resolutely modernist. Such is openly attempting to "fill out" the picture around the historical record, and the historical intertexts in *Riverrun* essentially take their place as segments of a cohesive, continuous narrative. Though there is a tension between the different kinds of discourses, there is not the openly dialogic play that characterizes Wiebe's use of intertexts in *Big Bear*. Such obviously believes in the possibility of historical reconstruction and in a historiographical preface to the book acknowledges his sources, finishing with this humanist note: "It is tempting to explain my obsession with writing about the Beothuk. Let me just say it is a kind of debt I owe to Nonosabasut, Demasduit, Shawnadithit, Doodebewshet and Longon – to whom I was introduced first through the pages of history – and to Osnahanut and the other persons in this book whom I met in dreams" (*Riverrun* ix). Such seems to see himself as setting the record straight and in the process compensating for, presumably, the terrible legacy of the extermination of the Beothuks; *Riverrun* is thus much more vulnerable to Tremblay's critique of historical revisionist fiction as both guilty and consolatory. While this is true to a degree of Wiebe as well, I would argue that *Big Bear* shows Wiebe to be far more cognizant of the literary, historiographical, and moral complexities of such a revisionist intent.

49 This position is different, I would argue, from the suggestion that revisionist histories are an attempt to solve history.

50 Rudy Wiebe, "Unearthing Language: An Interview With Rudy Wiebe and Robert Kroetsch," interview with Shirley Neuman, in *Voice in the Land*, ed. Keith, 237.

51 McHale, *Postmodernist Fiction*, 166.

52 Davey, *Post-National Arguments*, 54.

53 Rudy Wiebe, "'Looking at our Particular World'": An Interview With Rudy Wiebe," interview with Om P. Juneja et al., *World Literature Written in English* 31, no. 2 (1991): 7.

54 Rudy Wiebe, "Where the Voice Comes From," interview with Eli Mandel, in *Voice in the Land*, ed. Keith, 152.

55 van Toorn, *Rudy Wiebe*, 127.

56 Wiebe, "Looking," 8.

57 Goldie, *Fear and Temptation*, 192, 213.

58 Ibid., 214.

59 See van Toorn, *Rudy Wiebe*, 100.

60 Tompkins, *West of Everything*, 9.

61 Vanderhaeghe underlines the continuity between the two eras by also subverting such conventions in the twentieth-century sequences, in scenes such as the old hand Shorty teaching the greenhorn Harry how to shoot and the showdown in the main street – in front of Grauman's Egyptian Theatre – at the climax of the novel.

62 One exception is the recent popular history *How the Mounties Conquered the West*, in which David Cruise and Alison Griffiths dubiously inflate the death toll to between two hundred and two hundred and fifty by presuming that the wolfers decimated almost the entire population of the camp (203).

63 Useful for comparison are Goldring's "Whisky, Horses and Death," Paul Sharp's *Whoop-Up Country: The Canadian-American West, 1865–1885* (Minneapolis: University of Minnesota Press, 1955), and Wallace Stegner's *Wolf Willow* (New York: Viking, 1955).

64 Bakhtin, *Dialogic Imagination*, 332.

65 van Toorn, *Rudy Wiebe*, 15.

66 Hutcheon, "'Circling the Downspout,'" 171.

67 Donna Bennett, "English Canada's Postcolonial Complexities," 196.

68 Lawson, "Postcolonial Theory," 29.

69 Strong-Boag, "Writing About Women," 176.

70 Hughes, *The Historical Romance*, 14.

71 George Eliot, *The Mill on the Floss* VI.III.

72 Conrad and Finkel, *History of the Canadian Peoples*, xvii.

73 Scott, *Gender and the Politics of History*, 6.

74 Strong-Boag, "Writing About Women," 180.

75 See Pamela Banting's chapter on *Ana Historic*, "Unlimited Inc. corporation," in *Body Inc.: A Theory of Translation Poetics* (Winnipeg: Turnstone, 1995) for a discussion of Marlatt's attitude to language and etymology.

76 Tostevin, "Writing in the Space," 37.

77 Goldman, *Paths of Desire*, 113–14.

78 Davidson, *Writing Against the Silence*, 13–14.

79 Conrad and Finkel, *History*, xiv.

80 Howells, *Private and Fictional Worlds*, 122.

81 See Davidson, *Writing Against the Silence*, 14–15.

82 Marilyn Russell Rose, "Politics into Art," 220.

83 Willis, "Speaking the Silence," 242.

84 Kogawa, *Obasan*, 24.

85 Howells, *Private and Fictional Worlds*, 125.

86 Kogawa, *Obasan*, 31.

87 Benjamin, "Theses on the Philosophy of History," 258.

88 Ibid., 258–9.

89 Siemerling, *Discoveries of the Other*, 168.

90 Ondaatje, *In the Skin of a Lion*, 145.

91 The narrative's obsession with space, movement, and crossing boundaries, Spearey argues, serves to displace conventional models of
narrative, historiography, cultural identity, and politics: "Ondaatje's
deployment of the tropes of migration and metamorphosis points to
a deliberate spatialization – as opposed to, or more accurately, in
addition to, a historicization – of the investigation of social structures
and relations of power. While history and the manner in which events
are related in temporal terms provides a focus for many of the questions raised by the novel, we are not presented with an account of
its linear or cumulative progression" ("Mapping and Masking" 49).

92 Gallagher, "Marxism and The New Historicism," 43.

93 In all of these respects, Atwood's approach to Grace Marks's story
is strongly reminiscent of Sharon Pollock's 1981 historical metadrama,
Blood Relations (in *Blood Relations and Other Plays*, ed. Diane Bessai,
Edmonton: NeWest, 1981, 10–70), which is about the notorious (alleged)
New England axe-murderer Lizzie Borden. In her "Author's After-
word" to the novel, Atwood says of her use of historical material
that she has "of course fictionalized historical events (as did many
commentators on this case who claimed to be writing history)"
(*Alias Grace* 467), a description which is eminently applicable to
Pollock's handling of the likewise sensationalized Borden case.

94 Prentice et al., *Canadian Women: A History*, 129.

95 Atwood refers to the source for the story of Mary Whitney in the
"Author's Afterword" to *Alias Grace*, 466.

96 Grace Marks's and James McDermott's confessions are conveyed in
George Walton's contemporary account, *The Trials of James McDermott*.
In his confession, McDermott says, "I will not say how Mr. Kinnear
and Nancy Montgomery were killed, *but I should not have done it,*
if I had not been urged to do so by Grace Marks ... Grace Marks is
wrong in stating that she had no hand in the murder; she was the
means from beginning to end" (16). Before being hung, he reiterated
the truth of his confession, "and he wished further to state, that when
the housekeeper was thrown down the cellar, after being knocked
down, *Grace Marks* followed him into the cellar, and brought a piece
of white cloth with her; he held the housekeeper's hands, she being
then insensible, and *Grace Marks* tied the cloth tight round her neck
and strangled her" (16). Grace's version in her confession is of course
quite different: "he [McDermott] presently came to me and said he

had thrown her down the cellar and he said he wanted a handker-chief, I asked him what for, he said never mind, she is not dead yet, I gave him a piece of white cloth, and followed him to the trap door, he went down the stairs. I saw the body lying at the foot of the stairs, he said you can't come down here, went down himself and shut the trap-door after him – he came up in a few minutes, I asked him if she was dead, he said yes, and he had put her behind the barrels" (4).

97 Butler, *Gender Trouble*, 140.

98 Ibid., 147.

99 E. Elizabeth Rose, "Wheel of Mystery," 118.

100 Judith Knelman, however, takes issue with the accuracy of Atwood's presentation of Jordan as alienist. His use of hypnotism to recover memory is before its time and "Atwood strays even further from real-ity in giving Jordan the frame of reference for a diagnosis of 'double consciousness, with a distinct secondary personality, capable of acting without the knowledge of the first'" ("Can We Believe?" 682).

101 In *Life in the Clearings*, Moodie conveys the case in the form of an off-hand (and second-hand) account of McDermott's testimony (152–71), leading up to a glimpse of Grace Marks in Kingston Penitentiary that stresses the culpability lurking beneath her melancholy appearance. Later, in Toronto, Moodie portrays Grace as having been consumed and destabilized by that guilt: "It appears that even in the wildest bursts of her terrible malady, she is continually haunted by a memory of the past. Unhappy girl! When will the long horror of her punish-ment and remorse be over? When will she sit at the feet of Jesus, clothed with the unsullied garments of her righteousness, the stain of blood washed from her hand, and her soul redeemed, and pardoned, and in her right mind?" (224).

102 In an interview with Marilyn Snell, Atwood resists the characterization of Grace as victim, pointing out that, compared to Nancy Montgomery and Thomas Kinnear, she comes out of the situation fairly well. See Atwood, "Power and Non-power," an interview with Marilyn Snell, in *The Power to Bend Spoons*, ed. Beverley Daurio, 23.

103 In this respect *Alias Grace* is once again quite similar to *Blood Relations*, in which Lizzie Borden's actress friend is compelled to play Lizzie in a version of the events leading up to the murders.

104 Lovelady, "Private Voice, Passing," 58.

105 Kamboureli, Introduction to *Making a Difference*, 12.

106 Ibid.

107 Siemerling, "Writing Ethnicity: Introduction," 18.

108 The term "away" refers to a kind of possession by the faeries or Sidhe, who "have been, like the Angels, from before the making of the earth" and whose "own country is Tir-nan-Og ... under the ground

or under the sea, or it may not be far from any of us" (Lady Gregory, *Visions and Beliefs in The West of Ireland*, Gerrards Cross, Bucks.: Colin Smythe, 1970, 11, 9).

109 Jane Urquhart, "Jane Urquhart: On Becoming a Novelist," interview with Susan Zettell, *Canadian Forum* 70 (May 1991): 21.

110 The phrase is the title of Cohen's collection of poems, *Let Us Compare Mythologies* (Toronto: McClelland & Stewart, 1966).

111 Bhabha, "Of Mimicry and Man," 128. Bhabha emphasizes that such ambivalence opens up a space for resistance to colonial discourse. Such mimic men "are the inappropriate objects of a colonialist chain of command, authorized versions of otherness. But they are also … the figures of a doubling, the part-objects of a metonymy of colonial desire which alienates the modality and normality of those dominant discourses in which they emerge as 'inappropriate' colonial subjects" (ibid 129).

112 Slattery, *Assassination of D'Arcy McGee*, xii.

113 Kirwin, *Thomas D'Arcy McGee*, 10.

114 Skelton, *Life of Thomas D'Arcy McGee*, 439.

115 Ibid., 540.

116 Slattery, "*They Got to Find Mee Guilty*," 325–6.

117 McNaughton, "Magically Real," 44.

118 Chao, *Beyond Silence*, 186.

119 Ibid., 95.

120 Huggan, "The Latitudes of Romance," 43.

121 Bennett Lee, Introduction to *Many-Mouthed Birds*, 4.

122 Kay Anderson, *Vancouver's Chinatown*, 140. The Immigration Act was supported by then-prime minister Mackenzie King during a debate in the House of Commons with a metallurgical analogy indicative of the racialism prevalent at the time; King pointed out that when "two kinds of metals are in circulation as coinage, if one [is] of finer quality than the other, the baser metal tend[s] to drive the finer metal out of circulation" (qtd. in Anderson, 138).

123 Ibid., 141.

124 Hall, "Question of Cultural Identity," 629.

125 See Kealey, *Workers and Canadian History*, 330.

126 Douglas Cruikshank and Gregory Kealey, in Kealey, *Workers and Canadian History*, 368.

127 Kramer notes that MacDougal is likely based on the Reverend William Ivens, a minister at Winnipeg's McDougall Methodist Church ("1919 Winnipeg General Strike" 54).

128 Ibid., 64.

129 Palmer, *Working-Class Experience*, 203.

130 Morton, *Manitoba*, 369.

131 Fischlin, ""As sparrows do fall,'" 61.

132 Brown, *Unauthorized History*, 39.

133 Smith, *Let Us Rise!*, 52.

134 Morton, *Manitoba*, 371.

135 Palmer contends that the strike "revealed, as had no other single development in the 1895–1920 period, the power marshalled by the state and capital in the age of monopoly. It told, as well, of the price to be paid if that power was not recognized and combatted with workers' organizations of equal power, with class directives, with preparations for all eventualities, especially those of repression, and with extensions of workers' autonomy and authority" (204).

136 Kramer, "1919 Winnipeg General Strike," 64.

137 Taken from Mackenzie King's confession that he led "a very double life," the phrase serves as the title of Stacey's biography *A Very Double Life: The Private World of Mackenzie King*.

138 Robertson is presumably lampooning the rhetoric of the original strike, during which the "Kirkland Lake local was caught up in the mood of militancy of 1919 (it called its executive a 'soviet')" (Laurel Macdowell, *'Remember Kirkland Lake': The History and Effects of the Kirkland Lake Miners' Strike, 1941–42*, Toronto: University of Toronto Press, 1983, 60).

139 Along with the many figures referred to in the discussion of *Lily*, Robertson's portraits include Duncan Campbell Scott, Nellie McClung, Charles Bedaux, Norman Bethune, and William "Bible Bill" Aberhart.

140 Brown, *Unauthorized History*, 36.

141 It is uncertain whether in Esselwein's report Robertson is quoting a historical document. According to Greg Kealey and Reg Whitaker, RCMP bulletins from this period have been removed from the National Archives (*R.C.M.P. Security Bulletins. The Early Years, 1919–1929*, St John's: Canadian Committee on Labour History, 1994, 9).

142 Robertson's assessment of the party on this score is shared by others. Sawatsky writes of the party's positions during this time: "The Canadian stalwarts were mesmerized by Russia and Moscow could not impose policies or duties unpalatable enough for the Canadian party to reject or rebel" (*Men in the Shadows* 61).

143 Cf. Palmer's description in *Working-Class Experience* (226–7) of the early members of the Canadian Communist party (including most of those spoofed by Robertson), which clearly differs in tone from Robertson's. For instance, he describes Maurice Spector thus: "Spector was only twenty-three at the time of the Guelph meeting, but he was already a theoretician of stature" (227).

144 Palmer's review of the significance of the era is a little more moderate: "In creating one of the first truly mass movements of the unemployed

... workers of the 1930s raised the demand of 'work and wages' at a critical point in history when such a claim to essential human rights necessarily extended beyond the economistic. The resulting agitation certainly produced little in the way of lasting organization, and even less in terms of combatting the cause of depression" (ibid. 246). But he likewise sees the Communist party as missing a chance. He qualifies criticism of the party by noting that because "so many rank-and-file Communists were such dedicated and able organizers, and because they willingly defended the weak and members of the new industrial work force, a great deal of historic importance must be attached to their activities in the 1930s" (248). But in the course of the decade the party nonetheless became marginalized through its own adherence to the Comintern, its condemnation of socialists and other progressives, and by the opposition of employers and more mainstream labour organizations (247). Thus "the policy and practice of the party dictated that it would not lead a generally leftist upsurge. At the very moment that labour needed a political leadership of the left, the Communist Party was embroiled in confrontation with which only one segment of the Canadian working class could identify. In abdicating its larger responsibility and substituting for it ritual exhortations of revolution, the CPC helped create the conditions in which social democracy would experience its rebirth" (248).

145 Robertson's somewhat facetious depiction of Leopold stands in contrast to. Lorne and Caroline Brown's presentation of Leopold's counter-subversive activities much more seriously as an obvious breach of the law: "The involvement of the RCMP and Sergeant Leopold in prosecuting Communists led to some interesting questions in police ethics. If Communism was considered illegal by the authorities, then Leopold and others like him must have been guilty of breaking the law. As a prominent Communist activist under the name of Esselwein, Leopold had sold literature, organized meetings and recruited people to the party. Was he not then guilty of counselling people to commit what the authorities defined as a crime? Similarly, weren't all police and private agents who posed as militant advocates of violence and then assisted prosecuting those who followed their advice guilty? Such questions obviously neither interested nor bothered the RCMP" (*Unauthorized History*, 53–4). For an overview of Leopold's career, see Steve Hewitt, "Royal Canadian Mounted Spy: The Secret Life of John Leopold/Jack Esselwein," *Intelligence and National Security* 15, no. 1 (Spring 2000): 144–68.

146 Lorne and Caroline Brown argue that what "saved the RNWMP from abolition as a force was intense industrial and social unrest at the end of World War I. Events during this period caused great anxiety

in business and governmental circles, and the Mounted Police assured their own future by making themselves invaluable to the economic and political elite of the day" (Ibid. 36).

147 The RCMP's manipulation of the trek is not Robertson's invention. According to Lorne and Caroline Brown, "The RCMP were extremely active during the On-to-Ottawa Trek of the single unemployed which culminated in the Regina riot of July 1, 1935. The RCMP tried to discredit the trekkers and their leaders, they harrassed citizens who attempted to assist the trekkers, and they frustrated the government of Saskatchewan, which was vehemently opposed to federal plans to stop the trekkers in Regina at all costs. That the RCMP provoked the riot of July 1 had been proven beyond a doubt" (Ibid. 77).

148 Kogawa, *Obasan*, 226.

149 Granatstein, *Who Killed Canadian History?*, 59, 66.

150 Ibid., 100.

151 Ibid., 103.

152 Litvack, "Canadian Writing in English," 129.

153 Underhill, *Image of Confederation*, 2.

154 Butterfield, *Historical Novel*, 42.

155 Hall, "Question of Cultural Identity," 613.

156 Benedict Anderson defines the nation as "an imagined political community – and imagined as both inherently limited and sovereign" (*Imagined Communities* 15).

157 White, *Tropics of Discourse*, 91.

158 Kelley, *Reinventing Allegory*, 2.

159 Frye, *Anatomy of Criticism*, 89.

160 In *The Language of Allegory*, Quilligan makes a distinction between allegory, on the one hand, and allegoresis or allegorical criticism, in which "the critic treats the text in front of him as a veiled offering of a hidden message" (224). But it can be argued that all historical discourse and all historical fiction are necessarily both, interpreting the text of the past but also symbolically emplotting that interpretation in narrative.

161 McHale, *Postmodernist Fiction*, 145–6.

162 Appleby, Hunt, and Jacob, *Telling the Truth*, 245.

163 Slemon, "Monuments of Empire," 10–11.

164 Quilligan, *Language of Allegory*, 26.

165 Kamboureli, *"Biggest Modern Woman of the World,"* 8.

166 Gittings, "Collision of Discourse," 82.

167 Hall, "Question of Cultural Identity," 617.

168 Slemon, "Post-Colonial Allegory," 159.

169 Frye, *Anatomy*, 186.

170 Slemon, "Post-Colonial Allegory," 160.

171 Ibid., 161.

172 Frye, *Anatomy*, 200.

173 Beer, *Romance*, 10.

174 Though Mackenzie King resisted suggestions that he was actively working for Rockefeller's cause or promoting company unionism, Robertson's portrait of his involvement with Rockefeller in Colorado echoes that of some historians; for a detailed discussion, see Ferns and Ostry, *The Age of Mackenzie King*, 184–216.

175 Perhaps reflecting the influence of Findley's *The Wars* on Canadian literature generally, World War I has been a conspicuous concern of recent fiction, figuring in Thomas Wharton's *Icefields*, Ann-Marie MacDonald's *Fall on Your Knees* (1997), Jane Urquhart's *The Under-painter* (1997), and Jack Hodgins's *Broken Ground* (1998).

176 Arthur Lower, *Colony to Nation: A History of Canada*, 5th ed. (Toronto: McClelland & Stewart, 1977), 464.

177 Talbot's image of the emergence of Canada's nationality is taken from an open letter to his cousin, Henri Bourassa, criticizing Bourassa's stance toward Canada's participation in the war; cf. Papineau, "Open Letter," 210. For an overview of the exchange between the two, see Sandra Gwyn, *Tapestry of War*, 313–28.

178 Frye, *Anatomy*, 187. Gwyn says of Papineau that he "became for Canadians the symbol not only of Passchendaele, but of all the golden promise cut down by the Great War" (*Tapestry of War* 400).

179 Beer, *Romance*, 29.

180 According to Gwyn, the relationship between Papineau and Beatrice Fox developed to the point that the two agreed on an engagement (*Tapestry of War* 334), but, unlike Lily, Beatrice never came to meet Talbot before his death. While Beatrice's letters were destroyed, she saved Papineau's letters and later donated them in 1934 to the Army Historical Association, whence they were subsequently transferred to the National Archives.

181 Frye, *Anatomy*, 201.

182 Mackenzie King's diary has since been published by the University of Toronto Press in two volumes, *The Mackenzie King Diaries, 1893–1931* and *The Mackenzie King Diaries, 1932–1949*.

183 See Stacey, *Very Double Life*, 153.

184 J.L. Granatstein, qtd. in Barbara Wade Rose, "Fact and Fiction," *Books in Canada* 15, no. 6 (Aug./Sept. 1986): 10.

185 Heather Robertson, qtd. in Elspeth Cameron, "From Whitton to Willie," *Quill & Quire* 50, no. 27 (1984): 27.

186 Robertson, qtd. in Rose, "Fact and Fiction," 10.

187 Robertson, qtd. in Cameron, "From Whitton to Willie," 27.
188 Timothy Findley, "Interview with Timothy Findley," by Terry Goldie, *Kunapipi* 6, no. 1 (1984): 63.
189 Munslow, *Deconstructing History,* 75.
190 Beer, *Romance,* 79.
191 This experience is partially fictionalized, perhaps based on an incident in which Smallwood as a cub reporter stowed away on the H.M.S. *Cornwall* to report on its hunt for bootleggers; see Richard Gwyn, *Smallwood,* 13. The deaths of the men of the *S.S. Newfoundland,* however, were part of one of the most notorious incidents in Newfoundland sealing history. Kean was recognized as Newfoundland's most successful sealer for bringing in over 1 million pelts during his career. "While master of Bowring's *Stephano qv* in the spring of 1914, Kean was a central figure in the controversy over the *S.S. Newfoundland qv* sealing disaster and was held by some people to be responsible for the deaths of 78 of the ship's crew. Although exonerated by an inquiry, there was widespread criticism of his conduct in dropping the Newfoundland's crew off on the ice with a storm approaching" *Encyclopaedia of Newfoundland and Labrador,* vol. 3 (St John's: Harry Cuff Publications, 1991), s.v. "Kean, Abram."
192 Luc Sante, "O Canada!," review of *The Colony of Unrequited Dreams,* by Wayne Johnston, *The New York Times Book Review,* 25 July 1999, 6.
193 In *I Chose Canada,* Smallwood roots his eagerness for development in a desire to avoid a continuing colonial status: "We had been Britain's 'most ancient and loyal Colony.' It was at St. John's that the foundation of the British Empire had been laid in 1497. Our progress had been retarded, deliberately impeded, by official British policy. Settlement had been forbidden, and the Royal Navy had even been known to receive orders to go to Newfoundland and demolish every dwelling that had been unlawfully erected – and that meant all of them. It was not to be a Canadian colony that we had given up being a British colony!" (342).
194 Richard Gwyn, *Smallwood,* 209.
195 In *I Chose Canada* (88–9), Joey Smallwood observes that he did leave Bishop Feild school after being wrongly accused, though he confesses his inability to remember the source of the matter, and into that gap Johnston inserts the letter sent by Fielding's father. Fielding also later gets Smallwood a job as a journalist on the *Telegram* and is the one to convince him to drink a bottle of Pabst beer a day for 120 days, in an unsuccessful effort to gain weight. When Fielding travels to New York at the same time as Smallwood (though her intention is to see her children), her presence as his potential romantic interest is written over the historical Smallwood's relationship with Lillian Zahn, a

relationship that foundered after the two unsuccessfully tried to pass Smallwood off to her mother as an English Jew. "Smallwood, for once in his life, forgot his lines," Gwyn archly notes, and Lillian's mother afterwards confronted her: "I know he's a *goy*. You can't fool me. He's a *goy*" (30). Johnston also makes Fielding the lone holdout (and lone woman) among the 700 section men who sign up during Smallwood's unionizing drive. Finally, when Valdmanis bargains with Smallwood to get his charge reduced, Johnston has him use as bargaining power a copy of Fielding's journal, which he has had pilfered while she accompanied the two of them on a junket to Europe (Gwyn, 166–7). In Gwyn's account, Valdmanis, after having written an intercepted letter asking an industrialist friend to say the bribes he solicited were commissions for the Liberal Party, agreed to plead guilty in exchange for prosecution on only one of two charges against him.

196 Luc Sante indeed speculates that Fielding is perhaps "meant to be the incarnation of Newfoundland itself" because she is "physically large, with unvisited extremities and a nearly unknown heart, a bad drinking problem, blunt truth and savage wit" ("O Canada!" 6).

197 Madsen, "Fate of Allegory," 123.

198 Kelley, *Reinventing Allegory*, 249.

199 Madsen, "Fate of Allegory," 165–6.

200 Ibid., 166.

201 Ibid., 170.

202 Granatstein, *Who Killed Canadian History?*, 17.

203 Conrad and Finkel, *History*, xiv.

204 Granatstein, *Who Killed Canadian History?*, 101.

205 Bibby, *Mosaic Madness*, 104.

CHAPTER THREE

1 Wiebe, "Where is the Voice Coming From?" 135.

2 Ibid., 142.

3 Ibid., 143.

4 White, *Content of the Form*, ix.

5 Ibid.

6 de Certau, *Writing of History*, 35.

7 Hutcheon, *Canadian Postmodern*, 14.

8 Waugh, *Metafiction*, 11.

9 Hutcheon, *Canadian Postmodern*, 62.

10 York, *"Other Side of Dailiness,"* 84, 85.

11 Vauthier, "Dubious Battle of Storytelling," 35.

12 Findley, *The Wars*, 209.

13 Hutcheon, *Canadian Postmodern*, 72.

14 Findley, *The Wars*, 3.

15 Brydon, "'It could not be told,'" 66.

16 Davey, *Post-National Arguments*, 115.

17 Cobley, "Postmodernist War Fiction," 121.

18 Jones, *That Art of Difference*, 142.

19 Goldman, *Paths of Desire*, 113–14.

20 Marlatt, "Self-Representation and Fictionalysis," 204.

21 Kramer, "1919 Winnipeg General Strike," 53.

22 This is shorthand for the succinctly titled report of the commission headed by the Honorable Justice Robert Taschereau, *The Report of the Royal Commission to Investigate the Facts Relating to and the Circumstances Surrounding the Communication by Public Officials and Other Persons in Positions of Trust of Secret and Confidential Information to Agents of a Foreign Power* (Ottawa: E. Cloutier, 1946).

23 The phrase comes from Edward Herman and Noam Chomsky's analysis of the mass media, *Manufacturing Consent* (New York: Pantheon, 1988).

24 Indeed, one person Norman Robertson was going to contact was William Stephenson (the celebrated "Man from Intrepid" of British intelligence fame) in New York, who, Lily observes in a follow-up conversation, was running a top-secret cryptography centre called "the Examination Unit" next to King's house in Ottawa and perhaps exploiting King's superstition to keep him under Robertson's influence.

25 Kuester, *Framing Truths*, 92.

26 Ibid., 31.

27 In introducing the second edition, Prowse himself concedes of his *History* that, "notwithstanding all my efforts to bring the work within moderate compass, it grew into a ponderous volume" (b).

28 Ibid.

29 If the role of Prowse's book in *Colony*'s romantic intrigue symbolizes that the weight of history can be fatal, it is also literally so in the case of an old man who is killed when Smallwood's mother throws a copy of the substantial tome off the balcony of their cliffside home. She does so, moreover, because she has been pushed to the limit by Smallwood's father's obsession with what he takes to be Judge Prowse's condescending inscription to him in his copy and the exclusion of the likes of himself from the pages of the *History*.

30 Bloom, *Anxiety of Influence*, 91. Particularly interesting for historical fiction is one of Bloom's six "revisionary ratios," namely "kenosis," which involves repetition and "a movement towards discontinuity with the precursor" (14). Such a description is applicable not just to *Colony* but to Thomas Raddall's treatment of his primary source,

Simeon Perkins, in *His Majesty's Yankees* and Robertson's more parodic subversion of Mackenzie King's self-presentation in *The King Years* trilogy.

31 Prowse, *History*, 1st ed., 164.
32 Cf. Prowse, who describes Child thus: "In order to rightly appreciate the enormous influence of a monopolist like Child in the corrupt age of Charles II, we must try to picture to ourselves the president of one of the gigantic American trusts of our own time owning all the ministers of State, and the Courts, with unlimited money and unlimited power to bribe, and no questions asked about funds" (*History*, 1st ed., 189).
33 Munslow, *Deconstructing History*, 102.
34 Ibid., 163.
35 Jones, *That Art of Difference*, 13–14.
36 Ong, *Orality and Literacy*, 172.
37 Ibid., 78.
38 Ibid., 15.
39 Ibid., 12.
40 Ibid., 32–3.
41 Ibid., 82.
42 Wiebe, *Big Bear*, 138.
43 Ong, *Orality and Literacy*, 82.
44 Wiebe, *Big Bear*, 383.
45 Ong, *Orality and Literacy*, 167.
46 Ibid., 76.
47 Goldie, *Fear and Temptation*, 107.
48 Ibid., 110.
49 Ibid., 113.
50 Ibid., 122.
51 Ibid., 126.
52 Jack Hodgins, "An Interview With Jack Hodgins," interview with Geoff Hancock, *Canadian Fiction Magazine* 32/33 (1979/80): 61.
53 Keith, "Sources of Invention," 86.
54 Lecker, "Glut of Ghosts," 88.
55 Keith, "Sources of Invention," 89.
56 Tonkin, *Narrating Our Pasts*, 113.
57 Hodgins, Interview, 48.
58 Ibid., 50.
59 Munslow, *Deconstructing History*, 102.
60 Caunce, *Oral History*, 25.
61 Tonkin, *Narrating our Pasts*, 90.
62 Ong, *Orality and Literacy*, 131–2.
63 Shohat and Stam, *Unthinking Eurocentrism*, 120.

64 Keith, *Epic Fiction*, 96.
65 The historical Falcon, who was the brother-in-law of Métis leader
   Cuthbert Grant, composed "The Battle of Seven Oaks" in honour
   of the Métis victory in the first uprising of the Métis nation in 1816,
   a song that was sung for inspiration during the uprising of 1870 to
   remind supporters "of how their fathers had risen against oppression"
   and by Gabriel Dumont to rally his men at Fish-Creek (N. Brian
   Davis, *Poetry of the Canadian People*, vol. 1, 244).
66 Keith, *Epic Fiction*, 97.
67 Tonkin, *Narrating Our Pasts*, 12.
68 Davis, *Poetry*, 248.
69 Woodcock, "Riel & Dumont," 99.
70 Howells, "Rudy Wiebe's Art," 20.
71 See, for instance, Keith, *Epic Fiction*, 98–9.
72 As Vautier underlines, Wiebe's handling of heteroglossia is a very
   postmodern historiographic strategy: "by not giving the sources for
   the documents he uses, by treating them as just another aid in the
   storytelling process, the narrator subverts the concept of linear historiography and story, and makes the reader aware that *his* version of
   the past is being constructed" (*New World Myth* 74).
73 van Toorn argues that "Wiebe's authorial intentions decide how
   readers hear Falcon's voice; Falcon's intentions, in turn, help determine the reader's orientation towards the words uttered by Riel and
   other characters; and because Riel, too, incorporates others' words into
   his own speech, his intentions affect how readers interpret and evalu-
   ate them. Wiebe's practice of embedding ranks the voices into a com-
   positional hierarchy, with each voice subject to the authorial will of
   the speaker who quotes, and creates the context for, his words. As in
   an army, a vertical chain of command extends between the many
   voices which speak in Wiebe's text" (*Rudy Wiebe* 149). She qualifies
   this description of the novel's discursive hierarchy by noting that
   there is an important dialogism all the same; instead of a rigid subordination consistently sustained throughout the hierarchy, there is a
   certain amount of internal contestation (Ibid. 149–50).
74 Ibid., 153.
75 Ibid., 154.
76 Ong, *Orality and Literacy*, 155.
77 Vautier, *New World Myth*, 71.
78 van Toorn, *Rudy Wiebe*, 162.
79 Ong, *Orality and Literacy*, 14–15.
80 Goldie, *Fear and Temptation*, 109.
81 The tension between orality and literacy could be related to the very
   heart of Métis identity, which is an uneasy mix, as Falcon puts it,
   of "two heritages so rich that often one alone is more than you want,

when you feel one of them move in you like a living beast and the other whispers, sings between your ears with a beauty you would gladly sell your soul to hear until you die. Such doubleness, such sometimes half-and-half richness of nothing" (Wiebe, *Scorched-Wood People*, 112). The very heterogeneity of the narrative, van Toorn argues, inscribes these concerns with identity, as the "utterance itself becomes métis, multi-accentual, a site of social struggle, as several authorial wills compete to control its meaning. Within the space of the verbal sign, as in the geographical region of the North-West, disparate voices coexist in a fluctuating state of harmony, forging and breaking alliances with one another, clashing and then making peace" (*Rudy Wiebe* 141).

82 Ong, *Orality and Literacy*, 80.

83 Jaeger, "'Body of Lore,'" 42.

84 The scene at the falls is a close rendering of an episode in volume 2 of Cartwright's *Journal* (334–8), though Steffler's description of Cartwright's reaction to the slaughter suggests that he is shaken by something more than the fatigue noted in the *Journal*.

85 Throughout Cartwright's *Journal*, Mrs Selby is described as his house-keeper and is an entirely marginal figure in his chronicling of his voyages. Yet, shortly after she gave birth to a child on 21 April 1779, Cartwright tried her and his headman Richard Daubeney for carrying on "a criminal connexion" and subsequently "declared as formal a divorce between us as ever was pronounced in Doctors Commons" (442). As for the child, "I disowned it, and resolved never to make any provision for it, unless I should hereafter be compelled so to do by a judicial sentence" (443).

86 See Lawson, "Postcolonial Theory," 29.

87 Kathleen McConnell, "Textile Tropes," 94.

88 Ibid., 107, 108.

89 Tremblay, "Piracy, Penance," 169.

90 Jaeger, "'Body of Lore,'" 51.

91 Merkur, *Becoming Half Hidden*, 7.

92 See Ibid., 258.

93 Wiesel, "Myth and History," 23.

94 Eliade, *Myth and Reality*, 1.

95 Ibid., 18.

96 Ibid., 139.

97 Eliade, *Eternal Return*, 89.

98 Ibid., 89–90.

99 Ibid., 35.

100 Indeed, Eliade makes the point in passing that the work of modernists like Joyce and Eliot "is saturated with nostalgia for the myth of eternal repetition and, in the last analysis, for the abolition of time" (ibid. 153).

101 Eliade, *Myth and Reality*, 113.

102 Munslow, *Deconstructing History*, 4–5.

103 Fludernik, "History and Metafiction," 94.

104 Levi-Strauss, *Myth and Meaning*, 42–3.

105 Eliade, *Myth and Reality*, 8, 12.

106 See, for instance, Bruce Pirie, "The Dragon in the Fog: 'Displaced Mythology' in *The Wars*," in *Canadian Literature* 91 (1981): 70–9, and Peter Klovan, "'Bright and Good': Findley's *The Wars*" in *Canadian Literature* 91 (1981): 58–69.

107 Eliade, *Eternal Return*, 74, 75.

108 Eliade, *Myth and Reality*, 192.

109 Ibid., 192.

110 Hutcheon, *Canadian Postmodern*, 1.

111 Eliade, *Myth and Reality*, 191.

112 Vautier, *New World Myth*, 52.

113 See N.K. Sandars's introduction to *The Epic of Gilgamesh*, 20–1.

114 Vautier, *New World Myth*, xi.

115 Ibid., ix.

116 Ibid., xi.

117 See Gamlin, "Michael Ondaatje's *In the Skin of a Lion* and the Oral Narrative," and Beran, "Ex-centricity: Michael Ondaatje's *In the Skin of a Lion* and Hugh MacLennan's *Barometer Rising*."

118 *Epic of Gilgamesh*, 93.

119 Ibid., 111.

120 Ibid., 113.

121 Ibid.

122 Beran, "Ex-centricity," 77.

123 Fleishman, *English Historical Novel*, 14.

124 Vautier, *New World Myth*, 52.

125 For a discussion of the mythic intertexts of *Invention*, see Jan C. Horner, "Irish & Biblical Myth in Jack Hodgins' *The Invention of the World*," *Canadian Literature* 99 (1983): 6–18.

126 Lecker, "Glut of Ghosts," 88–9, 95.

127 See, for instance, Fink, "'If Words Won't Do, and Symbols Fail': Hodgins' Magic Reality," 122, and McCaig, "Brother XII and *The Invention of the World*," 135.

128 Fink, "'If Words Won't Do,'" 131.

129 See Keith, "Sources of Invention," 85–6, and McCaig, "Brother XII," 133–8, for discussions of the parallels between the two figures.

130 Fink, "'If Words Won't Do,'" 125.

131 Lecker, "Glut of Ghosts," 103.

132 Hodgins, Interview, 62.

133 Wiesel, "Myth and History," 22, 30.

134 Zamora and Faris, "Daiquiri Birds," 3.

135 Slemon, "Magic Realism as Postcolonial Discourse," 409.

136 Zamora and Faris, "Daiquiri Birds," 5–6.

137 Birch, "Irish Female Presence," 116.

138 Ellis, *Celtic Women*, 44.

139 Cooper, *Magical Realism*, 49.

140 Levi-Strauss, *Myth and Meaning*, 43.

141 Vautier, *New World Myth*, 35.

142 Ibid., 50.

143 Ibid., 35.

144 Cooper, *Magical Realism*, 33.

145 Eliade, *Eternal Return*, 43.

146 Ibid., 44, 46.

147 Ibid., 110–11

148 Ibid., 132.

149 Ibid., 160.

150 Tonkin, *Narrating Our Pasts*, 8.

151 Bakhtin, *Rabelais and his World*, 5–6.

152 McHale, *Postmodernist Fiction*, 174.

153 Ibid., 172.

154 Tonkin, *Narrating Our Pasts*, 3. Tonkin considers it "a cumbersome phrase, but more exact here than 'hostory'" (3).

155 See M. Keith Booker and Dubravka Juraga, *Bakhtin, Stalin, and Modern Russian Fiction: Carnival, Dialogism, and History* (Westport, Conn.: Greenwood, 1995), 3–11, for an overview of, and a response to, such critiques.

CHAPTER FOUR

1 Carr, *What is History?*, 28, 29.

2 de Certau, *Writing of History*, 36.

3 Jameson, "On Magic Realism," 303; *Postmodernism*, 284.

4 Jameson, *Postmodernism*, ix.

5 Ibid., 96.

6 Waugh, *Practising Postmodernism/Reading Modernism*, 6.

7 See Terry Eagleton, *The Illusions of Postmodernism* (Oxford: Blackwell Publishers, 1985), and Aijaz Ahmad, *In Theory: Classes, Nations, Literatures* (London: Verso, 1992), 127–30.

8 Waugh, *Practising Postmodernism*, 59.

9 Harvey, *Condition of Postmodernity*, 303.

10 Jameson, *Postmodernism*, 283.

11 Ibid., 283–4.

12 Jameson, "On Magic Realism," 311.

13 Ross, "Forays into Polyvocality," 176.

14 Zamora and Faris, "Daiquiri Birds," 2.

15 Compton, "Romancing the Landscape," 213.

16 My commentary here owes a debt to Shannon Smyrl's interesting discussion of the allegorical significance of this commercial activity in a paper at the 1998 Association for Canadian and Quebec Literatures conference, "The Trace of a Culture on a Nation: Global History and the Displaced Nation-State in Jane Urquhart's *Away*."

17 Hancock, "Magic or Realism," 43.

18 David Bennett, "Postmodernism and Vision," 264.

19 Manzoni, *On the Historical Novel*, 63, 65.

20 Jameson, *Postmodernism*, 325, 25.

21 Foster, "Postmodernism: A Preface," xv.

22 Featherstone, *Consumer Culture and Postmodernism*, 126.

23 According to Bruce West, on 2 December 1919, Ambrose Small sold out his theater chain, deposited a million dollars in his bank account, bought a newspaper, and was never seen again (*Toronto*, Toronto: Doubleday Canada, 1967, 237).

24 The phrase "self-consuming" owes its currency to Stanley Fish's *Self-Consuming Artifacts: The Experience of Seventeenth-Century Literature* (Berkeley: University of California Press, 1972).

25 Davey, *Post-National Arguments*, 153.

26 Bök, "The Secular Opiate," 13.

27 Sarris, "*In the Skin of a Lion*," 195–6. Sarris supports this observation by pointing out that Patrick in his revolutionary mode is associated with both darkness and bestiality and Harris is humanized under the influence of light (198–9).

28 Ibid., 200.

29 Michael Ondaatje, "Where the Personal and Historical Meet," interview with Cary Fagan, in *The Power to Bend Spoons*, ed. Beverly Daurio, 121.

30 Gamlin, "Oral Narrative," 77.

31 Spearey, "Mapping and Masking," 49.

32 Ibid., 53.

33 Ondaatje is fairly explicit about wanting to humanize Harris. In "Where the Historical and the Personal Meet" he describes how "Harris seemed to be going in the direction of total villain and then he got muted in that role." His thumbnail sketch of Harris is eminently sympathetic: "Historically he was quite a sweet guy. He was a photography fan. And he was very moral, very honourable" (120).

34 I discovered that Byrne was fictional the hard way, after trying to track down one of the sources cited in Wharton's acknowledgments, Yoshiro Kagami's "Edward Byrne: A Life in Ice," having assumed that

because the other sources were legitimate this one was too. I then decided to ask Tom Wharton, only to discover that not only was the source fabricated, but so was Byrne.

35 Stutfield and Collie, *Climbs & Exploration*, 30. As is the case with Byrne in *Icefields*, C.S. Thompson's backpack served to break his fall, but it was Collie, rather than the expedition guide, Bill Peyto, who descended into the crevasse to make the rescue.

36 Thompson opined that, "whatever scientific exploration or observation in future might be necessary on the summits of the Rocky Mountains, investigations made alone, sixty feet below the surface of the ice, in an inverted position, were extremely dangerous and even unworthy of record" (Ibid. 34).

37 The Collie expedition followed in the Earl of Southesk's footsteps, at one point finding "a tattered copy of *Hamlet*, a memento of Southesk's literary browsing by the campfire in the lonely valley" (Fraser, *Canadian Rockies*, 158).

38 Here Wharton's phrasing closely echoes the account of the discovery of the icefields in Stutfield and Collie's *Climbs & Exploration in the Canadian Rockies*. On 18 August 1898, Woolley and Collie ascended Athabasca Peak, and from there first viewed the icefields: "A new world was spread at our feet; to the westward stretched a vast ice-field probably never before seen by human eye, and surrounded by entirely unknown, unnamed, and unclimbed peaks" (107).

39 Clark, *Victorian Mountaineers*, 21.

40 In an interview, Wharton pointed out his desire to resist, through Byrne (in some ways modelled on Wharton himself, who started out in science), the dismissal of such a sense of the sublime as just another constructed perspective (Interview with author, Edmonton, 20 April 1999).

41 Harmon, *Columbia Icefield*, 86–8. As E.J. Hart notes, the Brewster family progressively monopolized the tourist business in the Rockies, their transportation service growing "from a small outfitting and guiding concern into North America's largest private sightseeing business, the Brewster Transport Company" (*The Selling of Canada: The CPR and the Beginnings of Canadian Tourism*, Banff: *Altitude Publishing*, 1983, 90).

42 In this respect, Byrne is somewhat different from the historical Stutfield and Collie, for whom discovery is prelude to commodification. In their account of the 1898 expedition, they write with a very Eurocentric, speculating tone of a tributary of the North Saskatchewan: "Taken altogether the place seems an ideal one for a tourist centre; and we may fairly anticipate that at the mouth of Bear Creek will be the Chamonix or Grindewald of the Canadian Alps in days to come, when the remoter peaks and valleys of this beautiful

region are made accessible to the outside world, and the new mountain playground of the American continent becomes no longer a dream but a reality" (89).

43 Jameson, *Postmodernism*, 315, 317.
44 The phrase "the tourist gaze" forms part of the title of John Urry's *The Tourist Gaze: Leisure and Travel in Contemporary Societies.*
45 Rojeck and Urry, "Transformations of Travel and Theory," 4.
46 Ibid.
47 Craik, "Culture of Tourism," 115.
48 Baudrillard, "Simulacra and Simulations," 167.
49 Ibid., 171.
50 Urry, *Tourist Gaze*, 86.
51 *Icefields* has won a number of prizes, including the Commonwealth Writers Prize for Best First Novel (Caribbean and Canadian Region) and the Writers Guild of Alberta Best First Book Award.
52 Jameson, *Postmodernism*, 206.
53 Jameson, *Postmodernism*, 23.
54 Ibid.
55 Ibid., 25.
56 Fludernik, "History and Metafiction," 93.
57 See Goldman, *Paths of Desire*, 63–100; Kamboureli, "*The Biggest Modern Woman of the World*"; and Heffernan, "Tracing the Travesty."
58 Heffernan, "Tracing the Travesty," 26.
59 Gittings, "Collision of Discourse," 83.
60 McHale, *Postmodernist Fiction*, 172.
61 Swan-Ryan, "Swan's Song," 8.
62 Goldman, *Paths of Desire*, 64.
63 Swan-Ryan, "Swan's Song," 8.
64 Heffernan, "Tracing the Travesty," 27.
65 Swan-Ryan, "Swan's Song," 8.
66 Various critics theorizing about the postmodern in Canada have stressed a centrifugal resistance to centralized authority and have asserted the importance of regional difference and autonomy. See, for instance, Hutcheon, *The Canadian Postmodern*, 19, and David Jordan, *New World Regionalism* (Toronto: University of Toronto Press, 1994), 8–9.
67 Blakeley, *Nova Scotia's Two Remarkable Giants*, 18.
68 Jameson, *Postmodernism*, 17.
69 Thiher, "Postmodern Fiction and History," 21.
70 Heffernan, "Tracing the Travesty," 5–6.
71 Goldman, *Paths of Desire*, 64.
72 McHale, *Postmodernist Fiction*, 96.
73 Ibid.

74 Ibid., 219

75 Ibid., 222.

76 Jameson, *Postmodernism*, 18.

77 Here Vanderhaeghe employs but also recuperates a technique that is a common strategy of postmodern historiographical metafiction. See McHale, *Postmodernist Fiction*, 17.

78 Baudrillard, "Simulacra," 167.

79 In "The Significance of the Frontier," Turner contends that a "perennial rebirth, this fluidity of American life, this expansion westward with its new opportunities, its continuous touch with the simplicity of primitive society, furnish the forces dominating American character" (2–3).

80 In *The Covered Wagon*, for instance, the film whose success Chance seeks to emulate, a key title reads, "The blood of America is the blood of the pioneers – the blood of lion-hearted men and women who carved a splendid civilisation out of an uncharted wilderness" (Vanderhaeghe, *The Englishman's Boy*, 230).

81 Neil Gabler, *An Empire of Their Own: How the Jews Invented Hollywood* (New York: Crown Publishers, 1988), 4.

82 See Lukács, *Historical Novel*, 303.

83 Butterfield, *Historical Novel*, 4.

84 Goldring, "Whisky, Horses and Death," 52–3. For a more detailed discussion of the novel's relationship to historical accounts, see my essay "Dances With Wolfers: Choreographing History in *The Englishman's Boy*," in *Essays in Canadian Writing* 67 (1999): 23–52.

85 Munslow, *Deconstructing History*, 98.

86 Ibid., 176.

87 See Iggers, *Historiography in the Twentieth Century*, 145, and Jacobs, *Character of Truth*, xvi.

88 Guy Vanderhaeghe, interview with Alan Twigg, in *Strong Voices: Conversations with 50 Canadian Authors* (Madeira Park, BC: Harbour Publishing, 1988), 273. Advances in film technology such as videos and computerization have certainly qualified the contrast Vanderhaeghe draws with the medium of print. It can be argued that it is now easier to "reread" film and to subject its effects to greater scrutiny, as well as that print often functions in a similarly impressionistic fashion as film.

89 That Vanderhaeghe has been commissioned to write a screenplay for a film version – which will necessitate a reworking of a written text according to imperatives of the image of which the novel itself is critical – deepens the irony.

90 Hatch, "Narrative Development," 81–2.

91 Jameson, *Postmodernism*, 286–7.

92 Hall, "Question of Cultural Identity," 622.

PERIOD PIECE

1 Goldie, "Blame Canada," 229.

2 Hulan, "Who's There?" 61–2

3 Boehmer, *Colonial & Postcolonial Literature*, 244.

4 Margeret Laurence, "Ivory Tower or Grassroots?: The Novelist as Socio-Political Being," in *A Political Art: Essays and Images in Honour of George Woodcock*, ed. W.H. New (Vancouver: University of British Columbia Press, 1978), 17.

5 Munslow, *Deconstructing History*, 69.

6 Featherstone, *Consumer Culture and Postmodernism*, 126.

7 Harvey, *Condition of Postmernity*, 299.

8 Ibid., 303.

9 Vanderhaeghe, *Englishman's Boy*, 326.

10 Mark Starowicz, "Ignore the past at your peril," *The Globe & Mail*, 20 September 2000, All.

11 Jack Hodgins, *Broken Ground* (Toronto: McClelland & Stewart, 1998); Fred Stenson, *The Trade* (Vancouver: Douglas & McIntyre, 2000); George Elliott Clarke, *George and Rue*, forthcoming from HarperCollins.

Bibliography

Allemano, Marina. *Historical Portraits and Visions*. New York: Garland Press, 1991.

Anderson, Benedict. *Imagined Communities: Reflections on the Origins and Spread of Nationalism*. London: Verso Press, 1983.

Anderson, Kay J. *Vancouver's Chinatown: Racial Discourse in Canada 1875–1980*. Montreal: McGill-Queen's University Press, 1991.

Appleby, Joyce, Lynn Hunt, and Margaret Jacob. *Telling the Truth About History*. New York: W.W. Norton, 1994.

Aristotle. *The Poetics*. Translated by Kenneth Telford. Chicago: Henry Regnery, 1961.

Ashcroft, Bill, Gareth Griffiths, and Helen Tiffin. *The Empire Writes Back: Theory and Practice in Post-Colonial Literatures*. New Accents Series. London: Routledge, 1989.

Atwood, Margaret. *Alias Grace*. Toronto: McClelland & Stewart, 1996.

– *In Search of* Alias Grace. Charles R. Bronfman Lecture in Canadian Studies, 21 November 1996. Ottawa: University of Ottawa Press, 1997.

Bakhtin, Mikhail M. *The Dialogic Imagination: Four Essays*. Ed. Michael Holquist, trans. Caryl Emerson and Michael Holquist. Austin: University of Texas Press, 1981.

– *Rabelais and His World*. Trans. Helene Iswolsky. Cambridge: MIT Press, 1968.

Barker, Francis, Peter Hulme, and Margaret Iversen. Introduction to *Colonial discourse / postcolonial theory*, 1–23. Essex Symposia Series. Manchester: Manchester University Press, 1994.

Barthes, Roland. "Historical Discourse." In *Introduction to Structuralism*, ed. Michael Lane, 145–55. New York: Basic Books, 1970.

Baudrillard, Jean. "Simulacra and Simulations." In *Selected Writings*, ed. Mark Poster, 166–84. Cambridge: Polity Press, 1988.

Beer, Gillian. *The Romance*. Critical Idiom Series. Vol. 10. London: Methuen, 1970.

Benjamin, Walter. "Theses on the Philosophy of History." In *Illuminations*, ed. Hannah Arendt, trans. by Harry Zohn, 255–66. New York: Harcourt, Brace & World, 1968.

Bennett, David. "Postmodernism and Vision: Ways of Seeing (at) the End of History." In *History and Post-war Writing*, ed. Theo D'haen and Hans Bertens, 259–79. Postmodern Studies Series. Vol. 3. Amsterdam: Rodopi, 1990.

Bennett, Donna. "English Canada's Postcolonial Complexities." *Essays on Canadian Writing* 52 (1994): 164–210.

Beran, Carol. "Ex-centricity: Michael Ondaatje's *In the Skin of a Lion* and Hugh MacLennan's *Barometer Rising*." *Studies in Canadian Literature* 18, no. 1 (1993): 71–84.

Bhabha, Homi. "DissemiNation: time, narrative, and the margins of the modern nation." In *Nation and Narration*, ed. Bhabha, 291–322. London: Routledge, 1990.

– "Of Mimicry and Man: The Ambivalence of Colonial Discourse." *October* 28 (1984): 125–33.

Bibby, Reginald W. *Mosaic Madness: Pluralism Without a Cause*. Toronto: Stoddart Press, 1990.

Birch, Libby. "The Irish Female Presence in Jane Urquhart's Fiction." *Canadian Woman Studies* 17, no. 3 (1997): 115–19.

Blakeley, Phyllis. *Nova Scotia's Two Remarkable Giants*. Windsor, N.S.: Lancelot Press, 1970.

Bloom, Harold. *The Anxiety of Influence: A Theory of Poetry*. Oxford: Oxford University Press, 1973.

Boehmer, Elleke. *Colonial & Postcolonial Literature: Migrant Metaphors*. Oxford: Oxford University Press, 1995.

Bök, Christian. "The Secular Opiate: Marxism as Ersatz Religion in Three Canadian Texts." *Canadian Literature* 147 (1995): 11–22.

Bowering, George. *Burning Water*. First pub. 1980. Toronto: Penguin Books, 1994.

Brown, Lorne and Caroline. *An Unauthorized History of the RCMP*. Toronto: James Lewis & Samuel, 1973.

Brydon, Diana. "Introduction: Reading Postcoloniality, Reading Canada." *Testing the Limits: Postcolonial Theories and Canadian Literature. Essays on Canadian Writing* 56 (1995): 1–19.

– "'It could not be told': Making Meaning in Timothy Findley's *The Wars*." *Journal of Commonwealth Literature* 21, no. 1 (1986): 62–79.

Butler, Judith. *Gender Trouble: Feminism and the Subversion of Identity.* Thinking Gender Series. London: Routledge, 1990.

Butterfield, Herbert. *The Historical Novel: an Essay.* Cambridge: Cambridge University Press, 1924.

Carnegie, James, Earl of Southesk. *Saskatchewan and the Rocky Mountains.* Edmonton: M.G. Hurtig, 1969.

Carr, Edward Hallett. *What Is History?* New York: Vintage Press, 1961.

Cartwright, George. *A Journal of Transactions and Events, During a Residence of Nearly Sixteen Years on the Coast of Labrador.* 3 vols. Newark: Allin and Ridge, 1792.

Caunce, Stephen. *Oral History and the Local Historian.* Approaches to Local History Series. London: Longman, 1994.

Chao, Lien. *Beyond Silence: Chinese Canadian Literature in English.* Toronto: TSAR Publications, 1997.

Clark, Ronald. *The Victorian Mountaineers.* London: B.T. Batsford, 1953.

Cobley, Evelyn. "Postmodernist War Fiction: Timothy Findley's *The Wars.*" *Canadian Literature* 147 (1995): 98–124.

Collingwood, Robin. *The Idea of History.* First pub. 1946. Oxford: Oxford University Press, 1966.

Compton, Anne. "Romancing the Landscape: Jane Urquhart's Fiction." In *Literature of Region and Nation: Proceedings of the 6th International Literature of Region and Nation Conference,* ed. Winnifred M. Bogaards, 211–29. Saint John: Social Sciences and Humanities Research Council, 1998.

Conrad, Margaret, and Alvin Finkel. *History of the Canadian Peoples.* Vol. 1. 2nd ed. Toronto: Copp Clark, 1998.

Cooper, Brenda. *Magical Realism in West African Fiction: Seeing with a third eye.* Routledge Research in Postcolonial Literatures Series. Vol. 1. London: Routledge, 1998.

Craik, Jennifer. "The Culture of Tourism." In *Touring Cultures: Transformations of Travel and Theory,* ed. Chris Rojek and John Urry, 113–36. London: Routledge, 1997.

Croce, Benedetto. *History as the Story of Liberty.* Trans. Sylvia Sprigge. London: Allen & Unwin, 1941.

Cruise, David, and Alison Griffiths. *The Great Adventure: How the Mounties Conquered the West.* Toronto: Penguin Books, 1996.

Daurio, Beverly, ed. *The Power to Bend Spoons: Interviews with Canadian Novelists.* Toronto: The Mercury Press, 1998.

Davey, Frank. *Post-National Arguments: The Politics of the Anglophone Novel Since 1967.* Theory/Culture Series. Toronto: University of Toronto Press, 1993.

Davidson, Arnold. *Writing Against the Silence: Joy Kogawa's Obasan.* Canadian Fiction Studies. Vol. 30. Toronto: ECW Press, 1993.

Davis, N. Brian, ed. *The Poetry of the Canadian People.* Vol. 1. Toronto: NC Press, 1976.

de Certeau, Michel. *The Writing of History.* Trans. Tom Conley. European Perspectives Series. New York: Columbia University Press, 1988.

Derrida, Jacques. *Of Grammatology.* Trans. Gayatri Chakravorty Spivak. Baltimore: Johns Hopkins University Press, 1974.

Duffy, Dennis. *Sounding the Iceberg: an essay on Canadian Historical Novels.* Toronto: ECW Press, 1986.

Eliade, Mircea. *Myth and Reality.* Trans. Willard Trask. World Perspectives Series. Vol. 31. New York: Harper & Row, 1963.

– *The Myth of the Eternal Return, or, Cosmos and History.* Trans. Willard Trask. Bollingen Series. Vol. 46. Princeton: Princeton University Press, 1954.

Ellis, Peter Berresford. *Celtic Women: Women in Celtic Society and Literature.* Grand Rapids: William B. Eerdmans Publishing, 1995.

Elton, G.R. *The Practice of History.* New York: Crowell, 1969.

The Epic of Gilgamesh, ed., trans. N.K. Sandars. Rev. ed. Harmondsworth: Penguin Books, 1964.

Featherstone, Mike. *Consumer Culture and Postmodernism.* Theory, Culture & Society Series. London: Sage Publications, 1991.

Ferns, H.S. and B. Ostry. *The Age of Mackenzie King: The Rise of the Leader.* London: Heinemann, 1953.

Findley, Timothy. *The Wars.* First pub. 1977. Markham, Ont.: Penguin Books, 1978.

Fink, Cecilia Coulas. "'If Words Won't Do, and Symbols Fail': Hodgins' Magic Reality." *Journal of Canadian Studies* 20, no. 2 (1985): 118–31.

Fischlin, Daniel. "'As sparrows do fall': Sweatman's *Fox* and Transforming the Socius." *Open Letter* 9, no. 4 (1995): 55–68.

Fleishman, Avrom. *The English Historical Novel: Walter Scott to Virginia Woolf.* Baltimore: Johns Hopkins Press, 1971.

Fludernik, Monika. "History and Metafiction: Experientiality, Causality, and Myth." In *Historiographic Metafiction in Modern American and Canadian Literature*, ed. Bernd Engler and Kurt Müller, 81–101. Beiträge zur Englischen Und Amerikanischen Literatur. Vol. 13. Paderborn: Ferdinand Schöningh, 1994.

Foster, Hal. "Postmodernism: A Preface." In *The Anti-Aesthetic: Essays on Postmodern Culture*, ix–xvi. Port Townsend: Bay Press, 1983.

Foucault, Michel. *The Archaeology of Knowledge.* Trans. A.M. Sheridan Smith. World of Man Series. London: Tavistock, 1972.

– "The Order of Discourse." In *Untying the Text: A Post-Structuralist Reader*, ed. Robert Young, 48–78. London: Routledge, 1981.

Franklin, John. *Narrative of the Journey to the Shores of the Polar Sea in the Years 1819, 20, 21 and 22.* Edmonton: M.G. Hurtig, 1969.

Fraser, Esther. *The Canadian Rockies: Early Travels and Explorations.* Edmonton: M.G. Hurtig, 1969.

Frye, Northrop. *Anatomy of Criticism: Four Essays.* Princeton: Princeton University Press, 1957.

Gallagher, Catherine. "Marxism and The New Historicism." In *The New Historicism*, ed. H. Aram Veeser, 37–48. London: Routledge, 1989.

Gamlin, Gordon. "Michael Ondaatje's *In the Skin of a Lion* and the Oral Narrative." *Canadian Literature* 135 (1992): 68–77.

Gittings, Christopher. "A Collision of Discourse: Postmodernisms and Post-Colonialisms in *The Biggest Modern Woman of the World*." *Journal of Commonwealth Literature* 24, no. 1 (1994): 81–91.

Goldie, Terry. "Blame Canada." *Where Is Here Now? Essays on Canadian Writing* 71 (2000): 224–31.

– *Fear and Temptation: The Image of the Indigene in Canadian, Australian, and New Zealand Literatures*. Montreal: McGill-Queen's University Press, 1989.

Goldman, Marlene. *Paths of Desire: Images of Exploration and Mapping in Canadian Women's Writing*. Theory/Culture Series. Toronto: University of Toronto Press, 1997.

Goldring, Philip. "Whisky, Horses and Death: The Cypress Hills Massacre and Its Sequel." *Canadian Historic Sites*, 43–70. Occasional Papers in Archeology and History Series. Vol. 21. Ottawa: Parks Canada, 1979.

Gossman, Lionel. "History and Literature: Reproduction or Signification." In *The Writing of History: Literary Form and Historical Understanding*, eds Robert H. Canary and Henry Kozicki, 3–39. Madison: University of Wisconsin Press, 1978.

Granatstein, J.L. *Who Killed Canadian History?* Toronto: HarperCollins, 1998.

Gwyn, Richard. *Smallwood: The Unlikely Revolutionary*. Toronto: McClelland & Stewart, 1968.

Gwyn, Sandra. *Tapestry of War: A Private View of Canadians in the Great War*. Toronto: HarperCollins, 1992.

Hall, Stuart. "The Question of Cultural Identity." In *Modernity: An Introduction to Modern Societies*, eds Hall et al., 595–634. Cambridge, Mass.: Blackwell, 1996.

Hancock, Geoff. "Magic or Realism: The Marvellous in Canadian Fiction." In *Magic Realism and Canadian Literature: Proceedings of the Conference on Magic Realist Writing in Canada*, eds Peter Hinchcliffe and Ed Jewinski, 30–48. Waterloo: University of Waterloo Press, 1986.

Harmon, Don and Bart Robinson. *Columbia Icefield: A Solitude of Ice*. Banff: Altitude Publishing, 1981.

Harvey, David. *The Condition of Postmodernity: An Enquiry into the Origins of Cultural Change*. Oxford: Basil Blackwell, 1989.

Hatch, Ronald. "Narrative Development in the Canadian Historical Novel." *Canadian Literature* 110 (1986): 79–96.

Heffernan, Teresa. "Tracing the Travesty: Constructing the Female Subject in Susan Swan's *The Biggest Modern Woman of the World*." *Canadian Literature* 133 (1992): 24–37.

Hodgins, Jack. *The Invention of the World*. Toronto: Macmillan, 1977.

Howells, Coral Ann. *Private and Fictional Worlds: Canadian Women Novelists of the 1970s and 1980s*. London: Methuen, 1987.

– "Rudy Wiebe's Art and Acts of Narrative in *The Scorched-Wood People*." In *Canadian Story and History 1885–1985*, eds Colin Nicholson and Peter Easingwood, 18–26. Edinburgh: Centre of Canadian Studies, 1985.

Huggan, Graham. "Decolonizing the Map: Post-Colonialism, Post-Structuralism and the Cartographic Connection." *Ariel* 20, no. 4 (1989): 115–31.

– "The Latitudes of Romance: Representations of Chinese Canada in Bowering's *To All Appearances* and Sky Lee's *Disappearing Moon Café*." *Canadian Literature* 140 (1994): 34–48.

Hughes, Helen. *The Historical Romance*. Popular Fictions Series. London: Routledge, 1993.

Hulan, Renée. "Who's There?" *Where Is Here Now? Essays on Canadian Writing* 71 (2000): 61–70.

Hutcheon, Linda. *The Canadian Postmodern: A Study of Contemporary English-Canadian Fiction*. Studies in Canadian Literature Series. Toronto: Oxford University Press, 1988.

– "'Circling the Downspout of Empire': Post-Colonialism and Postmodernism." *Ariel* 20, no. 4 (1989): 149–75.

– "History and/as Intertext." In *Future Indicative: Literary Theory and Canadian Literature*, ed. John Moss, 169–84. Reappraisals: Canadian Writers Series. Vol. 13. Ottawa: University of Ottawa Press, 1987.

– *A Poetics of Postmodernism: History, Theory, Fiction*. London: Routledge, 1988.

Iggers, Georg. *Historiography in the Twentieth Century: From Scientific Objectivity to the Postmodern Challenge*. Hanover: Wesleyan University Press, 1997.

Jacobs, Naomi. *The Character of Truth: Historical Figures in Contemporary Fiction*. Crosscurrents/Modern Critiques, Third Series. Carbondale, Ill.: Southern Illinois University Press, 1990.

Jaeger, Peter. "'The Land Created a Body of Lore': The Green Story in John Steffler's *The Afterlife of George Cartwright*." *English Studies in Canada* 21, no. 1 (1995): 41–54.

Jameson, Fredric. "On Magic Realism in Film." *Critical Inquiry* 12, no. 2 (1986): 301–25.

– *The Political Unconscious: Narrative as a Socially Symbolic Act*. Ithaca: Cornell University Press, 1981.

– *Postmodernism, or, The Cultural Logic of Late Capitalism*. Post-contemporary Interventions Series. Durham: Duke University Press, 1991.

JanMohamed, Abdul. "The Economy of Manichean Allegory: The Function of Racial Difference in Colonialist Literature." *"Race," Writing, and Difference. Critical Inquiry* 12, no. 1 (1985): 59–87.

Johnston, Wayne. *The Colony of Unrequited Dreams*. Toronto: McClelland & Stewart, 1998.

Jones, Manina. *That Art of Difference: 'Documentary-Collage' and English-Canadian Writing*. Theory/Culture Series. Toronto: University of Toronto Press, 1993.

Kaltembach, Michèle. "Explorations Into History: Rudy Wiebe's *A Discovery of Strangers*." *Études Canadiennes/Canadian Studies* 44 (1998): 77–87.

Kamboureli, Smaro. "*The Biggest Modern Woman of the World*: Canada as the Absent Spouse." *Studies in Canadian Literature* 16, no. 2 (1991): 1–16.

– Introduction to *Making a Difference: Canadian Multicultural Literature*, 1–16. Toronto: Oxford University Press, 1996.

Kealey, Gregory S. *Workers and Canadian History*. Montreal: McGill-Queen's University Press, 1995.

Keith, W.J. *Epic Fiction: The Art of Rudy Wiebe*. Edmonton: University of Alberta Press, 1981.

– "Jack Hodgins and the Sources of Invention." *Essays on Canadian Writing* 34 (1987): 81–91.

– ed. *A Voice in the Land: Essays by and about Rudy Wiebe*. Western Canadian Literary Documents Series. Vol. 2. Edmonton: NeWest Press, 1981.

Kelley, Theresa M. *Reinventing Allegory*. Cambridge Studies in Romanticism Series. Cambridge: Cambridge University Press, 1997.

Kerby, Anthony Paul. *Narrative and the Self*. Studies in Continental Thought Series. Bloomington: Indiana University Press, 1991.

King, William Lyon Mackenzie. *The Mackenzie King Diaries, 1893–1931*. Toronto: University of Toronto Press, 1973.

– *The Mackenzie King Diaries, 1932–1949*. Toronto: University of Toronto Press, 1980.

Kirwin, Bill. *Thomas D'Arcy McGee: Visionary of the Welfare State in Canada*. Monograph Series. Vol. 4. Calgary: Faculty of Social Welfare, 1981.

Knelman, Judith. "Can We Believe What the Newspapers Tell Us? Missing Links in *Alias Grace*." *University of Toronto Quarterly* 68, no. 2 (1999): 677–86.

Kogawa, Joy. *Obasan*. First pub. 1981. Markham, Ont.: Penguin Books, 1983.

Kramer, Reinhold. "The 1919 Winnipeg General Strike and Margaret Sweatman's *Fox*." *Canadian Literature* 160 (1999): 50–70.

Krans, Michael. "Writing For an Elsewhere: Author(ity) and Authenticity in the Texts of the First Franklin Expedition (1819–1822)." *Studies in Canadian Literature* 24, no. 1 (1999): 70–92.

Kristeva, Julia. "The Bounded Text." In *Desire in Language: A Semiotic Approach to Literature and Art*, ed. Leon S. Roudiez, trans. Thomas Gora and Alice Jardine, 36–63. European Perspectives Series. New York: Columbia University Press, 1980.

Kuester, Martin. *Framing Truths: Parodic Structures in Contemporary English-Canadian Historical Novels*. Theory/Culture Series. Toronto: University of Toronto Press, 1992.

LaCapra, Dominick. *History and Criticism*. Ithaca: Cornell University Press, 1985.

– *History, Politics, and the Novel*. Ithaca: Cornell University Press, 1987.

Lawson, Alan. "Postcolonial Theory and the 'Settler' Subject." *Testing the Limits: Postcolonial Theories and Canadian Literature. Essays on Canadian Writing* 56 (1995): 20–36.

Lecker, Robert. "Haunted by a Glut of Ghosts: Jack Hodgins' *The Invention of the World*." *Essays on Canadian Writing* 20 (1981): 86–105.

Lee, Bennett. Introduction to *Many-Mouthed Birds: Contemporary Writing by Chinese-Canadians*, eds Lee and Jim Wong-Chu, 1–8. Vancouver: Douglas & McIntyre, 1991.

Lee, Sky. *Disappearing Moon Café*. Vancouver: Douglas & McIntyre, 1990.

Levi-Strauss, Claude. *Myth and Meaning*. Toronto: University of Toronto Press, 1978.

Litvack, Leon. "Canadian Writing in English and Multiculturalism." In *English Postcoloniality: Literatures from Around the World*, eds Radhika Mohanran and Gita Rajan, 119–34. Contributions to the Study of World Literatures Series. Vol. 66. Westport, Conn.: Greenwood, 1996.

Lobb, Edward. "Imagining History: The Romantic Background of George Bowering's *Burning Water*." *Studies in Canadian Literature* 12, no. 1 (1987): 12–28.

Lovelady, Stephanie. "I Am Telling This to No One But You: Private Voice, Passing, and the Private Sphere in Margaret Atwood's *Alias Grace*." *Studies in Canadian Literature*, no. 24.2 (1999): 35–63.

Lukács, Gyorgy. *The Historical Novel*. Trans Hannah and Stanley Mitchell. London: Merlin Press, 1962.

Lyotard, Jean-Francois. *The Postmodern Condition: A Report on Knowledge*. Trans. Geoff Bennington and Brian Massumi. Theory of History and Literature Series. Vol. 10. Minneapolis: University of Minnesota Press, 1984.

MacLaren, I.S. "Retaining Captaincy of the Soul: Response to Nature in the First Franklin Expedition." *Essays on Canadian Writing* 28 (1994): 57–92.

Madsen, Deborah. "The Fate of Allegory in the Twentieth Century." In *Allegory in America*, 122–44. Studies in Literature and Religion Series. Houndmills, Hamps.: Macmillan, 1996.

Manzoni, Alessandro. *On the Historical Novel*. Trans. Sandra Bermann. Lincoln: University of Nebraska Press, 1984.

Marlatt, Daphne. *Ana Historic*. First pub. 1988. Toronto: House of Anansi, 1997.

– "Self-Representation and Fictionalysis." In *Collaboration in the Feminine: Writings on Women and Culture from Tessera*, ed. Barbara Godard, 202–6. Toronto: Second Story Press, 1994.

McCaig, Joann. "Brother XII and *The Invention of the World*." *Essays on Canadian Writing* 28 (1984): 128–40.

McClintock, Anne. "The angel of progress: pitfalls of the term 'postcolonialism.'" In *Colonial discourse / postcolonial theory,* eds Francis Barker, Peter Hulme, and Margaret Iversen, 253–66. Essex Symposia Series. Manchester: Manchester University Press, 1994.

McConnell, Kathleen. "Textile Tropes in *The Afterlife of George Cartwright.*" *Canadian Literature* 149 (1996): 91–109.

McHale, Brian. *Postmodernist Fiction.* New York: Methuen, 1987.

McNaughton, Janet. "Magically Real." Review of *Away,* by Jane Urquhart. *Books in Canada* 22, no. 7 (1993): 44.

Merkur, Dan. *Becoming Half Hidden: Shamanism and Initiation Among the Inuit.* Garland Reference Library of the Humanities Series. Vol. 1559. New York: Garland Publishing, 1992.

Moodie, Susanna. *Life in the Clearings*, ed. Robert McDougall. Toronto: Macmillan, 1959.

Moore, Brian. *Black Robe.* Toronto: McClelland & Stewart, 1985.

Morton, W.L. *Manitoba: A History.* Toronto: University of Toronto Press, 1957.

Munslow, Alun. *Deconstructing History.* London: Routledge, 1997.

Ondaatje, Michael. *In the Skin of a Lion.* First pub. 1987. Toronto: Vintage Press, 1997.

Ong, Walter J. *Orality and Literacy: The Technologizing of the Word.* New Accents Series. London: Routledge, 1982.

Palmer, Bryan D. *Working-Class Experience: Rethinking the History of Canadian Labour, 1800–1991.* Toronto: McClelland & Stewart, 1992.

Papineau, Talbot. "An Open Letter from Capt. Talbot Papineau to Mr. Henri Bourassa," 21 March 1916. Rpt. in *"a country nourished on self-doubt": Documents in Canadian History, 1867–1980*, ed. Thomas Thorner, 206–15. Peterborough: Broadview Press, 1998.

Polkinghorne, Donald. *Narrative Knowing and the Human Sciences.* SUNY Series in Philosophy of the Social Sciences. Albany: SUNY Press, 1988.

Prentice, Alison et al. *Canadian Women: A History.* Harcourt Brace Jovanovitch, 1988.

Prowse, D.W. *A History of Newfoundland from the English, Colonial, and Foreign Records.* London: Macmillan, 1895.

– *A History of Newfoundland from the English, Colonial, and Foreign Records.* 2nd ed. London: Eyre and Spottiswoode, 1896.

Quilligan, Maureen. *The Language of Allegory: Defining the Genre.* Ithaca: Cornell University Press, 1979.

Richardson, John. *Arctic Ordeal: The Journal of John Richardson, Surgeon-Naturalist with Franklin, 1820–22.* Ed. C. Stuart Houston. Montreal: McGill-Queen's University Press, 1984.

Robertson, Heather. *Igor: A Novel of Intrigue. The King Years.* Vol 3. Toronto: James Lorimer, 1989.

– *Lily: A Rhapsody in Red. The King Years.* Vol. 2. Toronto: James Lorimer, 1986.

– "Lust, Murder and 'Long Pig': Rudy Wiebe takes on the taboos of history." *Canadian Forum* 73, no. 837 (1995): 20–4.

– *Willie: A Romance. The King Years.* Vol. 1. Toronto: James Lorimer, 1983.

Rojek, Chris and John Urry. "Transformations of Travel and Theory." In *Touring Cultures: Transformations of Travel and Theory,* eds Rojek and Urry, 1–19. London: Routledge, 1997.

Rose, E. Elizabeth. "A Wheel of Mystery." Review of *Alias Grace*, by Margaret Atwood. *Fiddlehead* 191 (1997): 114–19.

Rose, Marilyn Russell. "Politics into Art: Kogawa's *Obasan* and the Rhetoric of Fiction." *Mosaic* 21, no. 3 (1988): 215–26.

Ross, Sheila. "Forays into Polyvocality." Review of *Bad Imaginings*, by Caroline Adderson, and *Away*, by Jane Urquhart. *Canadian Literature* 148 (1996): 175–7.

Sarris, Fotios. "*In the Skin of a Lion*: Michael Ondaatje's Tenebristic Narrative." *Essays on Canadian Writing* 44 (1991): 183–201.

Sawatsky, John. *Gouzenko: The Untold Story.* Toronto: Macmillan, 1984.

– *Men in the Shadows: The RCMP Security Service.* Toronto: Doubleday Canada, 1980.

Scott, Joan. *Gender and the Politics of History.* Gender and Culture Series. New York: Columbia University Press, 1988.

Shohat, Ella and Robert Stam. *Unthinking Eurocentrism: Multiculturalism and the Media.* SightLines Series. London: Routledge, 1994.

Siemerling, Winfried. *Discoveries of the Other: Alterity in the Work of Leonard Cohen, Hubert Aquin, Michael Ondaatje, and Nicole Brossard.* Theory/Culture Series. Toronto: University of Toronto Press, 1994.

– "Writing Ethnicity: Introduction." In *Writing Ethnicity: Cross-Cultural Consciousness in Canadian and Québecois Literature*, 1–32. Toronto: ECW Press, 1996.

Skelton, Isabel. *The Life of Thomas D'Arcy McGee.* Gardenvale: Garden City Press, 1925.

Slattery, T.P. *The Assassination of D'Arcy McGee.* Toronto: Doubleday Canada, 1968.

– *"They Got to Find Mee Guilty Yet".* Toronto: Doubleday Canada, 1972.

Slemon, Stephen. "Magic Realism as Postcolonial Discourse." In *Magical Realism: Theory, History, Community,* eds Lois Parkinson Zamora and Wendy B. Faris, 409–26. Durham, N.C.: Duke University Press, 1995.

– "Monuments of Empire: Allegory/Counter-Discourse/Post-Colonial Writing." *Kunapipi* 9, no. 3 (1987): 1–16.

– "Post-Colonial Allegory and the Transformation of History." *Journal of Commonwealth Literature* 23, no. 1 (1988): 157–68.

Smallwood, Joseph R. *I Chose Canada: The Memoirs of the Honourable Joseph R. "Joey" Smallwood.* Toronto: Macmillan, 1973.

Smith, Doug. *Let Us Rise! A History of the Manitoba Labour Movement.* Winnipeg: New Star Books, 1985.

Spearey, Susan. "Mapping and Masking: The Migrant Experience in Michael Ondaatje's *In the Skin of a Lion.*" *Journal of Commonwealth Literature* 29, no. 2 (1994): 45–60.

Stacey, C.P. *A Very Double Life: The Private World of Mackenzie King.* Toronto: Macmillan, 1976.

Steffler, John. *The Afterlife of George Cartwright.* Toronto: McClelland & Stewart, 1992.

Strong-Boag, Veronica. "Writing About Women." In *Writing About Canada: A Handbook for Modern Canadian History,* ed. John Schulz, 175–200. Scarborough: Prentice-Hall Canada, 1990.

Stutfield, Hugh E.M. and J. Norman Collie. *Climbs & Exploration in the Canadian Rockies.* London: Longmans, Green & Co., 1903.

Such, Peter. *Riverrun.* Toronto: Clarke, Irwin, 1973.

Swan, Susan. *The Biggest Modern Woman of the World.* Toronto: Lester & Orpen Dennys, 1983.

Swan-Ryan, Linda. "A Swan's Song." *MacLean's* 29 October 1984, 8.

Sweatman, Margaret. *Fox.* Winnipeg: Turnstone Press, 1991.

Thiher, Allen. "Postmodern Fiction and History." In *History and Post-war Writing,* ed. Theo D'haen and Hans Bertens, 9–31. Postmodern Studies Series. Vol. 3. Amsterdam: Rodopi, 1990.

Tompkins, Jane. *West of Everything: The Inner Life of Westerns.* Oxford: Oxford University Press, 1992.

Tonkin, Elizabeth. *Narrating Our Pasts: The Social Construction of Oral History.* Cambridge Studies in Oral and Literate Culture Series. Vol. 22. Cambridge: Cambridge University Press, 1992.

Tostevin, Lola Lemire. "Writing in the Space That is Her Mother's Face." *Line* 13 (1989): 32–9.

Tremblay, Tony. "Piracy, Penance, and other Penal Codes: A Morphology of Postcolonial Revision in Three Recent Texts by Rudy Wiebe, John Steffler, and Joan Clark." *English Studies in Canada* 23, no. 2 (1997): 159–73.

Turner, Frederick Jackson. "The Significance of the Frontier in American History." In *The Frontier in American History,* 1–38. First pub. 1893. New York: Holt, 1953.

Underhill, Frank H. *The Image of Confederation.* Massey Lectures, Third Series. Toronto: Canadian Broadcasting Company, 1964.

Urquhart, Jane. *Away.* Toronto: McClelland & Stewart, 1993.

Urry, John. *The Tourist Gaze: Leisure and Travel in Contemporary Societies.* Theory, Culture & Society Series. London: Sage Publications, 1990.

van Toorn, Penny. *Rudy Wiebe and the Historicity of the Word.* Edmonton: University of Alberta Press, 1995.

Vancouver, George. *A Voyage of Discovery to the North Pacific Ocean and Round the World 1791–1795.* 4 vols. Ed. W. Kaye Lamb. London: Hakluyt Society, 1984.

Vanderhaeghe, Guy. *The Englishman's Boy.* Toronto: McClelland & Stewart, 1996.

Vauthier, Simone. "The Dubious Battle of Storytelling: Narrative Strategies in Timothy Findley's *The Wars.*" In *Gaining Ground: European Critics on Canadian Literature*, eds Robert Kroetsch and Reingard M. Nischik, 11–39. Western Canada Documents Series. Vol 4. Edmonton: NeWest Press, 1985.

Vautier, Marie. *New World Myth: Postmodernism and Postcolonialism in Canadian Fiction.* Montreal: McGill-Queen's University Press, 1998.

Walton, George. *The Trials of James McDermott, and Grace Marks, at Toronto, Upper Canada, November 3rd and 4th, 1843; for the Murder of Thomas Kinnear, Esquire, and his Housekeeper Nancy Montgomery,* etc. Toronto: Star and Transcript Office, 1843. CIHM/ICMH Microfiche Series. Canadian Institute for Historical Microreproductions, 1987.

Waugh, Patricia. *Metafiction: The Theory and Practice of Self-Conscious Fiction.* New Accents Series. London: Methuen, 1984.

– *Practising Postmodernism/Reading Modernism.* Interrogating Texts Series. London: Edward Arnold, 1992.

Wharton, Thomas. *Icefields.* Nunatuk Fiction Series. Edmonton: NeWest Press, 1995.

White, Hayden. *The Content of the Form: Narrative Discourse and Historical Representation.* Baltimore: Johns Hopkins University Press, 1987.

– *Metahistory: The Historical Imagination in Nineteenth-Century Europe.* Baltimore: Johns Hopkins University Press, 1973.

– *Tropics of Discourse: Essays in Cultural Criticism.* Baltimore: Johns Hopkins University Press, 1978.

– "The Value of Narrativity in the Representation of Reality." *Critical Inquiry* 7 (1980): 6–27.

Wiebe, Rudy. *A Discovery of Strangers.* Toronto: McClelland & Stewart, 1994.

– *The Scorched-Wood People.* New Canadian Library Series. Vol. 156. Toronto: McClelland & Stewart, 1977.

– *The Temptations of Big Bear.* First pub. 1973. New Canadian Library Series. Toronto: McClelland & Stewart, 1995.

– "Where is the Voice Coming From?" In *Where is the Voice Coming From?*, 135–43. Toronto: McClelland & Stewart, 1974.

Wiesel, Eli. "Myth and History." In *Myth, Symbol, and Reality,* ed. Alan Olson, 20–30. Boston University Studies in Philosophy and Religion Series. Vol. 1. Notre Dame: University of Notre Dame Press, 1980.

Willis, Gary. "Speaking the Silence: Joy Kogawa's *Obasan.*" *Studies in Canadian Literature* 12, no.2 (1987): 239–49.

Woodcock, George. "Riel & Dumont." Review of *The Scorched-Wood People,* by Rudy Wiebe. *Canadian Literature* 77 (1978): 98–100.

York, Lorraine. *"The Other Side of Dailiness: Photography in the Works of Alice Munro, Timothy Findley, Michael Ondaatje, and Margaret Laurence.* Toronto: ECW Press, 1988.

Young, Robert. *White Mythologies: Writing History and the West.* London: Routledge, 1990.

Zamora, Lois Parkinson and Wendy B. Faris. "Daiquiri Birds and Flaubertian Parrot(ie)s." Introduction to *Magical Realism: Theory, History, Community,* 1–11. Durham, N.C.: Duke University Press, 1995.

Index